MUTTS

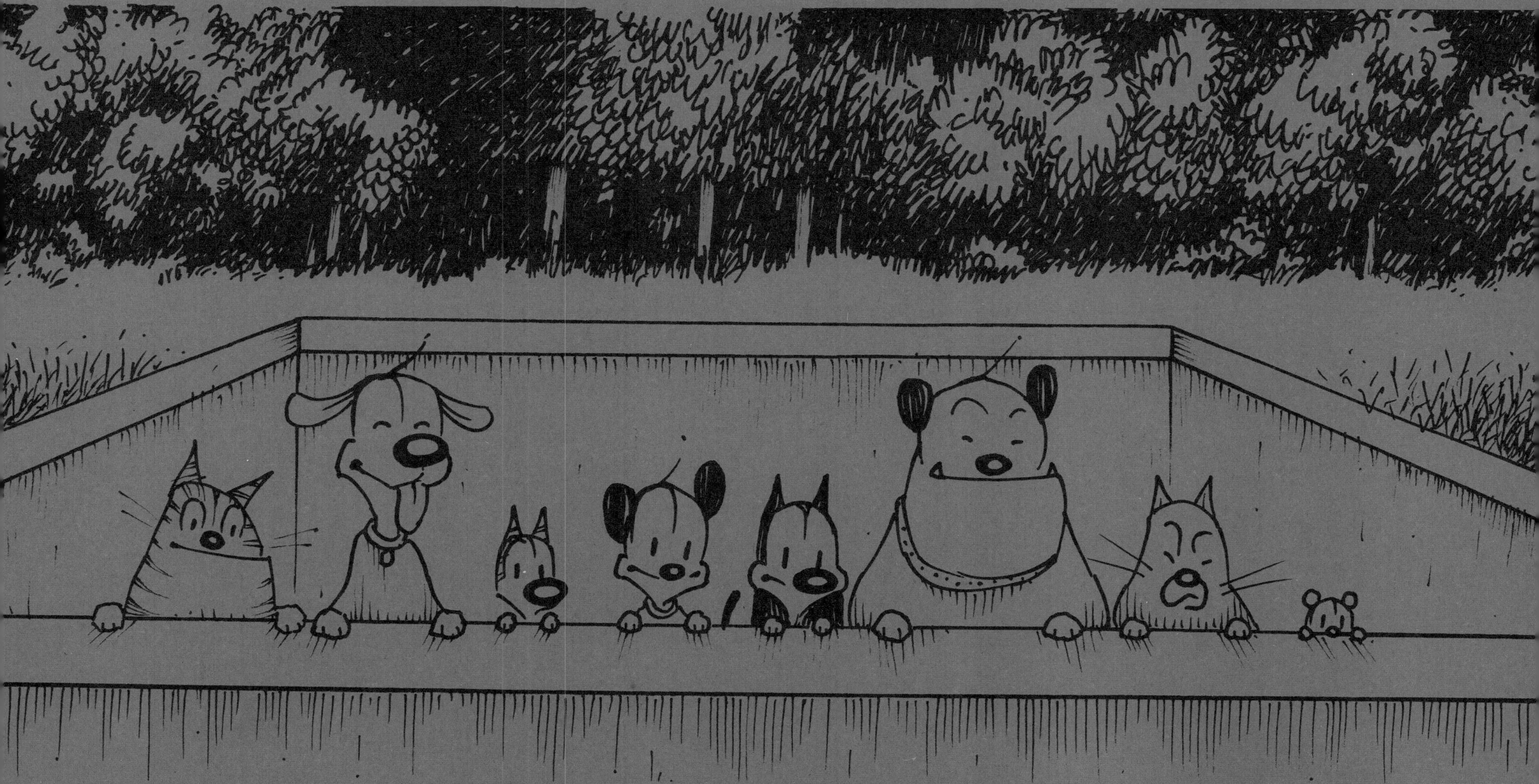

HOT DOGS, HOT CATS

PATRICK McDONNELL

Andrews McMeel PUBLISHING®

Other Books by Patrick McDonnell

The Best of Mutts

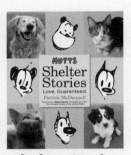

Shelter Stories

Mutts

Cats and Dogs: Mutts II

More Shtuff: Mutts III

Yesh!: Mutts IV

Our Mutts: Five

A Little Look-See: Mutts VI

What Now: Mutts VII

I Want to Be the Kitty: Mutts VIII

Dog-Eared: Mutts IX

Who Let the Cat Out: Mutts X

Everyday Mutts

Animal Friendly

Call of the Wild

Stop and Smell the Roses

Earl & Mooch

Our Little Kat King

Bonk!

A Shtinky Little Christmas

Cat Crazy

Living the Dream

Playtime

Year of Yesh

#LoveMutts

You've Got Those Wild Eyes Again, Mooch

Mutts Sundays

Sunday Mornings

Sunday Afternoons

Sunday Evenings

Mutts is distributed internationally by King Features Syndicate, Inc. For information, write to King Features Syndicate, Inc., 300 West Fifty-Seventh Street, New York, New York 10019, or visit www.KingFeatures.com.

20 21 22 23 24 POA 10 9 8 7 6 5 4 3 2 1

ISBN: 978-1-5248-5228-3

Library of Congress Control Number: 2019946595

Printed on recycled paper.

Mutts can be found on the Internet at **www.mutts.com.**

Special thanks to one of my favorites, Cal Schenkel, for the book's cover inspiration, which is based on his design for Frank Zappa's *Hot Rats* album. Cover art direction by Jeff Schulz.

ATTENTION: SCHOOLS AND BUSINESSES

Andrews McMeel books are available at quantity discounts with bulk purchase for educational, business, or sales promotional use. For information, please e-mail the Andrews McMeel Publishing Special Sales Department: specialsales@amuniversal.com.

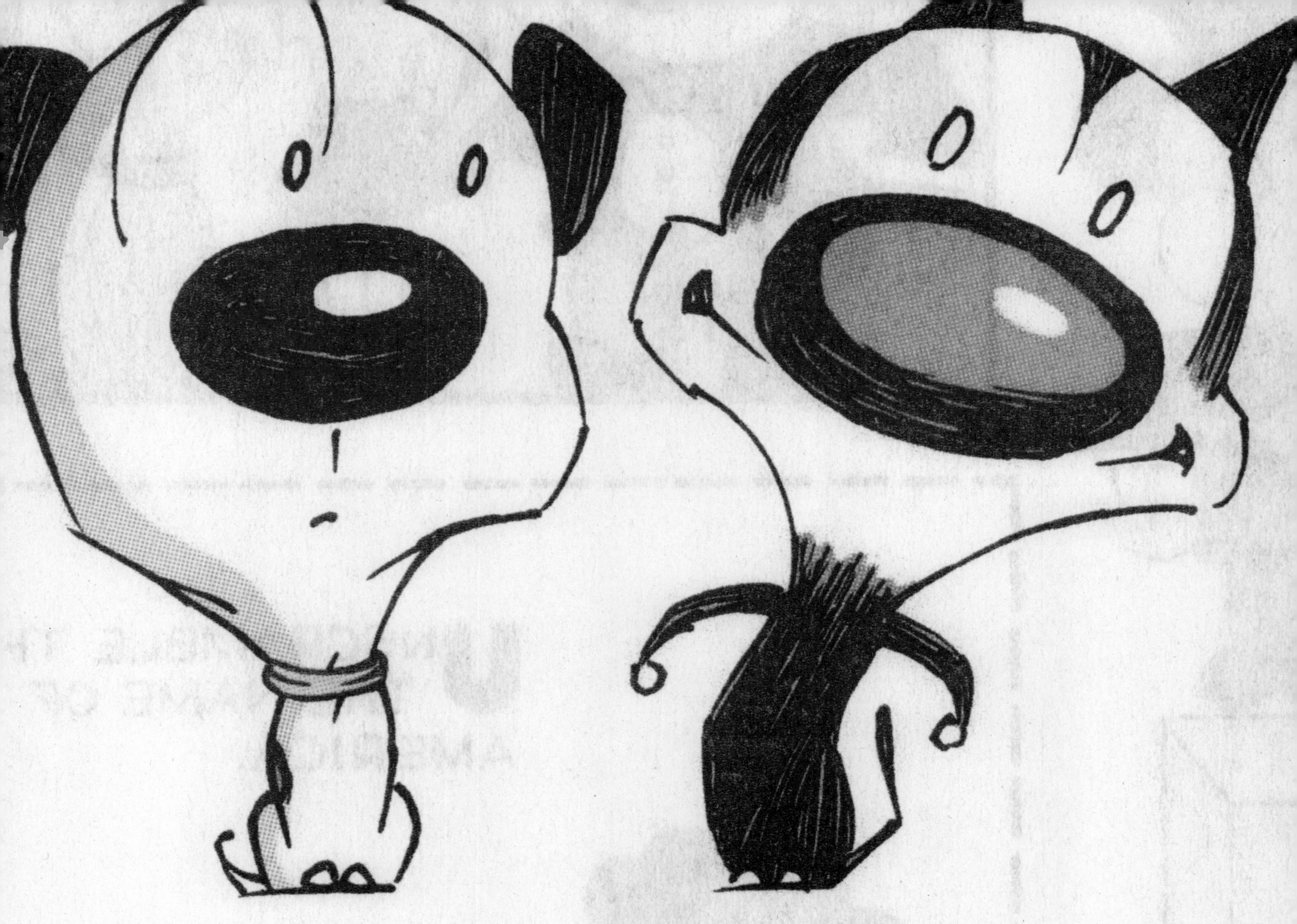

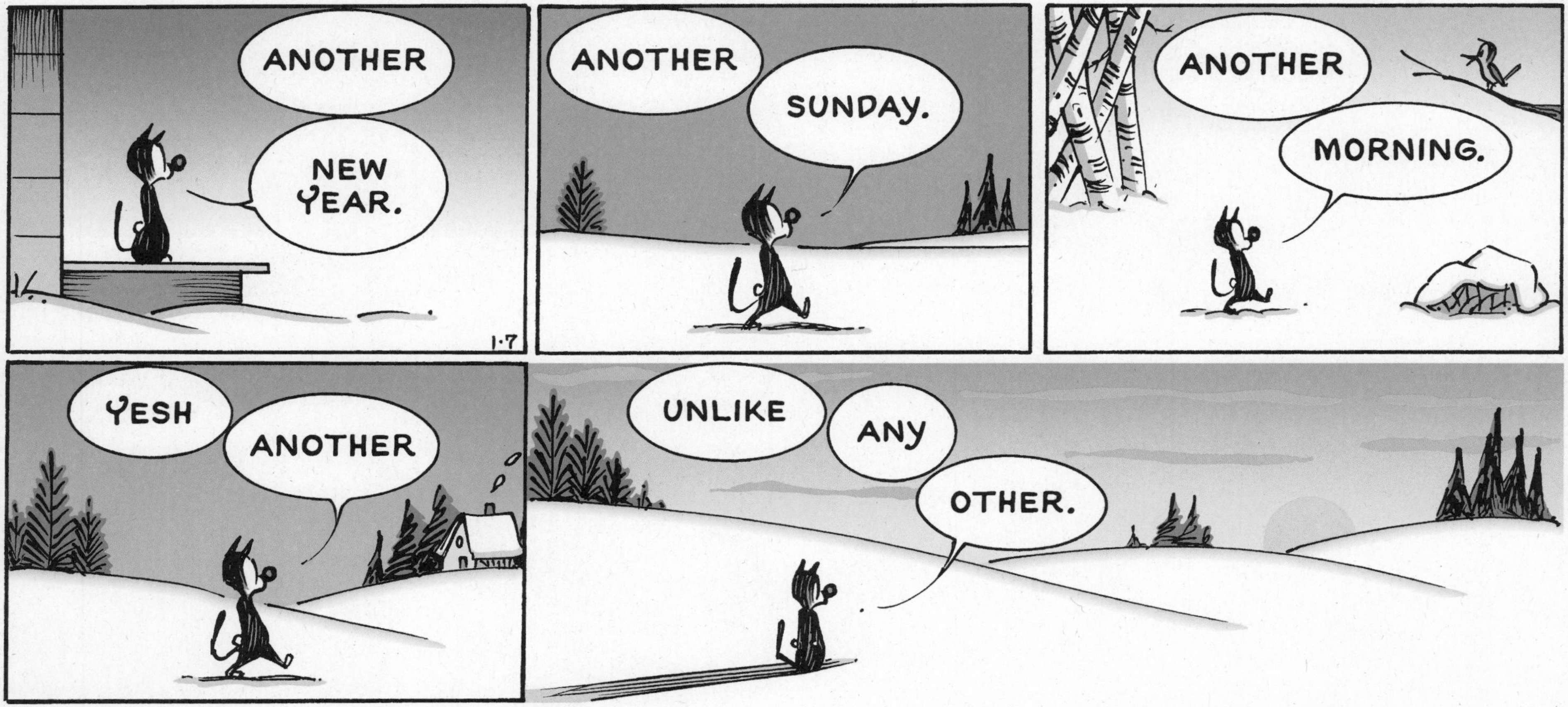
ANOTHER
NEW YEAR.
1·7
ANOTHER
SUNDAY.
ANOTHER
MORNING.
YESH
ANOTHER
UNLIKE
ANY
OTHER.

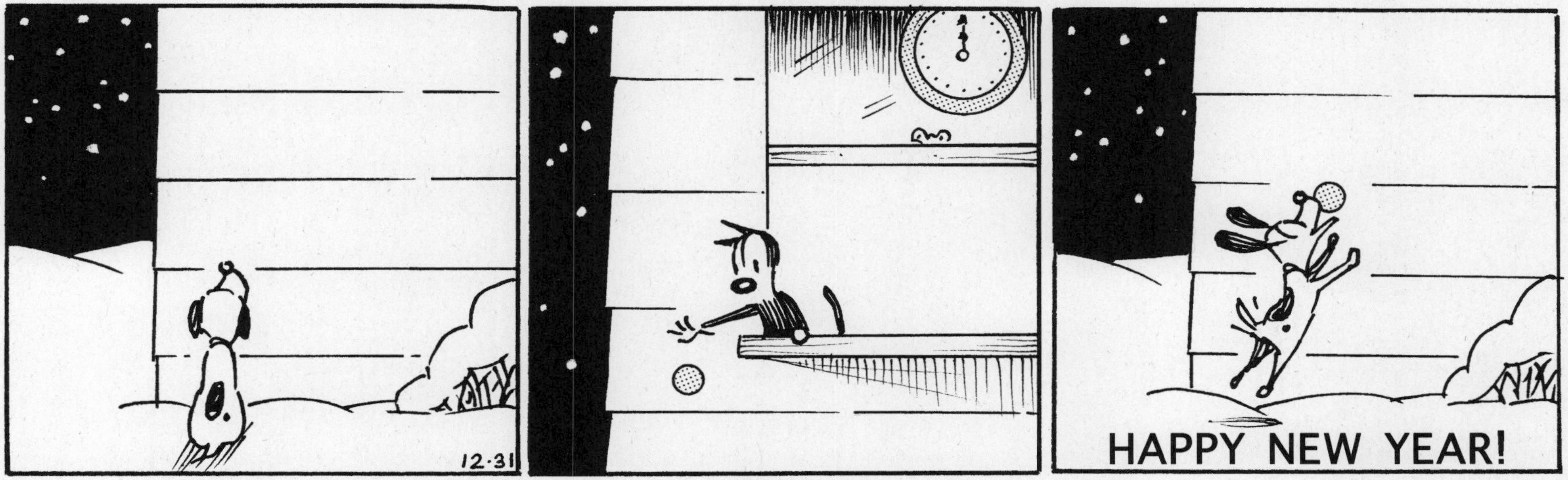
12·31
HAPPY NEW YEAR!

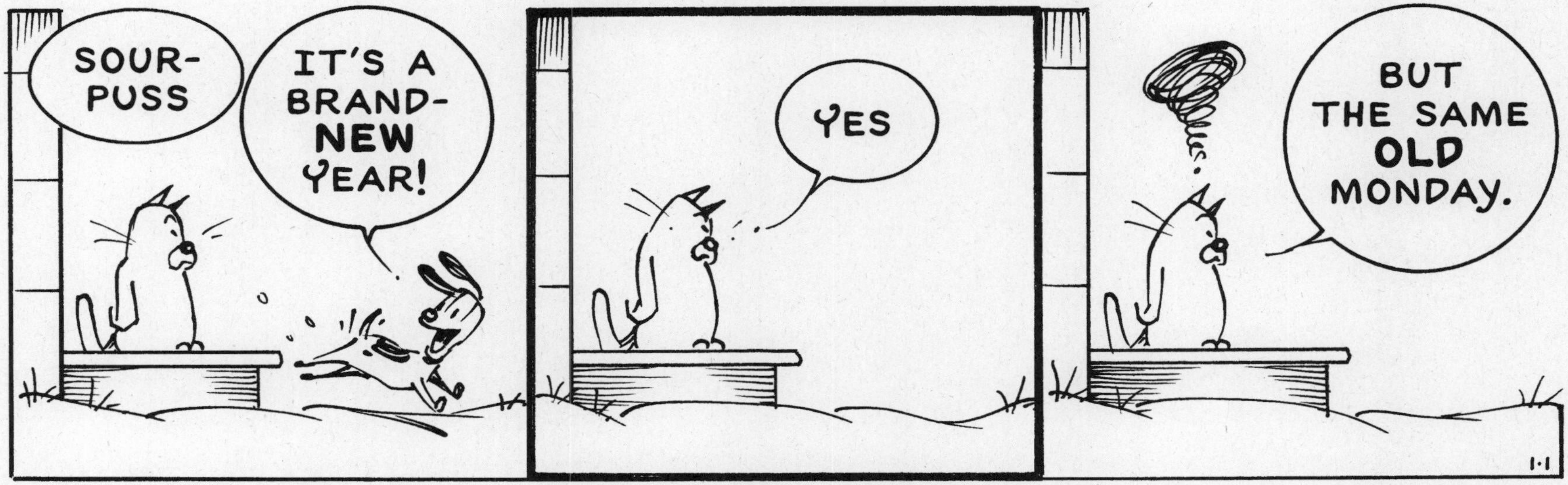
SOUR-PUSS
IT'S A BRAND-NEW YEAR!
YES
BUT THE SAME OLD MONDAY.
1·1

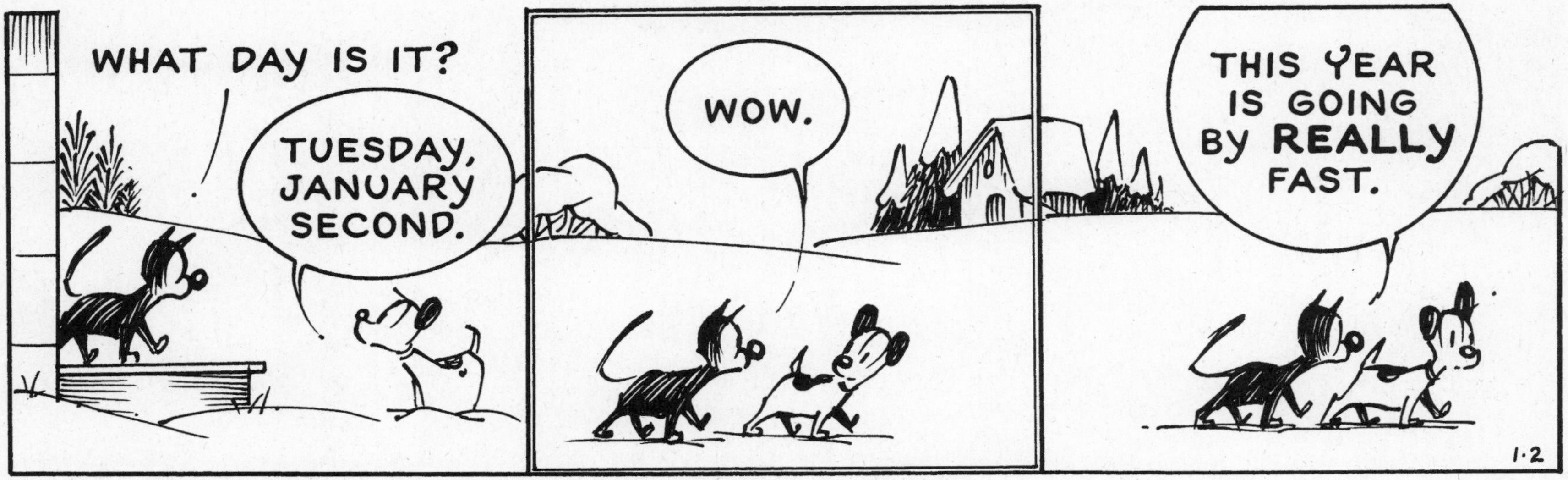
WHAT DAY IS IT?
TUESDAY, JANUARY SECOND.
WOW.
THIS YEAR IS GOING BY **REALLY** FAST.
1·2

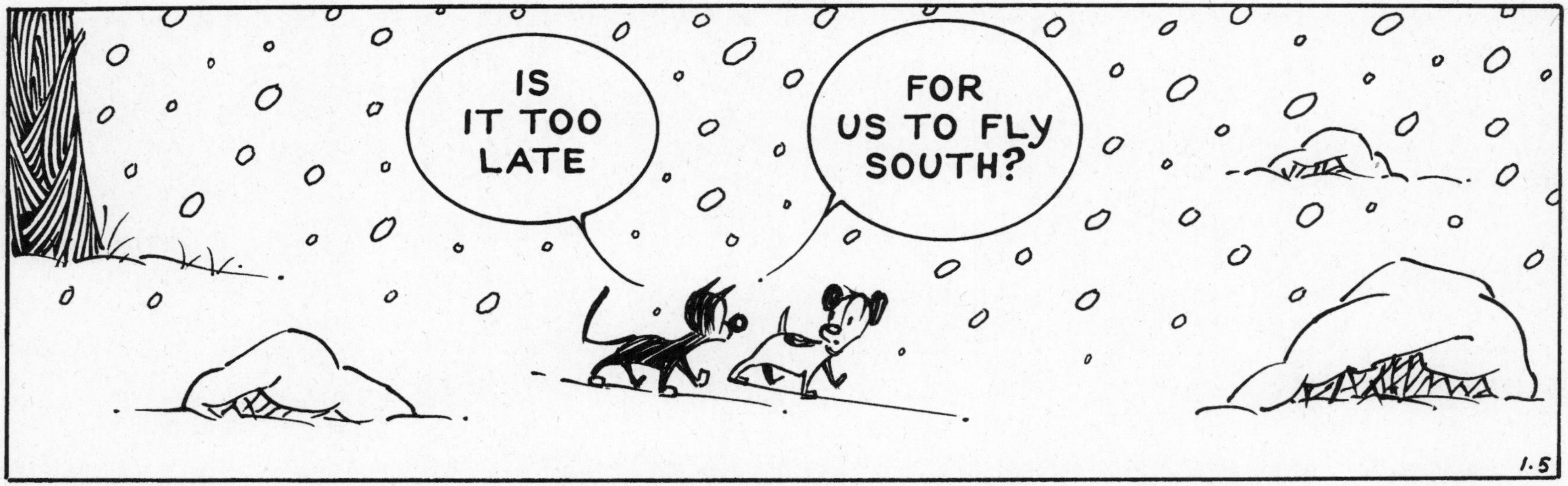
IS IT TOO LATE
FOR US TO FLY SOUTH?
1·5

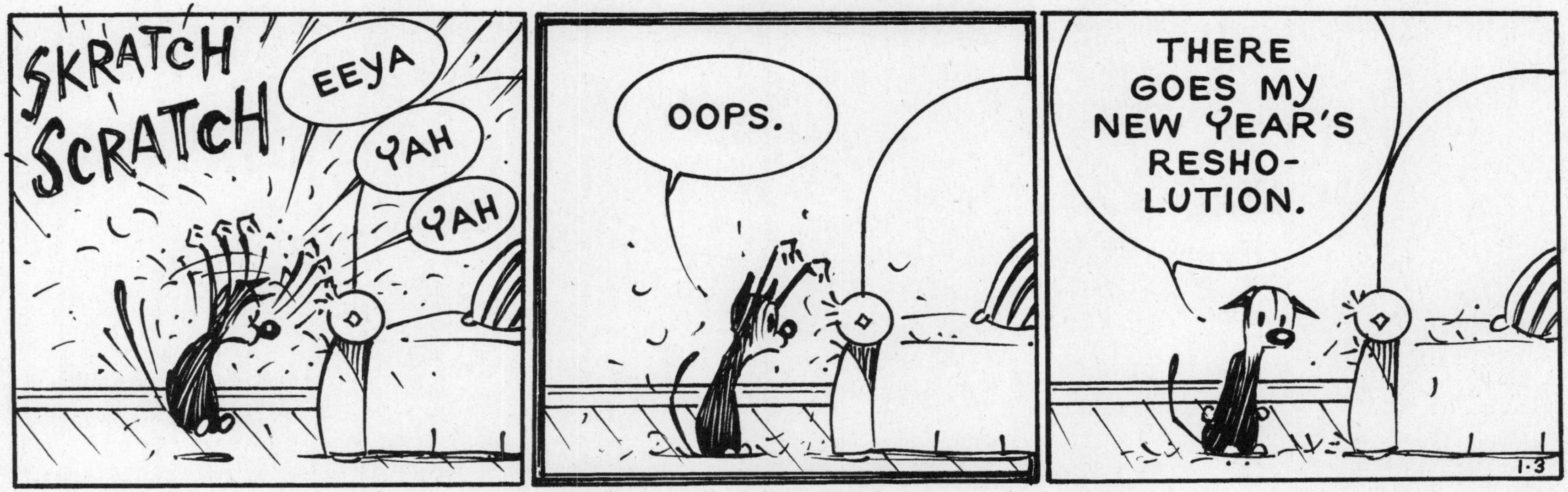
SKRATCH
SCRATCH
EEYA
YAH
YAH
OOPS.
THERE GOES MY NEW YEAR'S RESHO-LUTION.
1·3

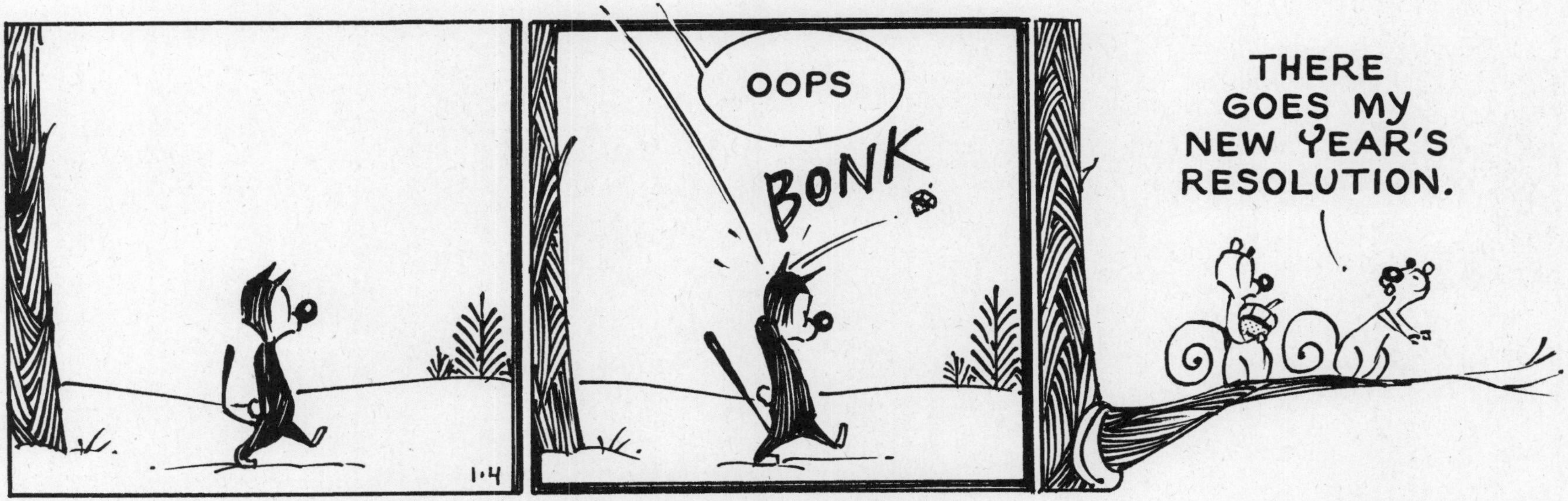
1·4
OOPS
BONK
THERE GOES MY NEW YEAR'S RESOLUTION.

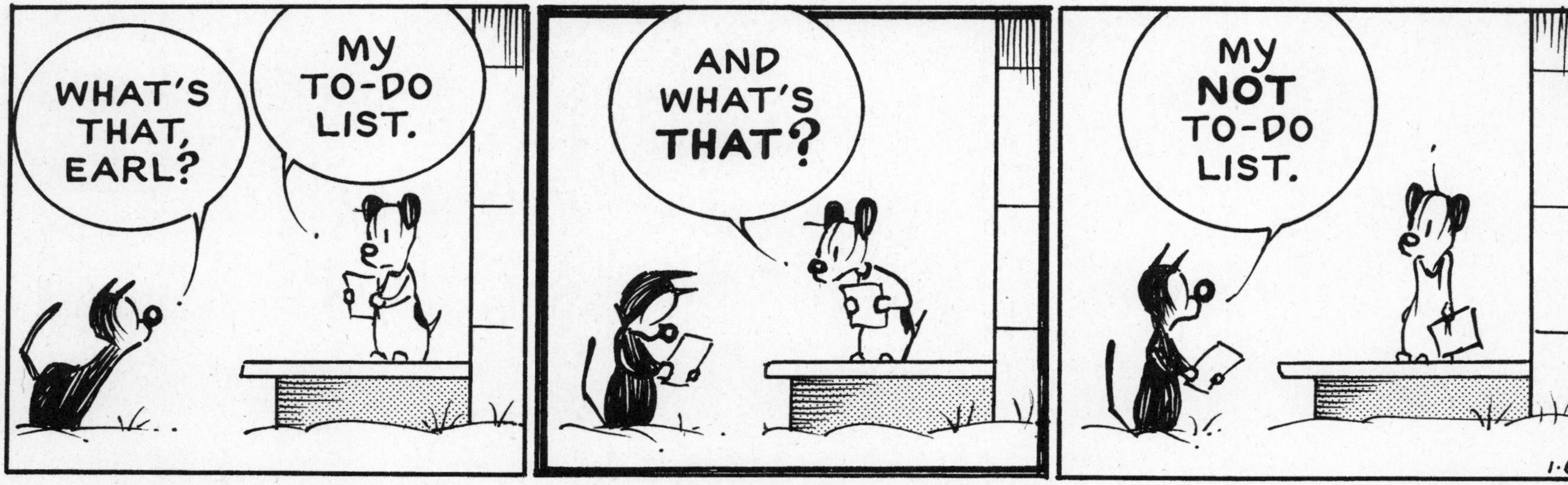
WHAT'S THAT, EARL?
MY TO-DO LIST.
AND WHAT'S THAT?
MY NOT TO-DO LIST.
1·6

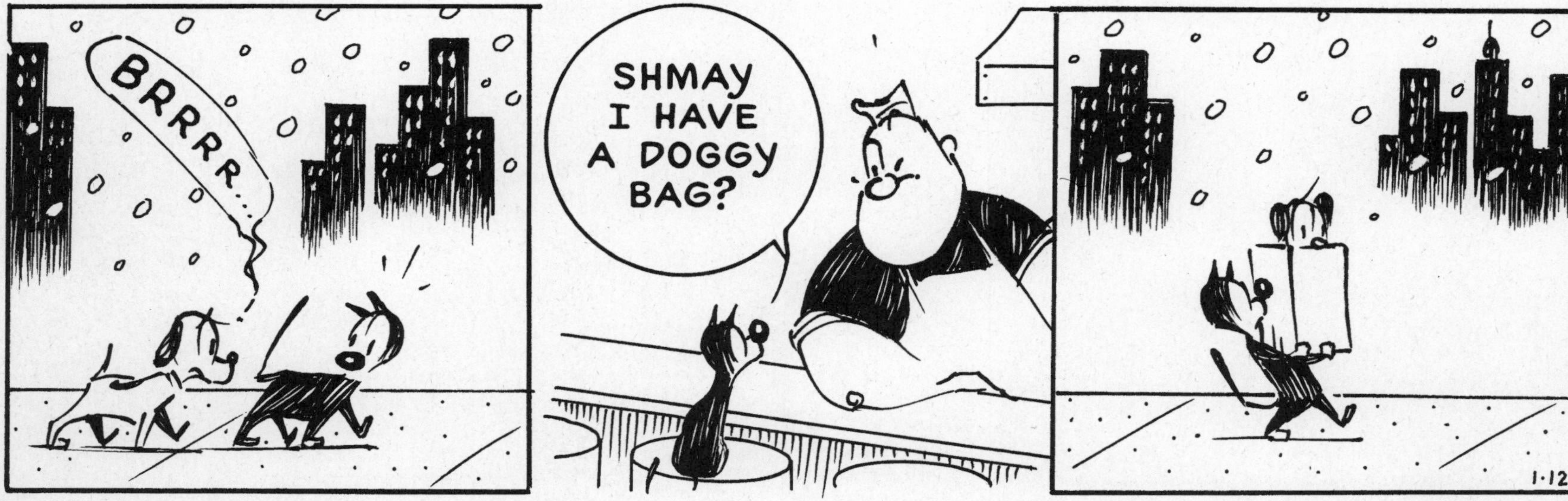
BRRRRR...
SHMAY I HAVE A DOGGY BAG?
1·12

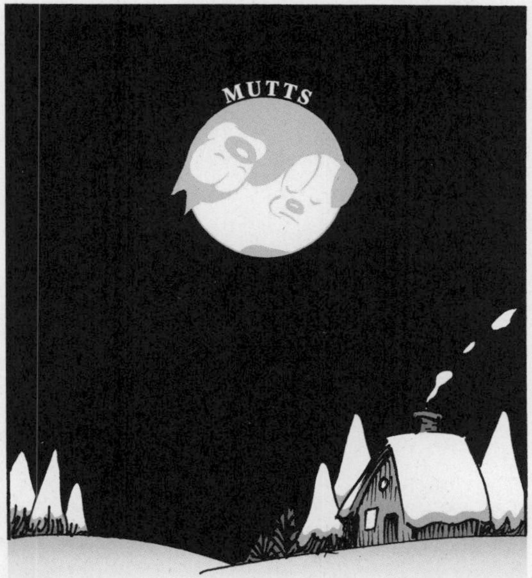
MUTTS

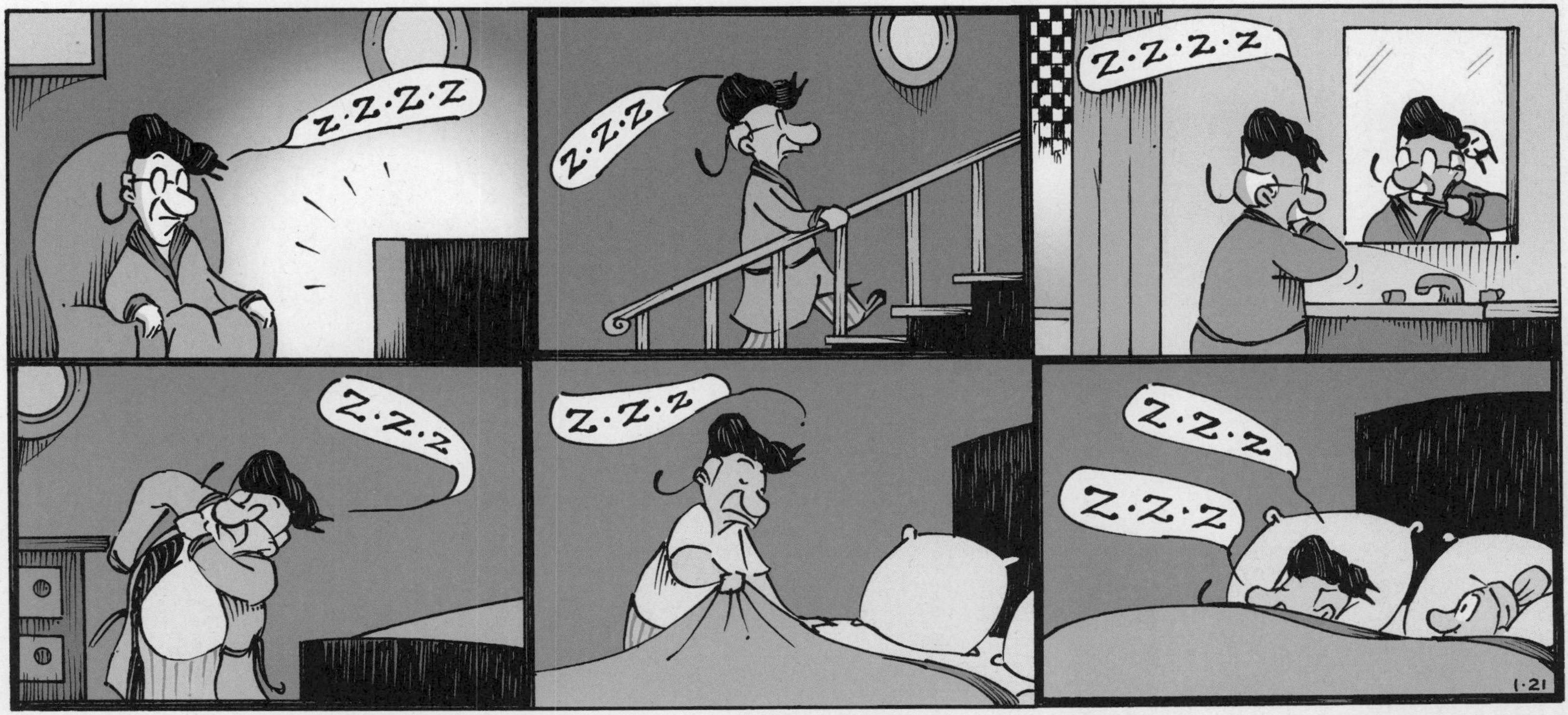
Z·Z·Z·Z
Z·Z·Z
Z·Z·Z·Z
Z·Z·Z
Z·Z·Z
Z·Z·Z
Z·Z·Z
1·21

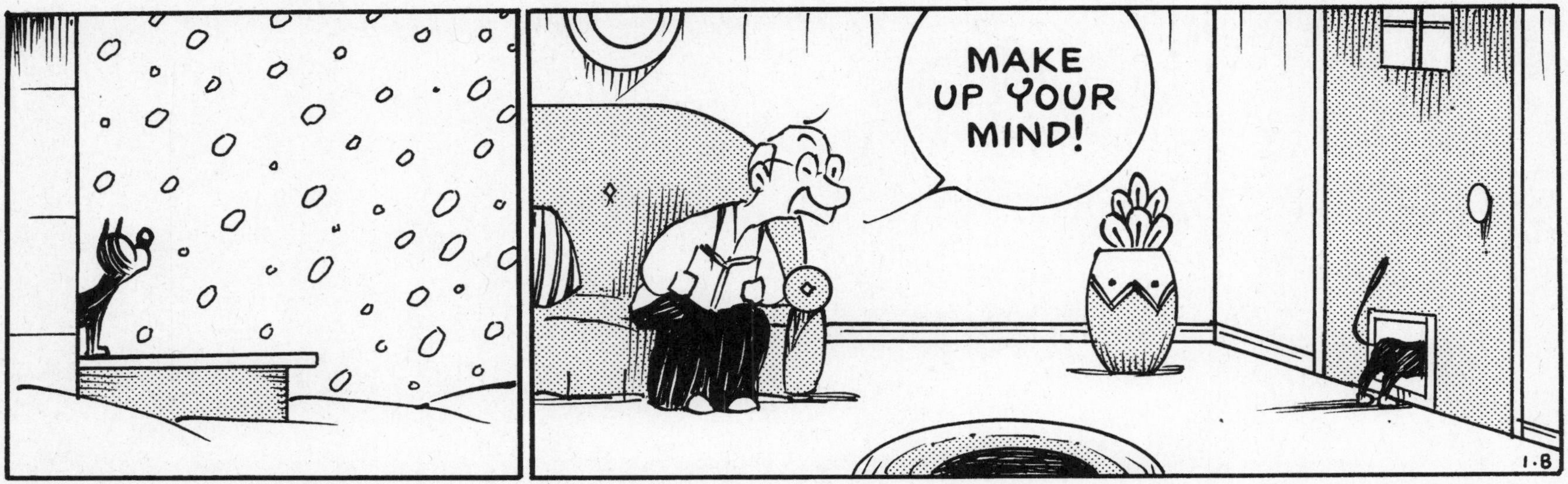
MAKE UP YOUR MIND!
1·8

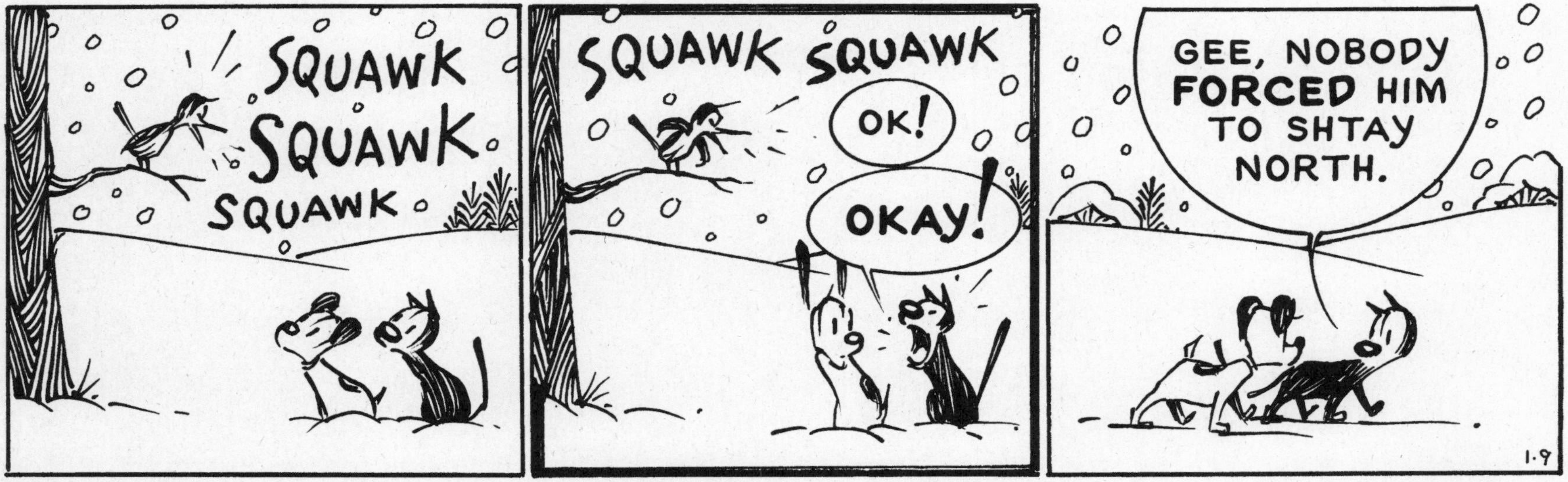
SQUAWK
SQUAWK
SQUAWK
SQUAWK SQUAWK
OK!
OKAY!
GEE, NOBODY FORCED HIM TO SHTAY NORTH.
1·9

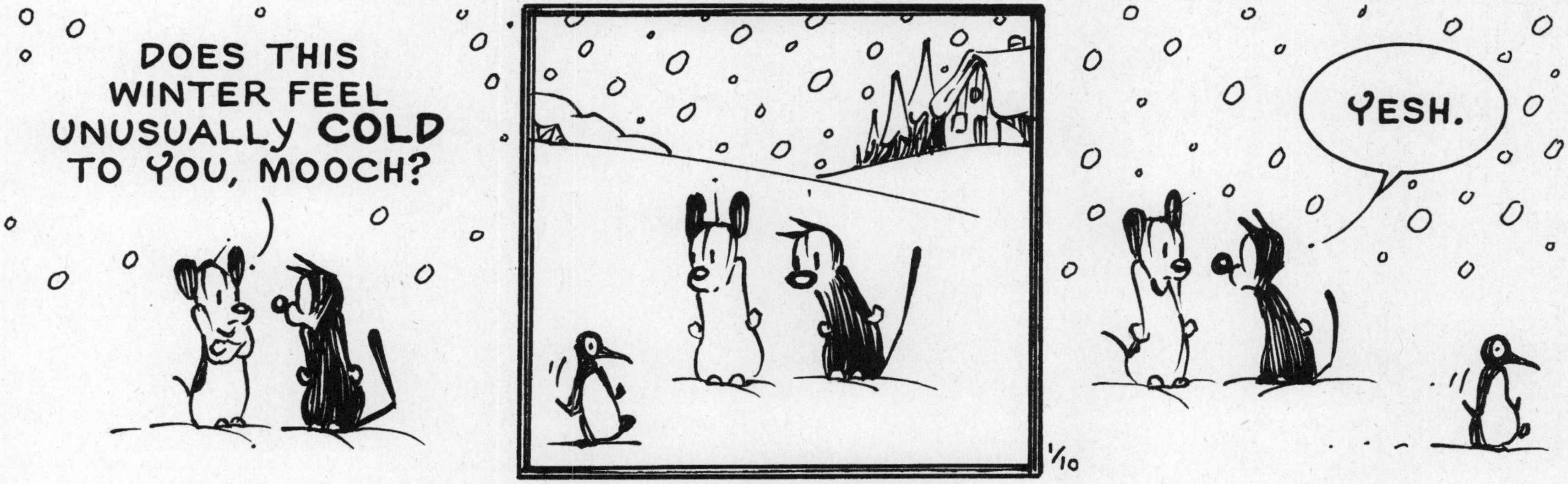
DOES THIS WINTER FEEL UNUSUALLY COLD TO YOU, MOOCH?
YESH.
1/10

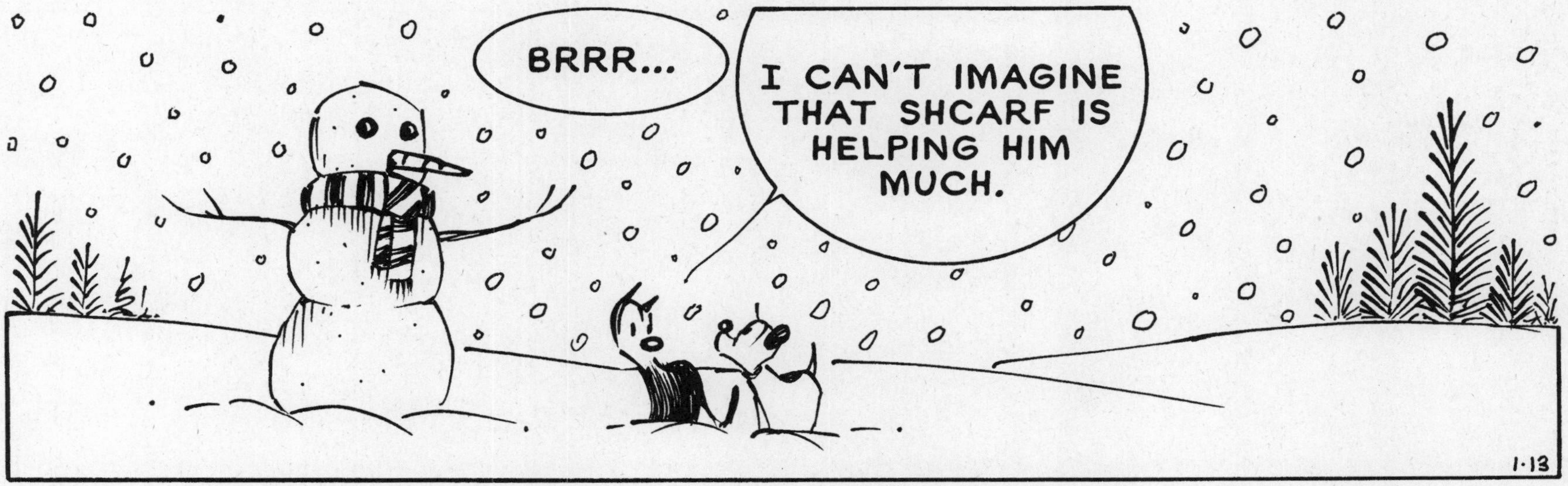
BRRR...
I CAN'T IMAGINE THAT SHCARF IS HELPING HIM MUCH.
1·13

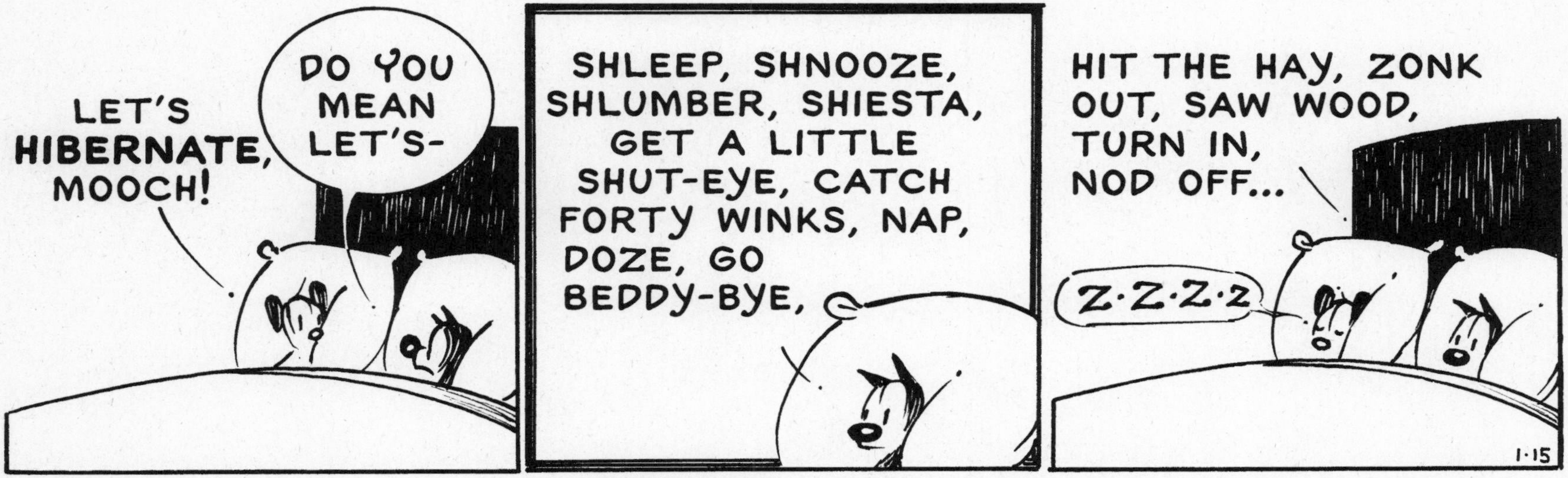
LET'S HIBERNATE, MOOCH!
DO YOU MEAN LET'S-
SHLEEP, SHNOOZE, SHLUMBER, SHIESTA, GET A LITTLE SHUT-EYE, CATCH FORTY WINKS, NAP, DOZE, GO BEDDY-BYE,
HIT THE HAY, ZONK OUT, SAW WOOD, TURN IN, NOD OFF...
Z·Z·Z·Z
1·15

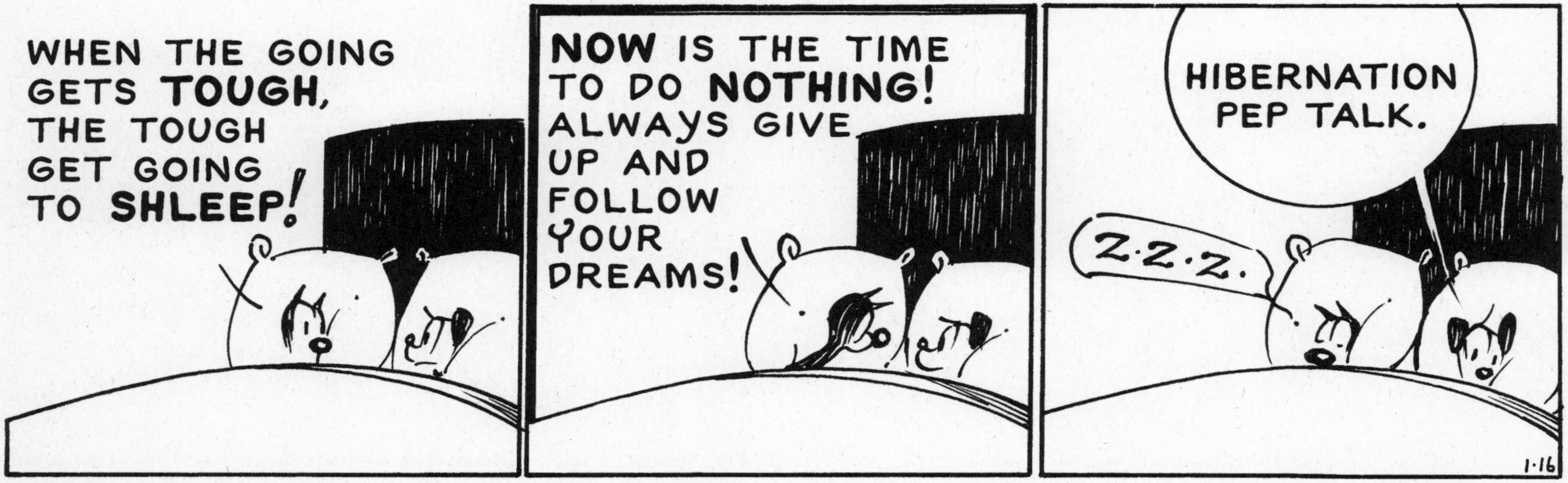
WHEN THE GOING GETS TOUGH, THE TOUGH GET GOING TO SHLEEP!
NOW IS THE TIME TO DO NOTHING! ALWAYS GIVE UP AND FOLLOW YOUR DREAMS!
HIBERNATION PEP TALK.
Z·Z·Z.
1·16

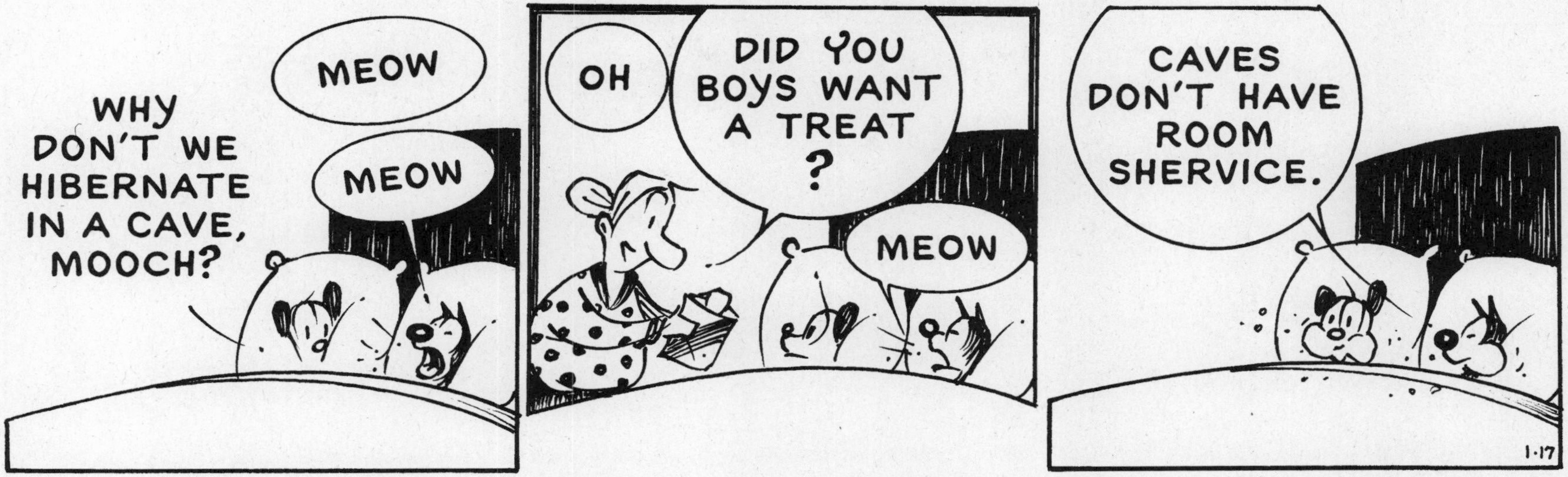
WHY DON'T WE HIBERNATE IN A CAVE, MOOCH?
MEOW
MEOW
OH
DID YOU BOYS WANT A TREAT ?
MEOW
CAVES DON'T HAVE ROOM SHERVICE.
1·17

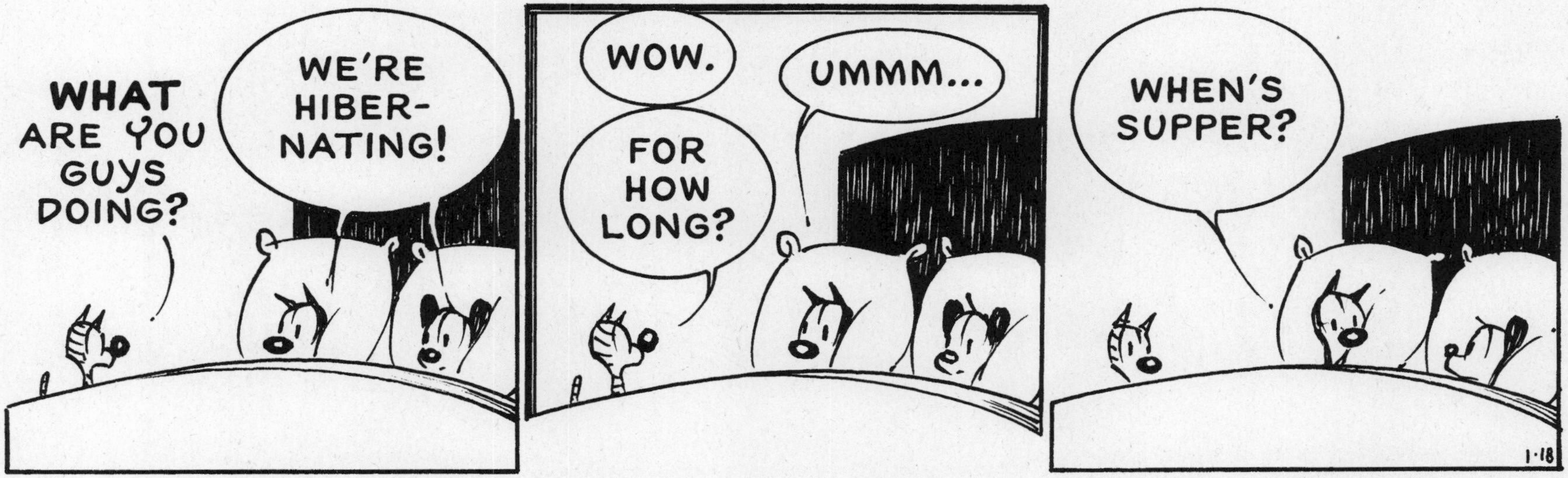
WHAT ARE YOU GUYS DOING?
WE'RE HIBER-NATING!
WOW.
FOR HOW LONG?
UMMM...
WHEN'S SUPPER?
1·18

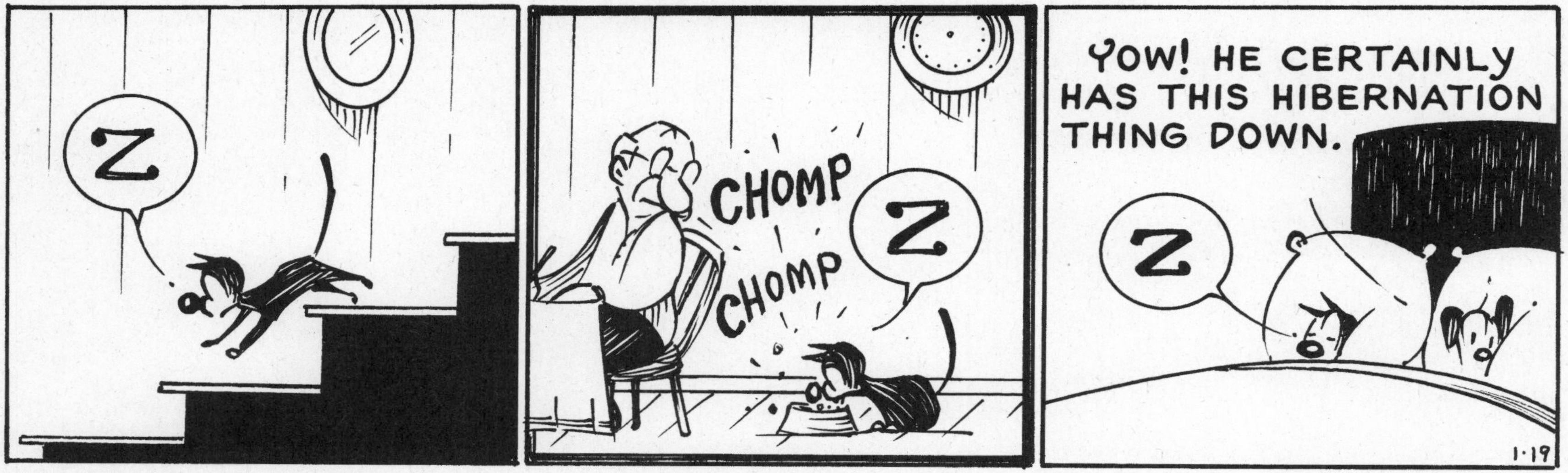
Z
CHOMP
CHOMP
Z
YOW! HE CERTAINLY HAS THIS HIBERNATION THING DOWN.
Z
1·19

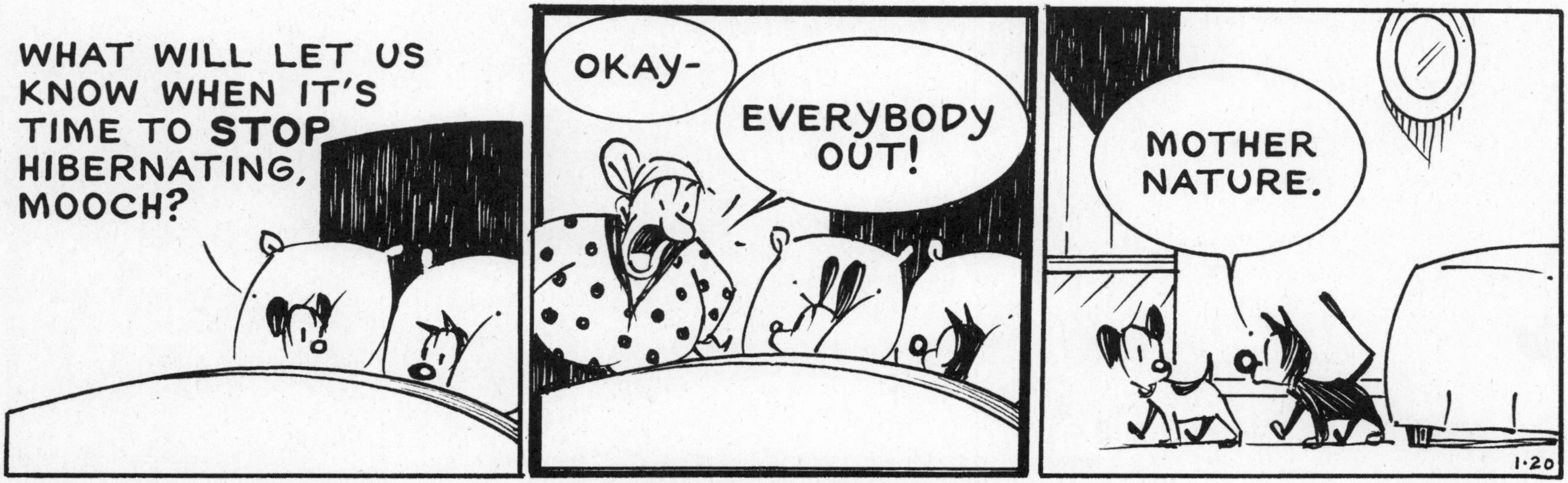
WHAT WILL LET US KNOW WHEN IT'S TIME TO **STOP** HIBERNATING, MOOCH?
OKAY-
EVERYBODY OUT!
MOTHER NATURE.
1·20

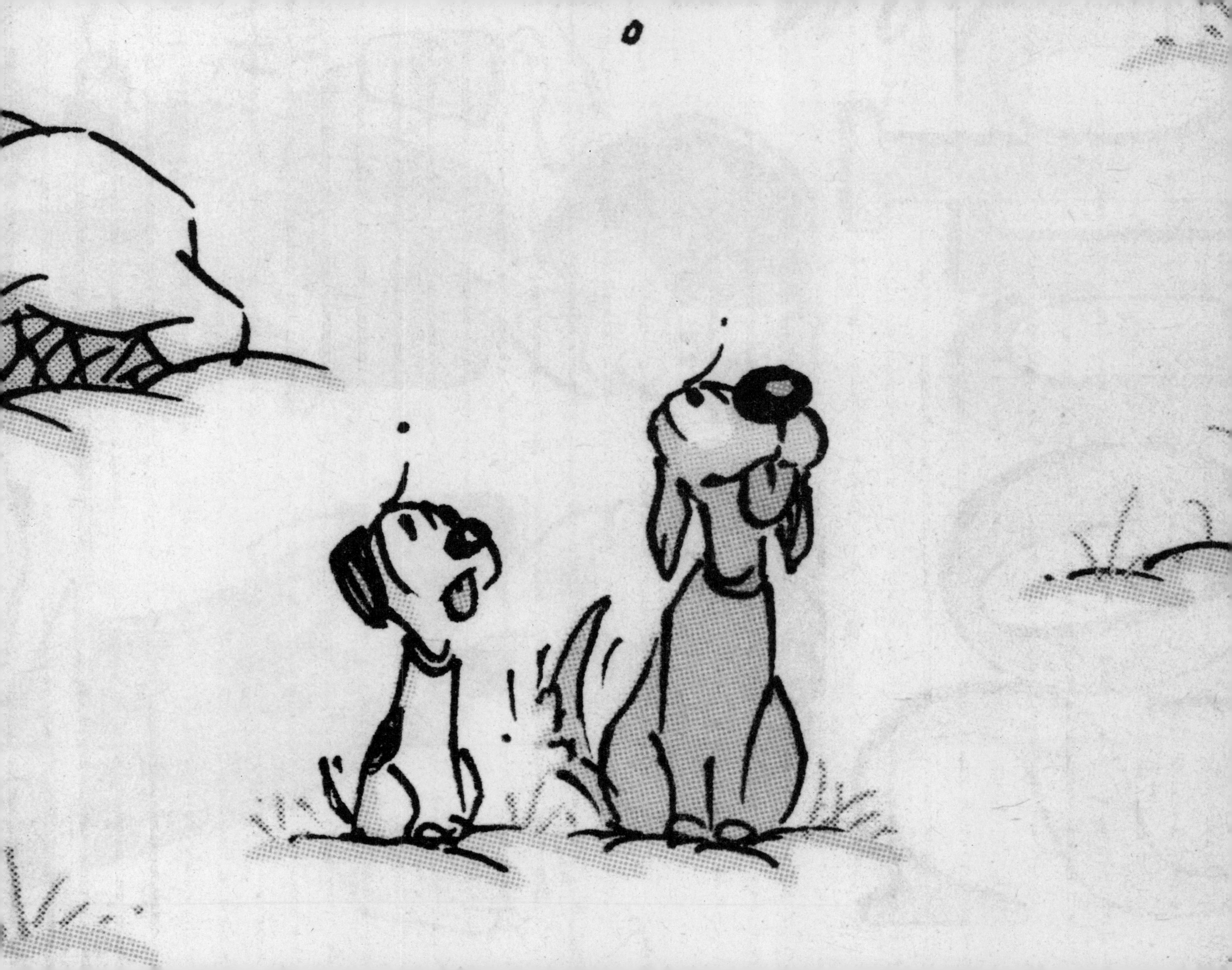

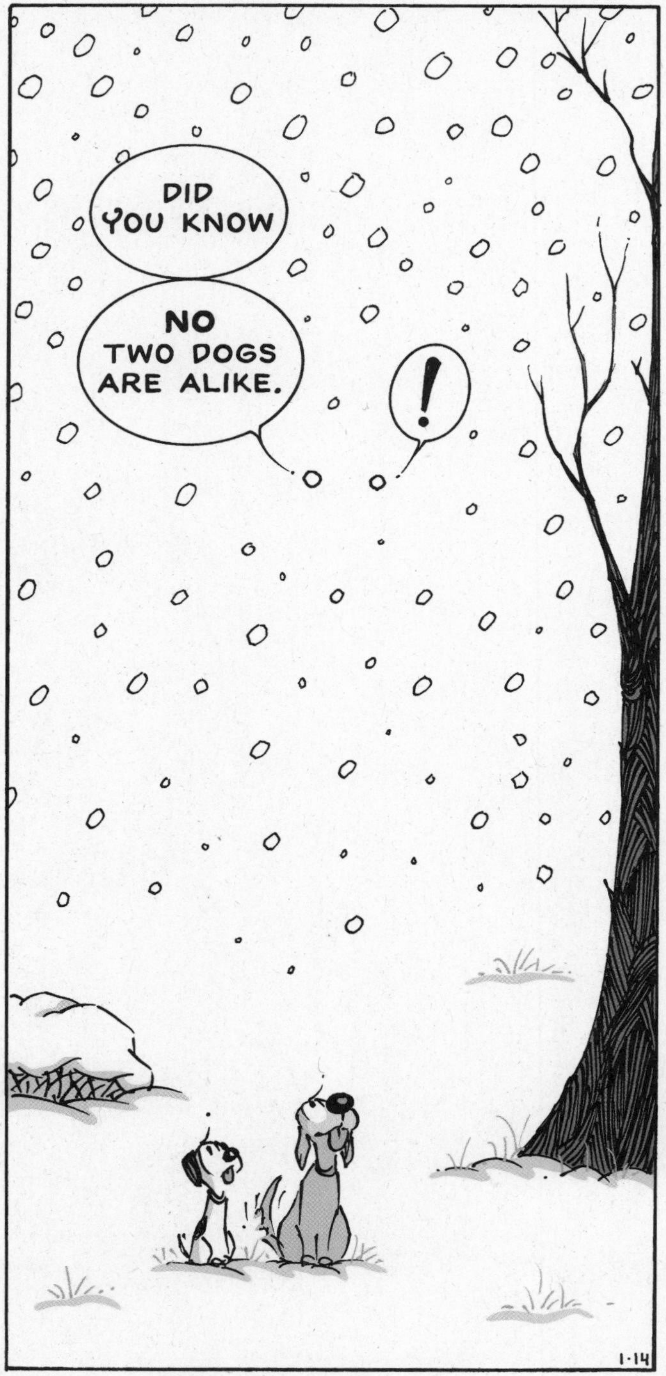
DID YOU KNOW
NO TWO DOGS ARE ALIKE.
!
1·14

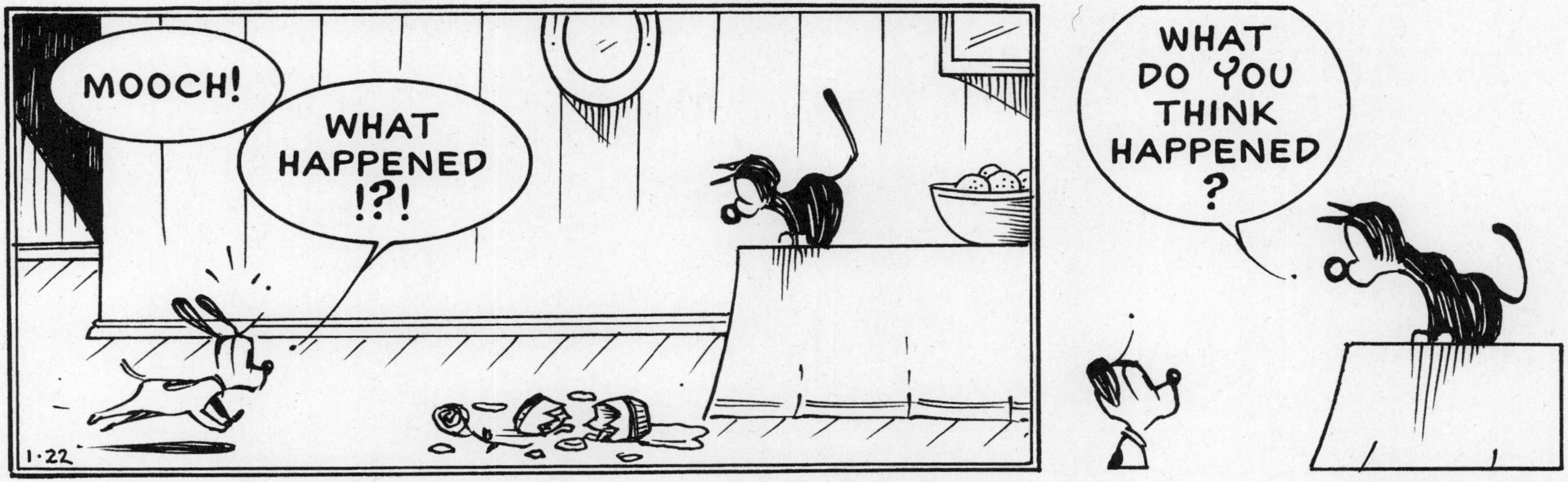
MOOCH!
WHAT HAPPENED !?!
WHAT DO YOU THINK HAPPENED ?
1·22

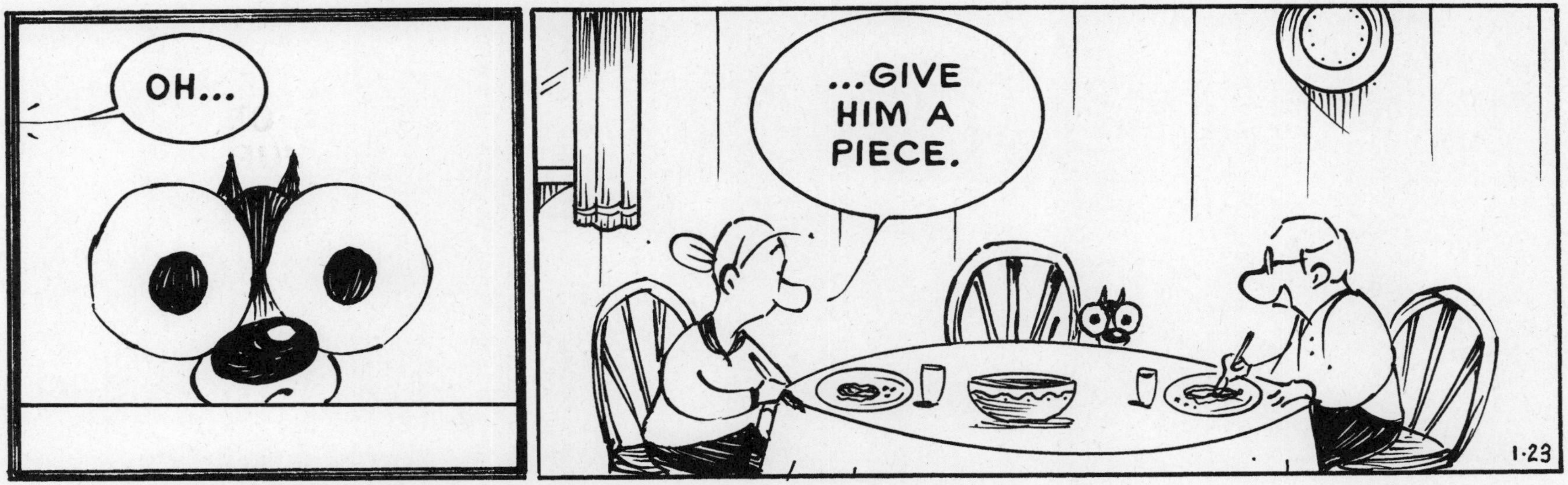
OH...
...GIVE HIM A PIECE.
1·23

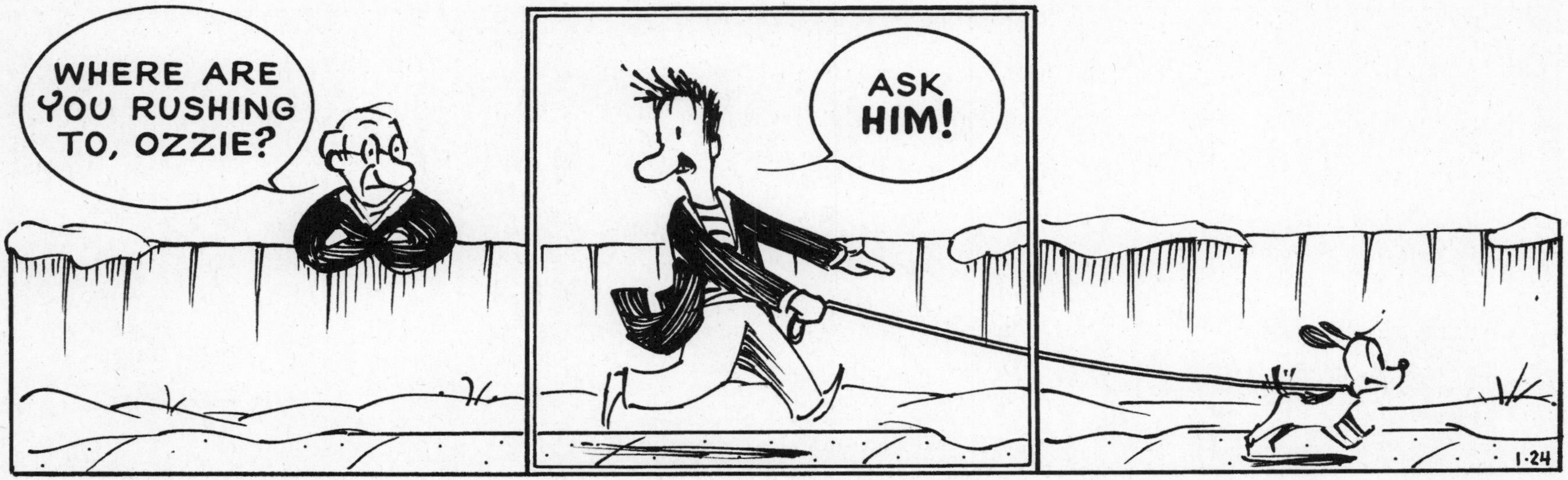
WHERE ARE YOU RUSHING TO, OZZIE?
ASK HIM!
1·24

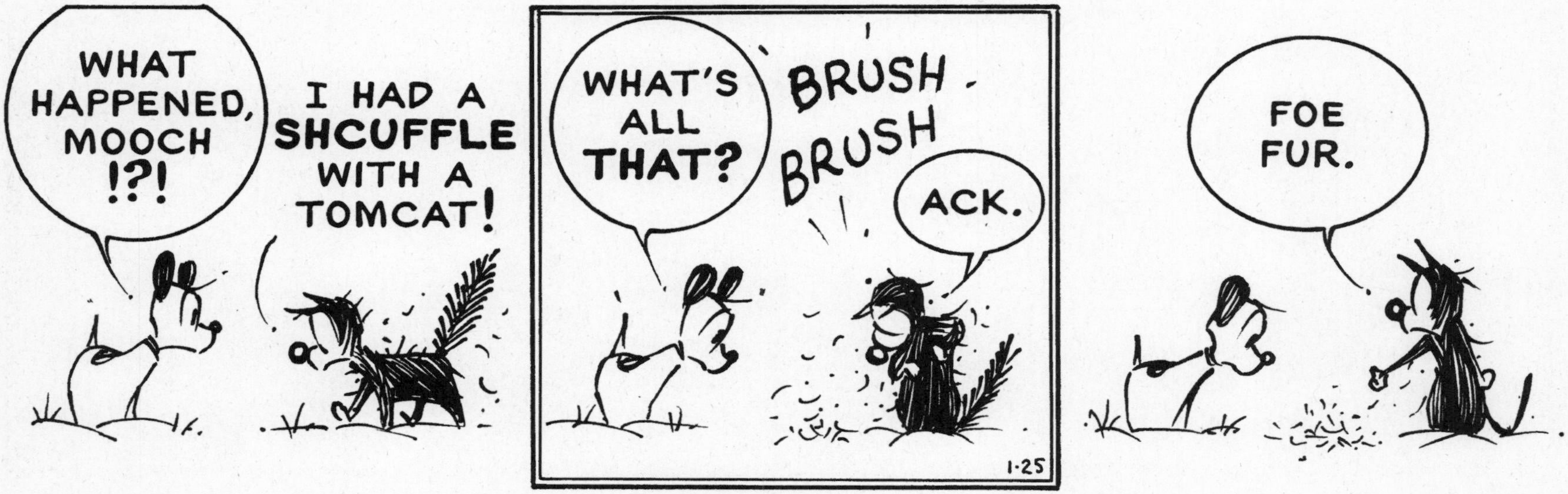
WHAT HAPPENED, MOOCH !?!
I HAD A SHCUFFLE WITH A TOMCAT!
WHAT'S ALL THAT?
BRUSH BRUSH
ACK.
1·25
FOE FUR.

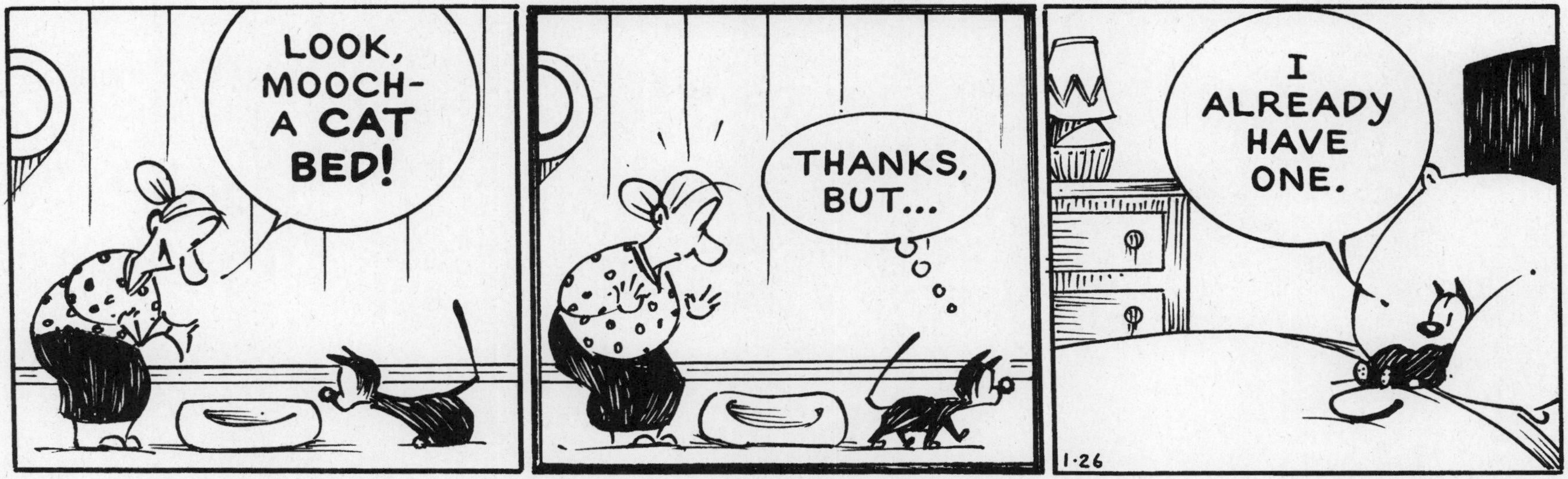
LOOK, MOOCH- A CAT BED!
THANKS, BUT...
I ALREADY HAVE ONE.
1·26

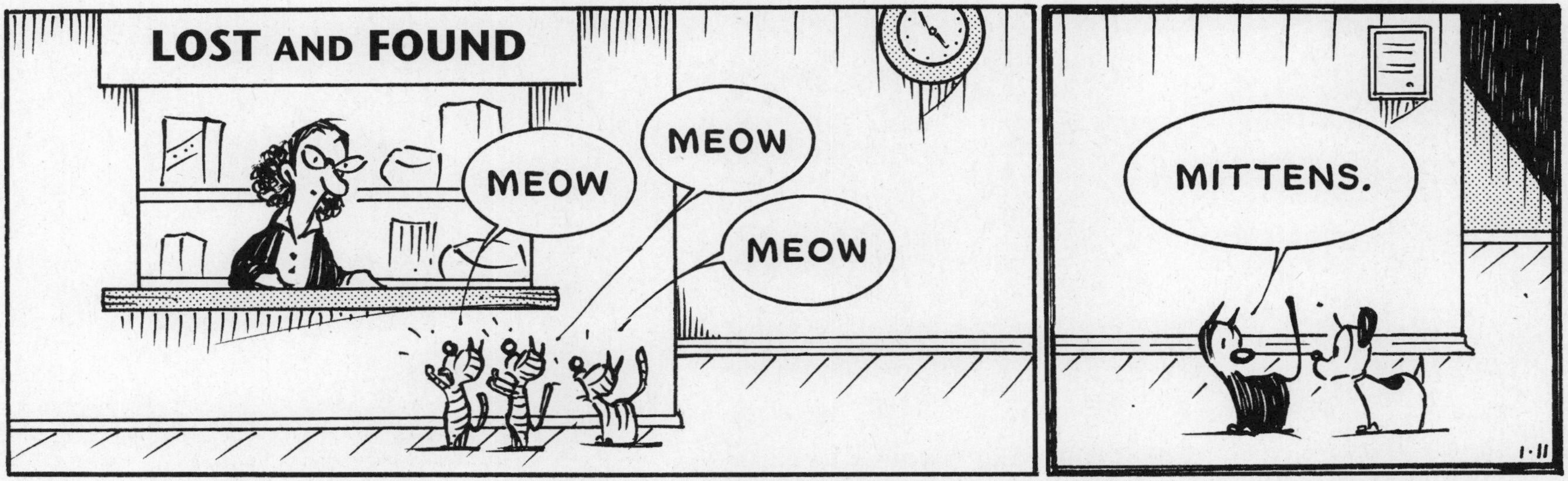
LOST AND FOUND
MEOW
MEOW
MEOW
MITTENS.
1·11

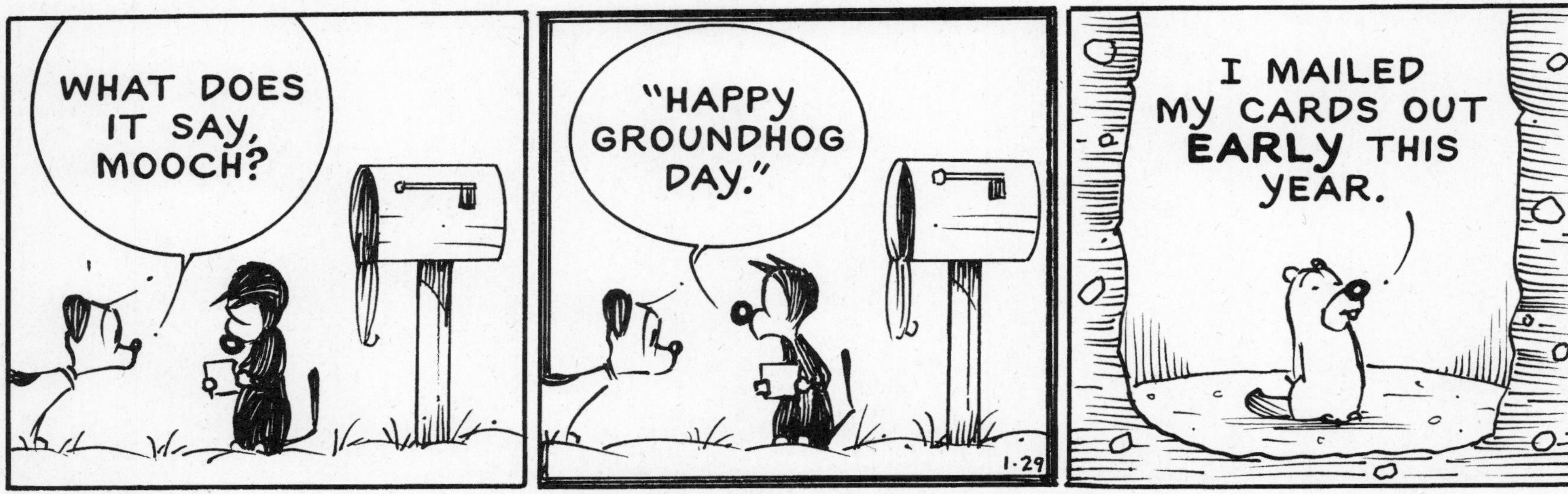
WHAT DOES IT SAY, MOOCH?
"HAPPY GROUNDHOG DAY."
1·29
I MAILED MY CARDS OUT **EARLY** THIS YEAR.

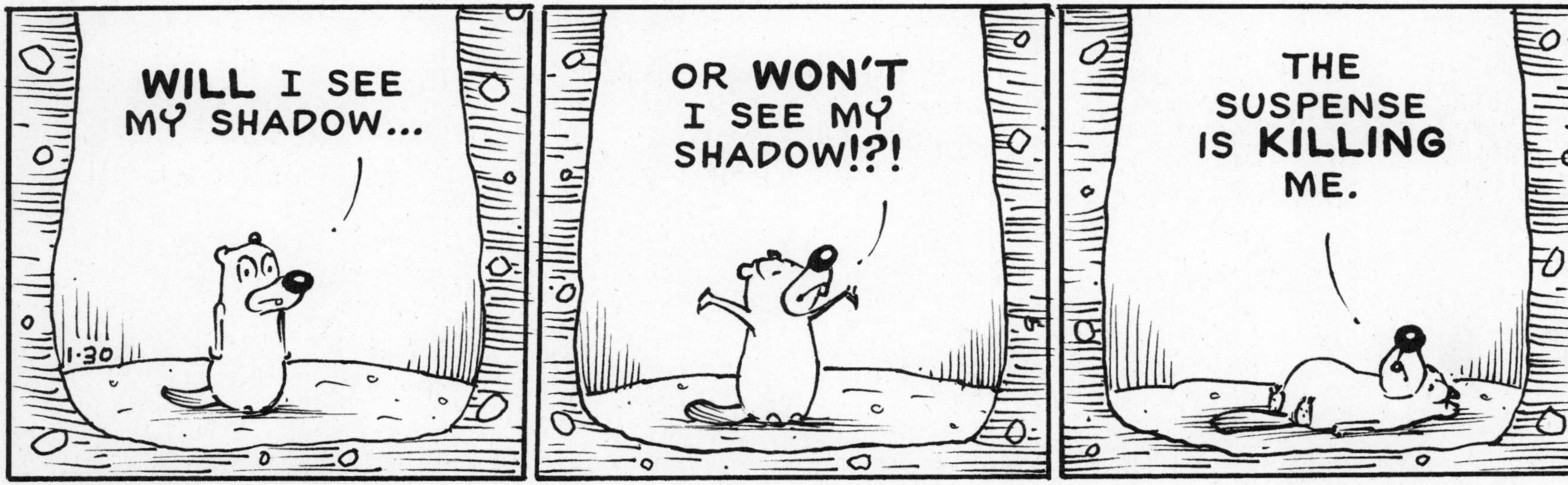
WILL I SEE MY SHADOW...
1·30
OR **WON'T** I SEE MY SHADOW!?!
THE SUSPENSE IS **KILLING** ME.

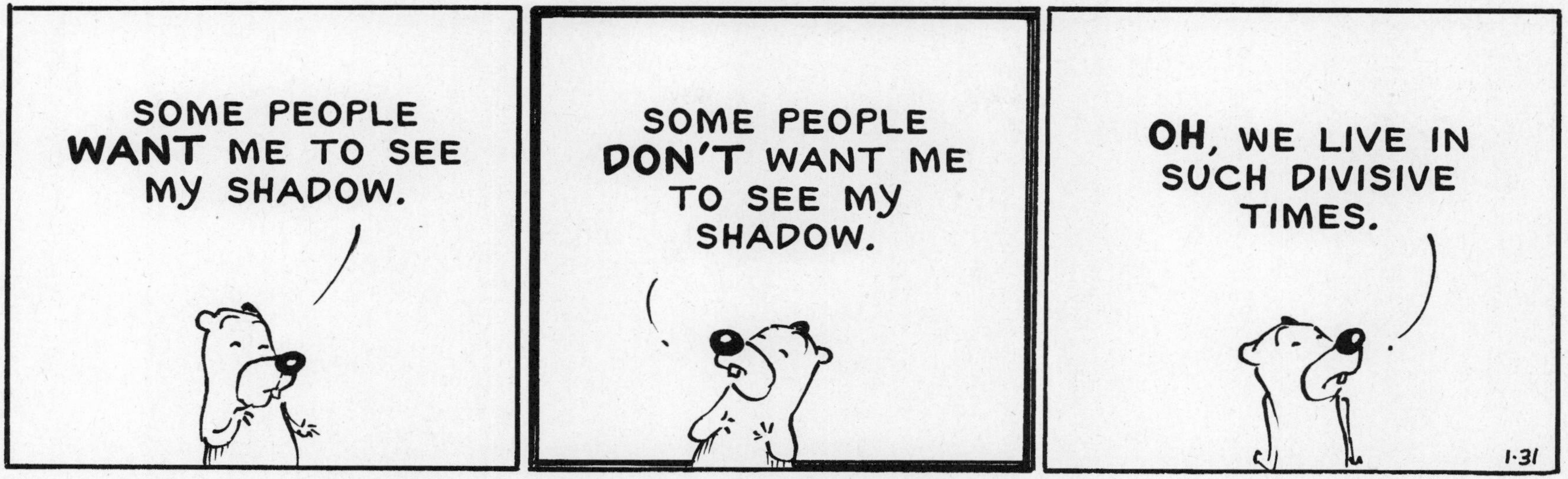
SOME PEOPLE **WANT** ME TO SEE MY SHADOW.
SOME PEOPLE **DON'T** WANT ME TO SEE MY SHADOW.
OH, WE LIVE IN SUCH DIVISIVE TIMES.
1·31

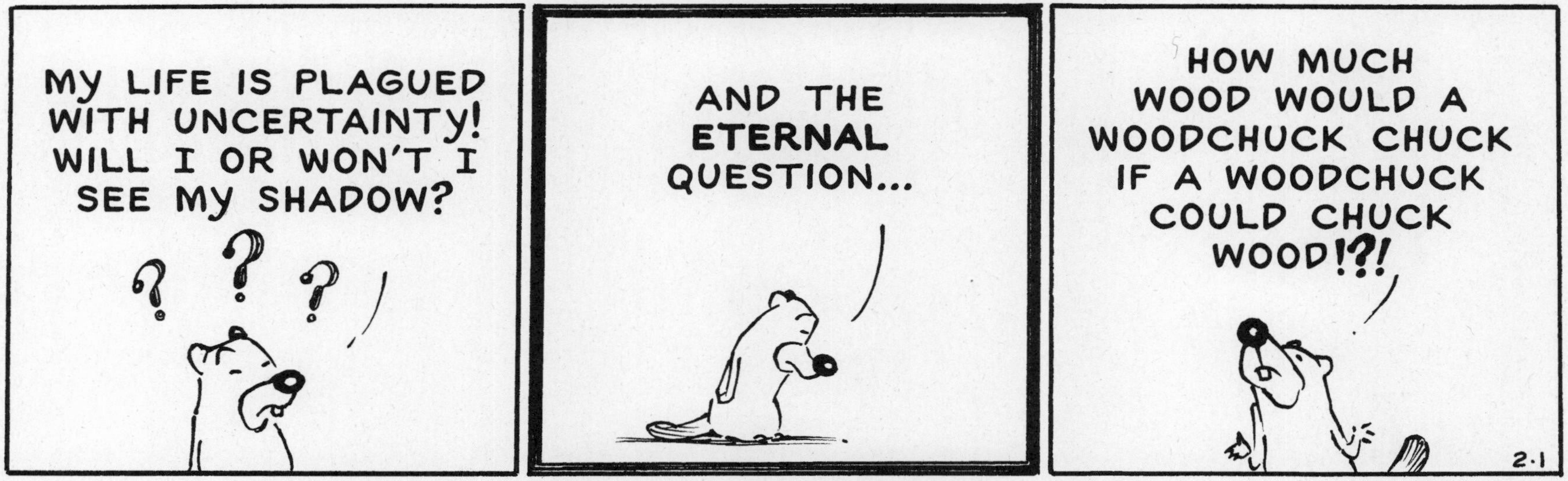
MY LIFE IS PLAGUED WITH UNCERTAINTY! WILL I OR WON'T I SEE MY SHADOW?
? ? ?
AND THE **ETERNAL** QUESTION...
HOW MUCH WOOD WOULD A WOODCHUCK CHUCK IF A WOODCHUCK COULD CHUCK WOOD!?!
2·1

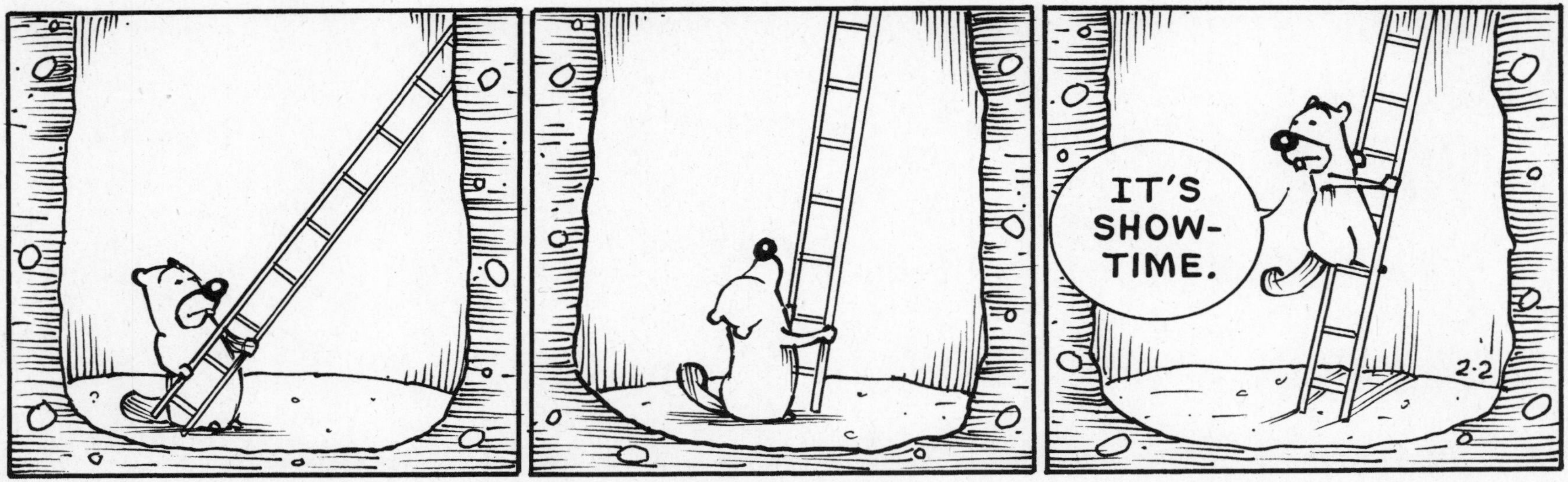
IT'S SHOW-TIME.
2·2

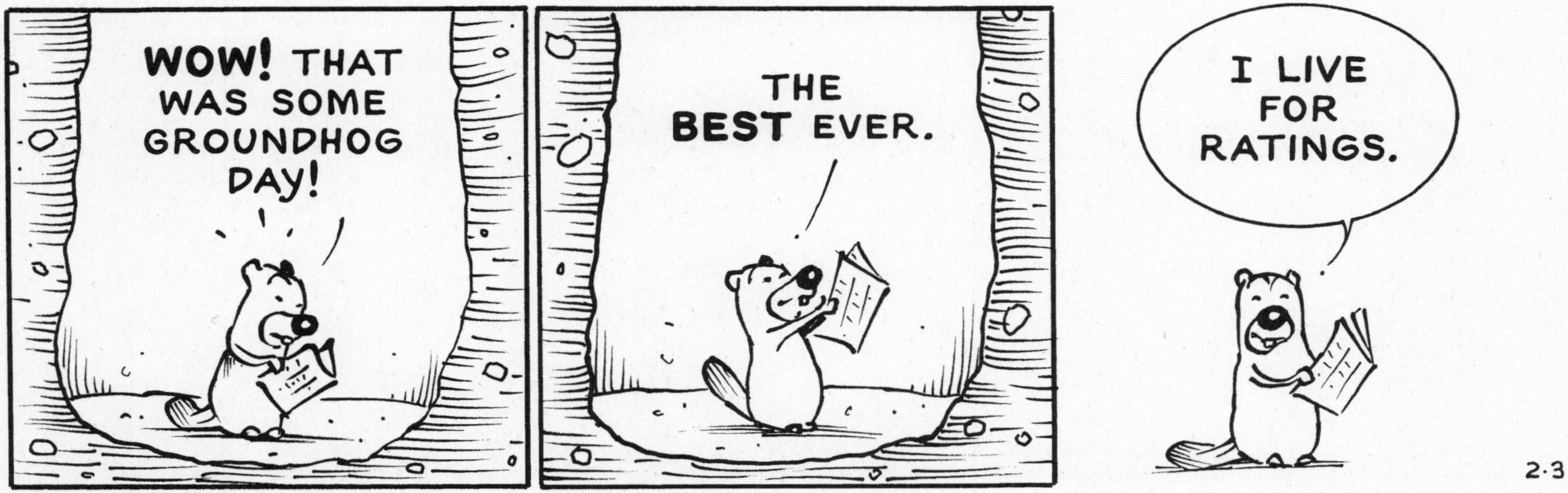
WOW! THAT WAS SOME GROUNDHOG DAY!
THE BEST EVER.
I LIVE FOR RATINGS.
2·3

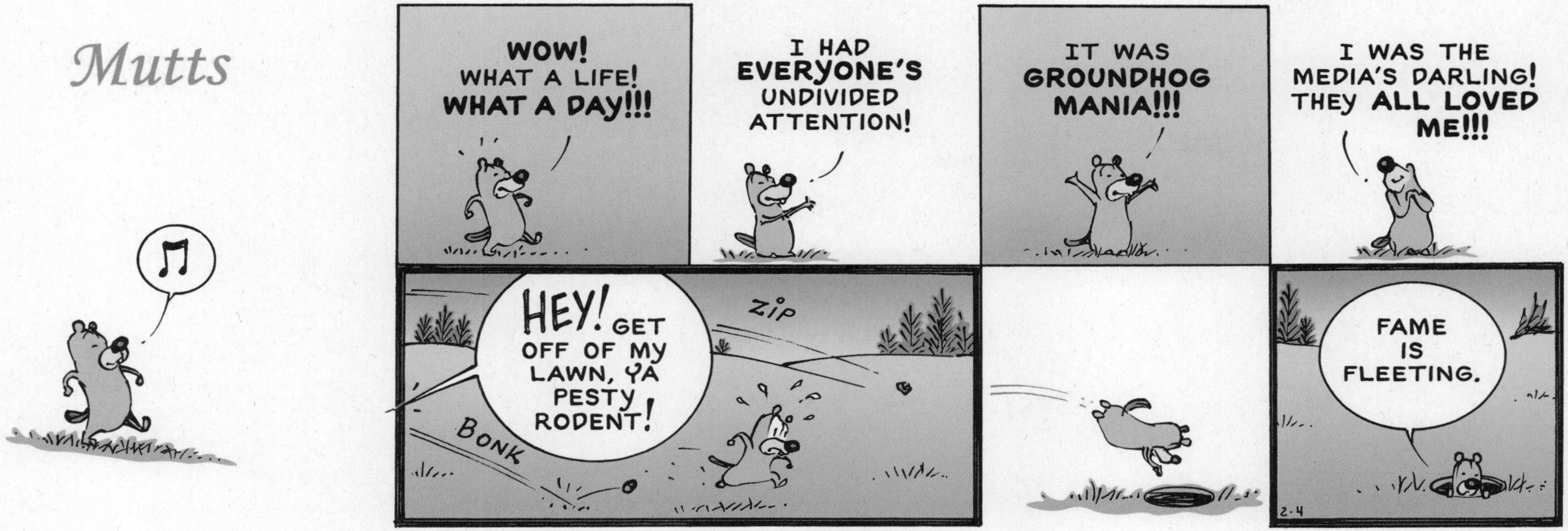
Mutts
♫
WOW! WHAT A LIFE! WHAT A DAY!!!
I HAD EVERYONE'S UNDIVIDED ATTENTION!
IT WAS GROUNDHOG MANIA!!!
I WAS THE MEDIA'S DARLING! THEY ALL LOVED ME!!!
HEY! GET OFF OF MY LAWN, YA PESTY RODENT!
ZIP
BONK
FAME IS FLEETING.
2·4

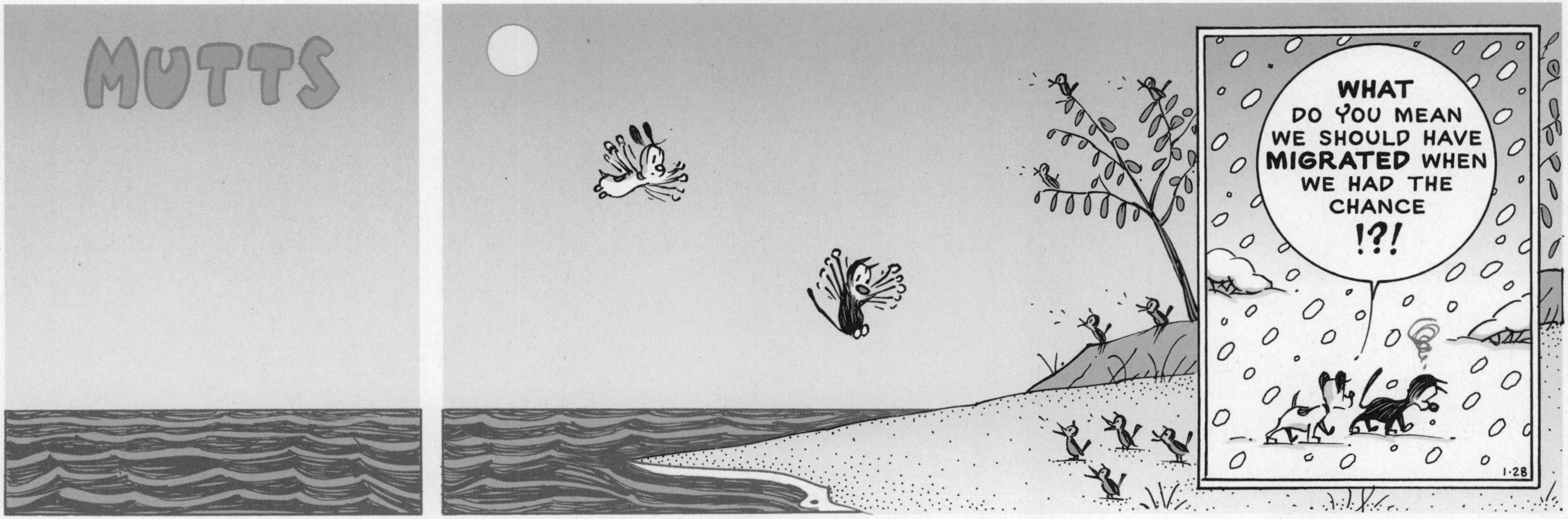
MUTTS
WHAT DO YOU MEAN WE SHOULD HAVE MIGRATED WHEN WE HAD THE CHANCE !?!
1·28

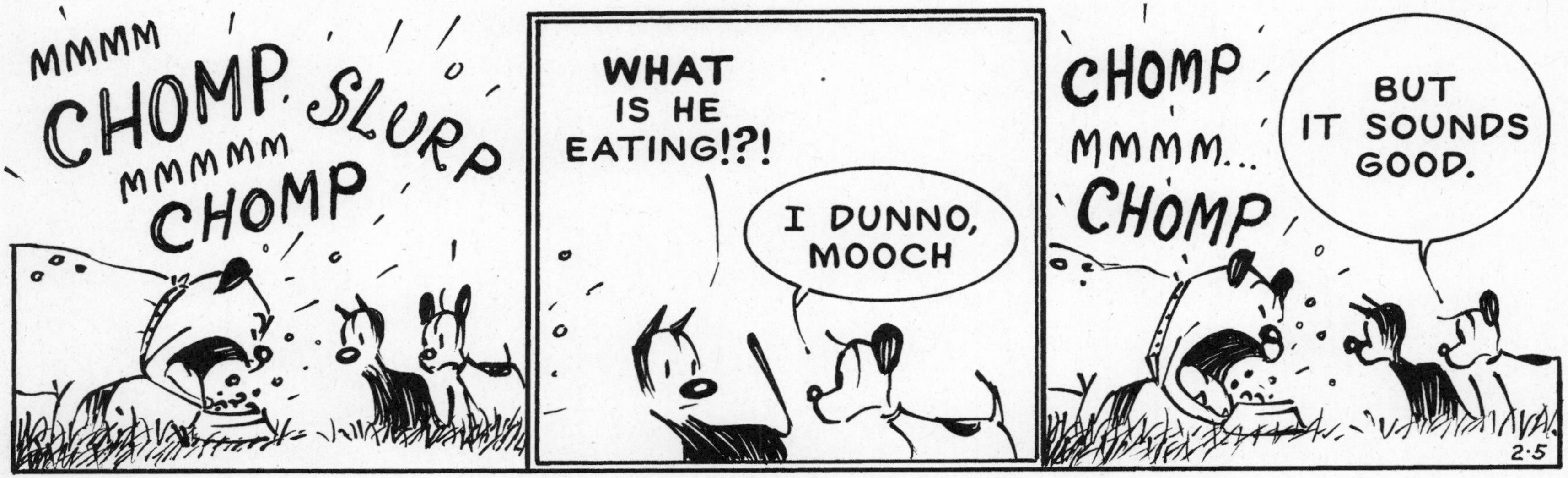
MMMM
CHOMP
SLURP
MMMMMM
CHOMP
WHAT IS HE EATING!?!
I DUNNO, MOOCH
CHOMP
MMMM...
CHOMP
BUT IT SOUNDS GOOD.
2·5

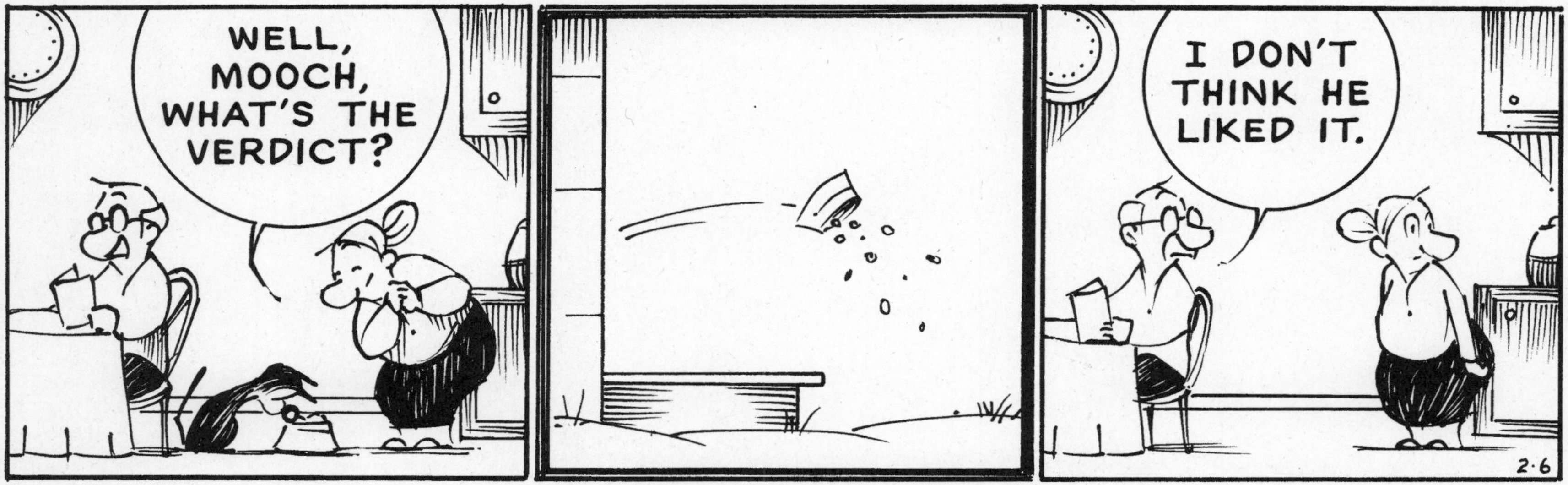
WELL, MOOCH, WHAT'S THE VERDICT?
I DON'T THINK HE LIKED IT.
2·6

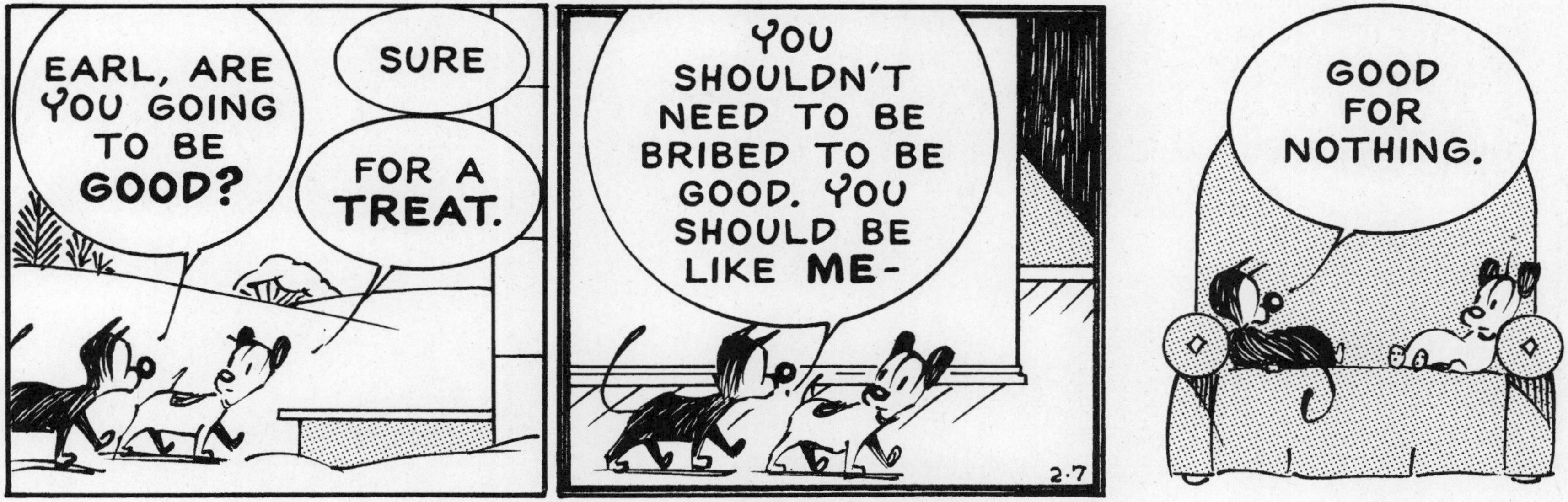
EARL, ARE YOU GOING TO BE **GOOD?**
SURE
FOR A **TREAT.**
YOU SHOULDN'T NEED TO BE BRIBED TO BE GOOD. YOU SHOULD BE LIKE **ME**-
2·7
GOOD FOR NOTHING.

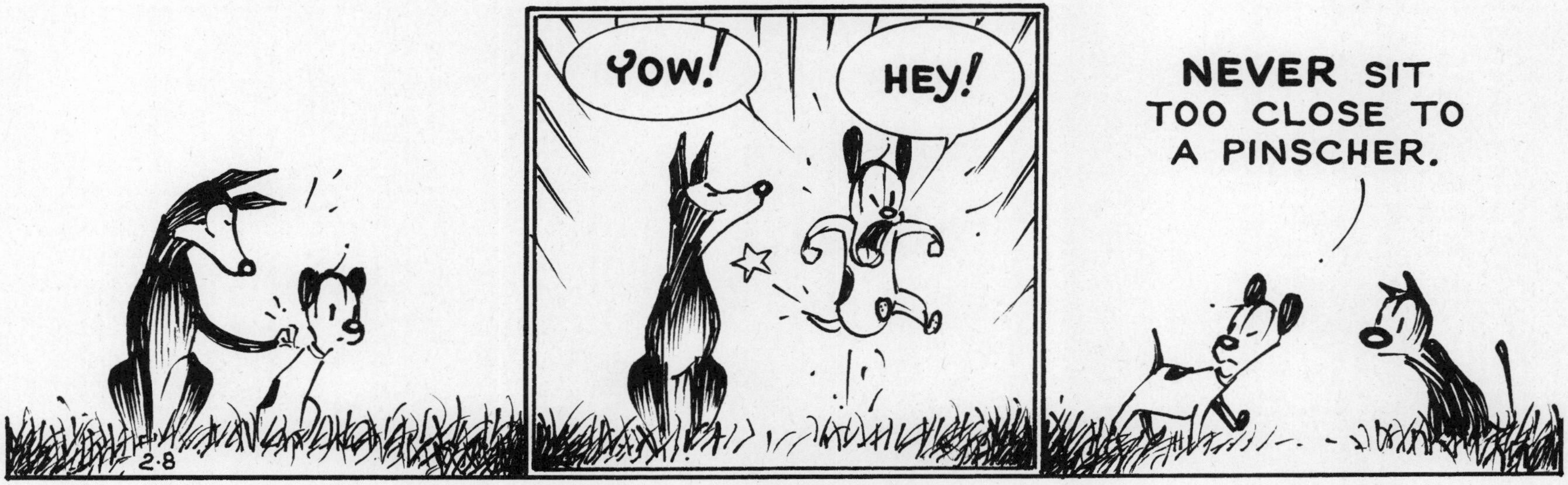
2·8
YOW!
HEY!
NEVER SIT TOO CLOSE TO A PINSCHER.

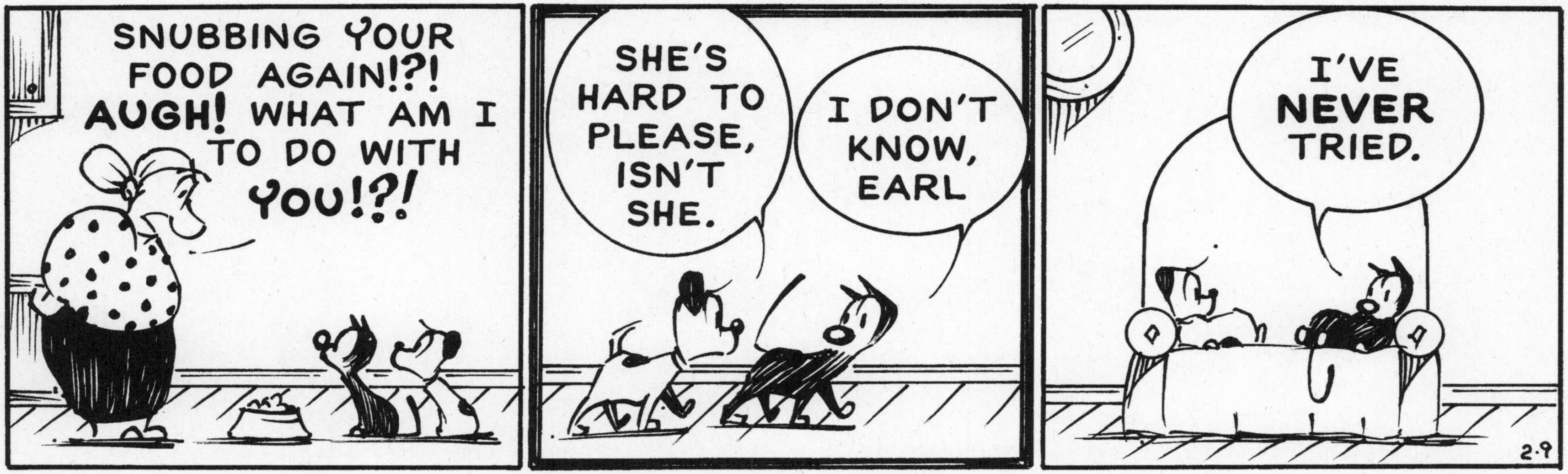
SNUBBING YOUR FOOD AGAIN!?! AUGH! WHAT AM I TO DO WITH YOU!?!
SHE'S HARD TO PLEASE, ISN'T SHE.
I DON'T KNOW, EARL
I'VE NEVER TRIED.
2·9

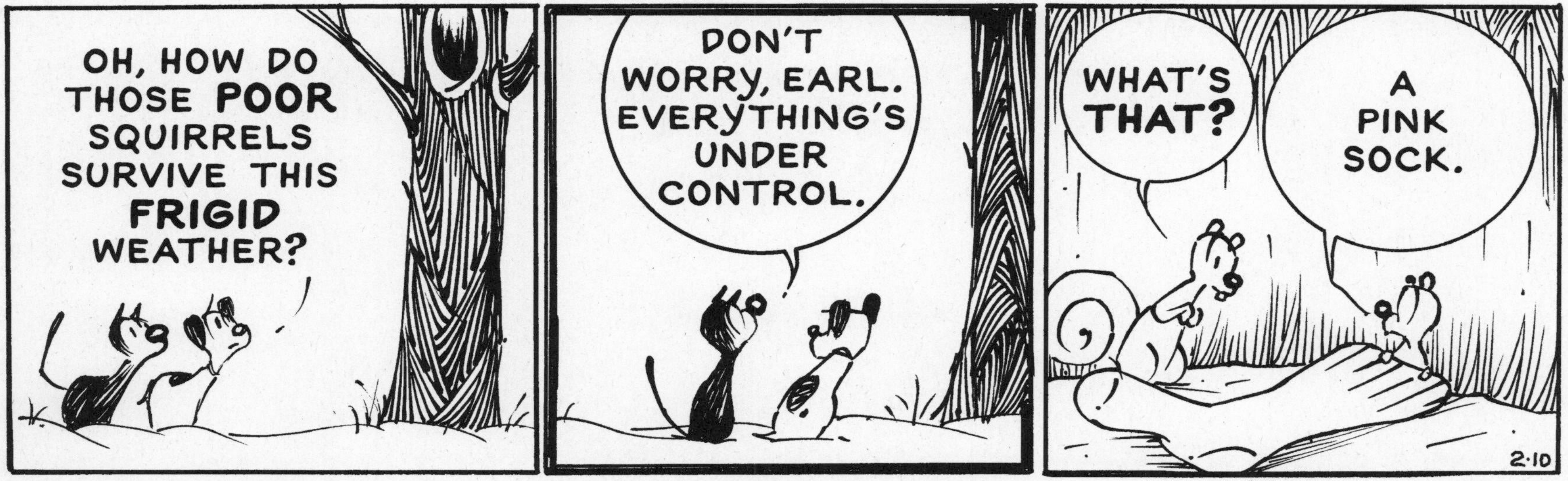
OH, HOW DO THOSE POOR SQUIRRELS SURVIVE THIS FRIGID WEATHER?
DON'T WORRY, EARL. EVERYTHING'S UNDER CONTROL.
WHAT'S THAT?
A PINK SOCK.
2·10

MUTTS

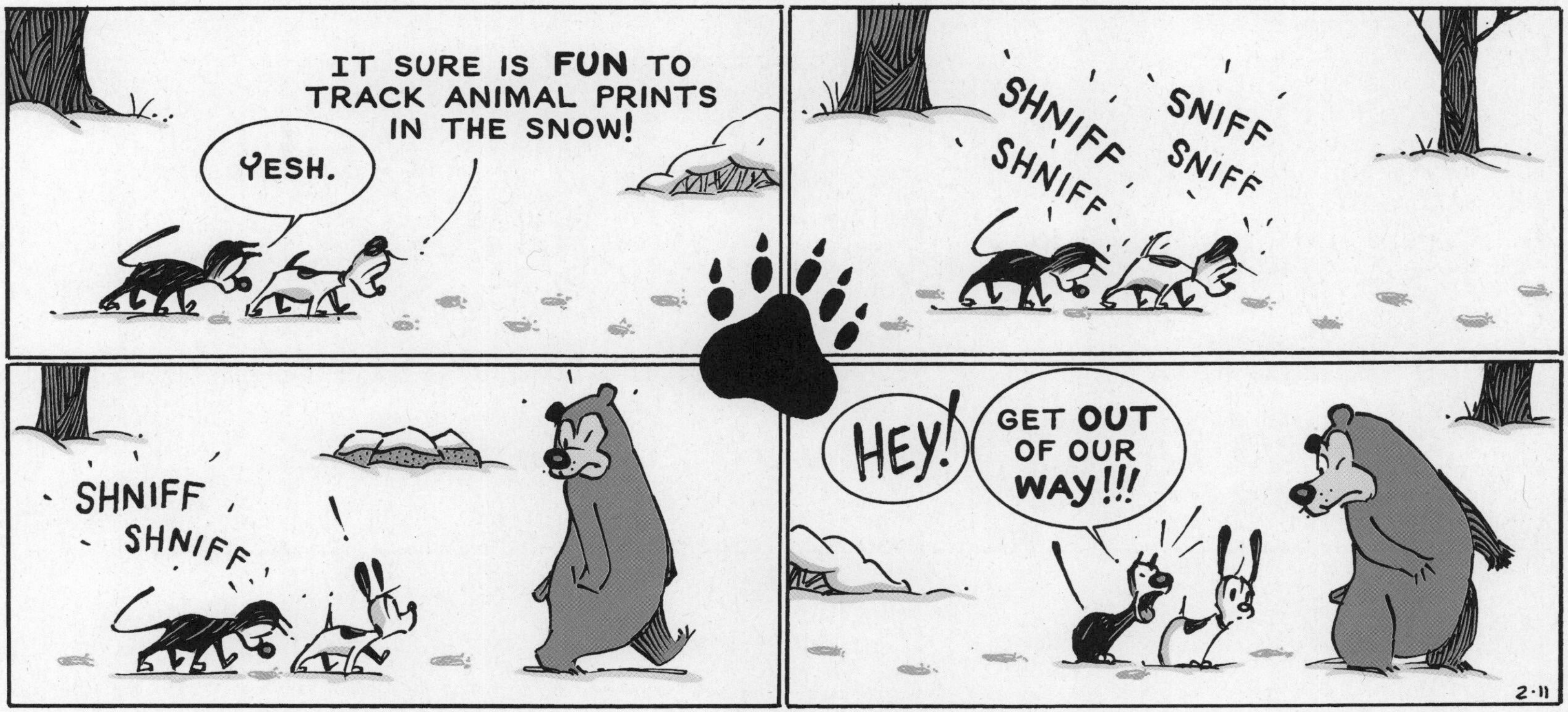
IT SURE IS FUN TO TRACK ANIMAL PRINTS IN THE SNOW!
YESH.
SHNIFF SHNIFF
SNIFF SNIFF
SHNIFF SHNIFF
HEY!
GET OUT OF OUR WAY!!!
2·11

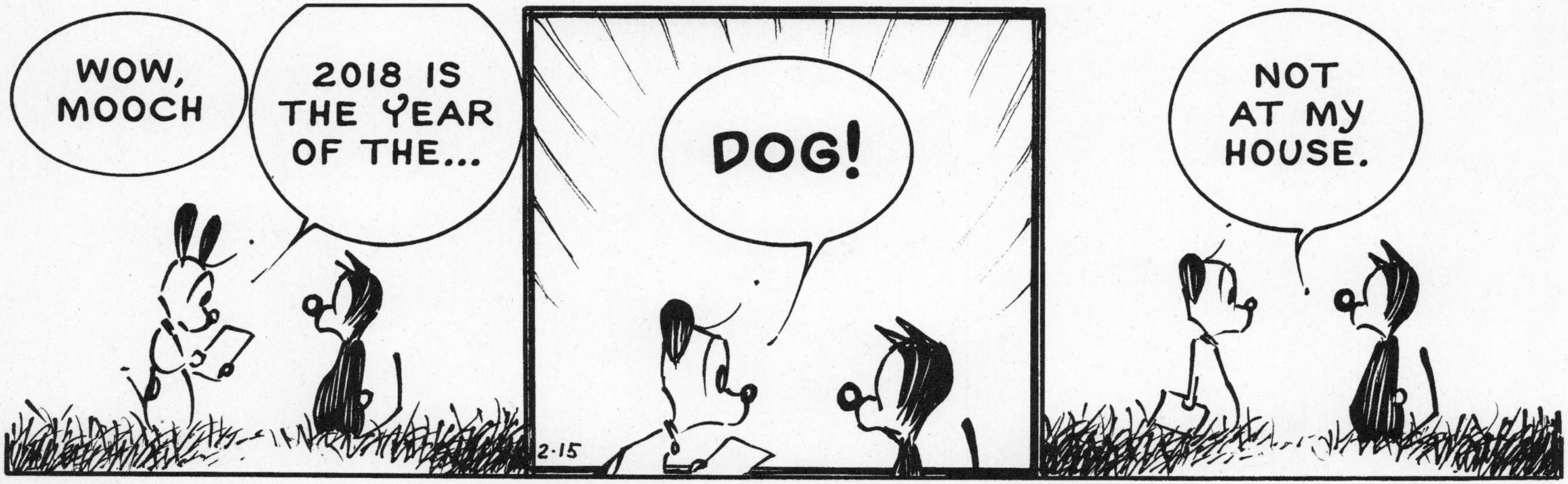
WOW, MOOCH
2018 IS THE YEAR OF THE...
DOG!
NOT AT MY HOUSE.
2·15

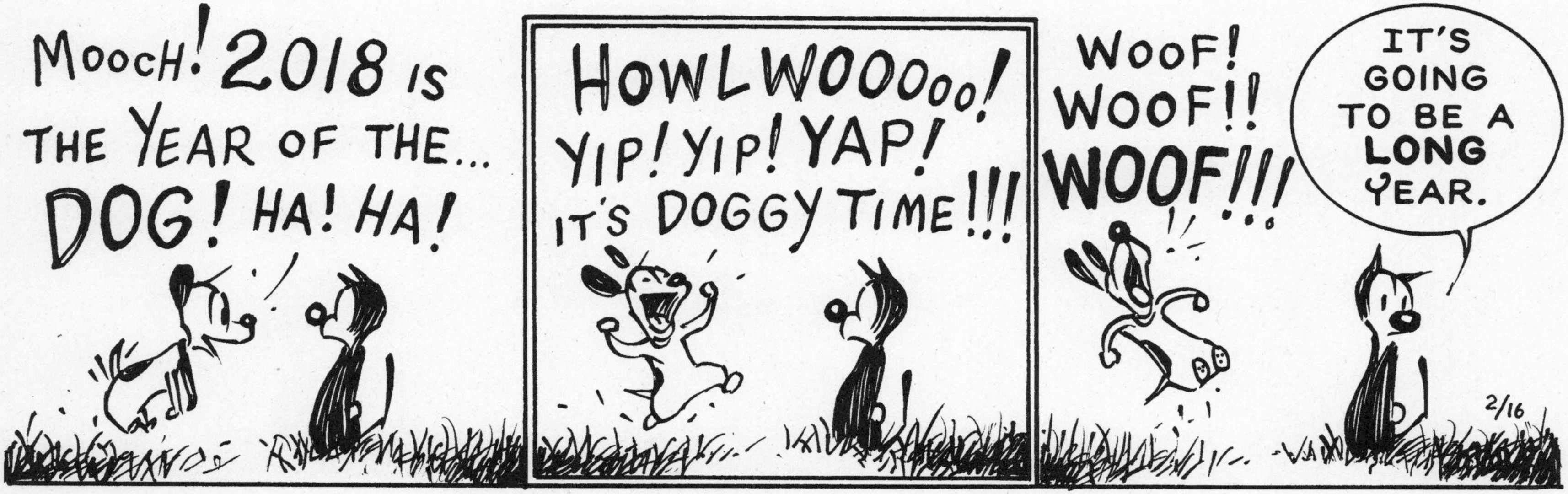
MOOCH! 2018 IS THE YEAR OF THE... DOG! HA! HA!
HOWLWOOOooo! YIP! YIP! YAP! IT'S DOGGY TIME!!!
WOOF! WOOF!! WOOF!!!
IT'S GOING TO BE A LONG YEAR.
2/16

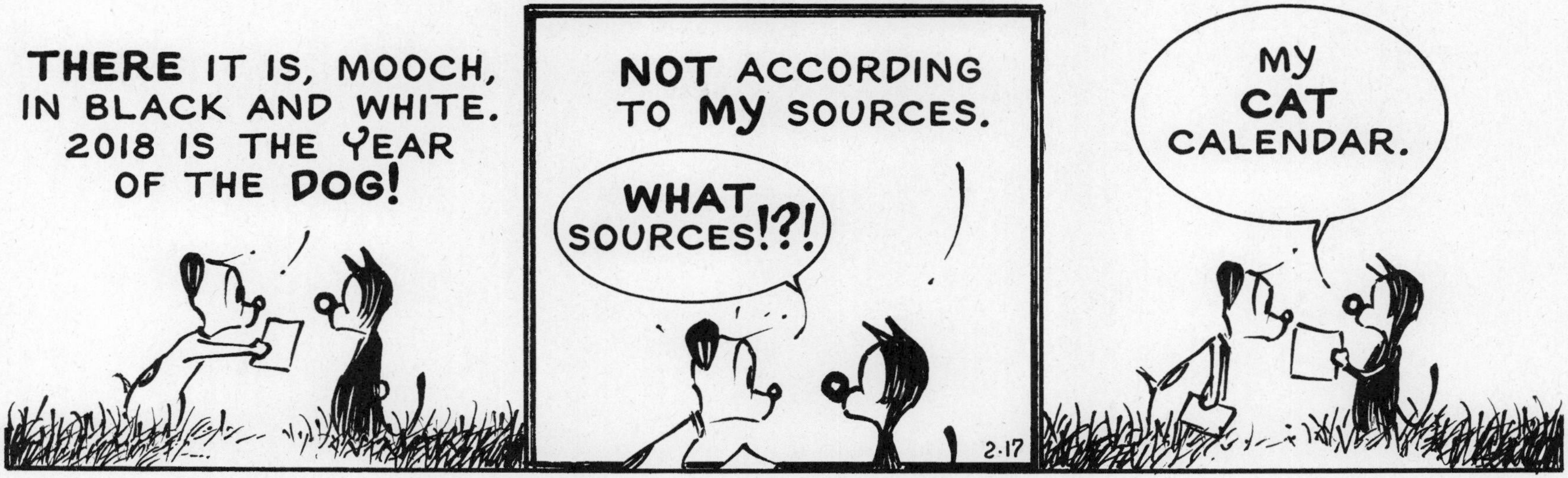
THERE IT IS, MOOCH, IN BLACK AND WHITE. 2018 IS THE YEAR OF THE DOG!
NOT ACCORDING TO MY SOURCES.
WHAT SOURCES!?!
MY CAT CALENDAR.
2·17

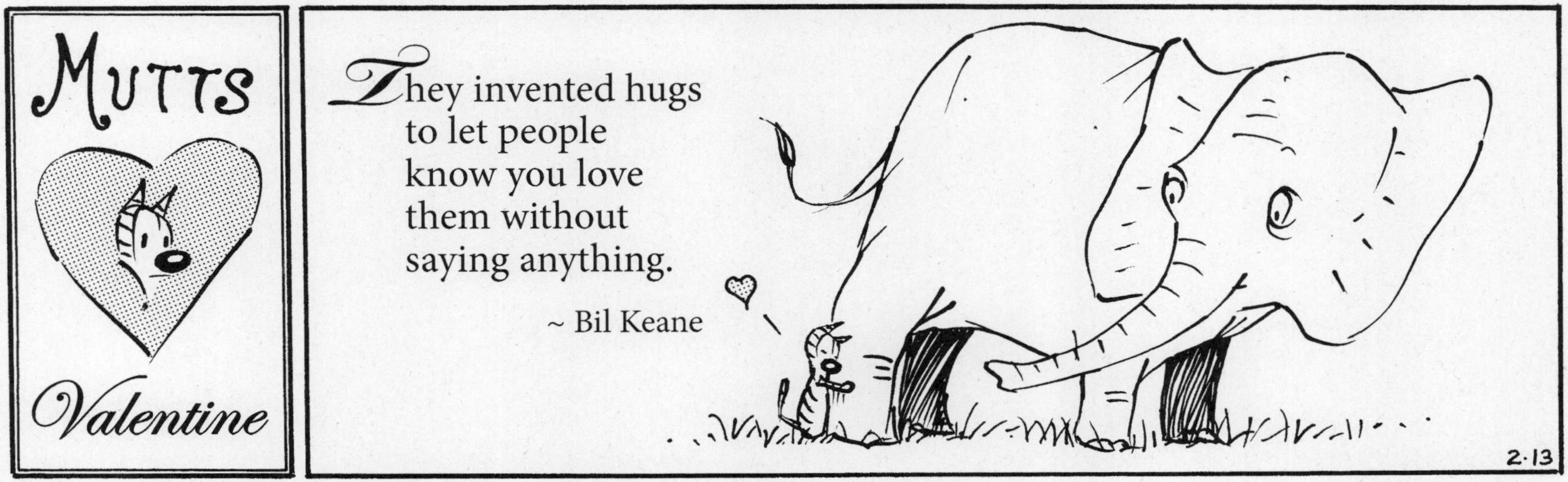
MUTTS
Valentine
They invented hugs to let people know you love them without saying anything.
~ Bil Keane
2·13

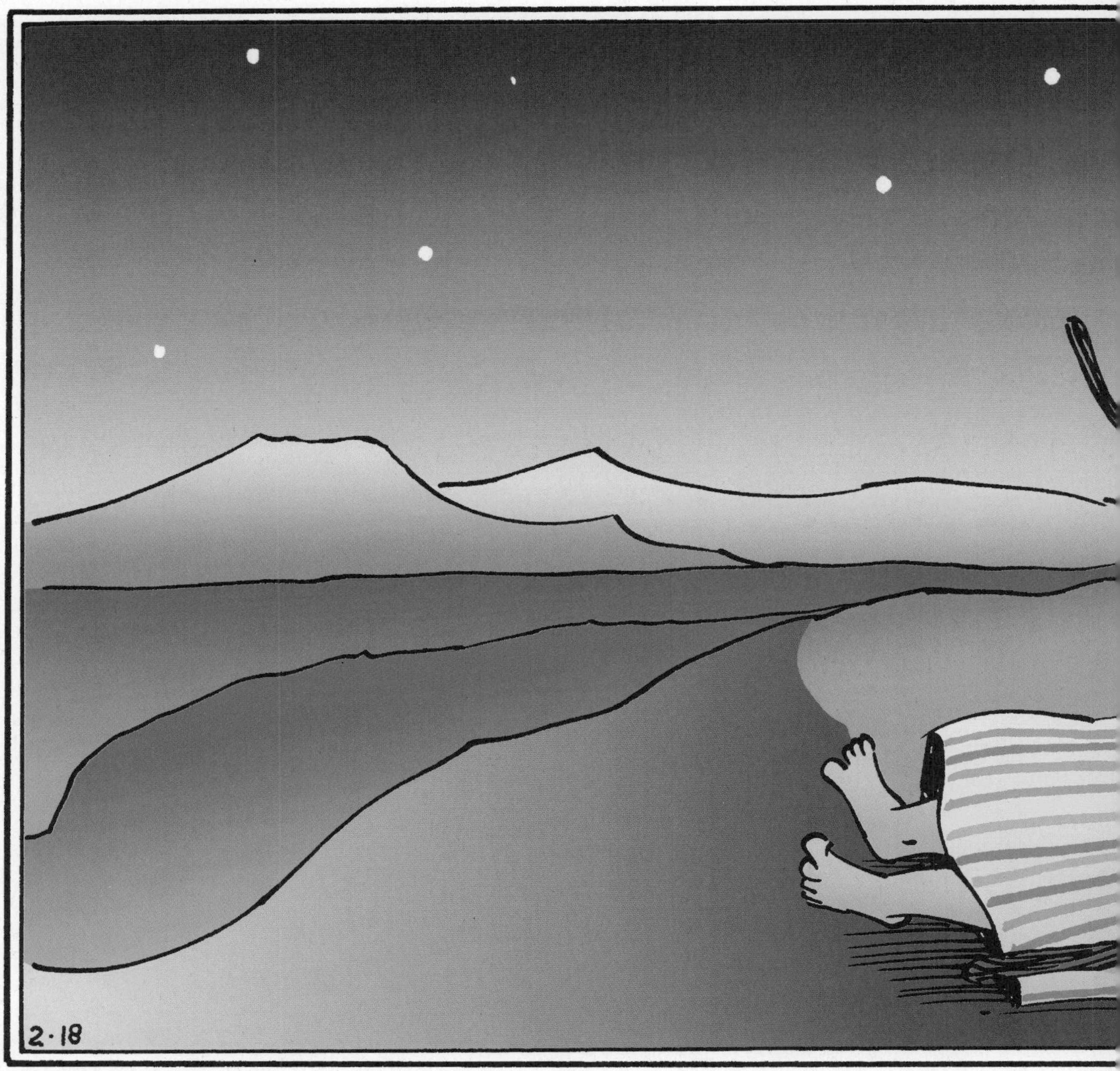
2·18

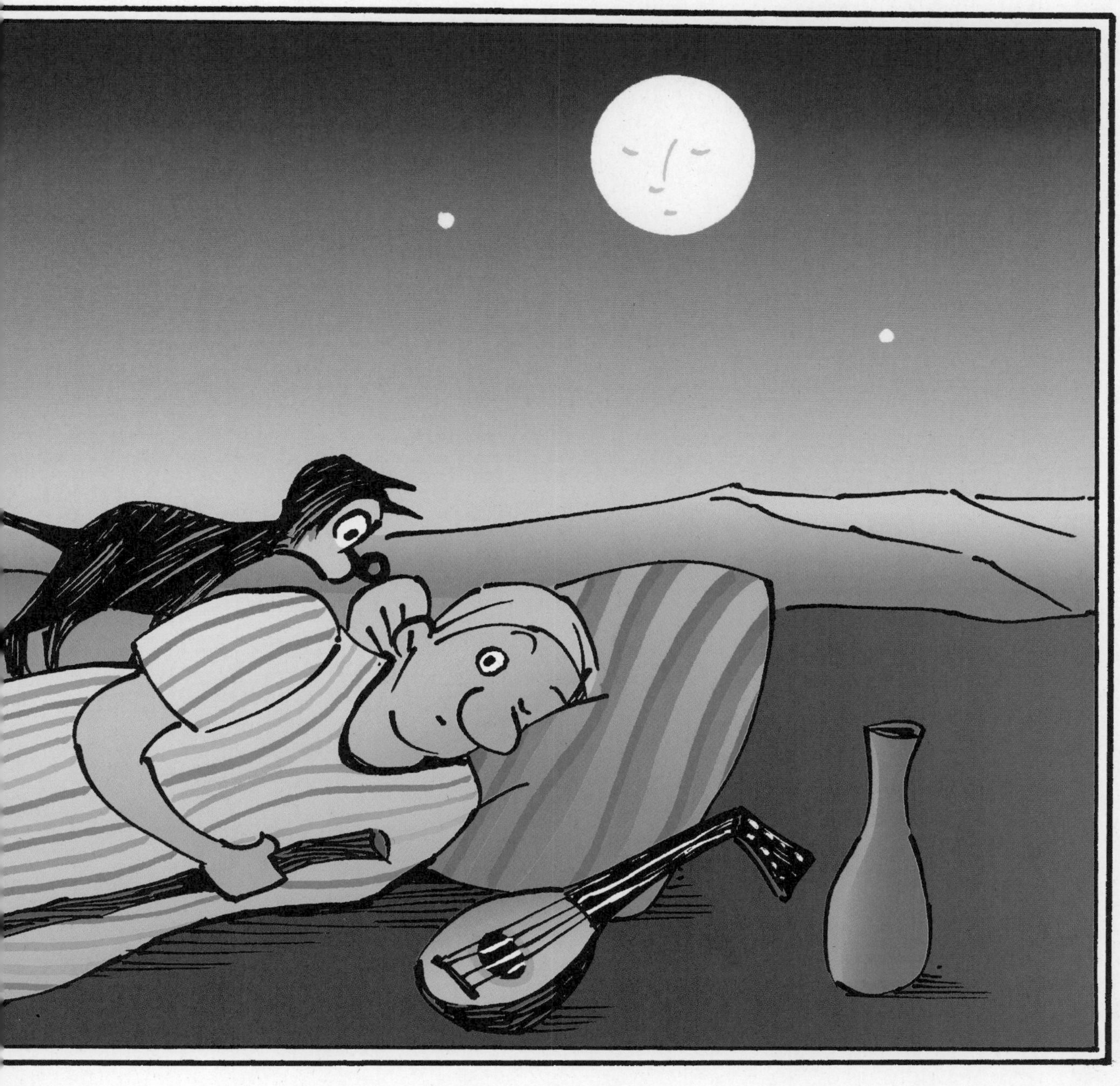

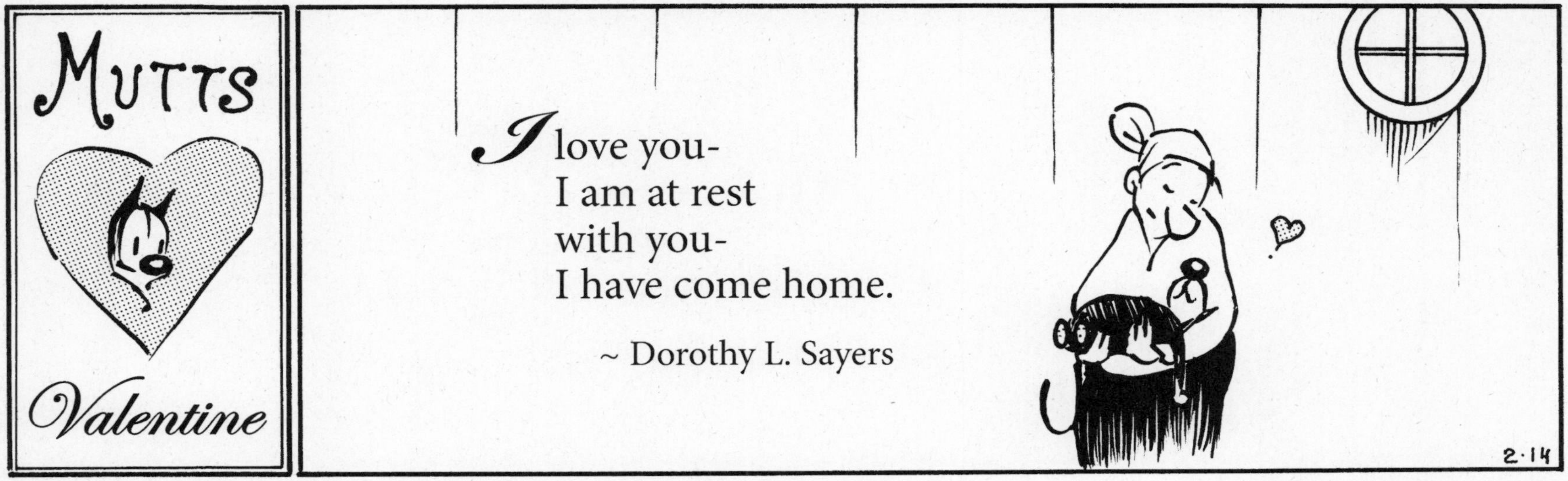
MUTTS
Valentine
I love you-
I am at rest
with you-
I have come home.
~ Dorothy L. Sayers
2·14

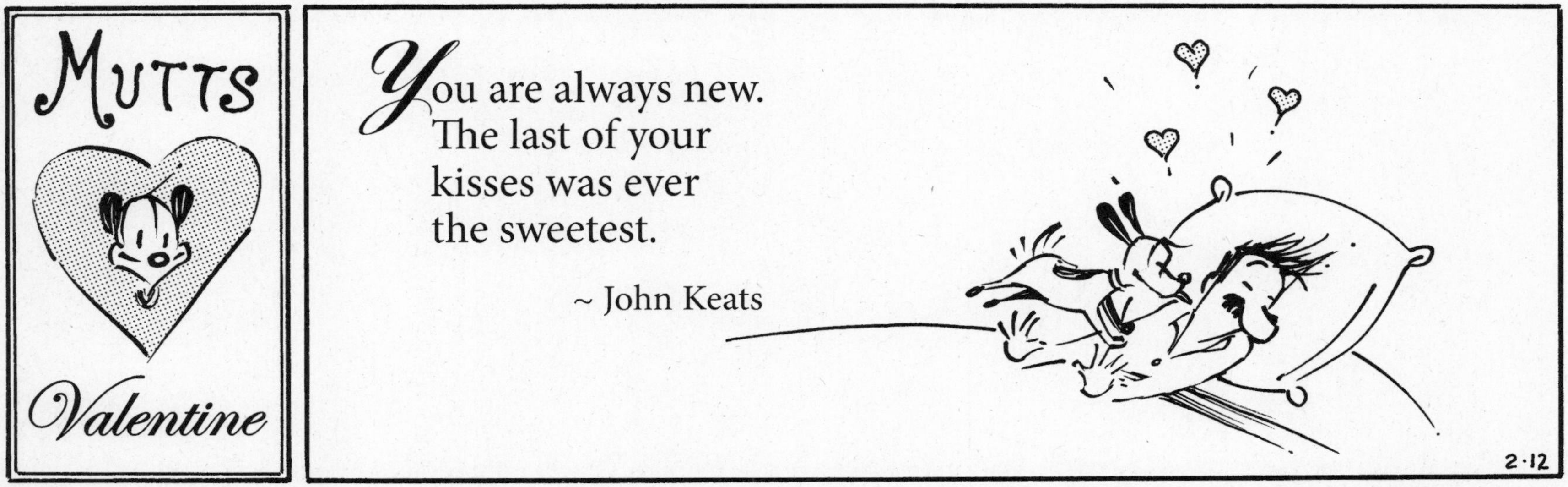
MUTTS
Valentine
You are always new.
The last of your
kisses was ever
the sweetest.
~ John Keats
2·12

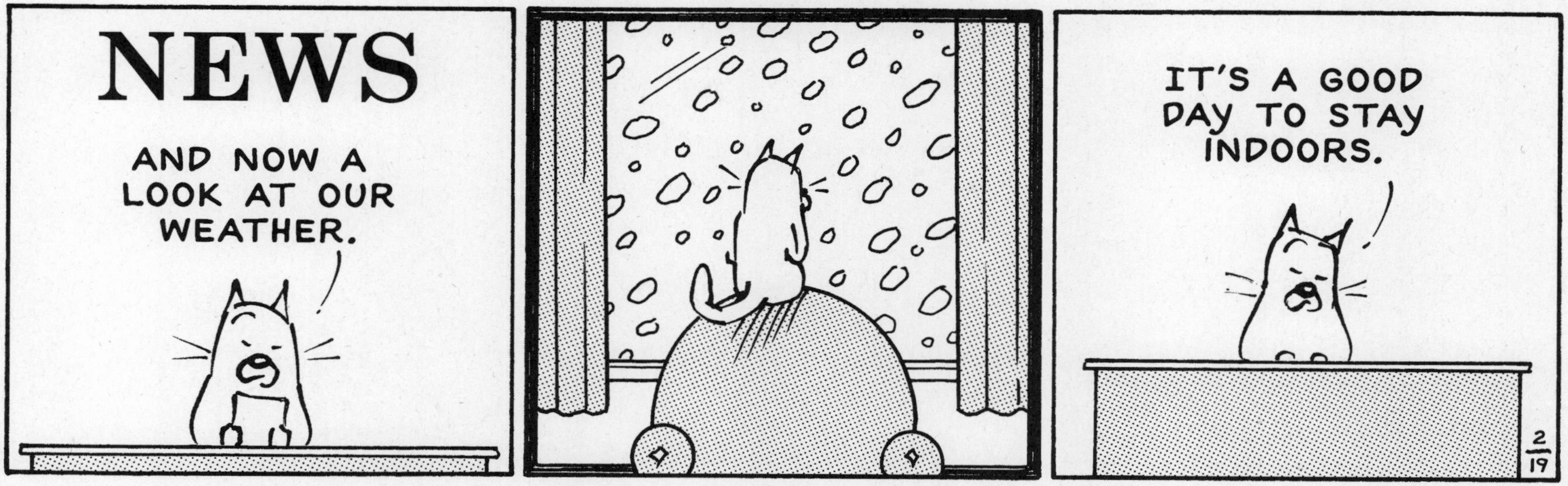
NEWS
AND NOW A LOOK AT OUR WEATHER.
IT'S A GOOD DAY TO STAY INDOORS.
2/19

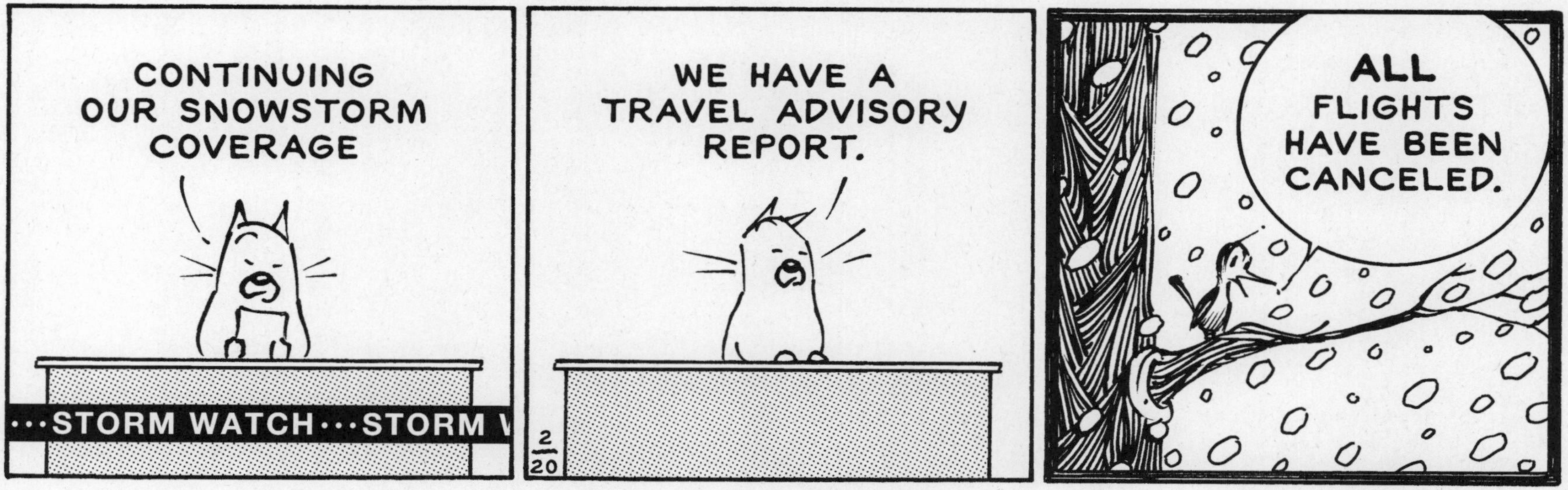
CONTINUING OUR SNOWSTORM COVERAGE
···STORM WATCH···STORM
WE HAVE A TRAVEL ADVISORY REPORT.
2/20
ALL FLIGHTS HAVE BEEN CANCELED.

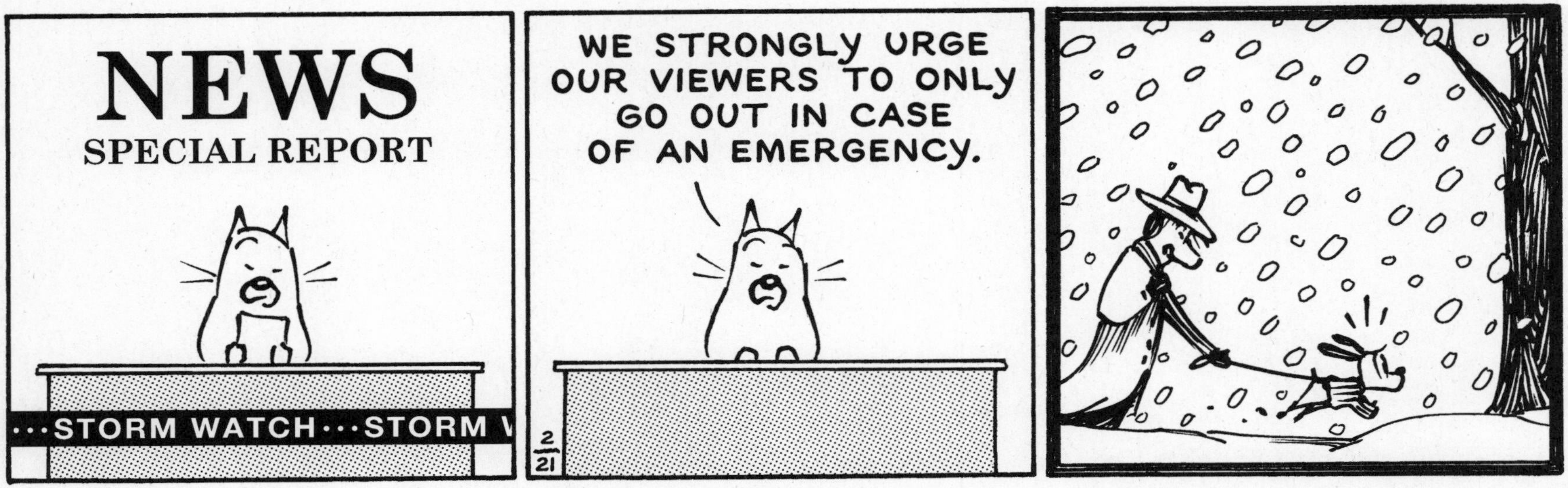
NEWS
SPECIAL REPORT
···STORM WATCH···STORM
WE STRONGLY URGE OUR VIEWERS TO ONLY GO OUT IN CASE OF AN EMERGENCY.
2/21

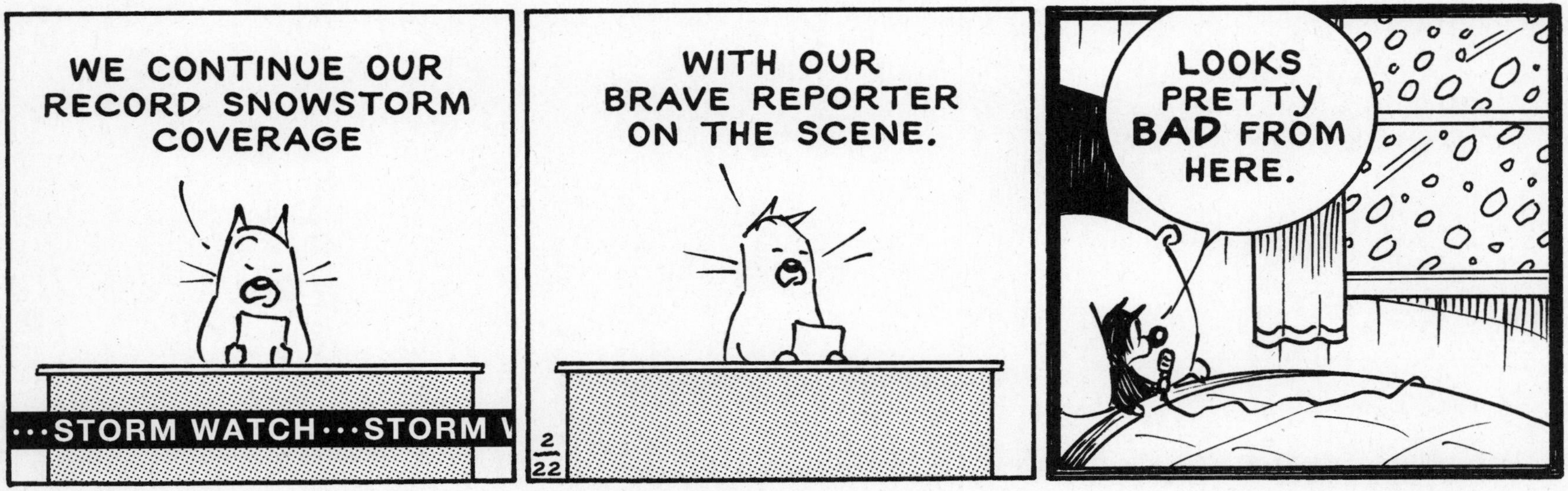
WE CONTINUE OUR RECORD SNOWSTORM COVERAGE
···STORM WATCH···STORM
WITH OUR BRAVE REPORTER ON THE SCENE.
2/22
LOOKS PRETTY BAD FROM HERE.

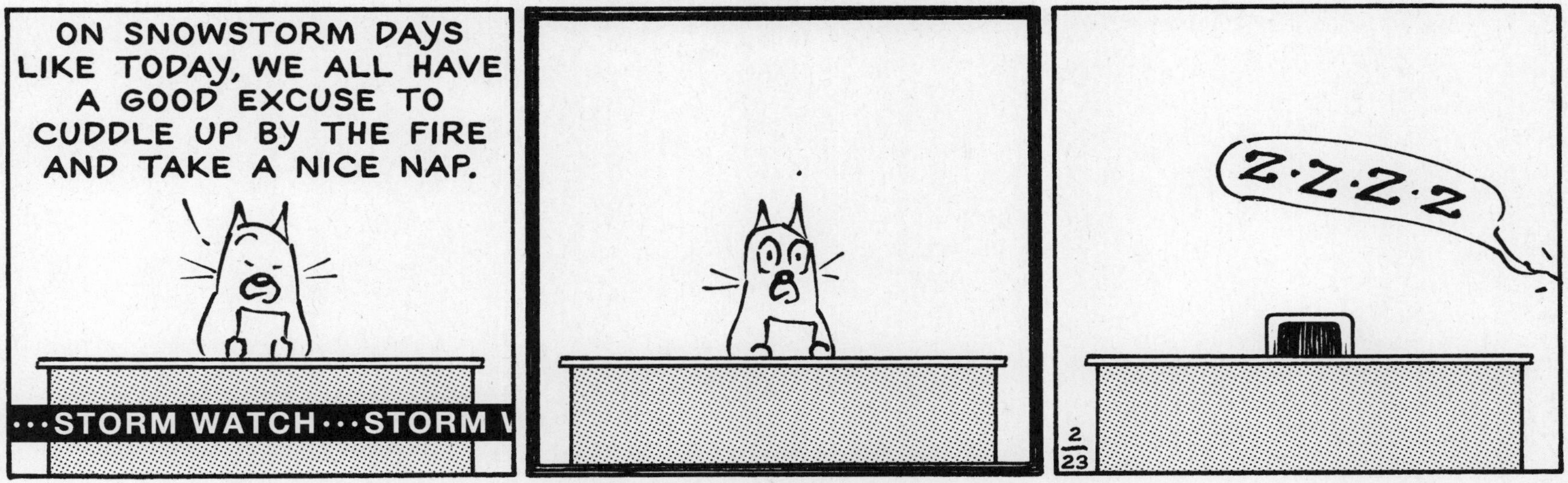
ON SNOWSTORM DAYS LIKE TODAY, WE ALL HAVE A GOOD EXCUSE TO CUDDLE UP BY THE FIRE AND TAKE A NICE NAP.
···STORM WATCH···STORM W
Z·Z·Z·Z
2/23

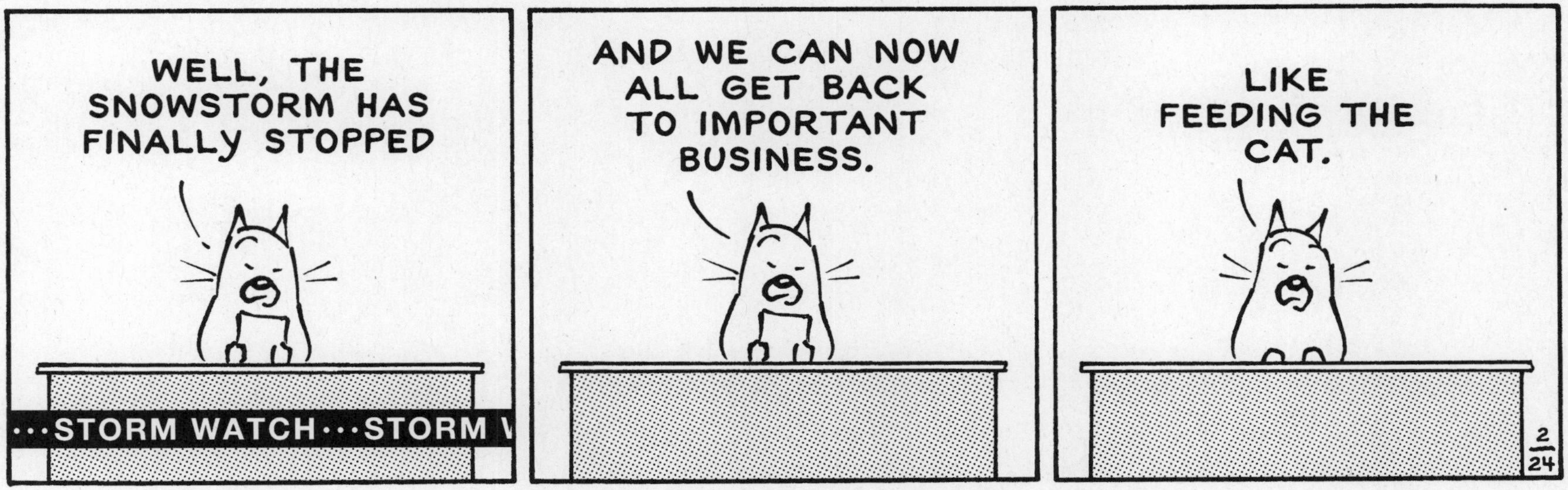
WELL, THE SNOWSTORM HAS FINALLY STOPPED
···STORM WATCH···STORM W
AND WE CAN NOW ALL GET BACK TO IMPORTANT BUSINESS.
LIKE FEEDING THE CAT.
2/24

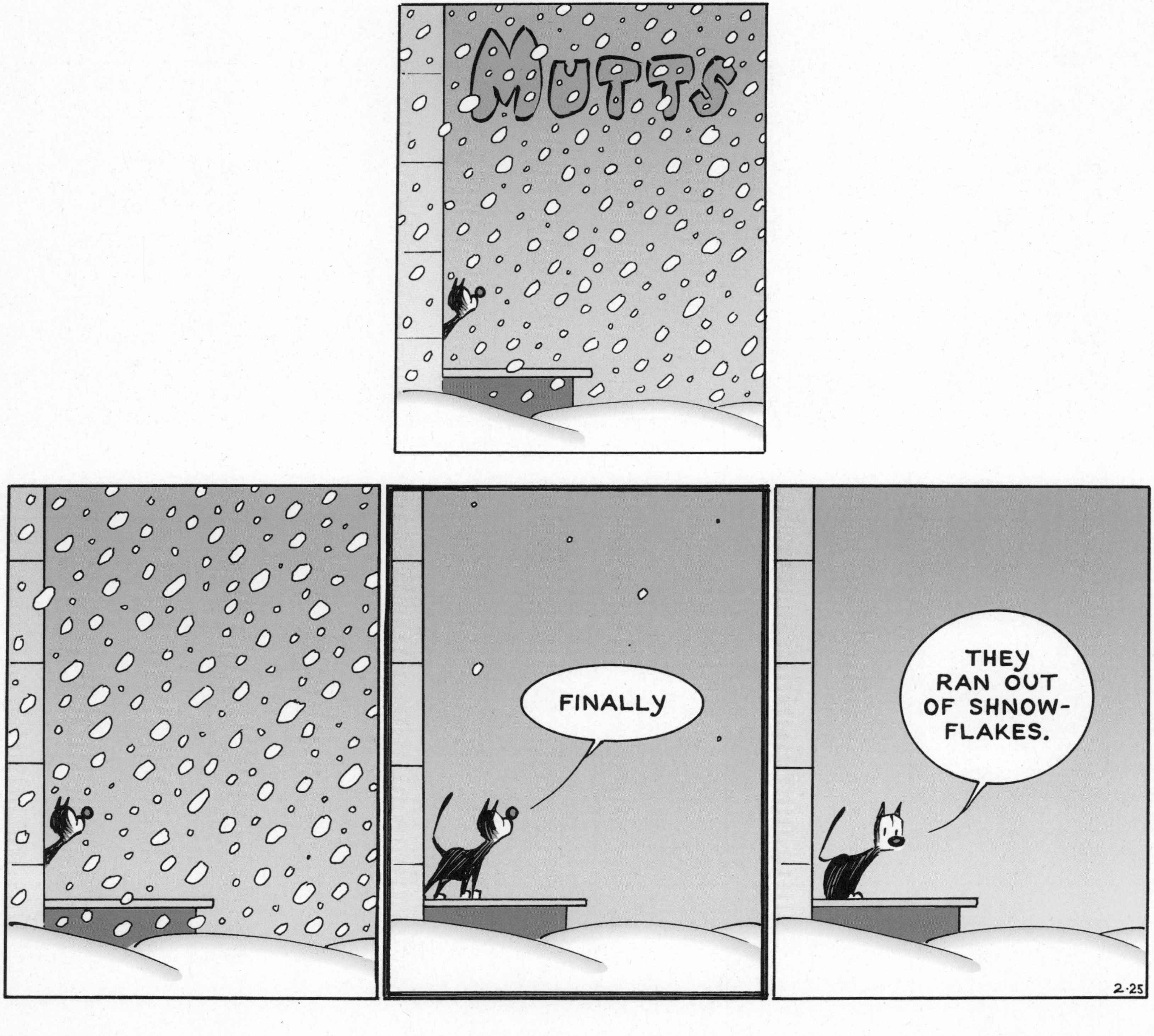
MUTTS
FINALLY
THEY RAN OUT OF SHNOW-FLAKES.
2-25

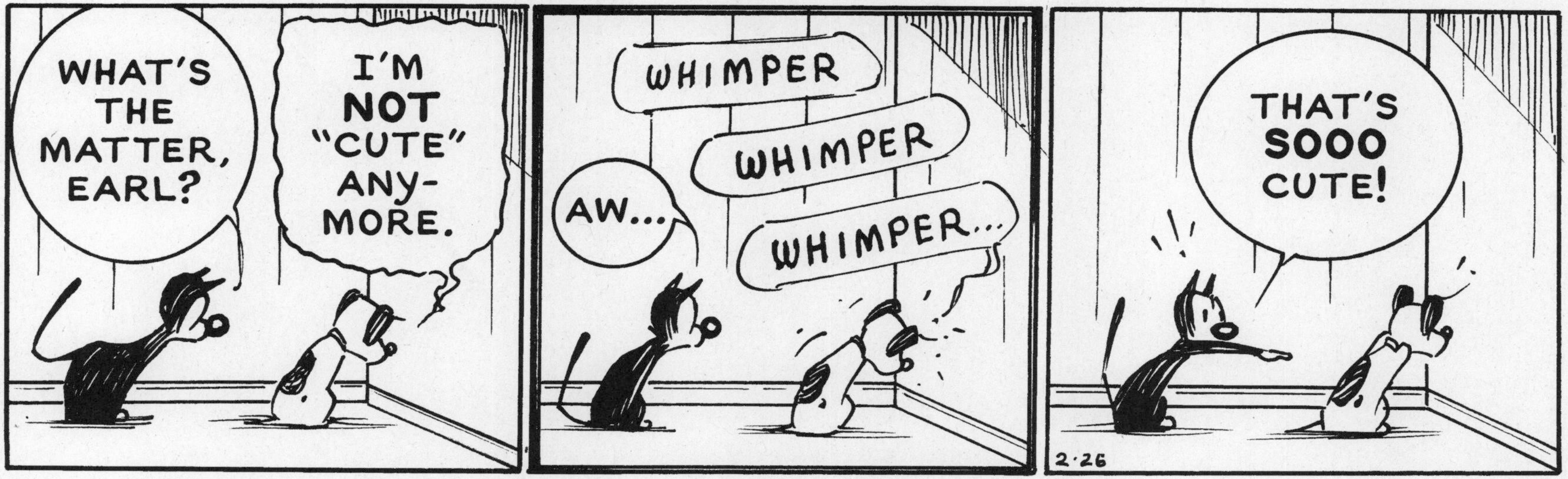
WHAT'S THE MATTER, EARL?
I'M NOT "CUTE" ANY-MORE.
WHIMPER
WHIMPER
AW...
WHIMPER...
THAT'S SOOO CUTE!
2·26

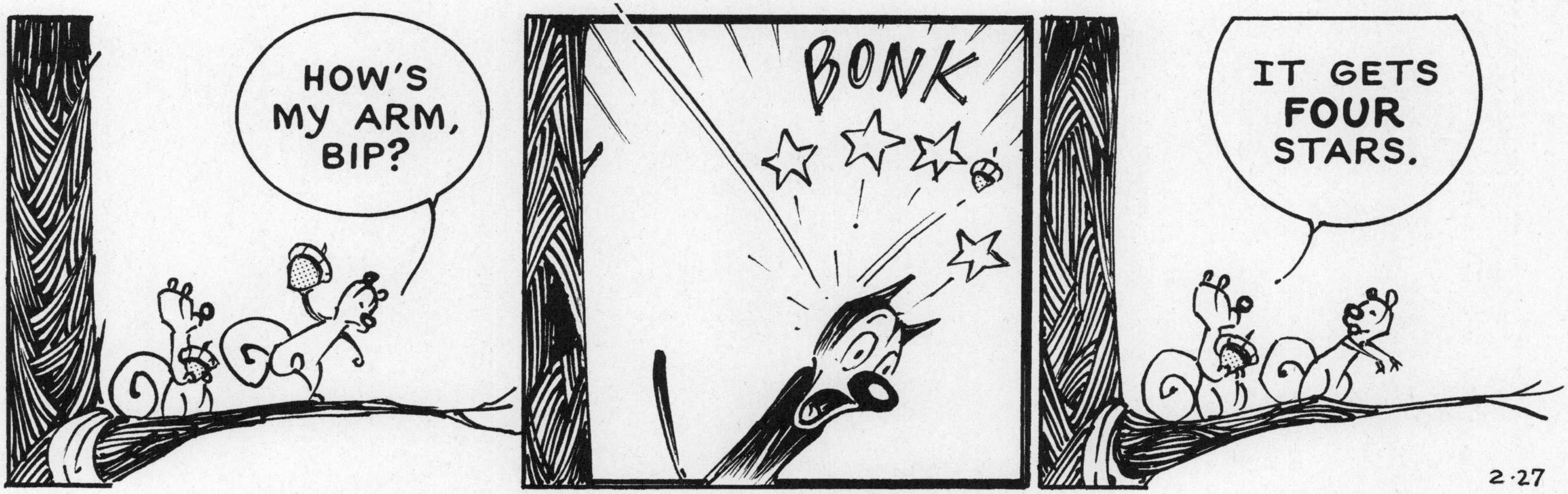
HOW'S MY ARM, BIP?
BONK
IT GETS FOUR STARS.
2·27

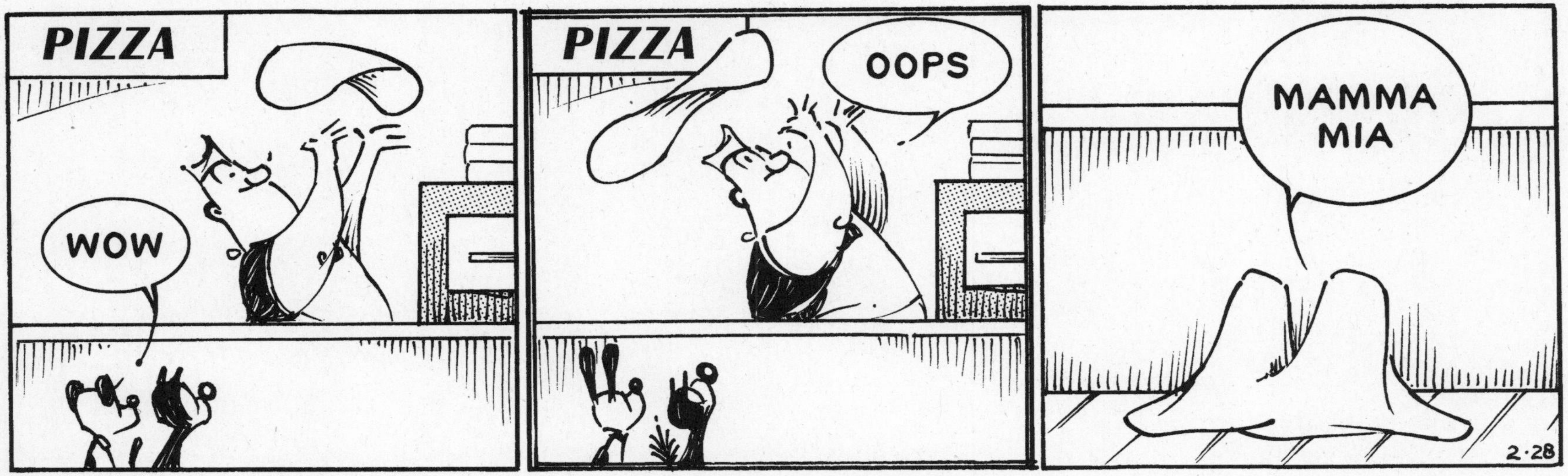
PIZZA
WOW
PIZZA
OOPS
MAMMA MIA
2·28

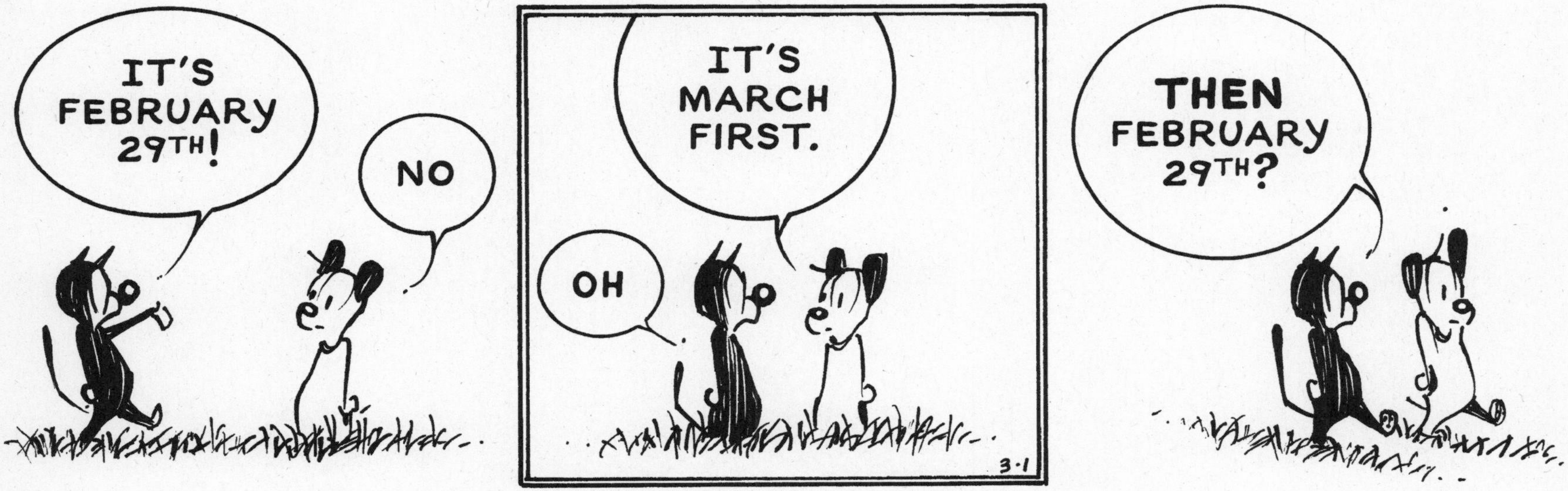
IT'S FEBRUARY 29TH!
NO
IT'S MARCH FIRST.
OH
3·1
THEN FEBRUARY 29TH?

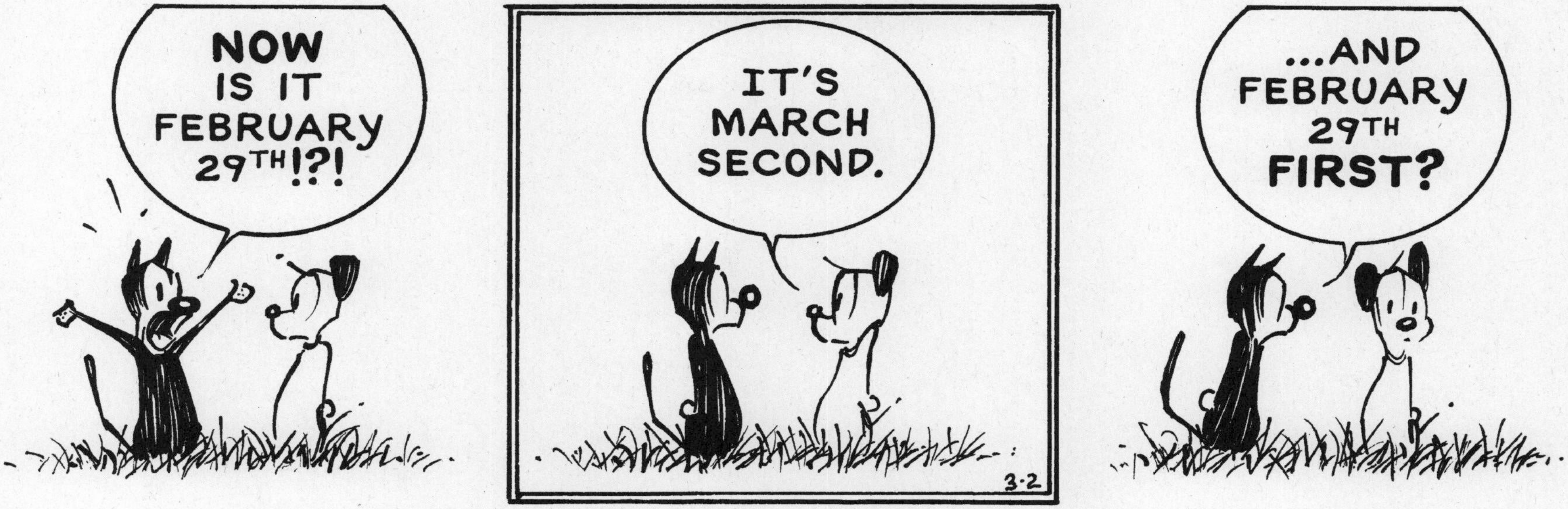
NOW IS IT FEBRUARY 29TH!?!
IT'S MARCH SECOND.
...AND FEBRUARY 29TH FIRST?
3·2

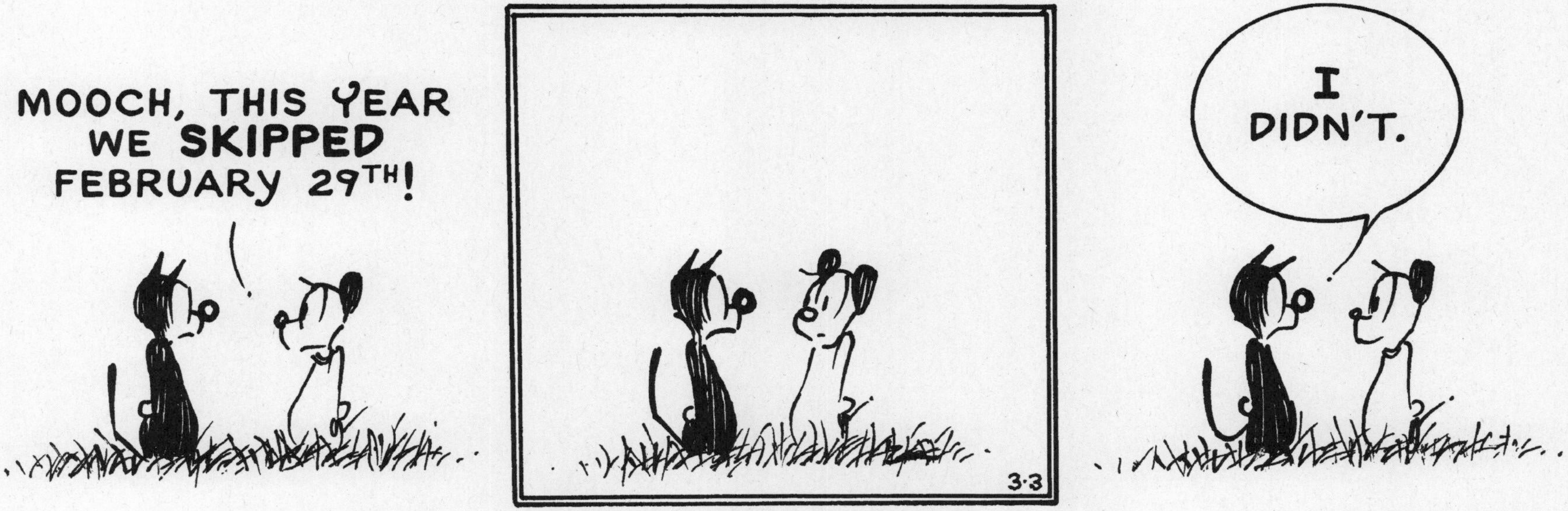
MOOCH, THIS YEAR WE SKIPPED FEBRUARY 29TH!
I DIDN'T.
3·3

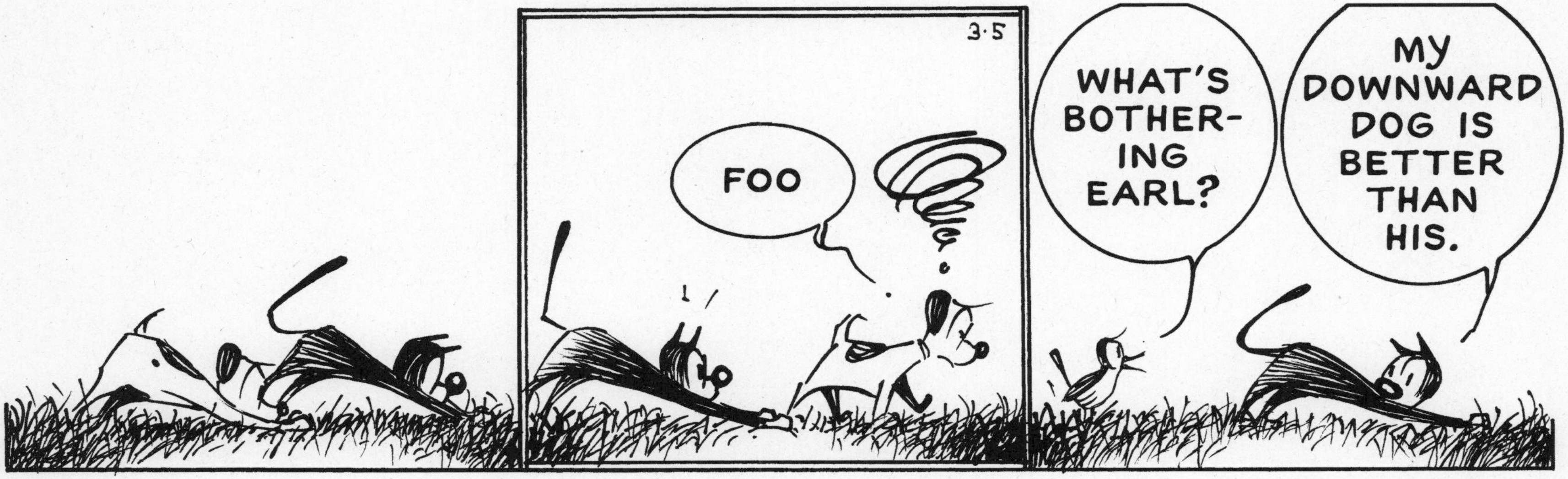
3·5
FOO
WHAT'S BOTHER-ING EARL?
MY DOWNWARD DOG IS BETTER THAN HIS.

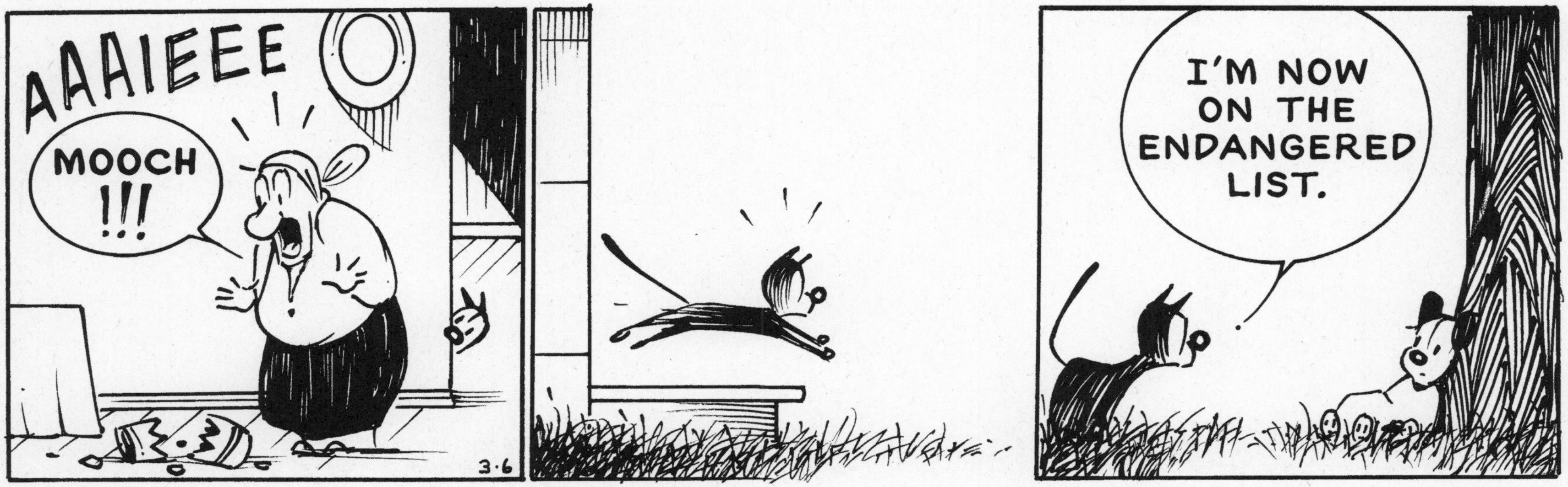
AAAIEEE
MOOCH !!!
3·6
I'M NOW ON THE ENDANGERED LIST.

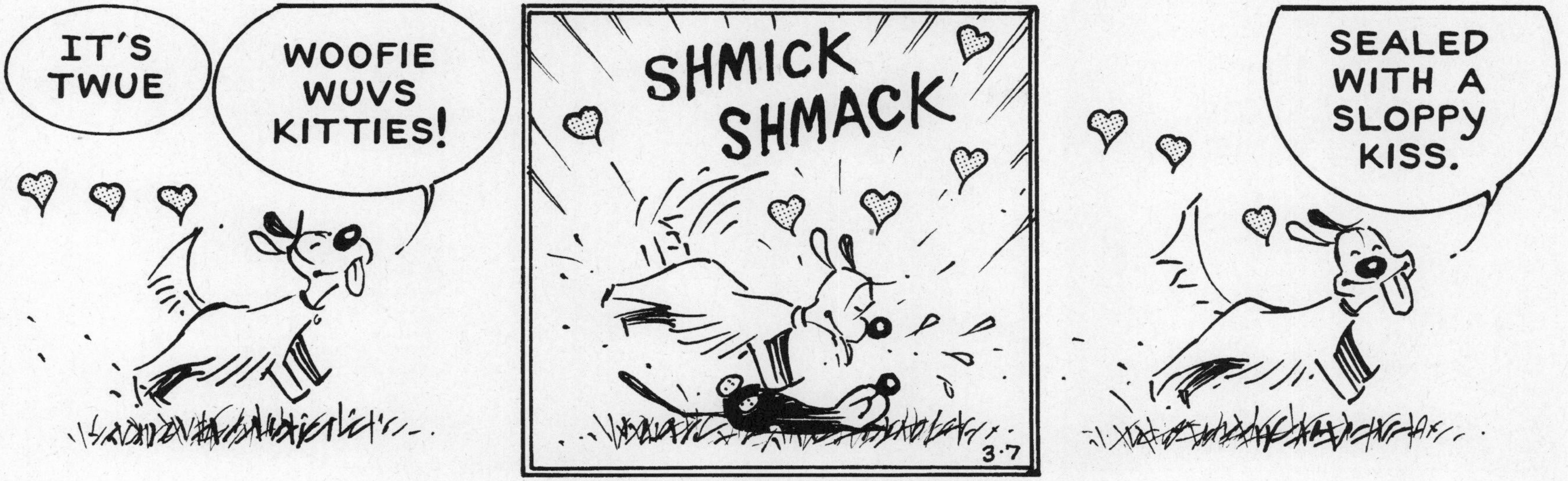
IT'S TWUE
WOOFIE WUVS KITTIES!
SHMICK SHMACK
3·7
SEALED WITH A SLOPPY KISS.

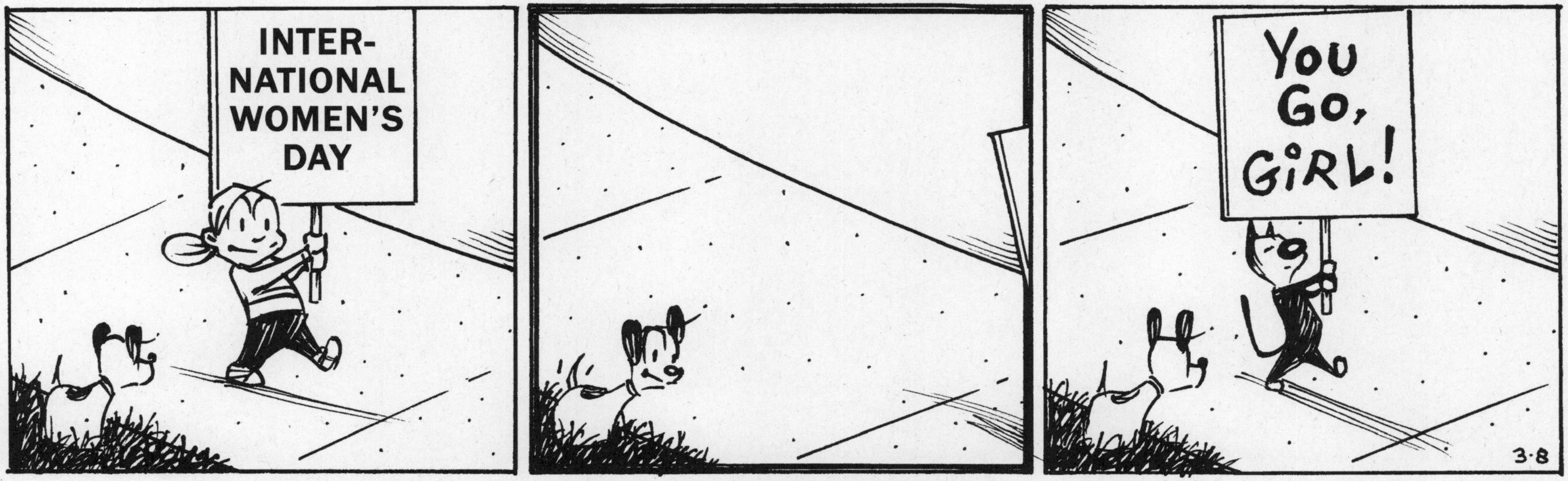
INTER-NATIONAL WOMEN'S DAY
YOU GO, GIRL!
3·8

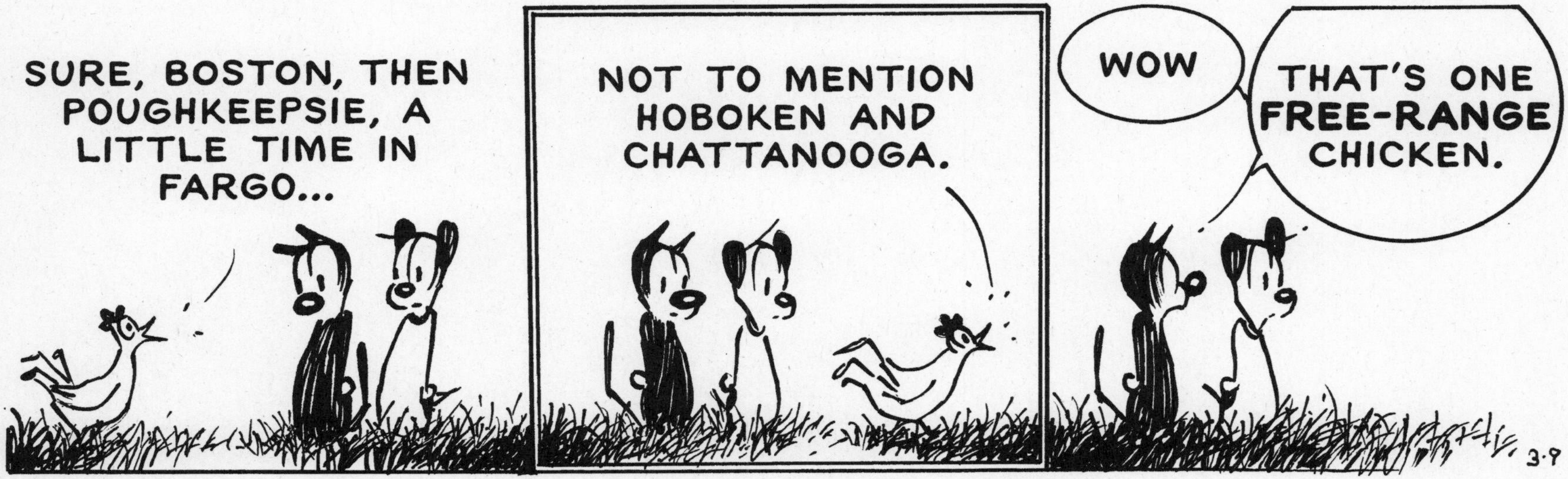
SURE, BOSTON, THEN POUGHKEEPSIE, A LITTLE TIME IN FARGO...
NOT TO MENTION HOBOKEN AND CHATTANOOGA.
WOW
THAT'S ONE **FREE-RANGE** CHICKEN.
3·9

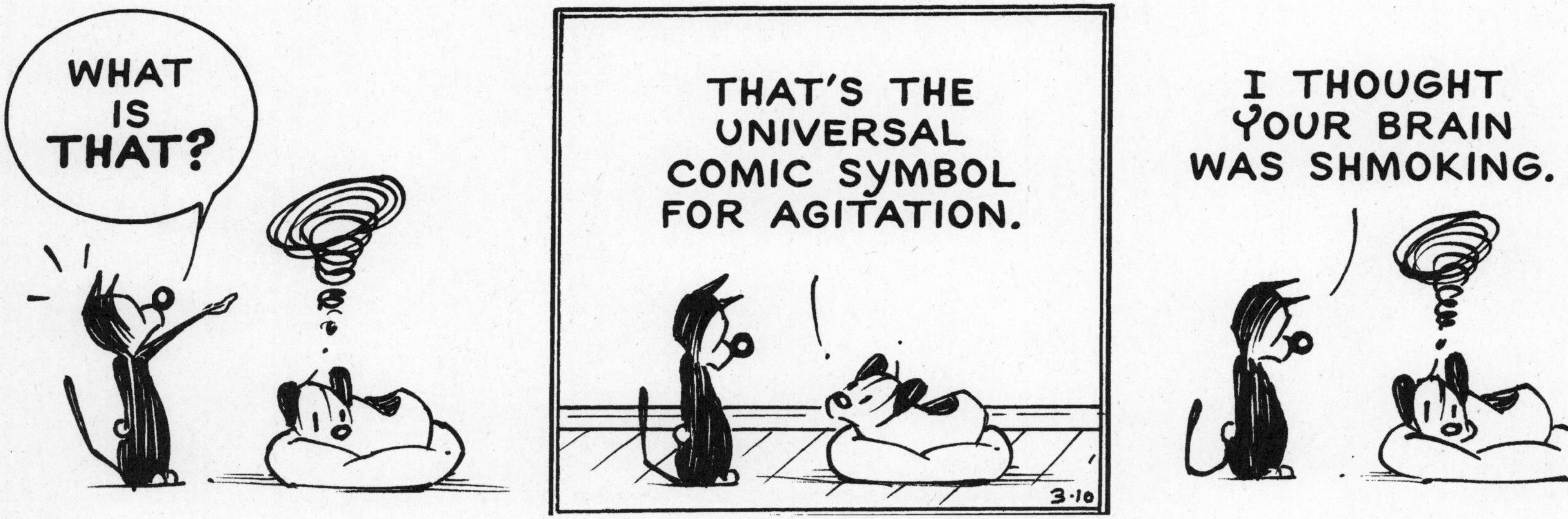
WHAT IS **THAT?**
THAT'S THE UNIVERSAL COMIC SYMBOL FOR AGITATION.
I THOUGHT YOUR BRAIN WAS SHMOKING.
3·10

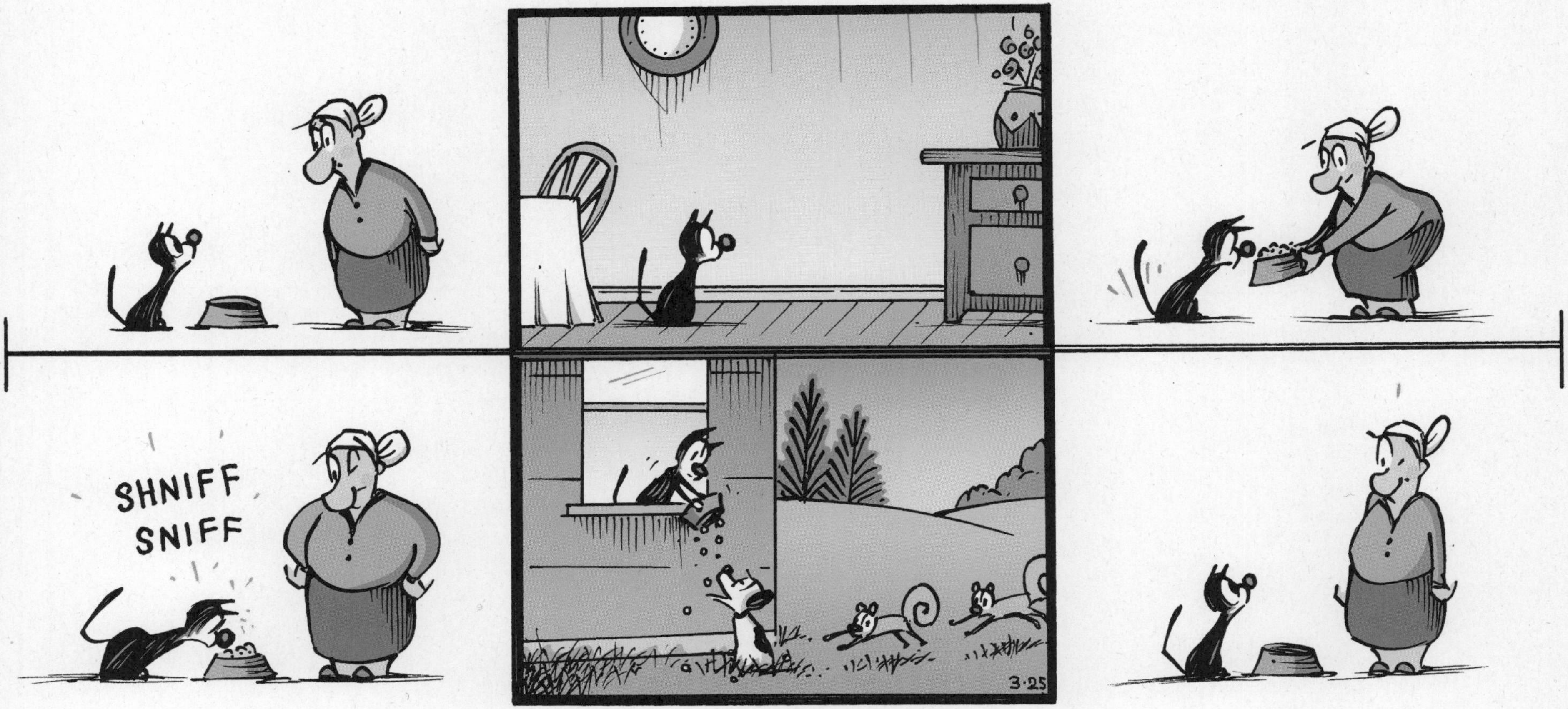
SHNIFF
SNIFF
3·25

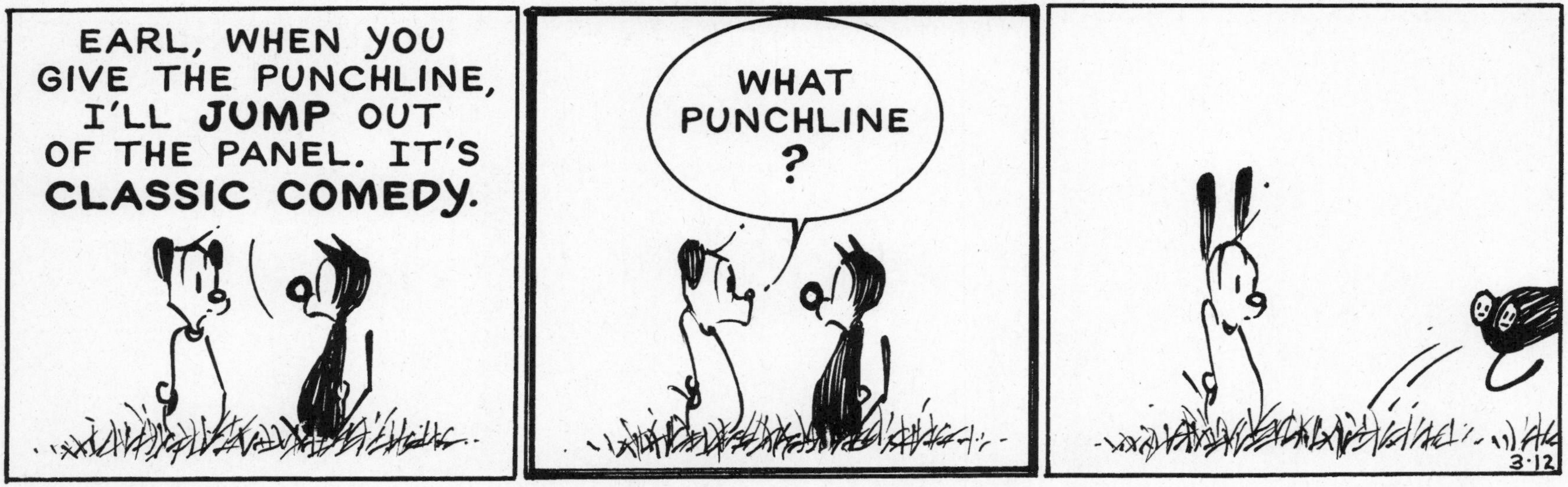
EARL, WHEN YOU GIVE THE PUNCHLINE, I'LL JUMP OUT OF THE PANEL. IT'S CLASSIC COMEDY.
WHAT PUNCHLINE ?
3·12

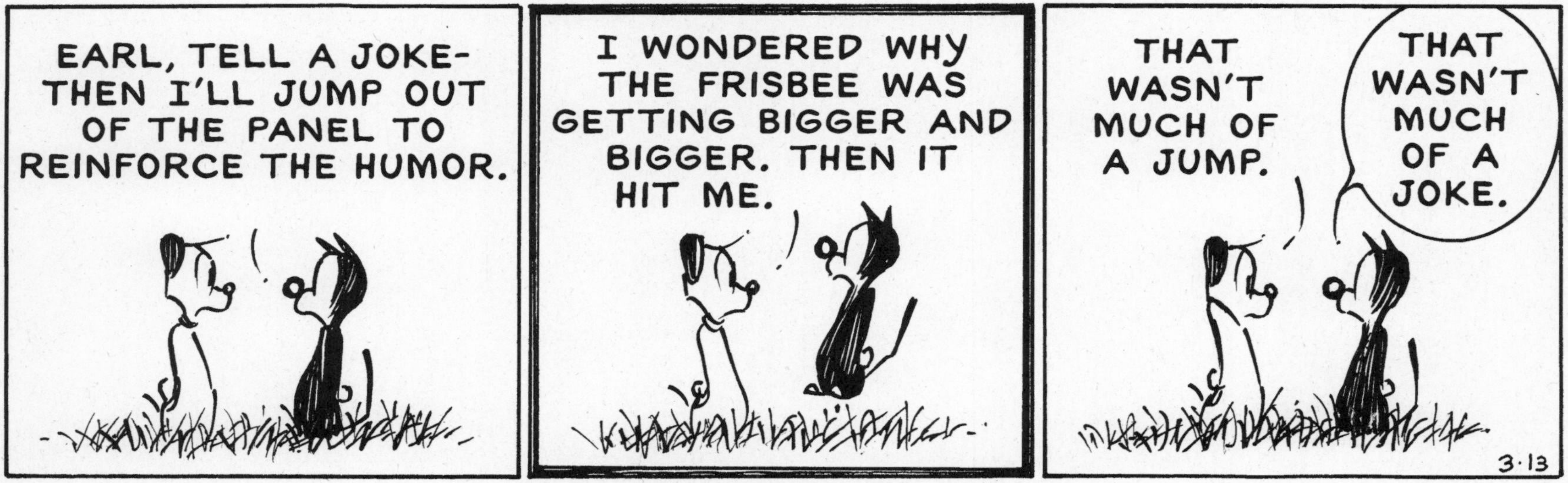
EARL, TELL A JOKE- THEN I'LL JUMP OUT OF THE PANEL TO REINFORCE THE HUMOR.
I WONDERED WHY THE FRISBEE WAS GETTING BIGGER AND BIGGER. THEN IT HIT ME.
THAT WASN'T MUCH OF A JUMP.
THAT WASN'T MUCH OF A JOKE.
3·13

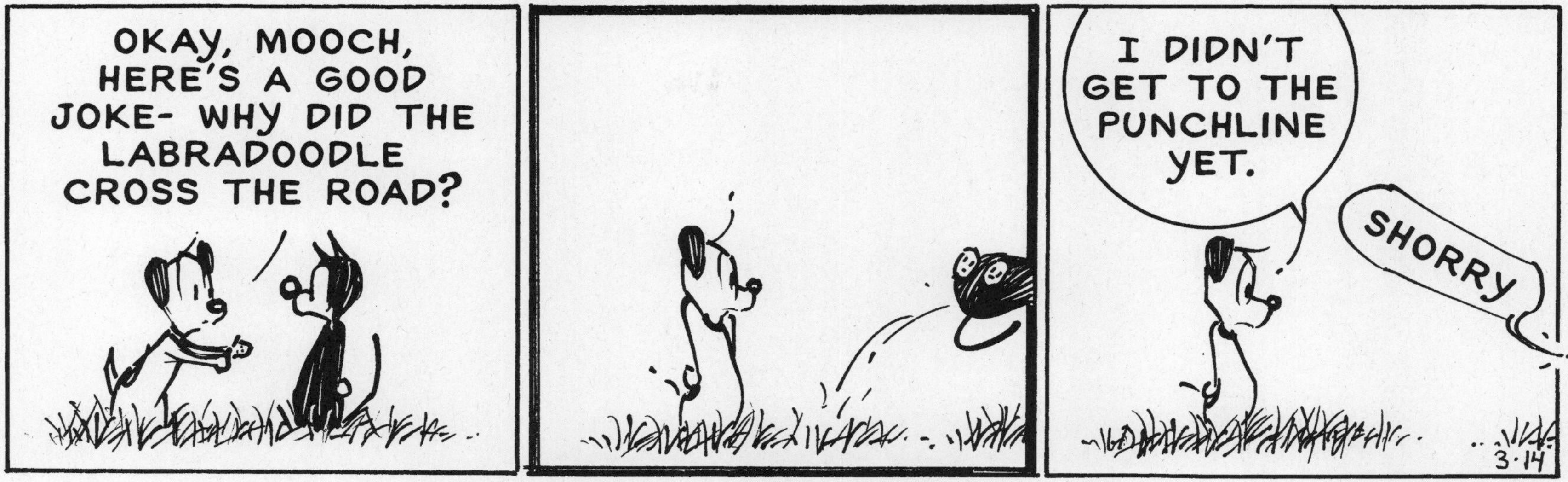
OKAY, MOOCH, HERE'S A GOOD JOKE- WHY DID THE LABRADOODLE CROSS THE ROAD?
I DIDN'T GET TO THE PUNCHLINE YET.
SHORRY
3·14

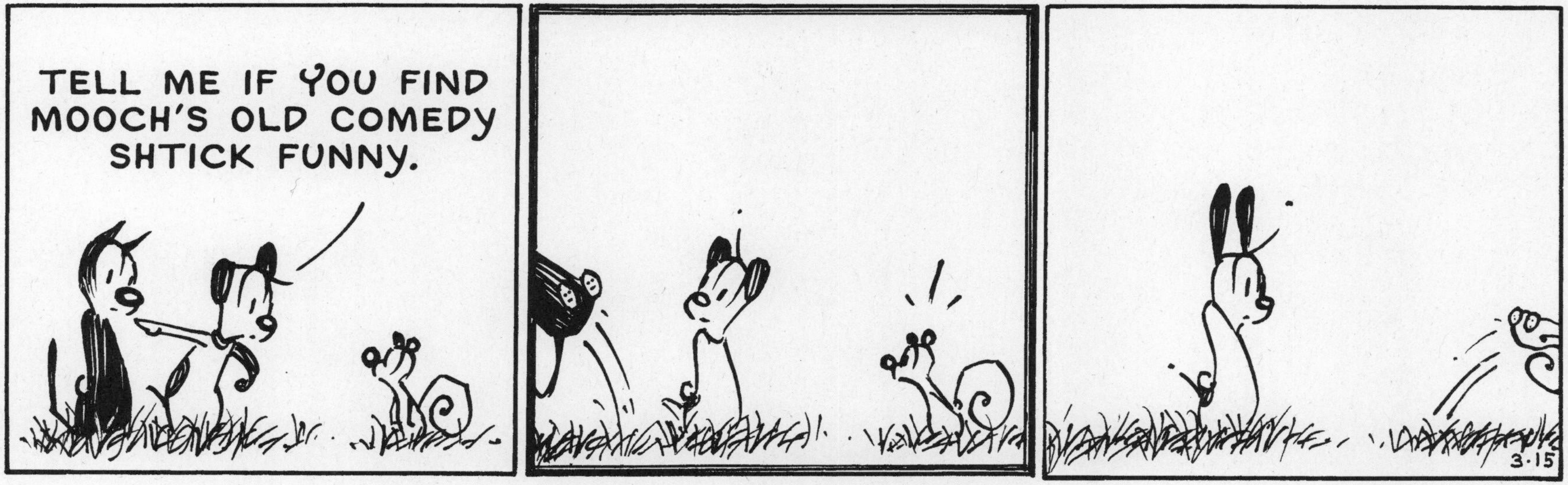
TELL ME IF YOU FIND MOOCH'S OLD COMEDY SHTICK FUNNY.
3·15

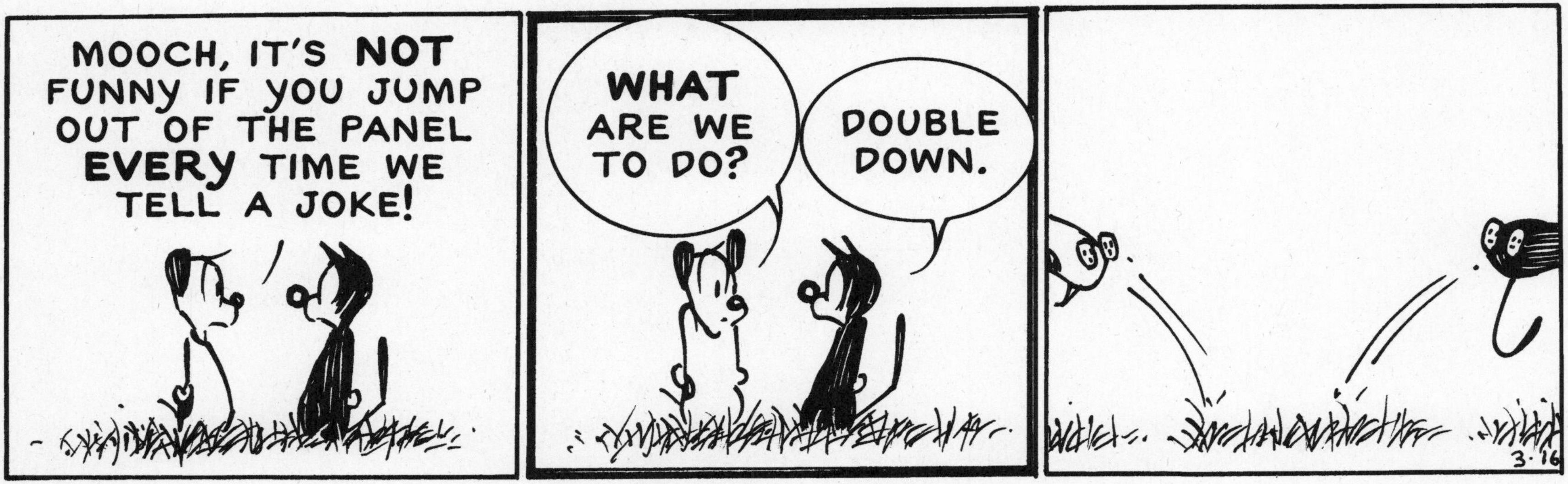
MOOCH, IT'S NOT FUNNY IF YOU JUMP OUT OF THE PANEL EVERY TIME WE TELL A JOKE!
WHAT ARE WE TO DO?
DOUBLE DOWN.
3·16

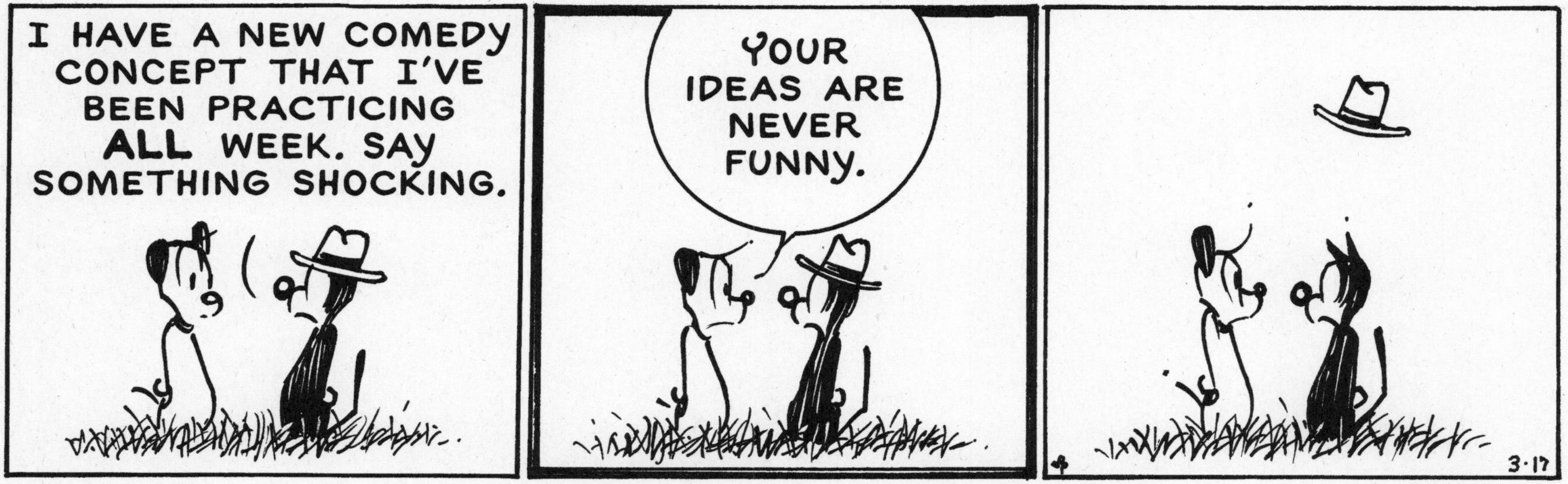
I HAVE A NEW COMEDY CONCEPT THAT I'VE BEEN PRACTICING ALL WEEK. SAY SOMETHING SHOCKING.
YOUR IDEAS ARE NEVER FUNNY.
3·17

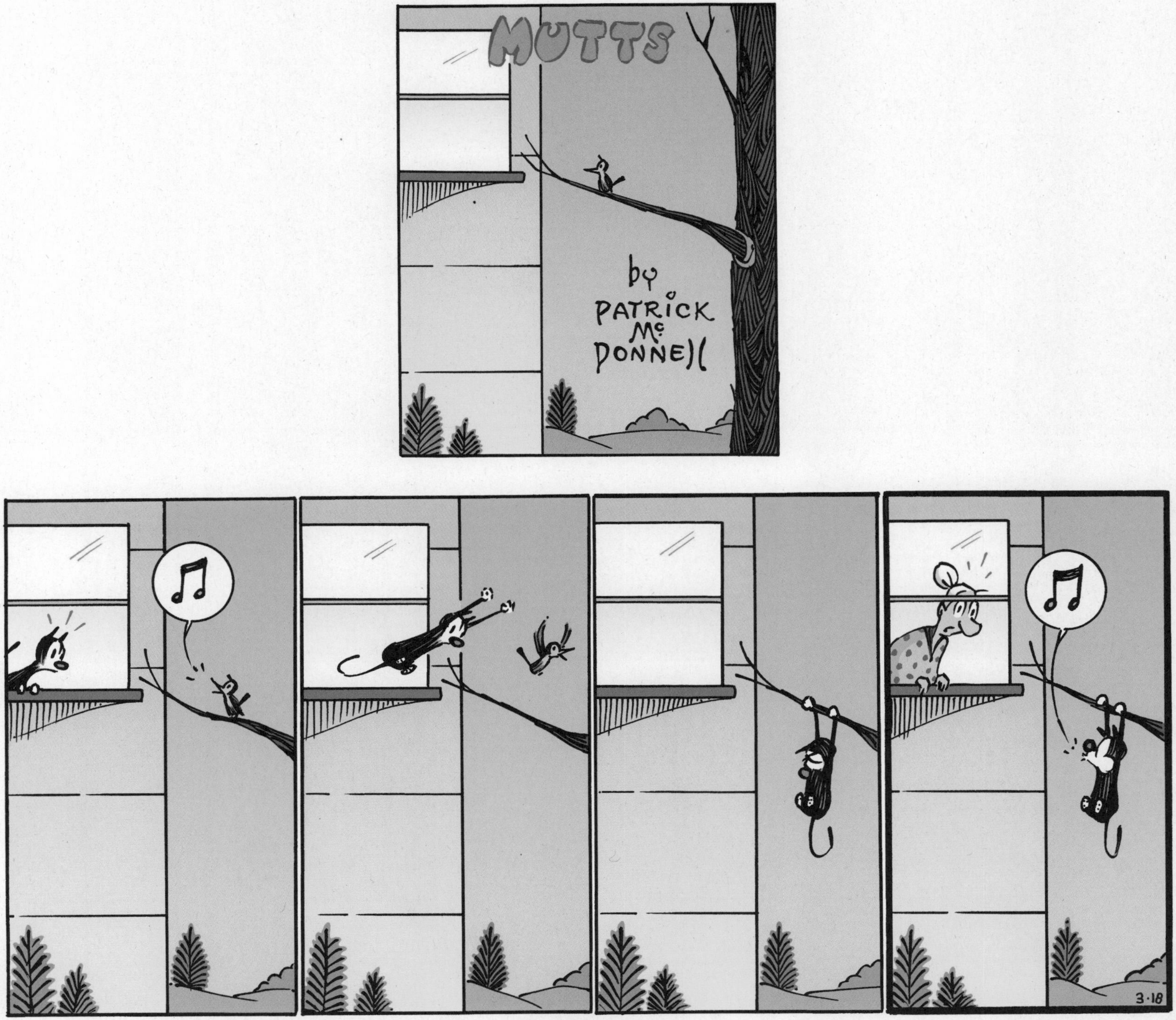
MUTTS
by PATRICK Mc DONNELL
3·18

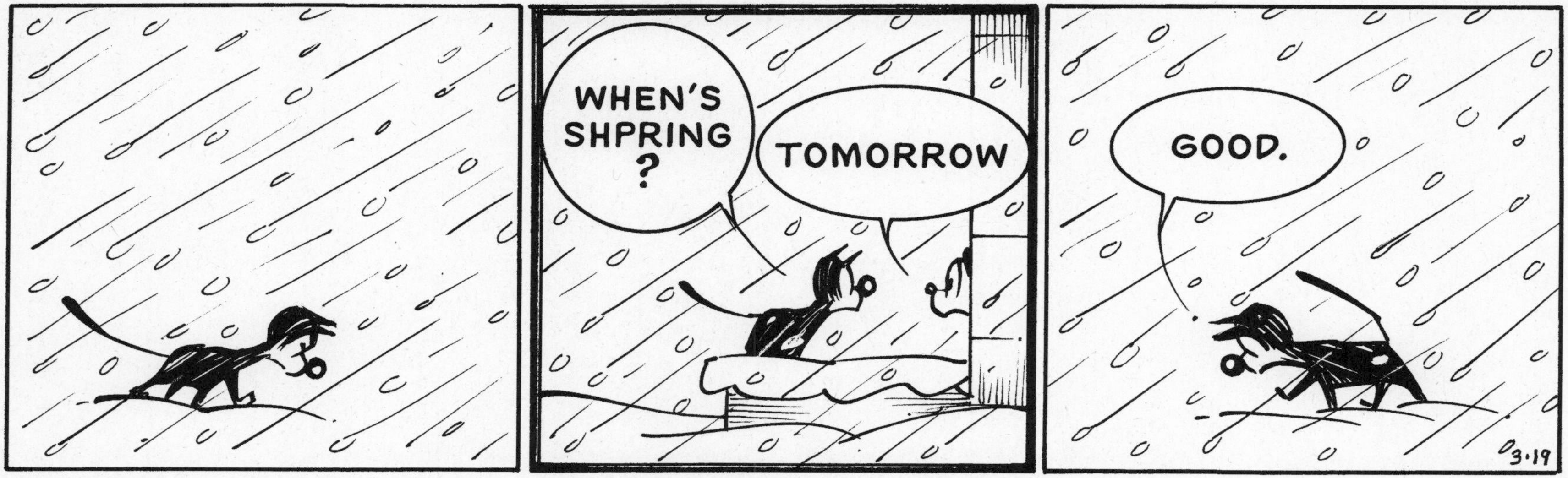
WHEN'S SHPRING ?
TOMORROW
GOOD.
3·19

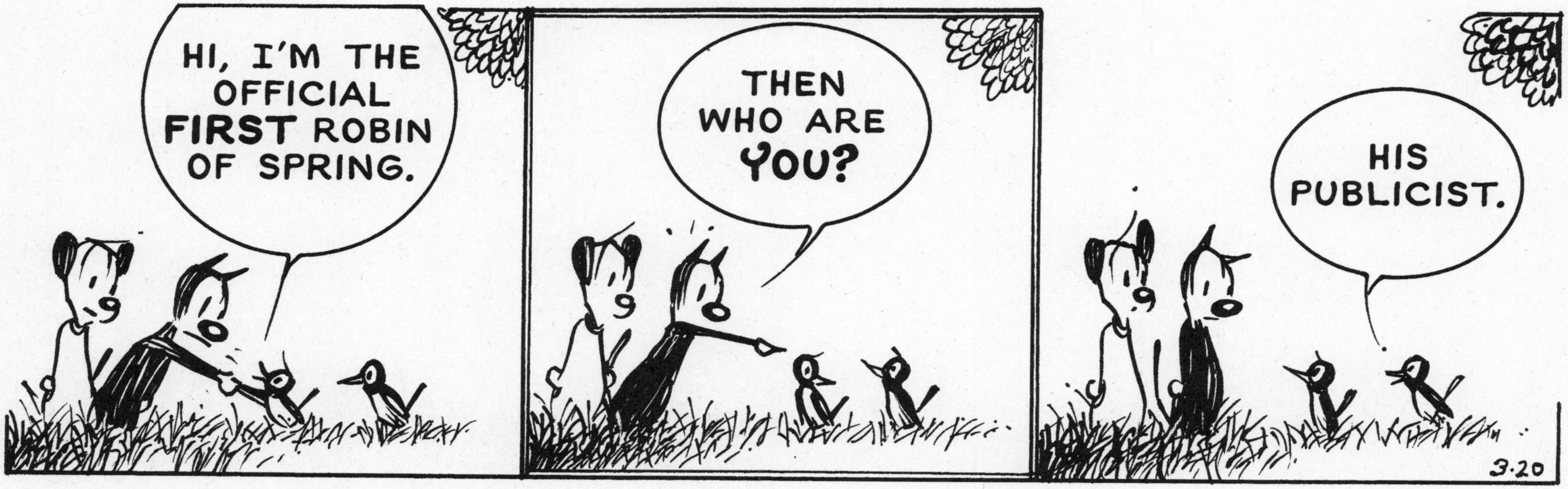
HI, I'M THE OFFICIAL **FIRST** ROBIN OF SPRING.
THEN WHO ARE **YOU?**
HIS PUBLICIST.
3·20

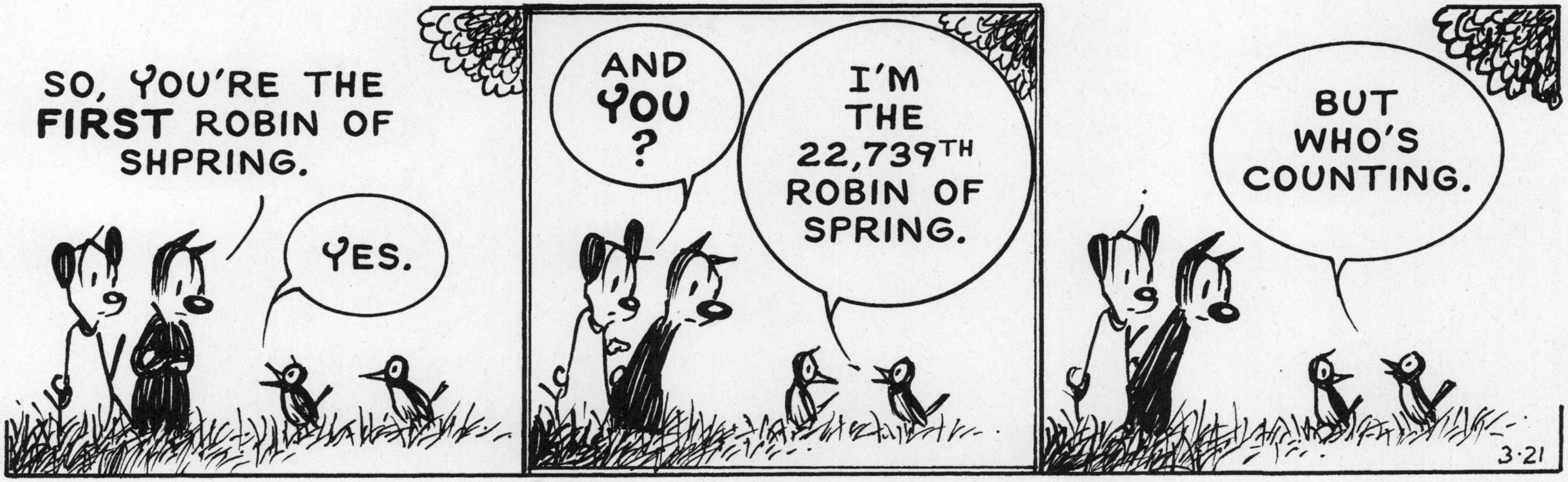
SO, YOU'RE THE FIRST ROBIN OF SHPRING.
YES.
AND YOU ?
I'M THE 22,739TH ROBIN OF SPRING.
BUT WHO'S COUNTING.
3·21

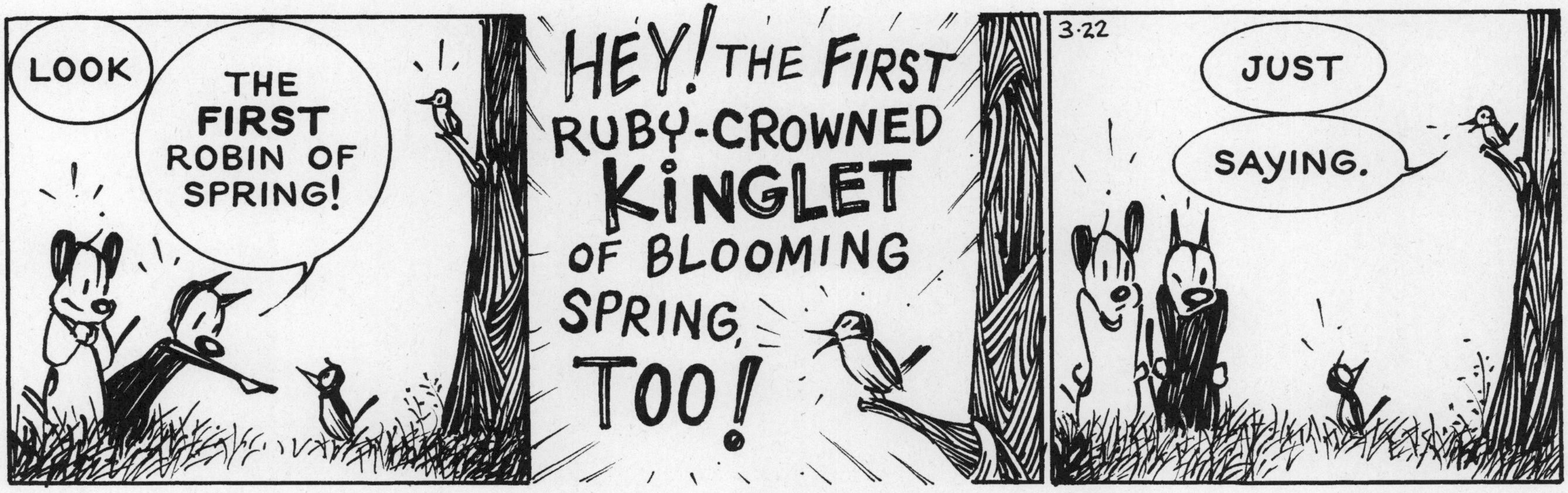
LOOK
THE FIRST ROBIN OF SPRING!
HEY! THE FIRST RUBY-CROWNED KINGLET OF BLOOMING SPRING, TOO!
3·22
JUST
SAYING.

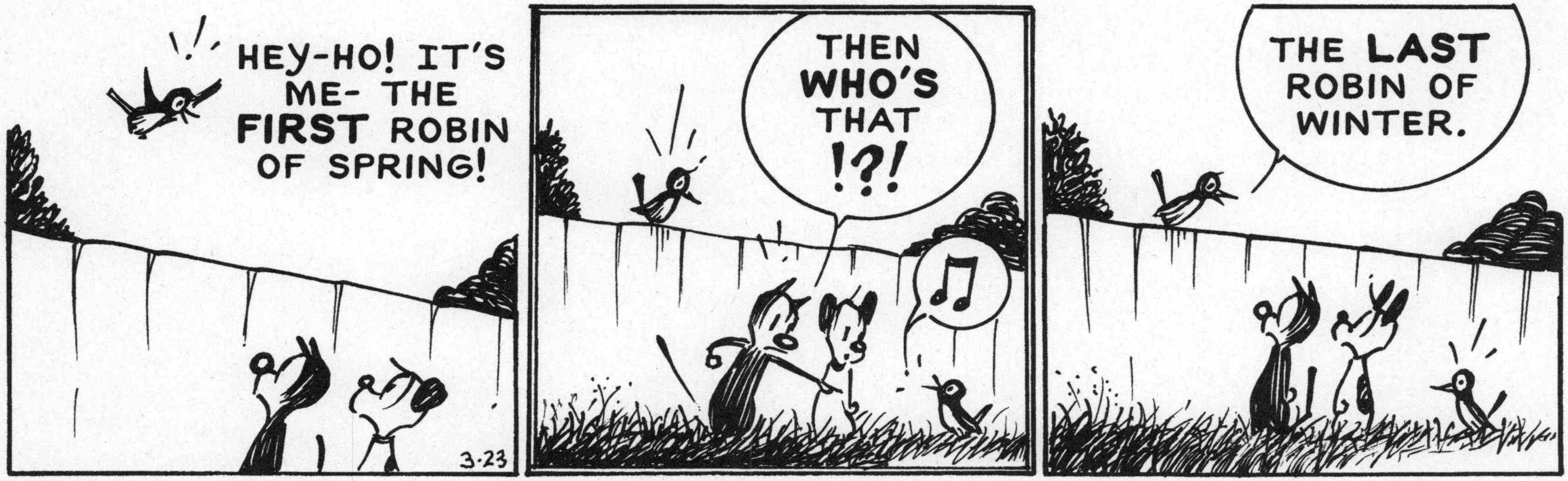
HEY-HO! IT'S ME- THE FIRST ROBIN OF SPRING!
3·23
THEN WHO'S THAT !?!
♫
THE LAST ROBIN OF WINTER.

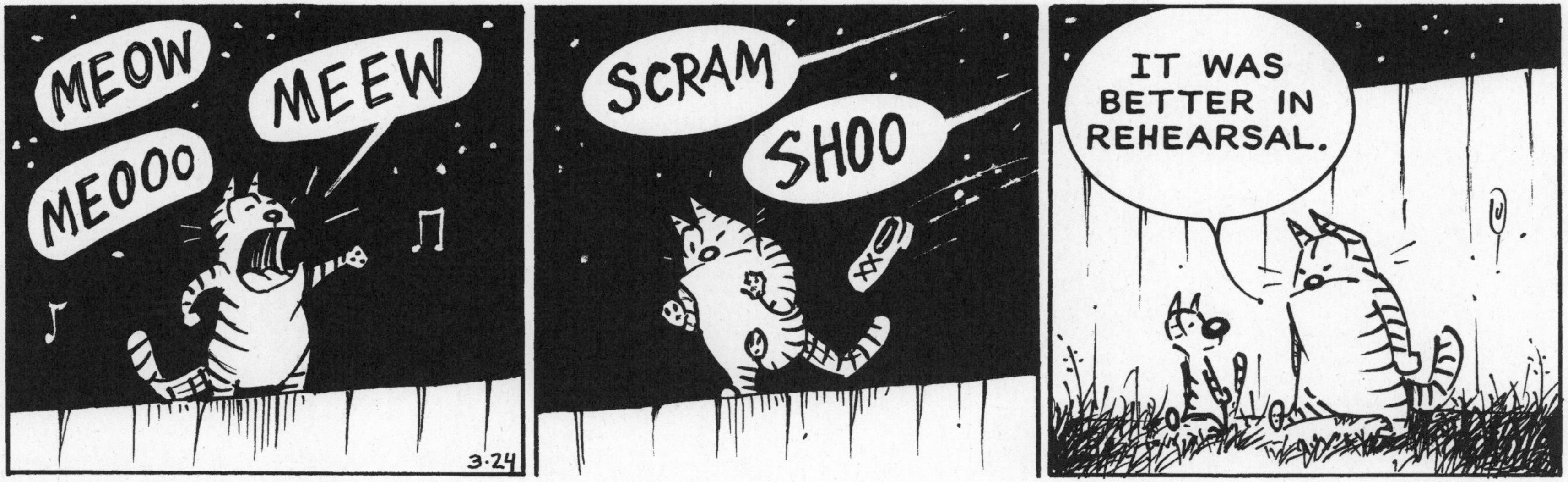
MEOW
MEEW
MEOOO
3·24
SCRAM
SHOO
IT WAS BETTER IN REHEARSAL.

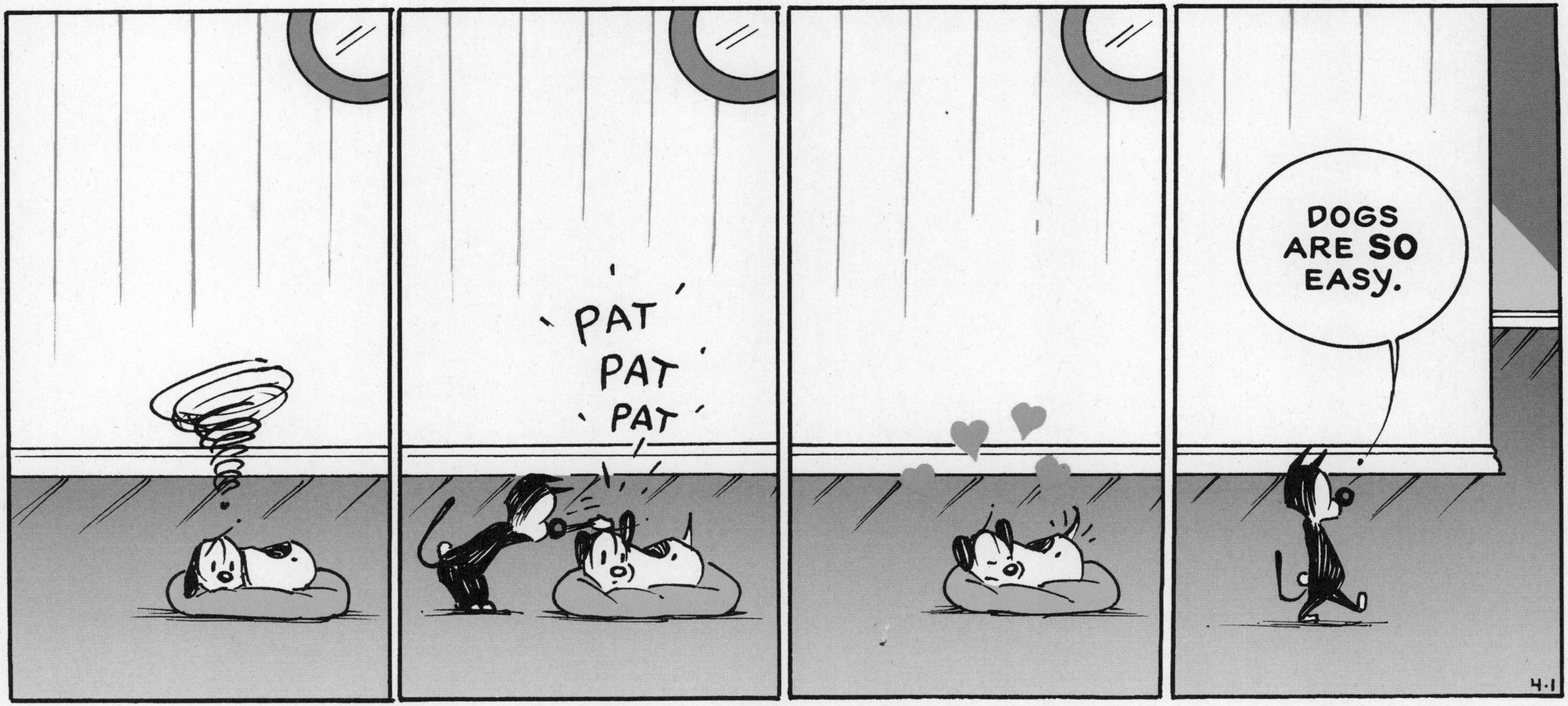
PAT
PAT
PAT
DOGS ARE SO EASY.
4.1

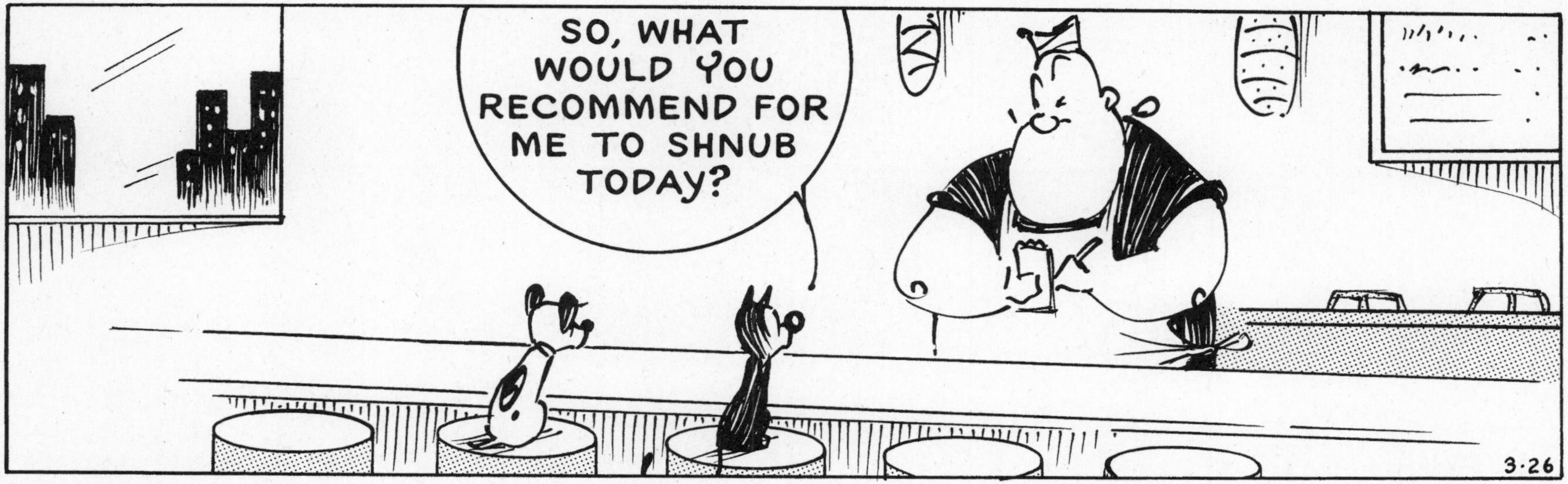
SO, WHAT WOULD YOU RECOMMEND FOR ME TO SHNUB TODAY?
3·26

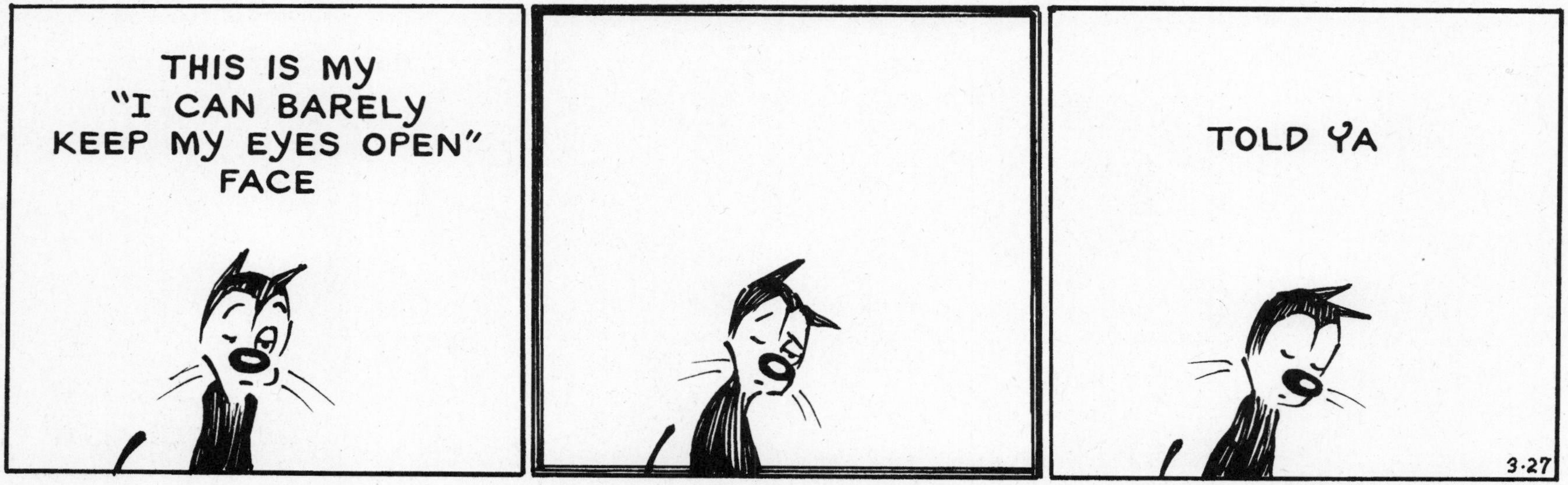
THIS IS MY "I CAN BARELY KEEP MY EYES OPEN" FACE
TOLD YA
3·27

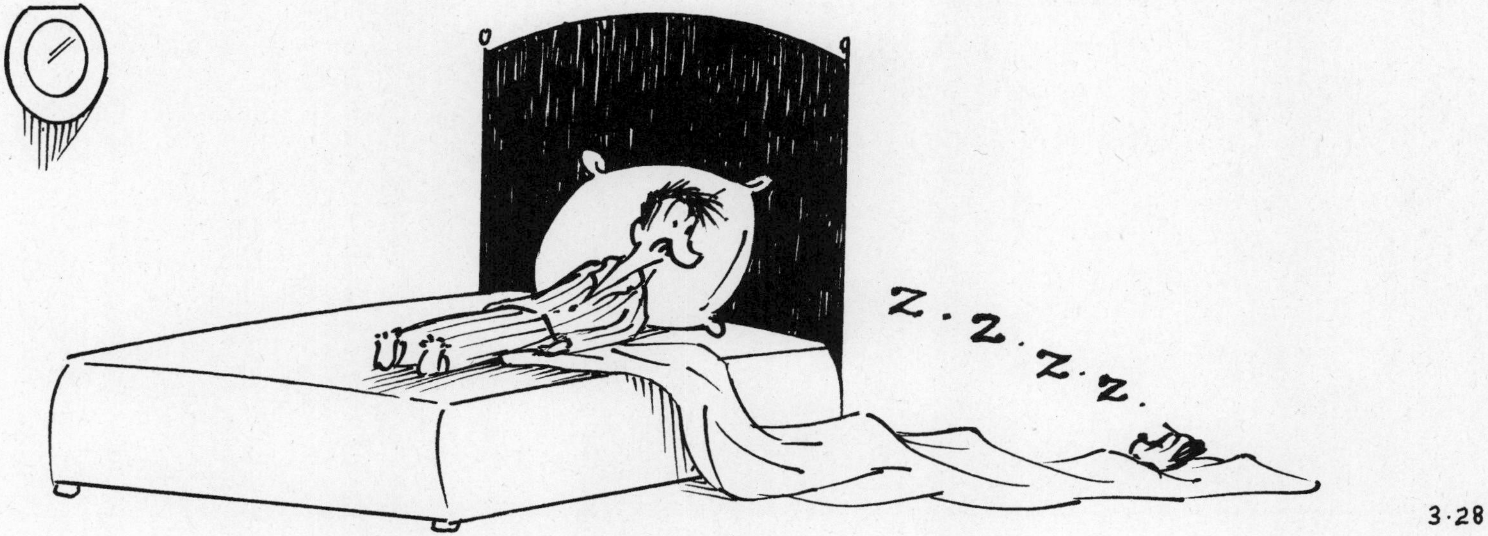
Z · Z · Z · Z ·
3·28

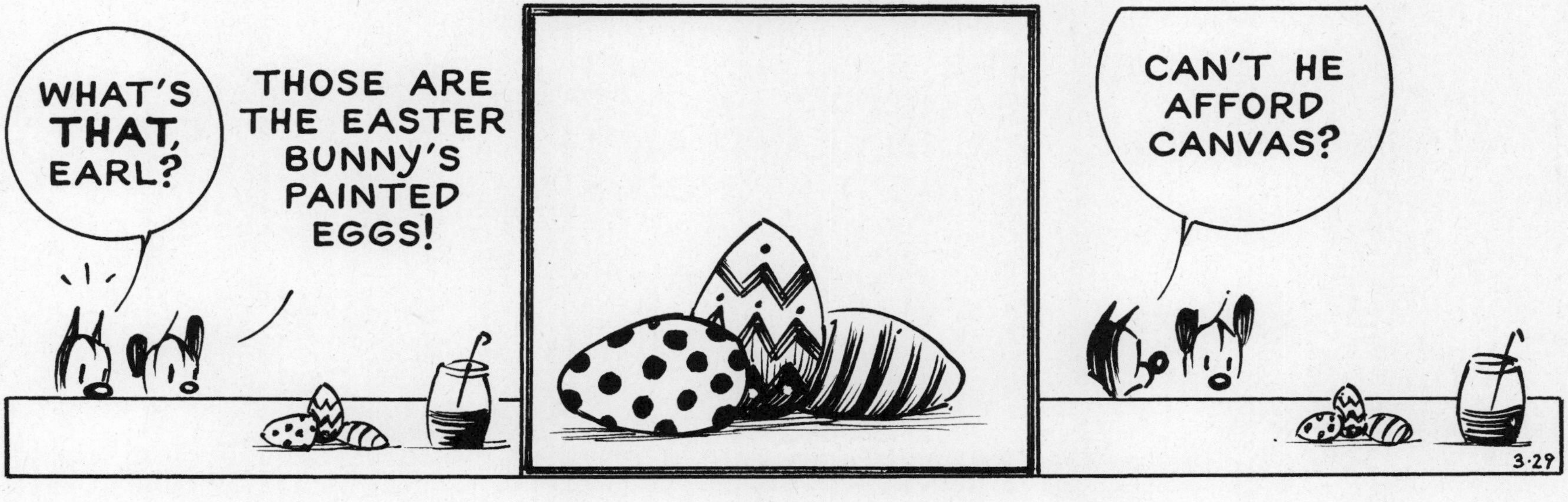
WHAT'S THAT, EARL?
THOSE ARE THE EASTER BUNNY'S PAINTED EGGS!
CAN'T HE AFFORD CANVAS?
3·29

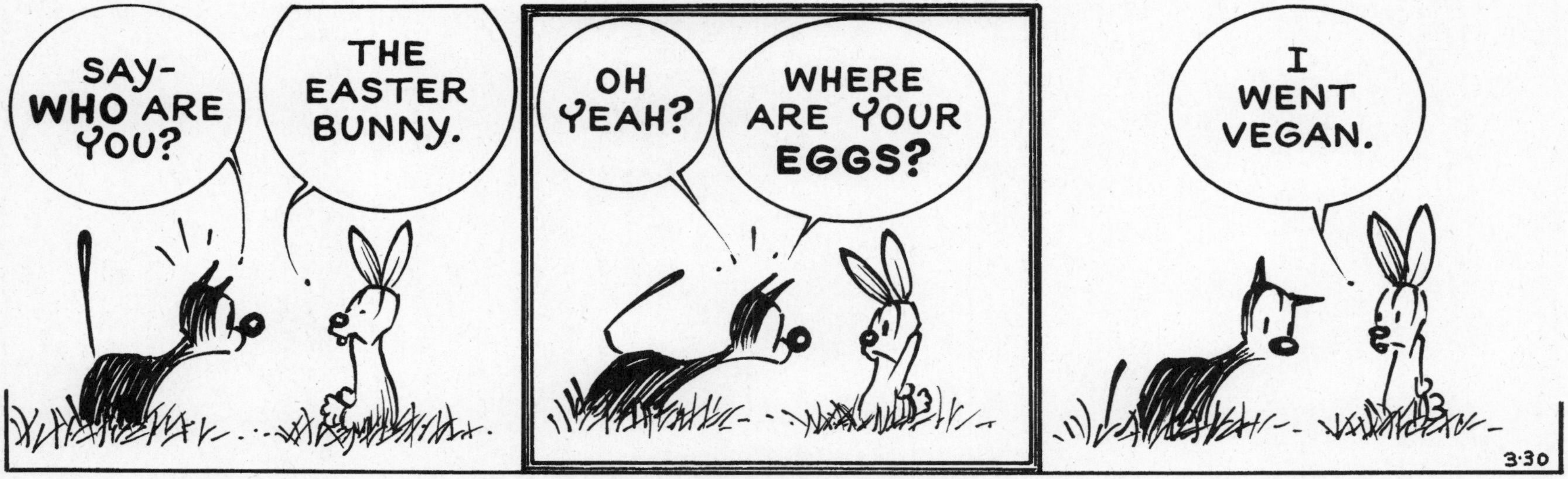
SAY- WHO ARE YOU?
THE EASTER BUNNY.
OH YEAH?
WHERE ARE YOUR EGGS?
I WENT VEGAN.
3·30

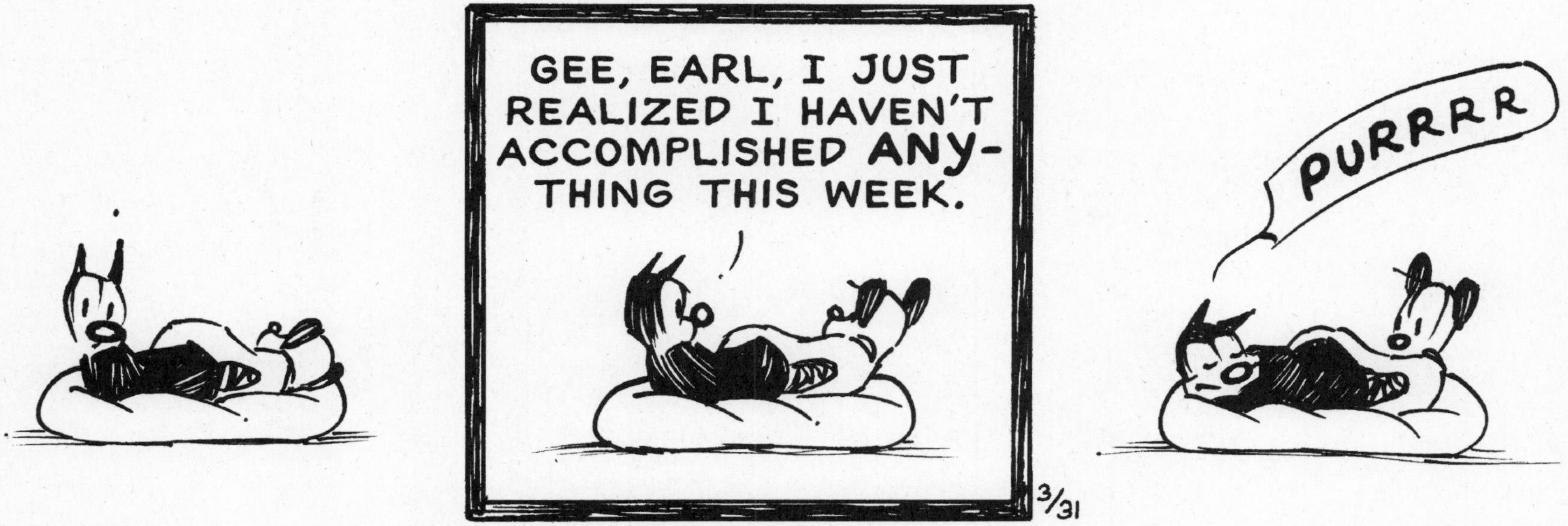
GEE, EARL, I JUST REALIZED I HAVEN'T ACCOMPLISHED ANY-THING THIS WEEK.
PURRRR
3/31

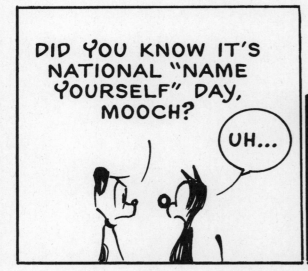

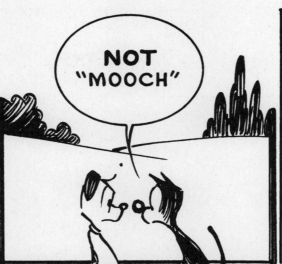

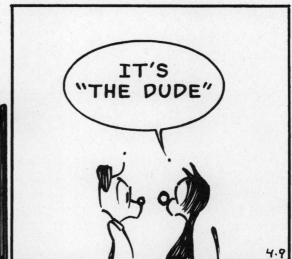

DID YOU KNOW IT'S NATIONAL "NAME YOURSELF" DAY, MOOCH?
UH...
NOT "MOOCH"
IT'S "THE DUDE"
4·9

Never, never be afraid to do what's right, especially if the well-being of a person or animal is at stake. Society's punishments are small compared to the wounds we inflict on our soul when we look the other way.

~ attributed to Martin Luther King, Jr.

4·4

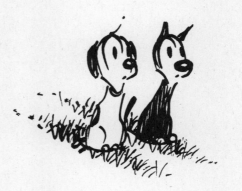

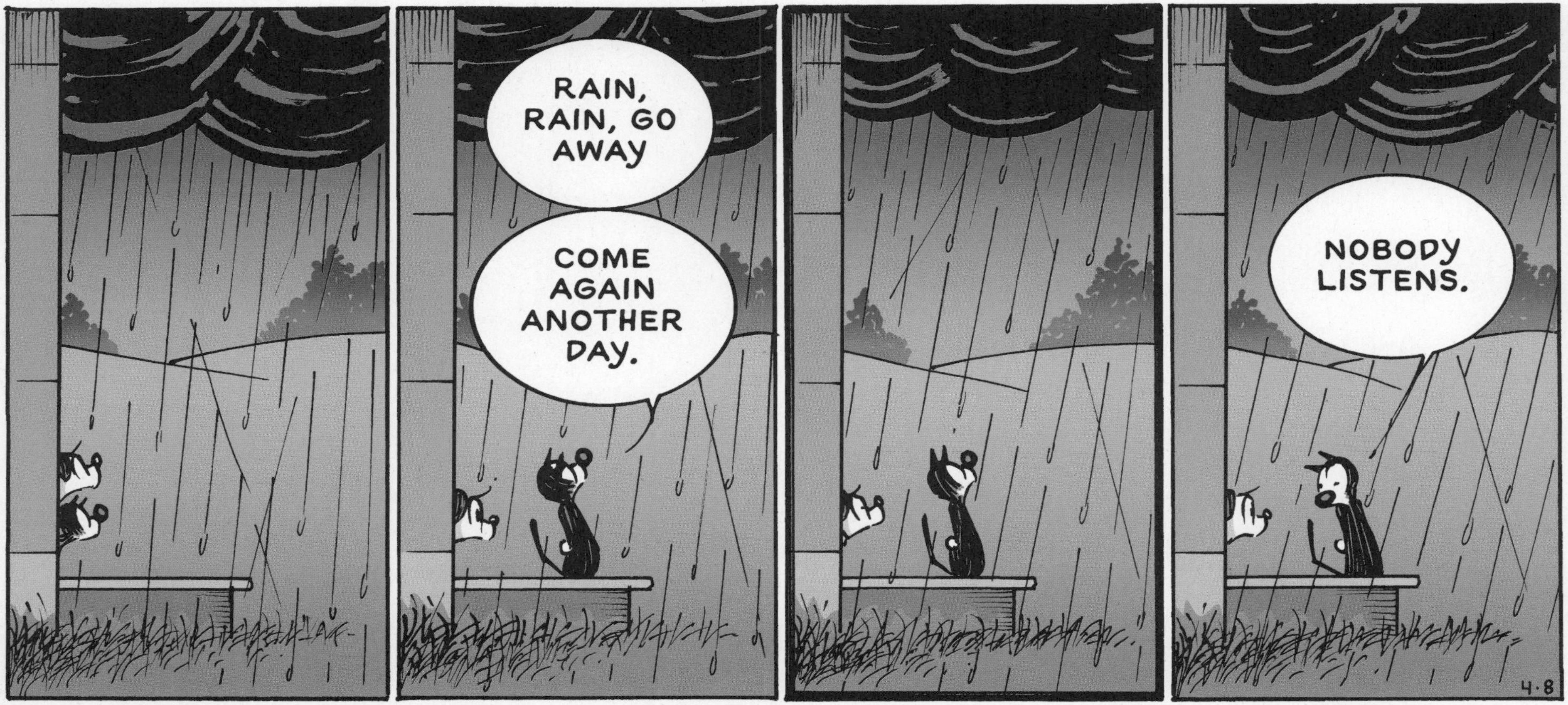
RAIN, RAIN, GO AWAY
COME AGAIN ANOTHER DAY.
NOBODY LISTENS.
4·8

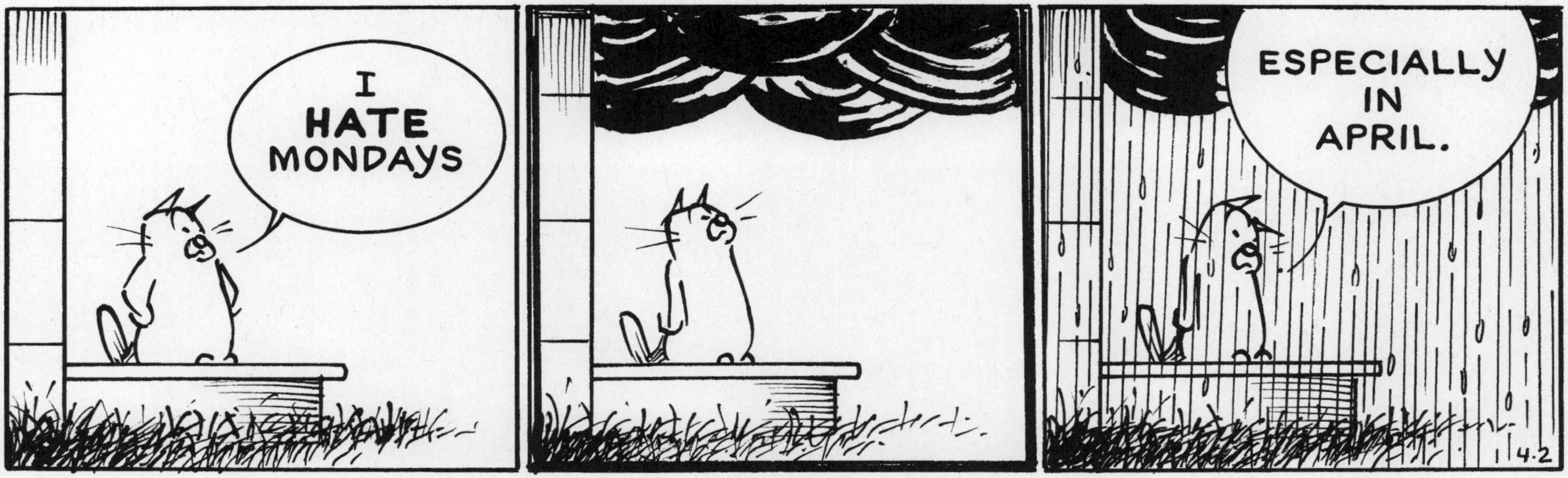
I HATE MONDAYS
ESPECIALLY IN APRIL.
4·2

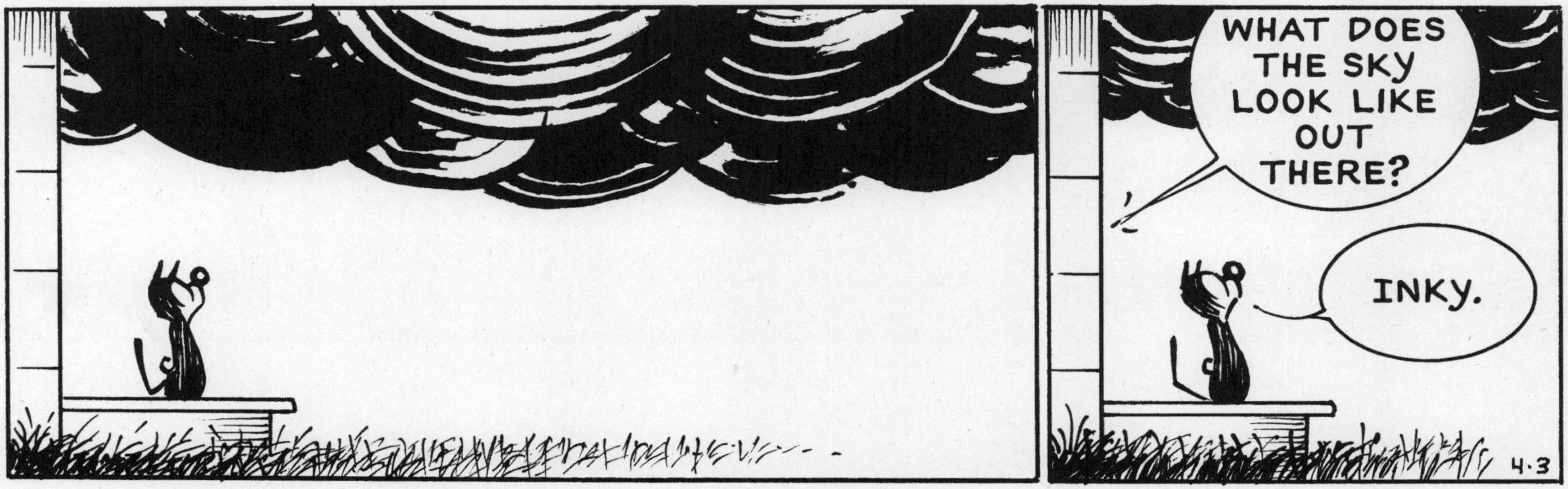
WHAT DOES THE SKY LOOK LIKE OUT THERE?
INKY.
4·3

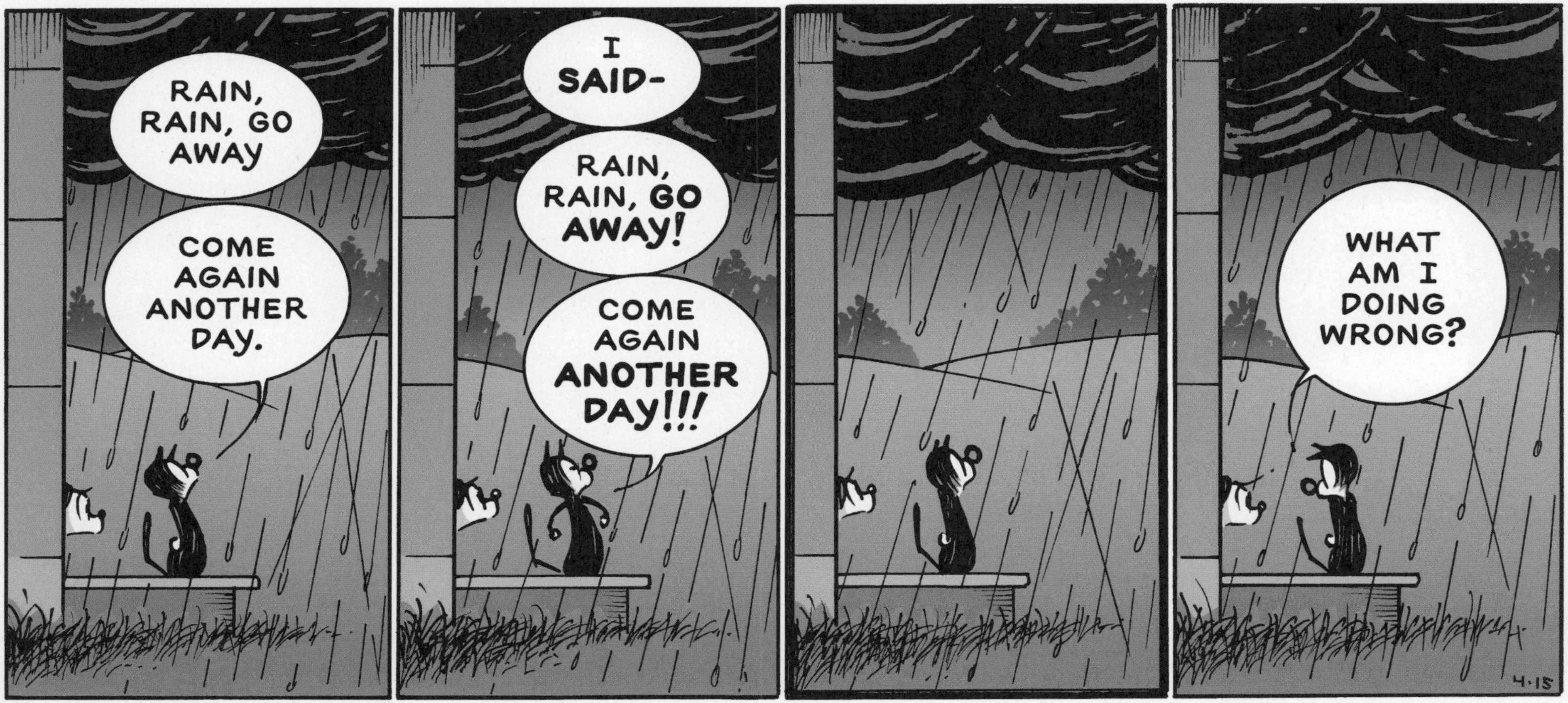
RAIN, RAIN, GO AWAY
COME AGAIN ANOTHER DAY.
I SAID-
RAIN, RAIN, GO AWAY!
COME AGAIN ANOTHER DAY!!!
WHAT AM I DOING WRONG?
4·15

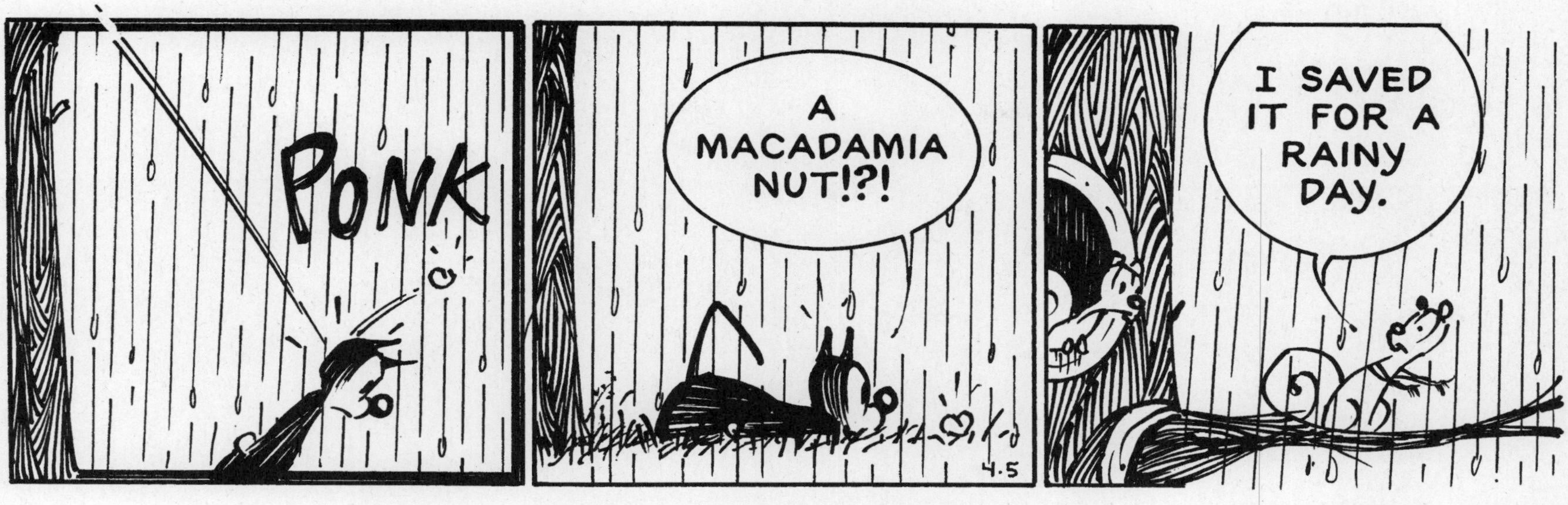
PONK
A MACADAMIA NUT!?!
I SAVED IT FOR A RAINY DAY.
4.5

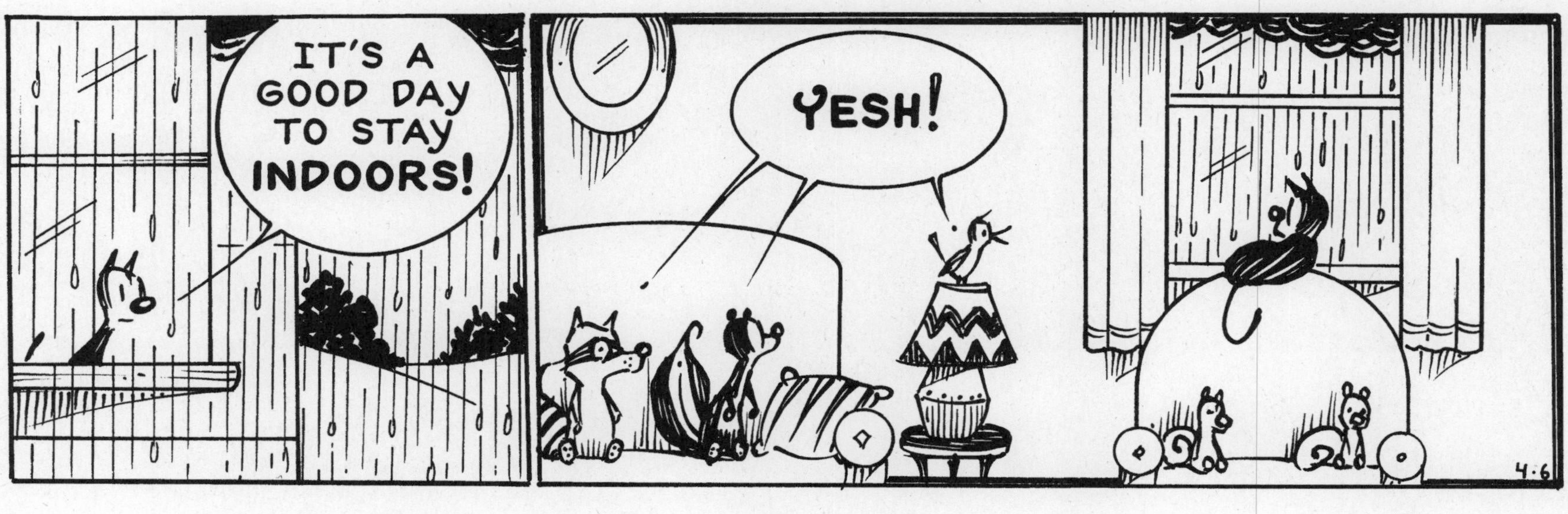
IT'S A GOOD DAY TO STAY INDOORS!
YESH!
4.6

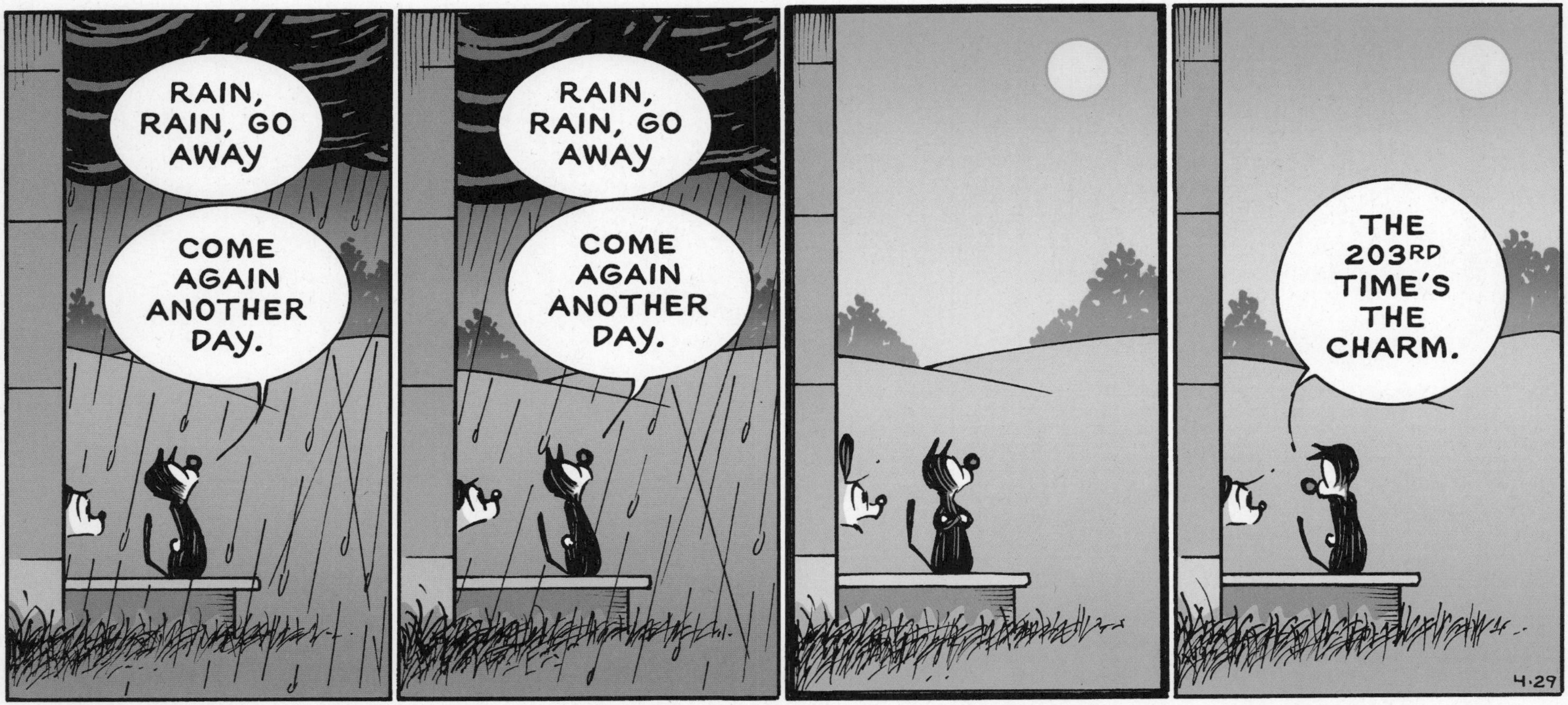
RAIN, RAIN, GO AWAY
COME AGAIN ANOTHER DAY.
RAIN, RAIN, GO AWAY
COME AGAIN ANOTHER DAY.
THE 203RD TIME'S THE CHARM.
4.29

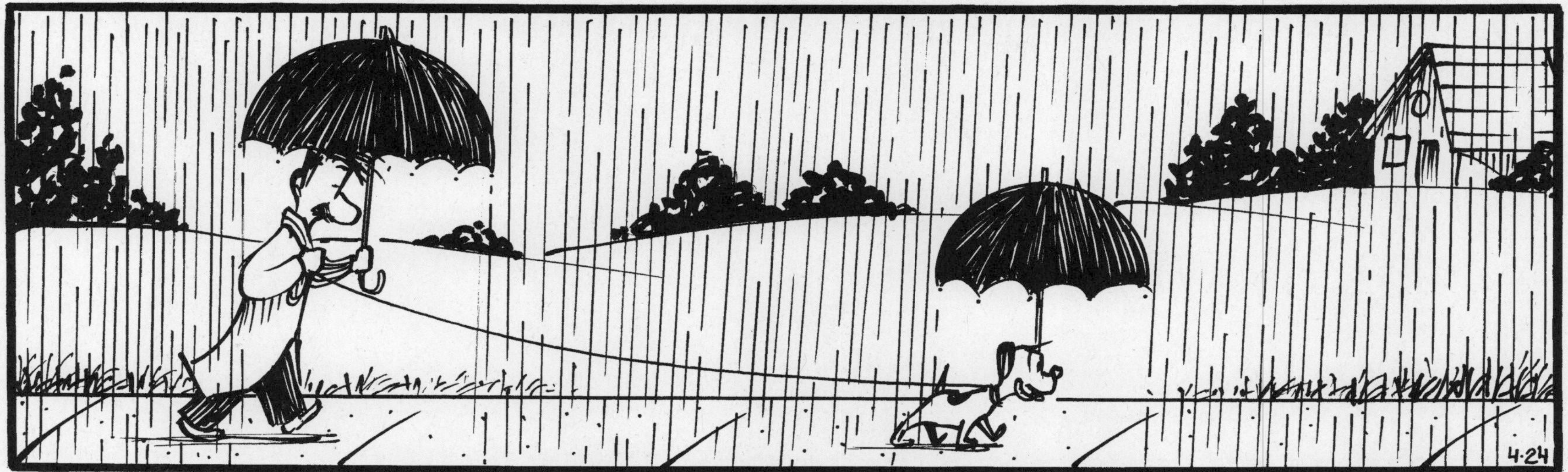
4·24

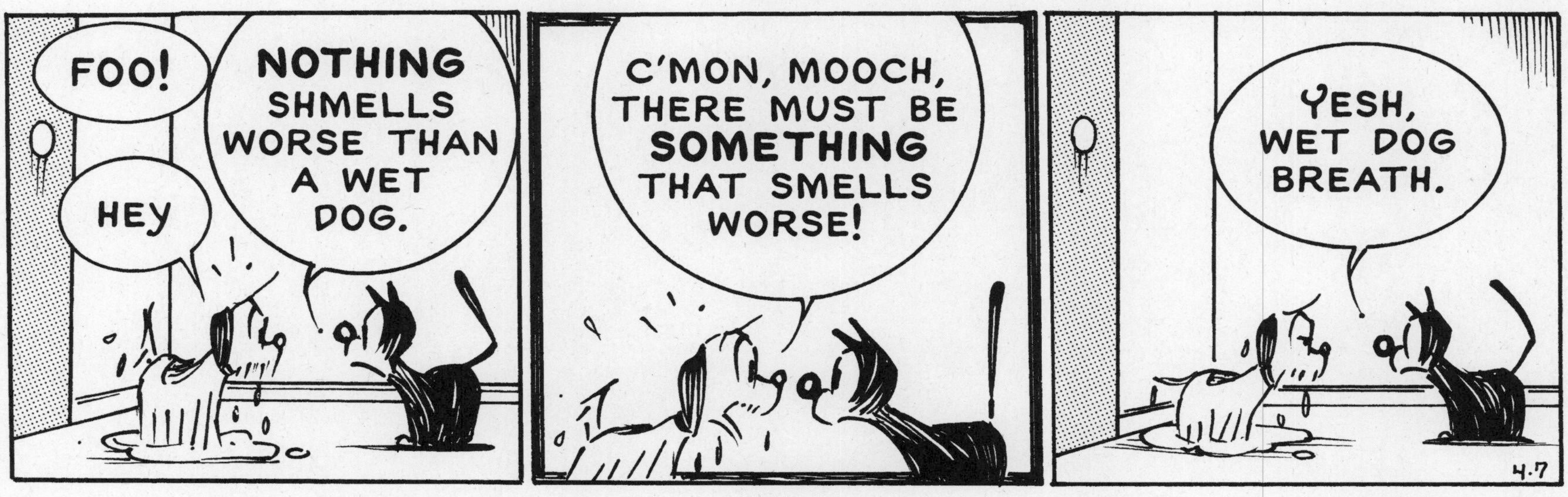
FOO!
HEY
NOTHING SHMELLS WORSE THAN A WET DOG.
C'MON, MOOCH, THERE MUST BE **SOMETHING** THAT SMELLS WORSE!
YESH, WET DOG BREATH.
4·7

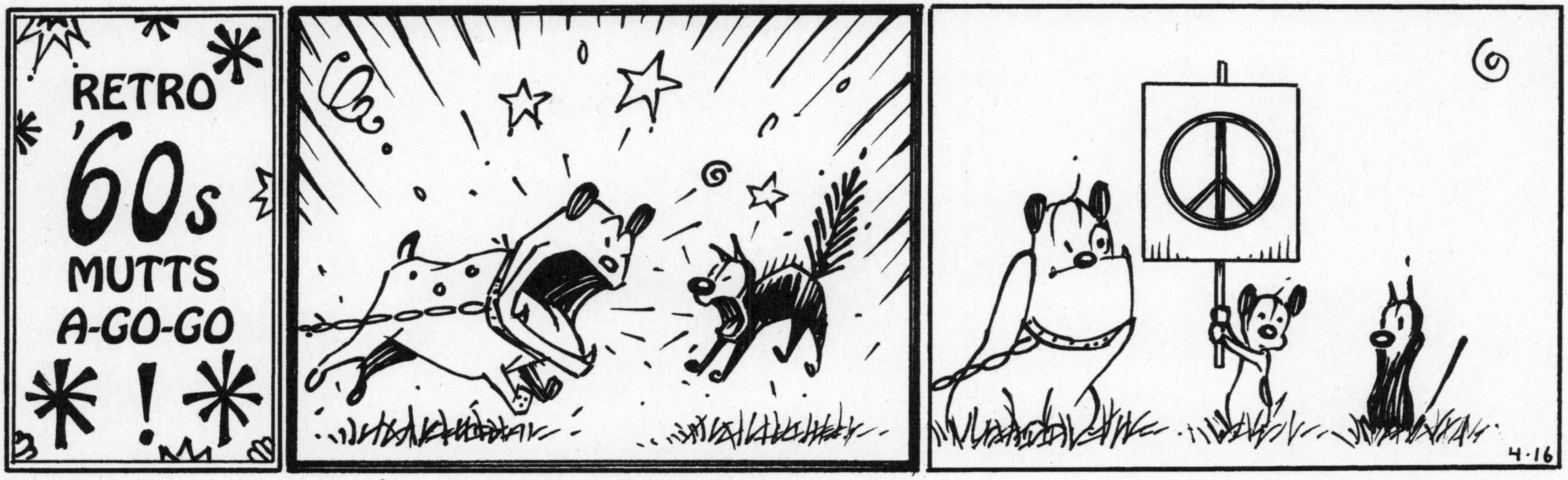
RETRO
'60s
MUTTS
A-GO-GO
4·16

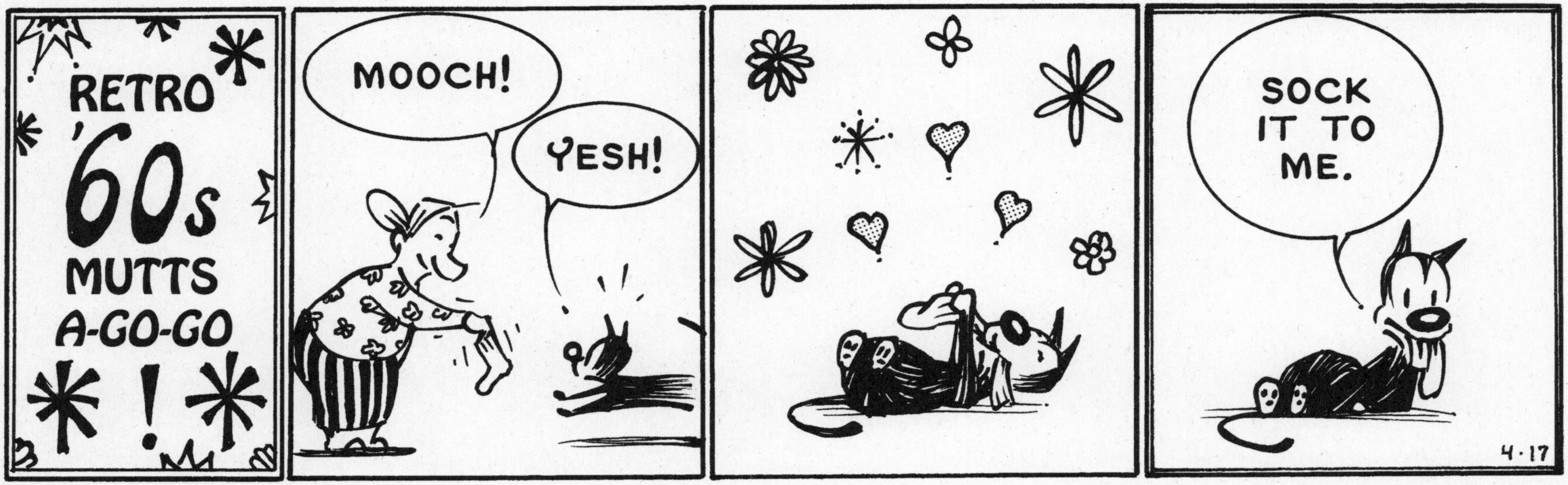
RETRO
'60s
MUTTS
A-GO-GO
MOOCH!
YESH!
SOCK IT TO ME.
4·17

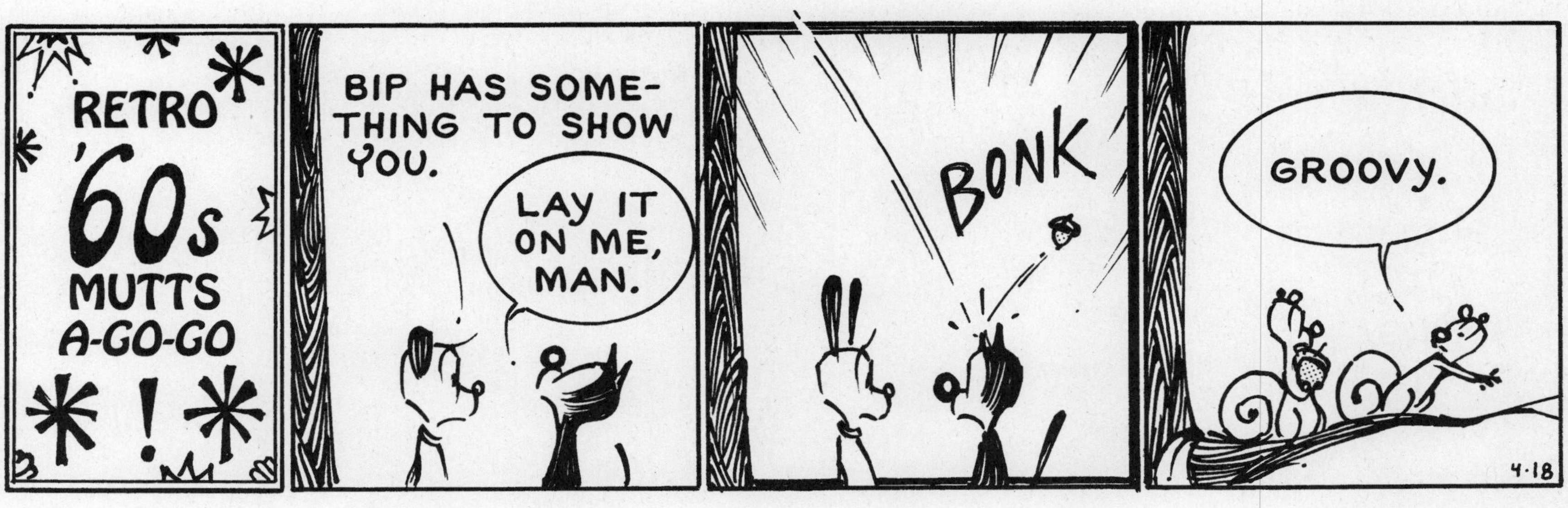
RETRO '60s MUTTS A-GO-GO !
BIP HAS SOME-THING TO SHOW YOU.
LAY IT ON ME, MAN.
BONK
GROOVY.
4·18

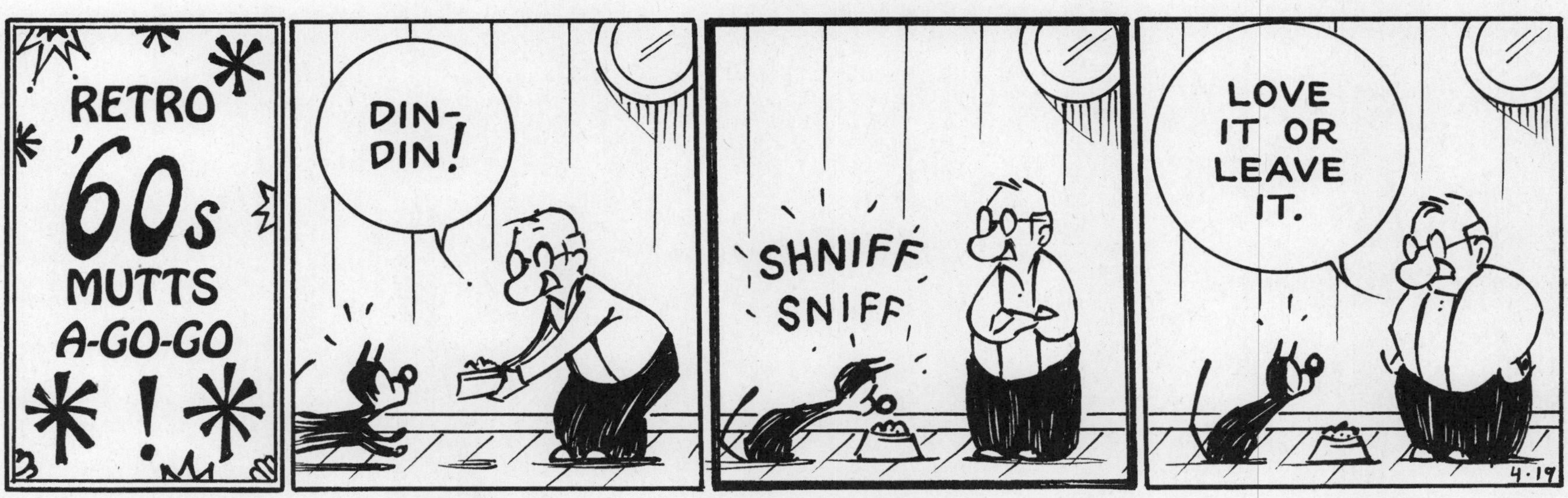
RETRO '60s MUTTS A-GO-GO !
DIN-DIN!
SHNIFF SNIFF
LOVE IT OR LEAVE IT.
4·19

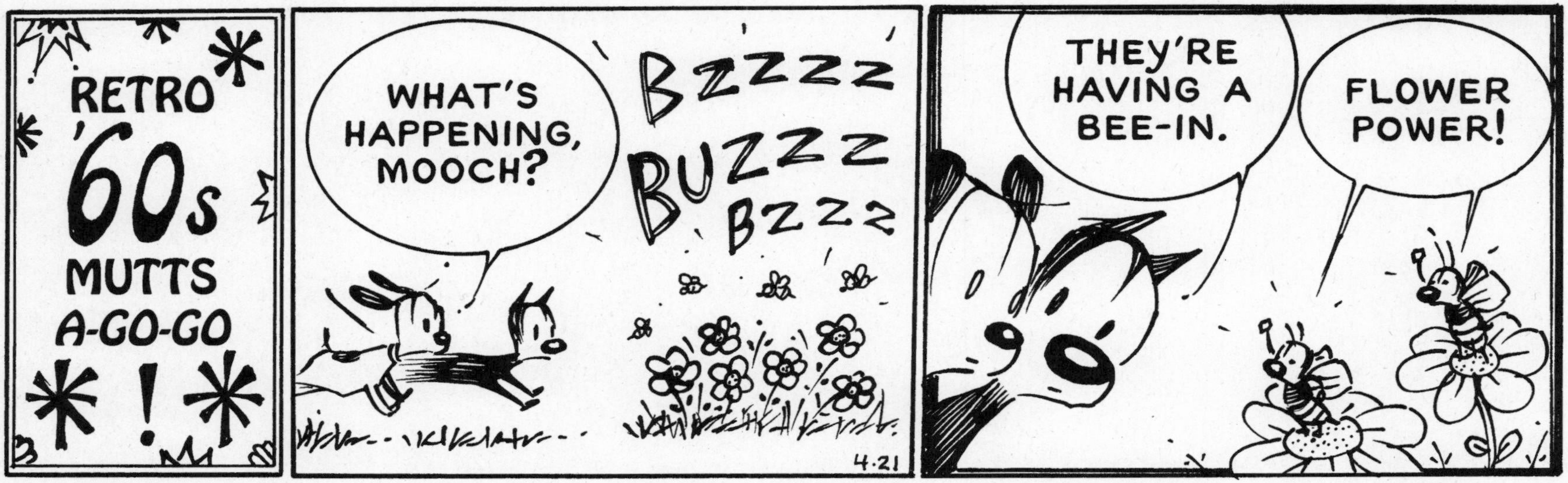
RETRO '60s MUTTS A-GO-GO !
WHAT'S HAPPENING, MOOCH?
BZZZZ BUZZZ BZZZ
4.21
THEY'RE HAVING A BEE-IN.
FLOWER POWER!

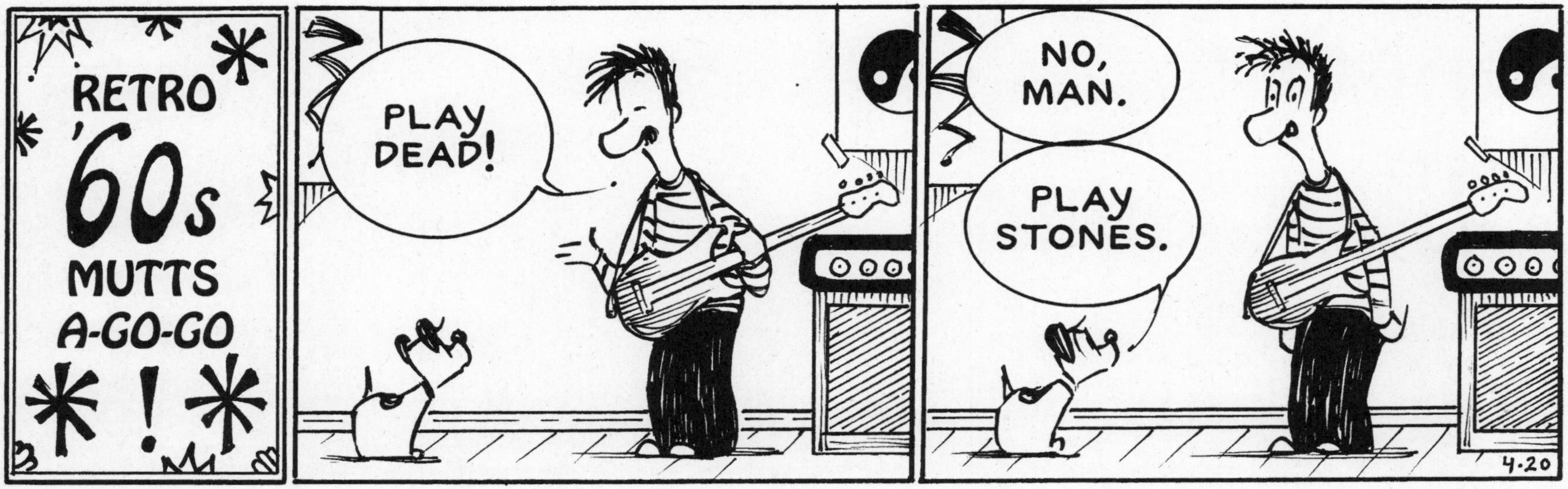
RETRO '60s MUTTS A-GO-GO !
PLAY DEAD!
NO, MAN.
PLAY STONES.
4.20

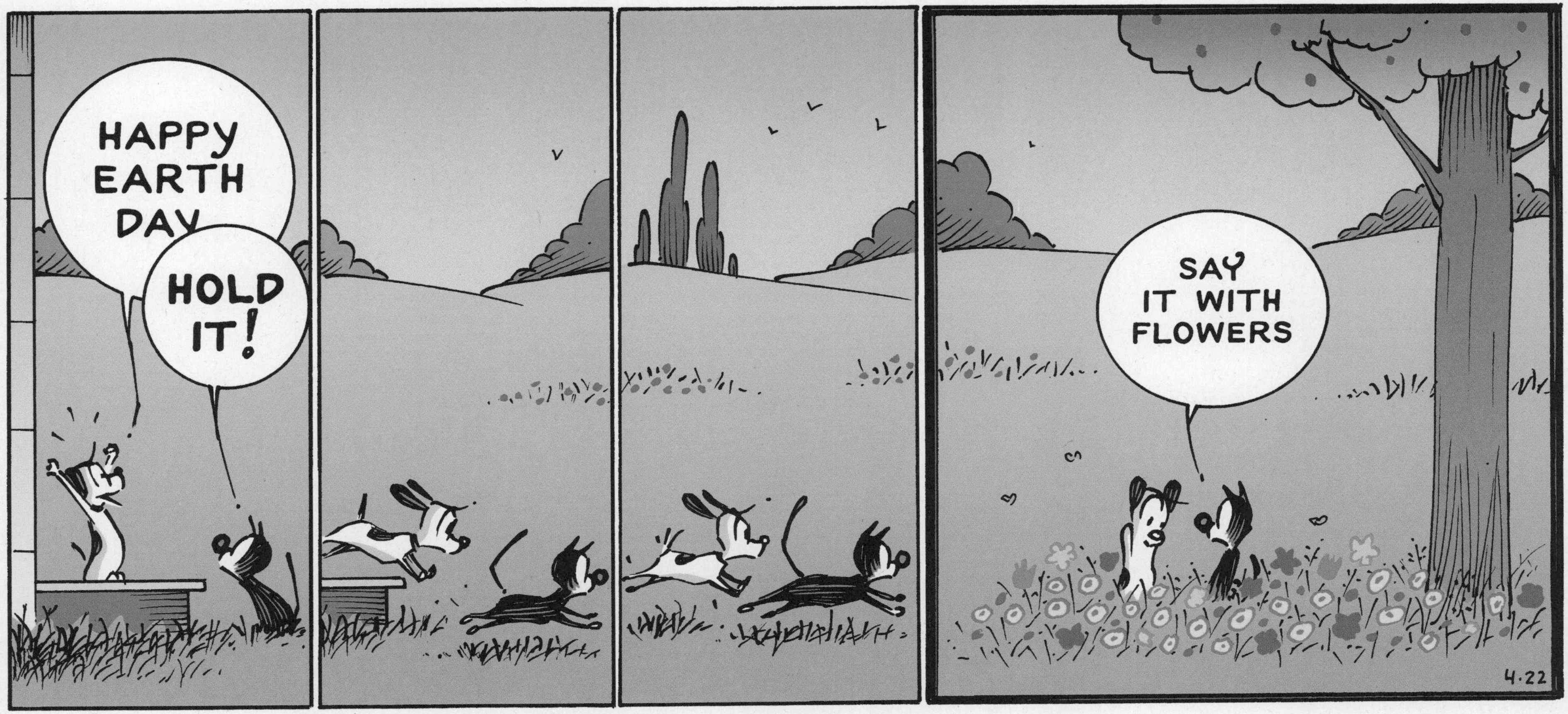
HAPPY EARTH DAY
HOLD IT!
SAY IT WITH FLOWERS
4·22

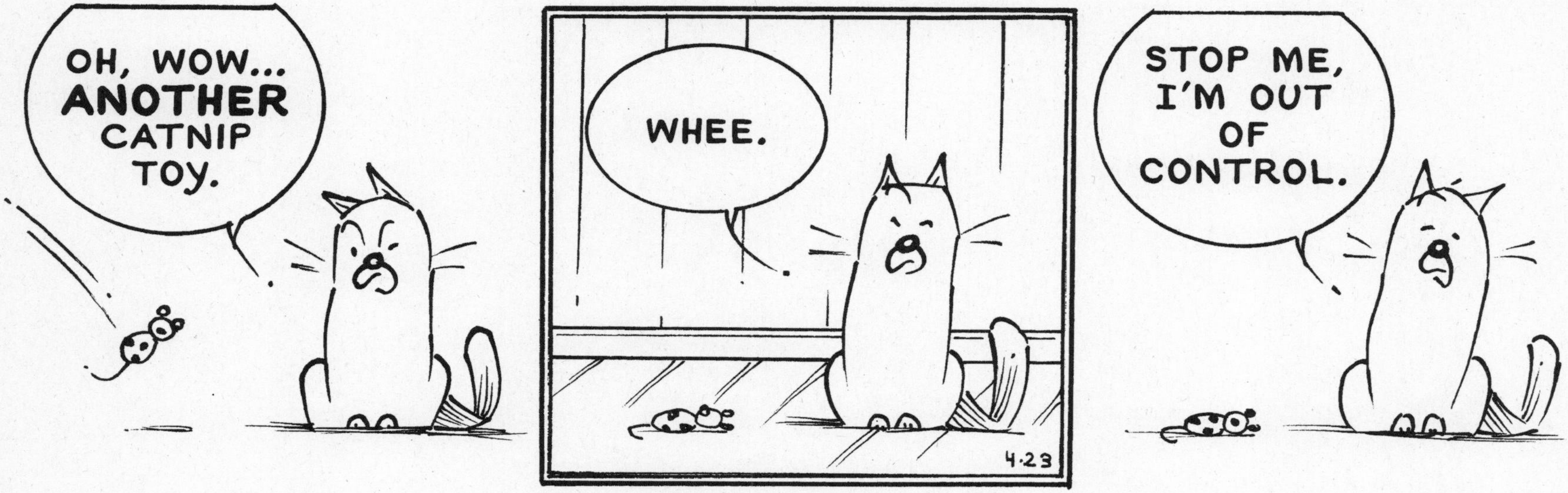
OH, WOW... **ANOTHER** CATNIP TOY.
WHEE.
STOP ME, I'M OUT OF CONTROL.
4·23

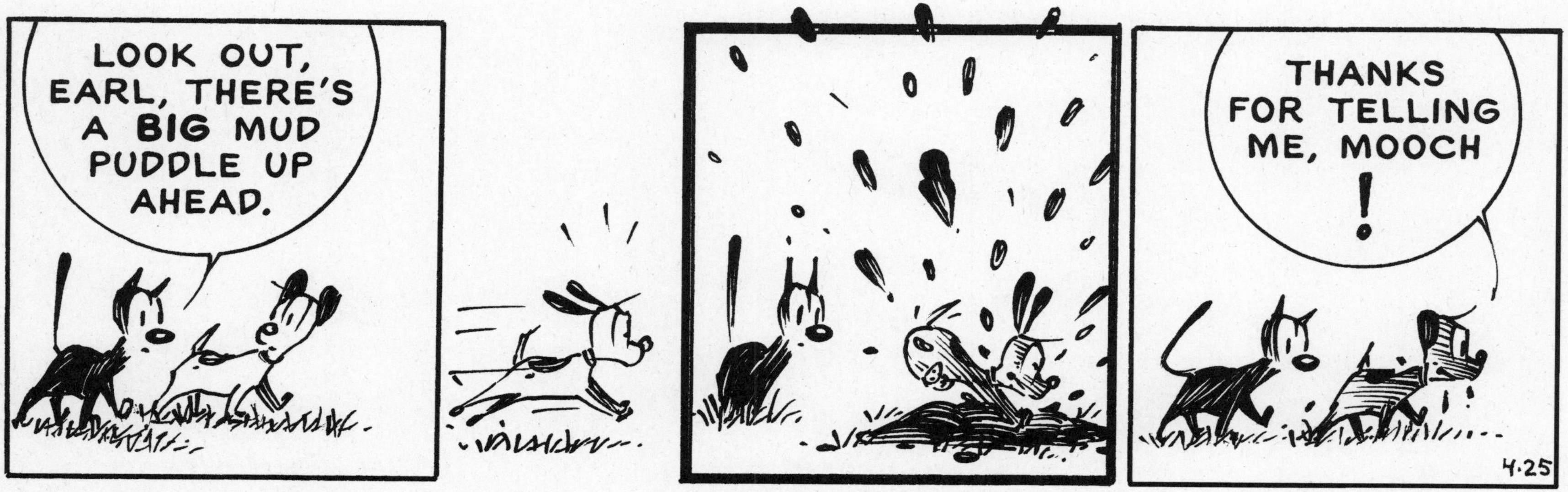
LOOK OUT, EARL, THERE'S A **BIG** MUD PUDDLE UP AHEAD.
THANKS FOR TELLING ME, MOOCH !
4·25

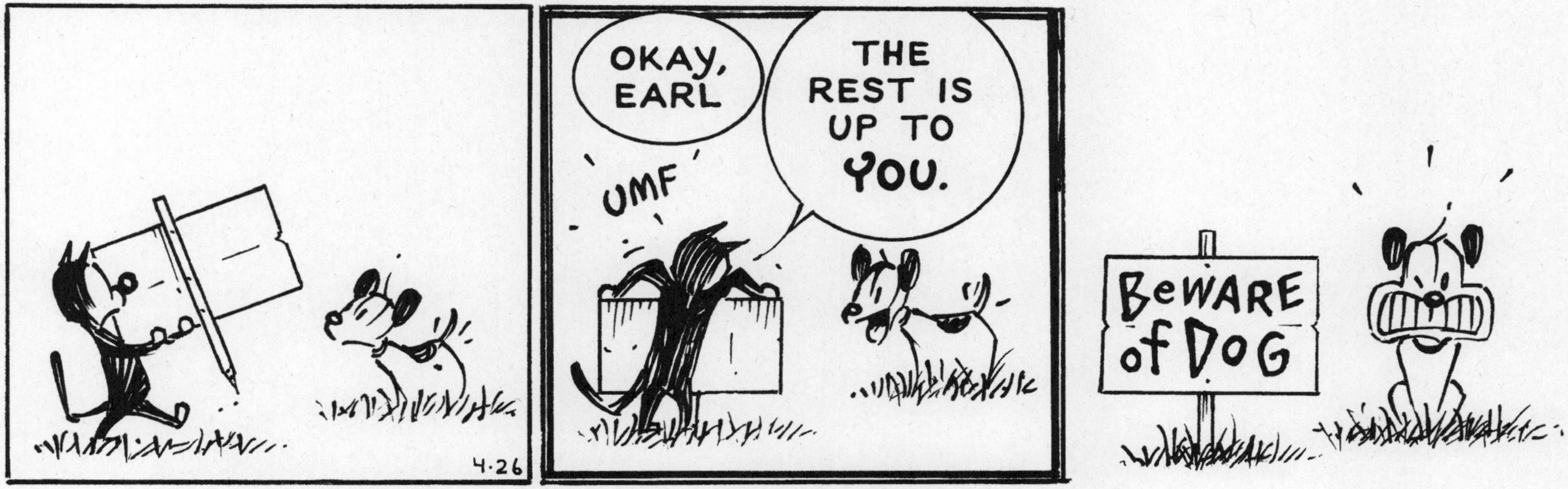
4·26
OKAY, EARL
THE REST IS UP TO YOU.
UMF
BeWARE of DOG

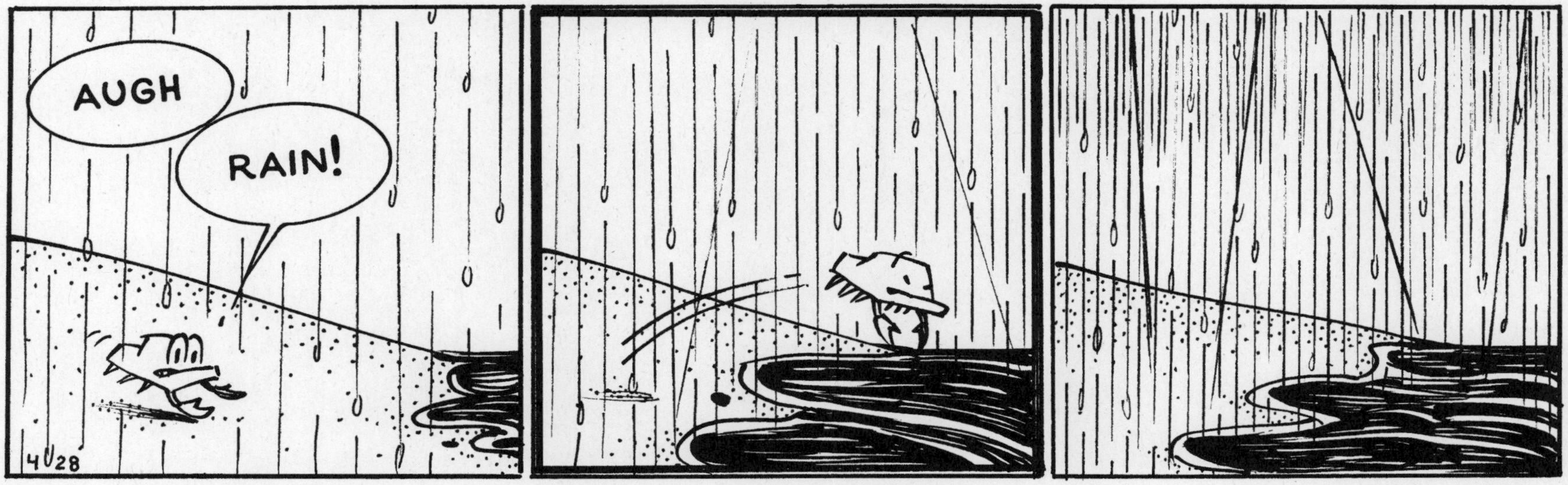
AUGH
RAIN!
4/28

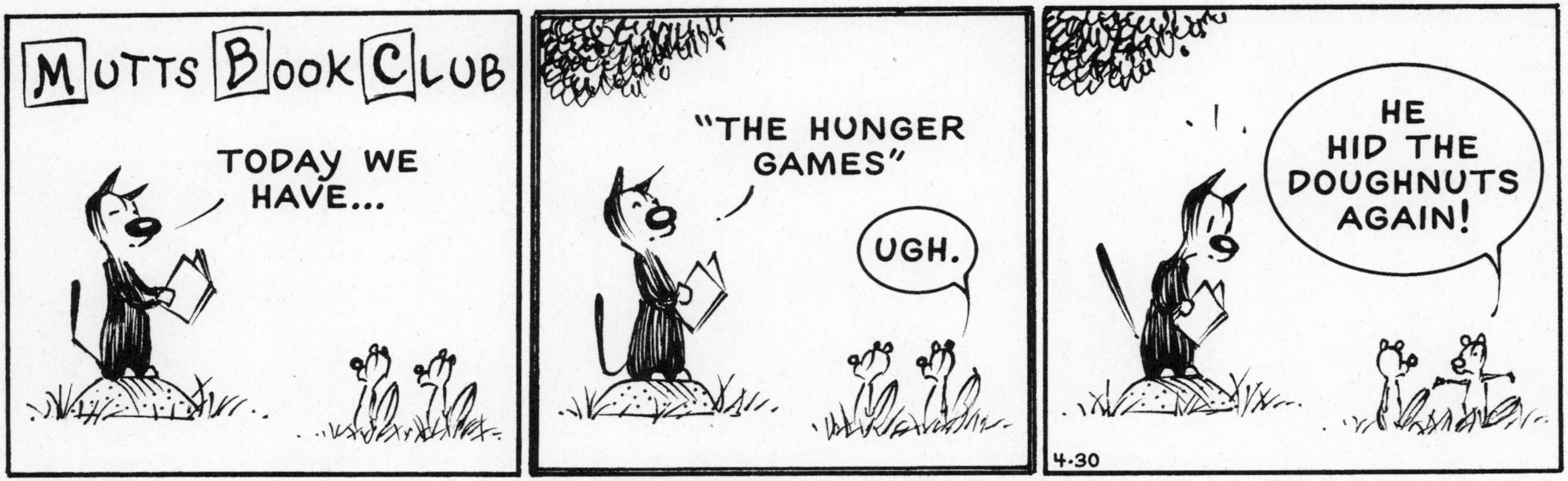
MUTTS BOOK CLUB
TODAY WE HAVE...
"THE HUNGER GAMES"
UGH.
HE HID THE DOUGHNUTS AGAIN!
4·30

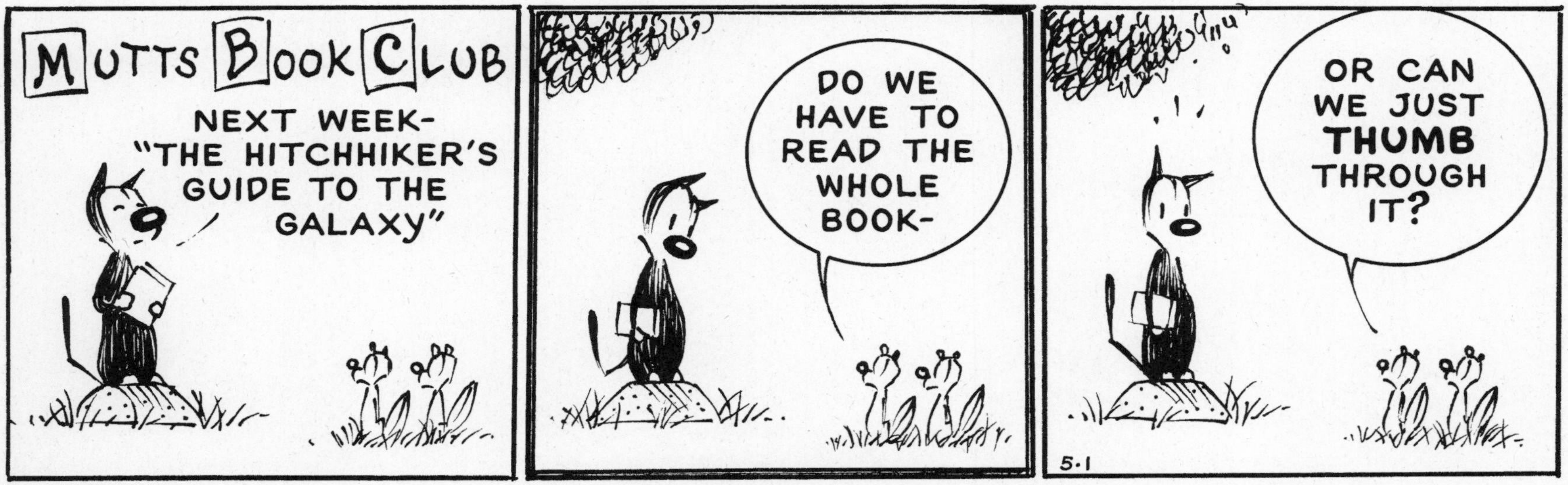
MUTTS BOOK CLUB
NEXT WEEK- "THE HITCHHIKER'S GUIDE TO THE GALAXY"
DO WE HAVE TO READ THE WHOLE BOOK-
OR CAN WE JUST THUMB THROUGH IT?
5·1

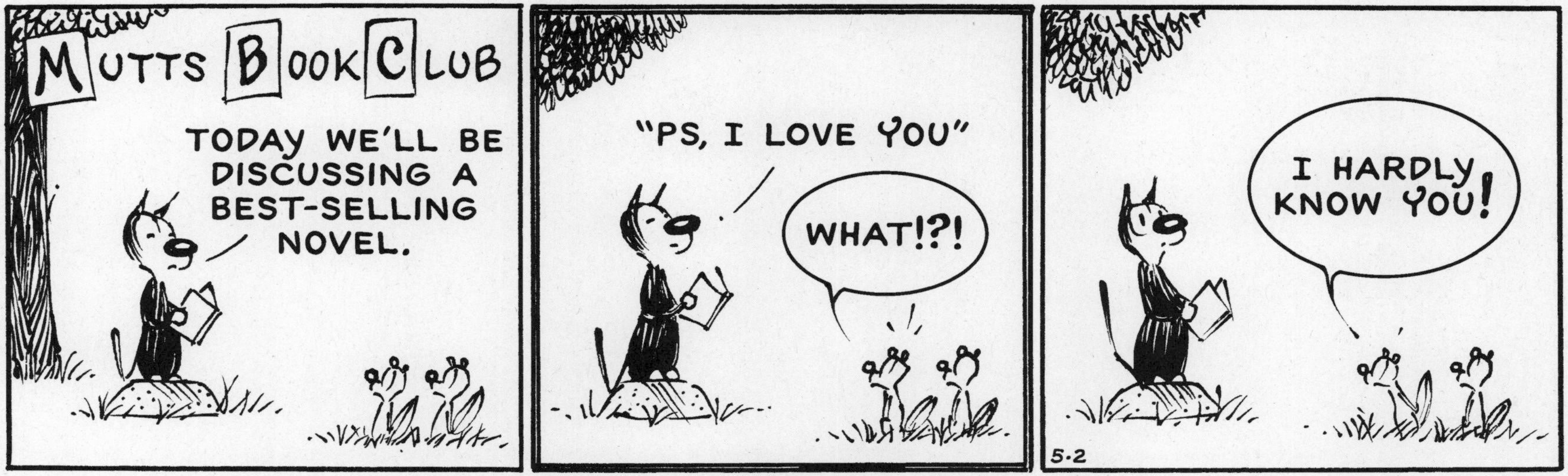
MUTTS BOOK CLUB
TODAY WE'LL BE DISCUSSING A BEST-SELLING NOVEL.
"PS, I LOVE YOU"
WHAT!?!
I HARDLY KNOW YOU!
5·2

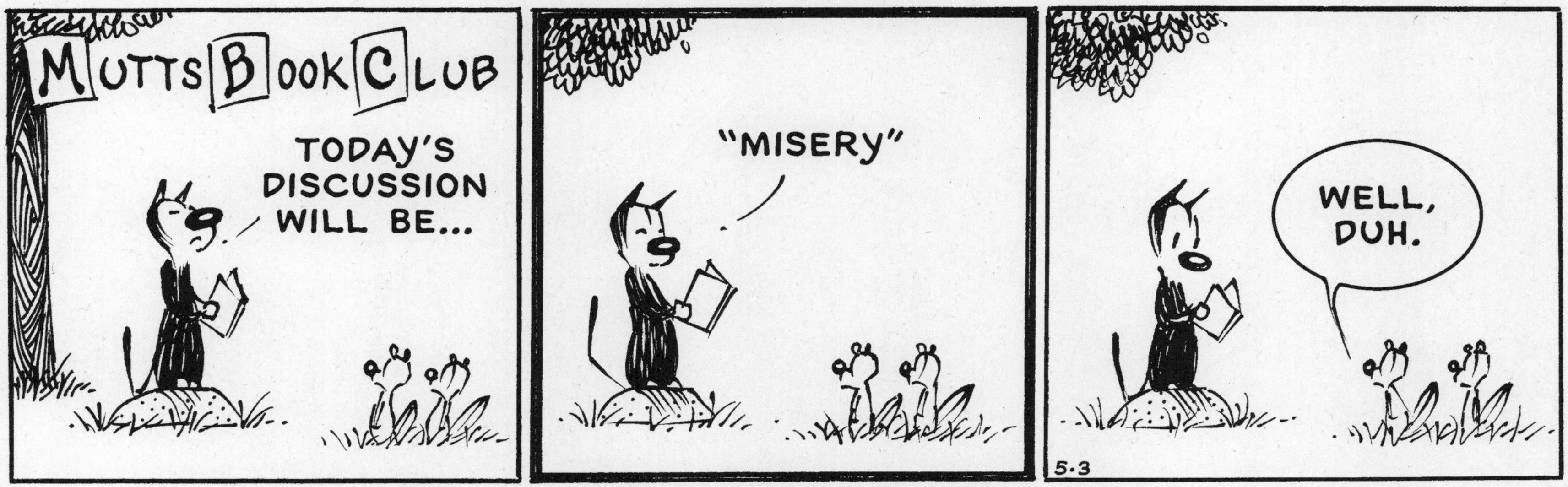
MUTTS BOOK CLUB
TODAY'S DISCUSSION WILL BE...
"MISERY"
WELL, DUH.
5·3

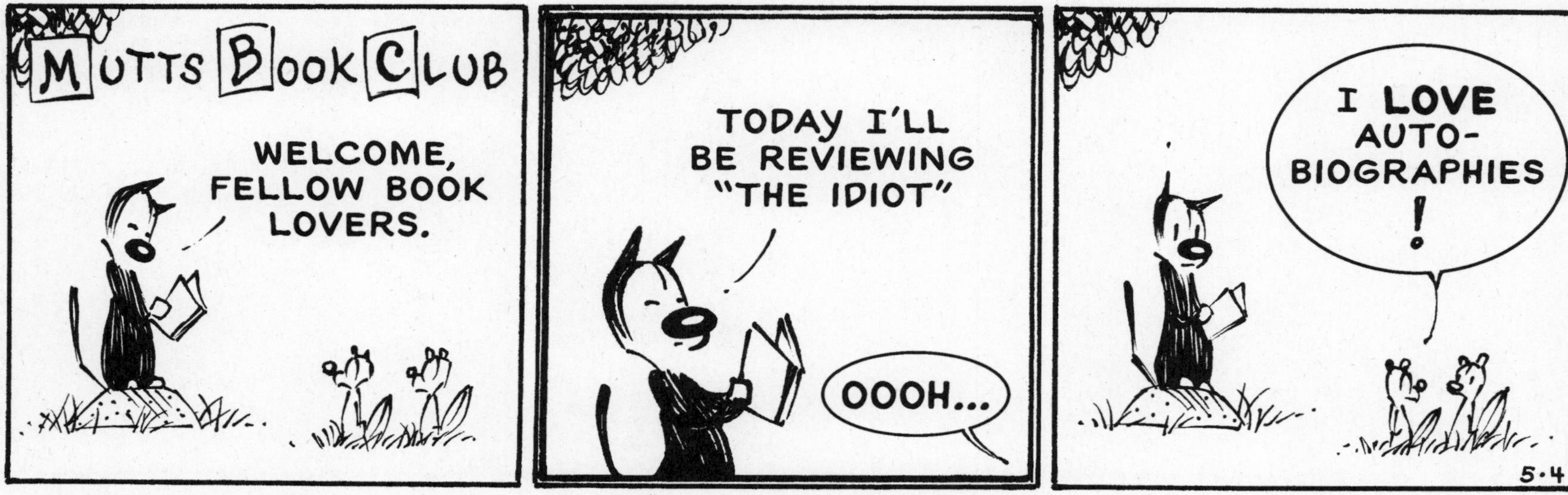
MUTTS BOOK CLUB
WELCOME, FELLOW BOOK LOVERS.
TODAY I'LL BE REVIEWING "THE IDIOT"
OOOH...
I LOVE AUTO-BIOGRAPHIES !
5·4

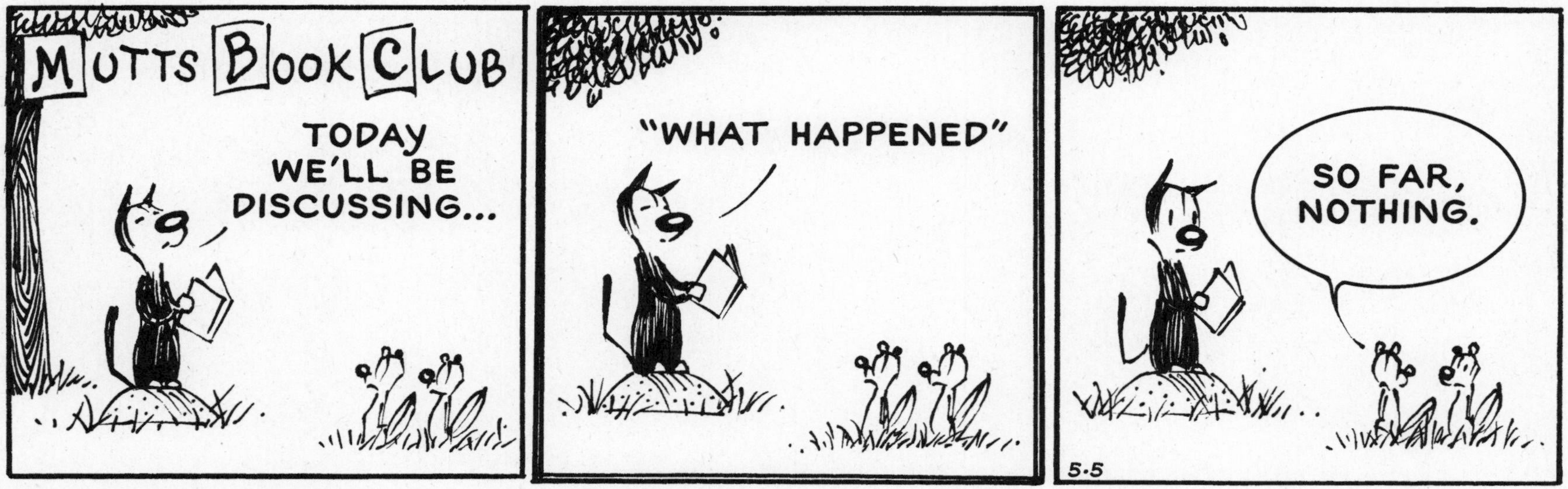
MUTTS BOOK CLUB
TODAY WE'LL BE DISCUSSING...
"WHAT HAPPENED"
SO FAR, NOTHING.
5·5

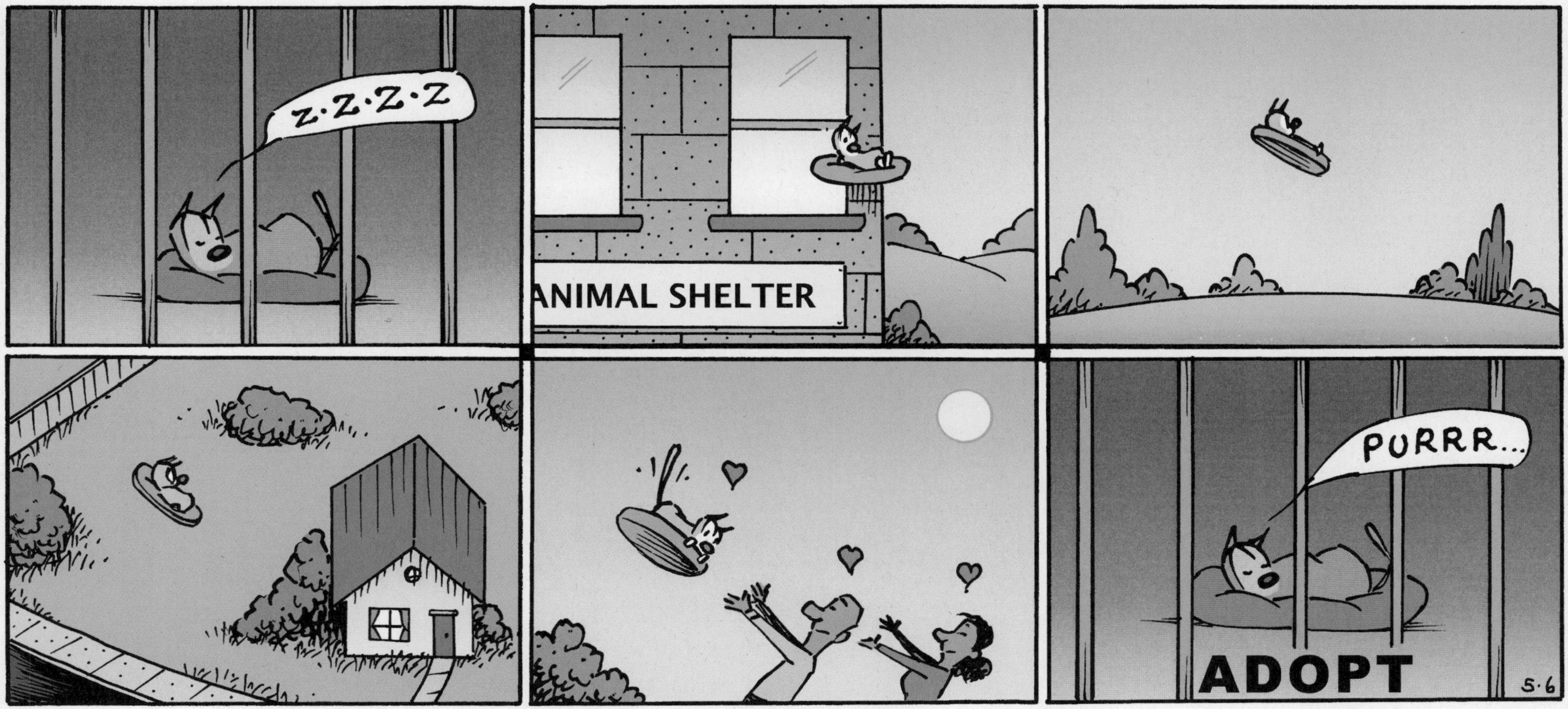
Z·Z·Z·Z
ANIMAL SHELTER
PURRR...
ADOPT
5·6

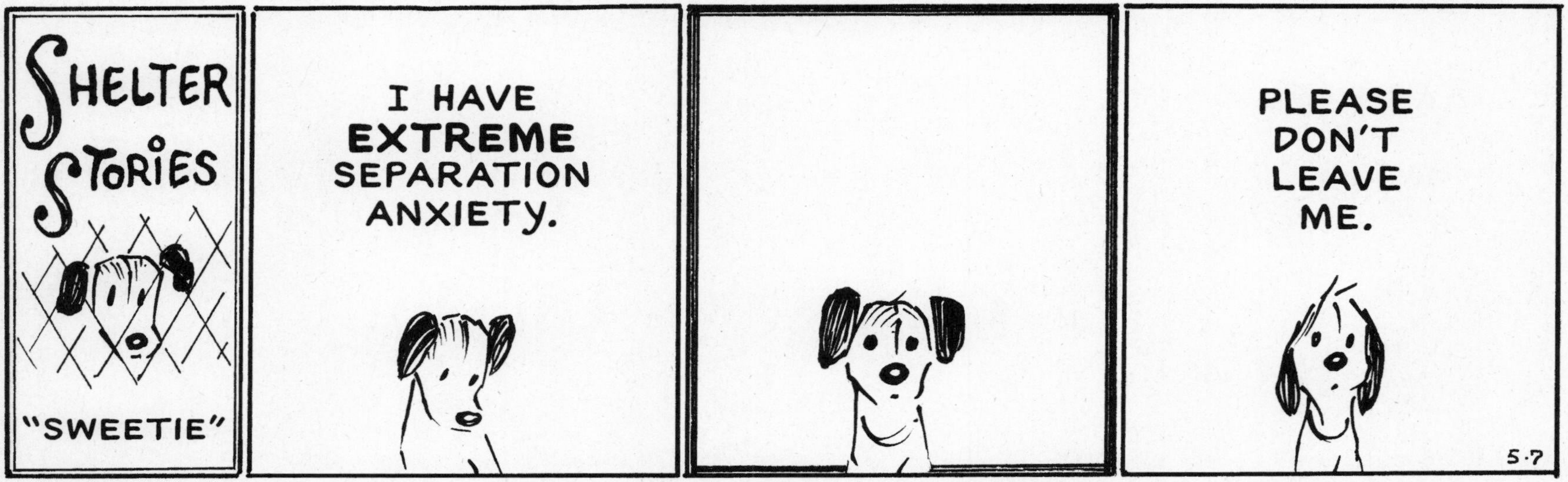
SHELTER STORIES
"SWEETIE"
I HAVE **EXTREME** SEPARATION ANXIETY.
PLEASE DON'T LEAVE ME.
5·7

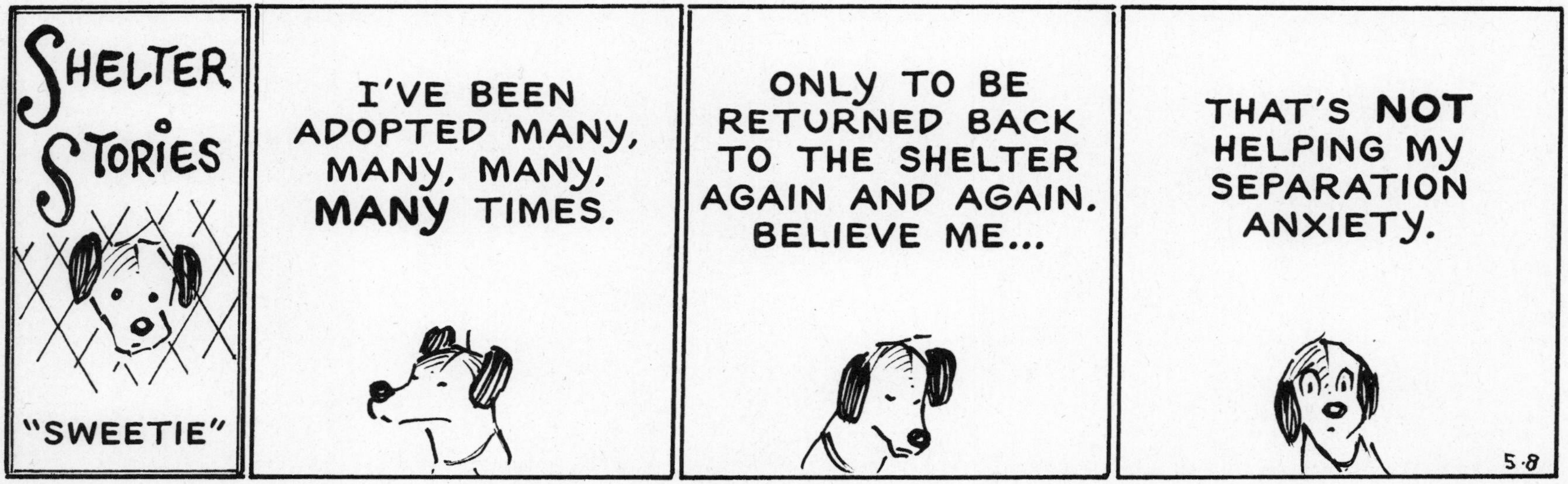
SHELTER STORIES
"SWEETIE"
I'VE BEEN ADOPTED MANY, MANY, MANY, **MANY** TIMES.
ONLY TO BE RETURNED BACK TO THE SHELTER AGAIN AND AGAIN. BELIEVE ME...
THAT'S **NOT** HELPING MY SEPARATION ANXIETY.
5·8

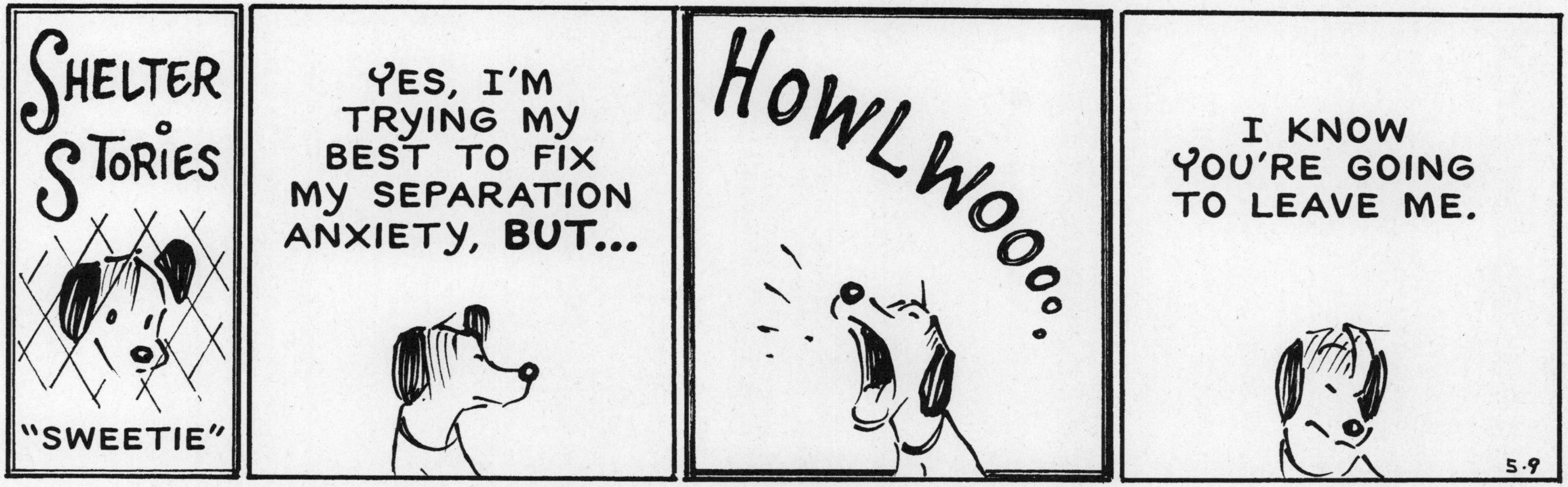
SHELTER STORIES
"SWEETIE"
YES, I'M TRYING MY BEST TO FIX MY SEPARATION ANXIETY, BUT...
HOWLWOOOO
I KNOW YOU'RE GOING TO LEAVE ME.
5·9

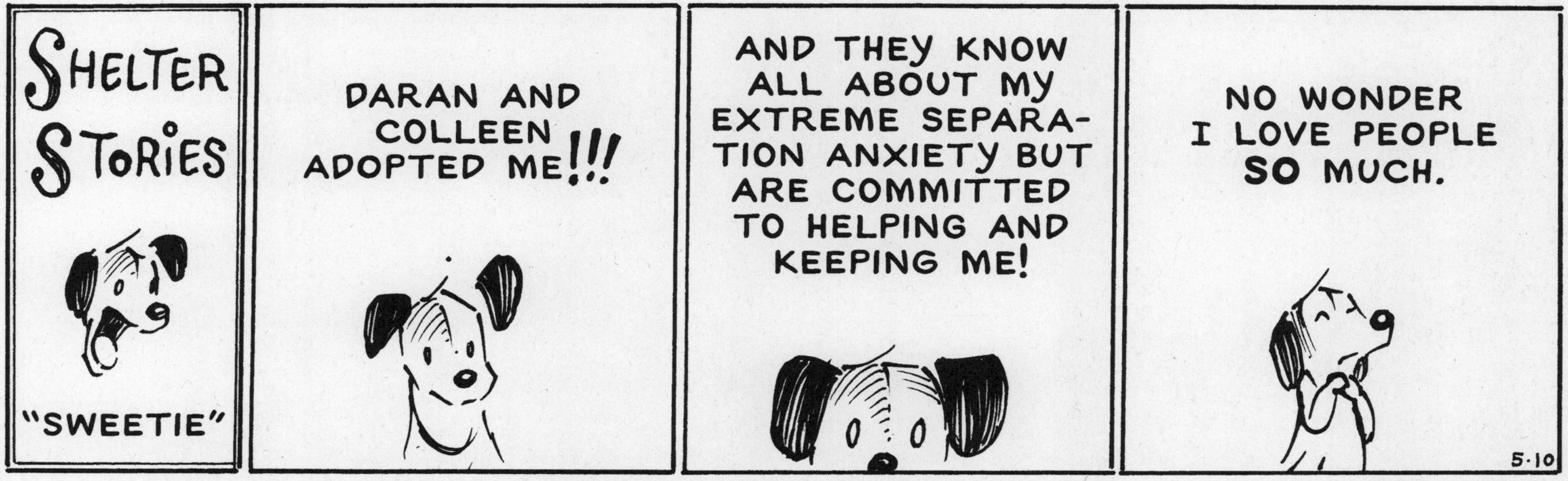
SHELTER STORIES
"SWEETIE"
DARAN AND COLLEEN ADOPTED ME!!!
AND THEY KNOW ALL ABOUT MY EXTREME SEPARATION ANXIETY BUT ARE COMMITTED TO HELPING AND KEEPING ME!
NO WONDER I LOVE PEOPLE SO MUCH.
5·10

Strip 1:

SHELTER STORIES

"SWEETIE"

DARAN AND COLLEEN ARE THE **BEST**.

FOR MY SEPA-RATION ANXIETY, THEY FOUND A GREAT DAYCARE AND THEY TRY TO TAKE ME EVERYWHERE SO I'M **ALWAYS** WITH THEM.

THEY **UNDERSTAND** ME.

5·11

Strip 2:

SHELTER STORIES

"SWEETIE"

YES. AS A "SPECIAL NEEDS" DOG, I ADMIT I WAS A HANDFUL.

BUT WITH A LITTLE CARE AND UNDERSTANDING AND LOTS OF PATIENCE...

I'M NOW A **BIG** HANDFUL OF **LOVE**.

5·12

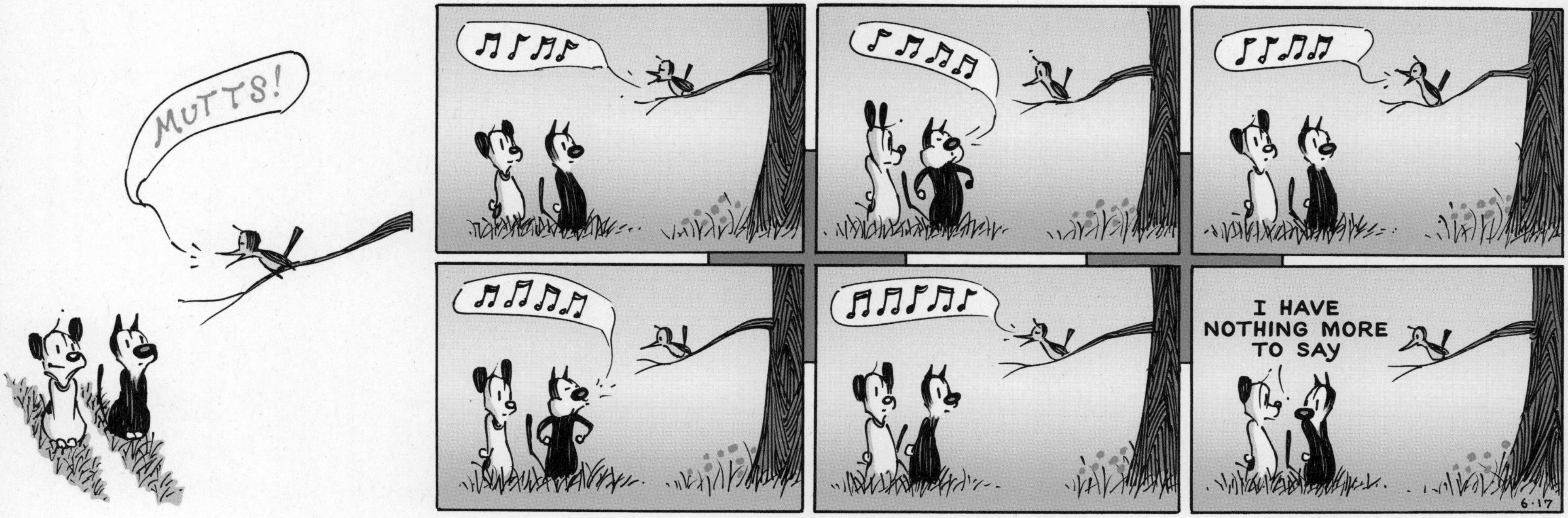
MUTTS!
I HAVE NOTHING MORE TO SAY
6·17

MUTTS
Patrick McDonnell

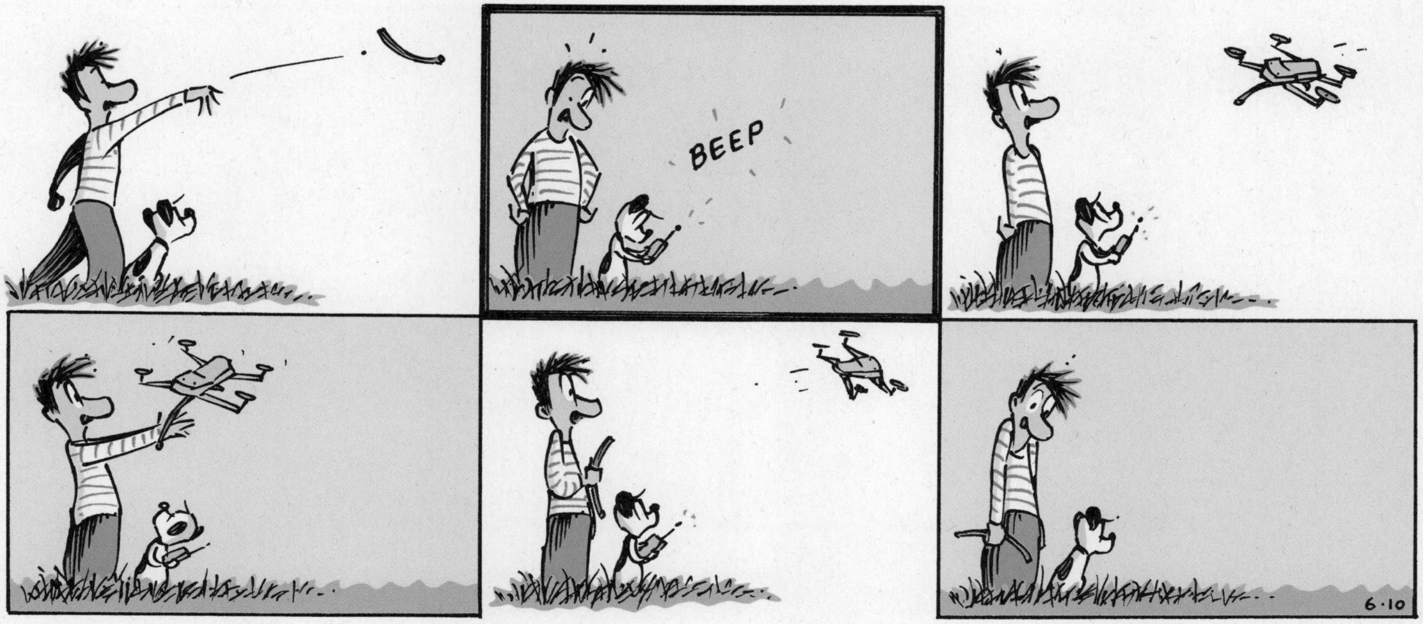
BEEP
6·10

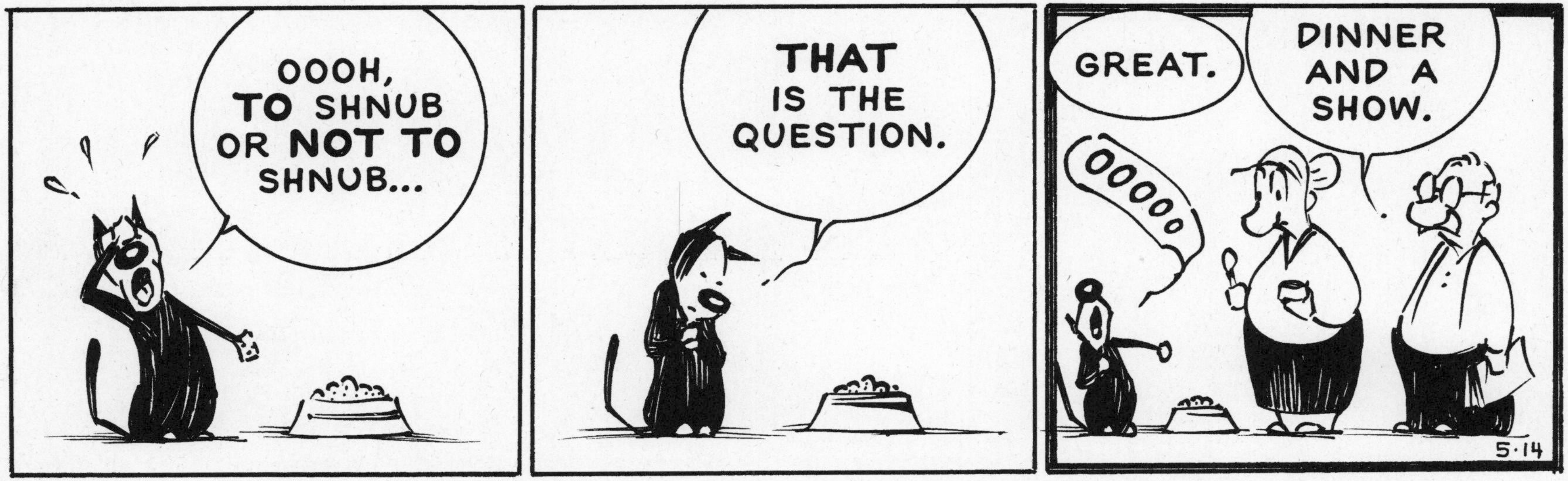
OOOH, TO SHNUB OR NOT TO SHNUB...
THAT IS THE QUESTION.
OOOOO
GREAT.
DINNER AND A SHOW.
5·14

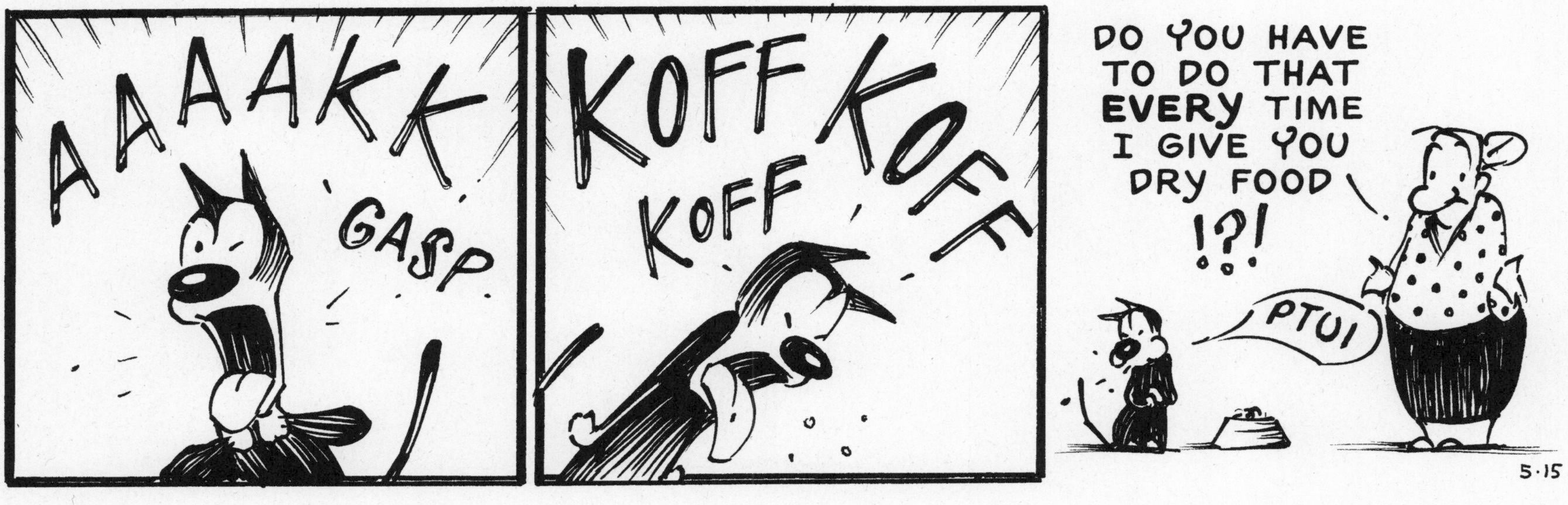
AAAAKK
GASP
KOFF KOFF
KOFF
DO YOU HAVE TO DO THAT EVERY TIME I GIVE YOU DRY FOOD !?!
PTUI
5·15

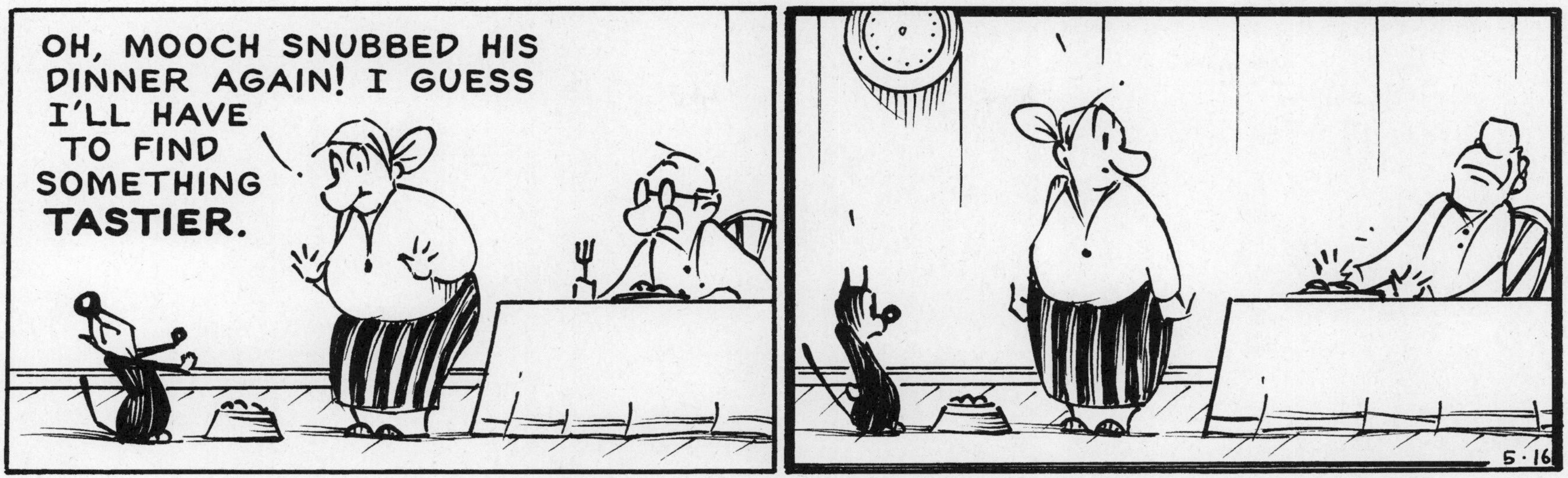
OH, MOOCH SNUBBED HIS DINNER AGAIN! I GUESS I'LL HAVE TO FIND SOMETHING TASTIER.
5·16

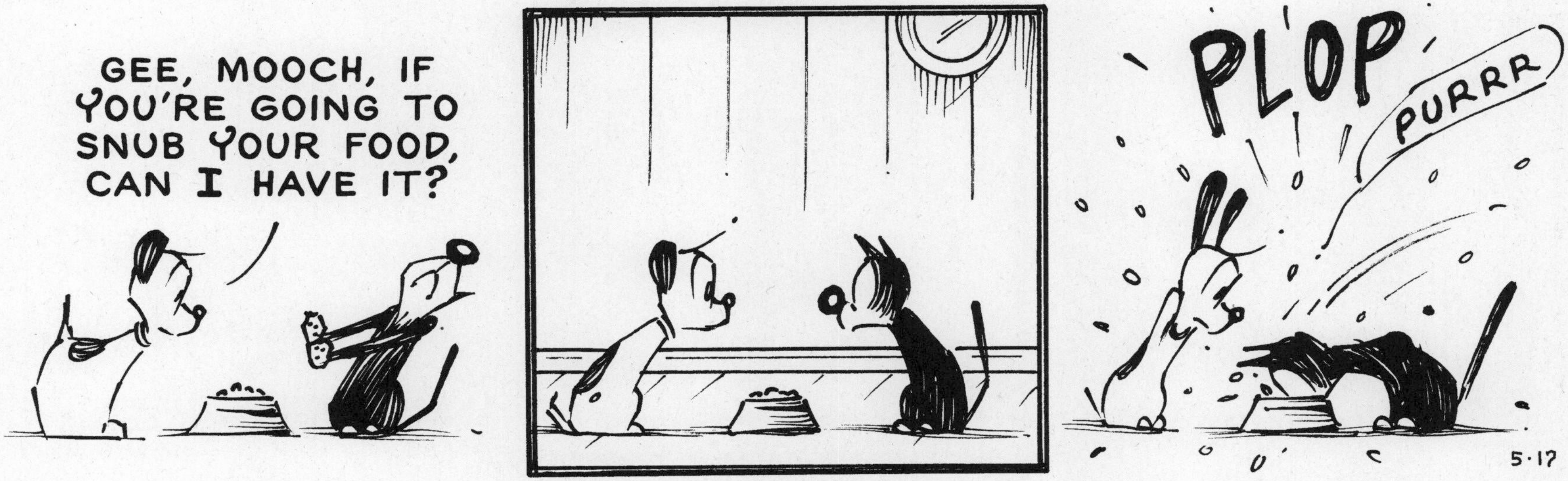
GEE, MOOCH, IF YOU'RE GOING TO SNUB YOUR FOOD, CAN I HAVE IT?
PLOP
PURRR
5·17

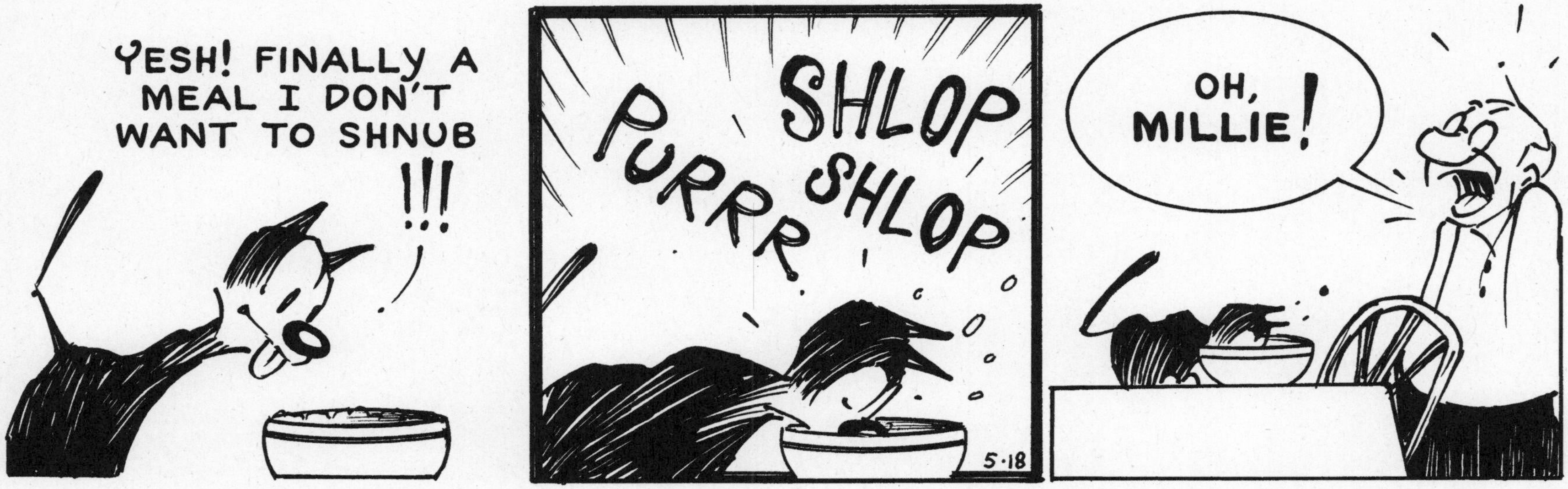
YESH! FINALLY A MEAL I DON'T WANT TO SHNUB !!!
SHLOP
PURRR
SHLOP
5·18
OH, MILLIE!

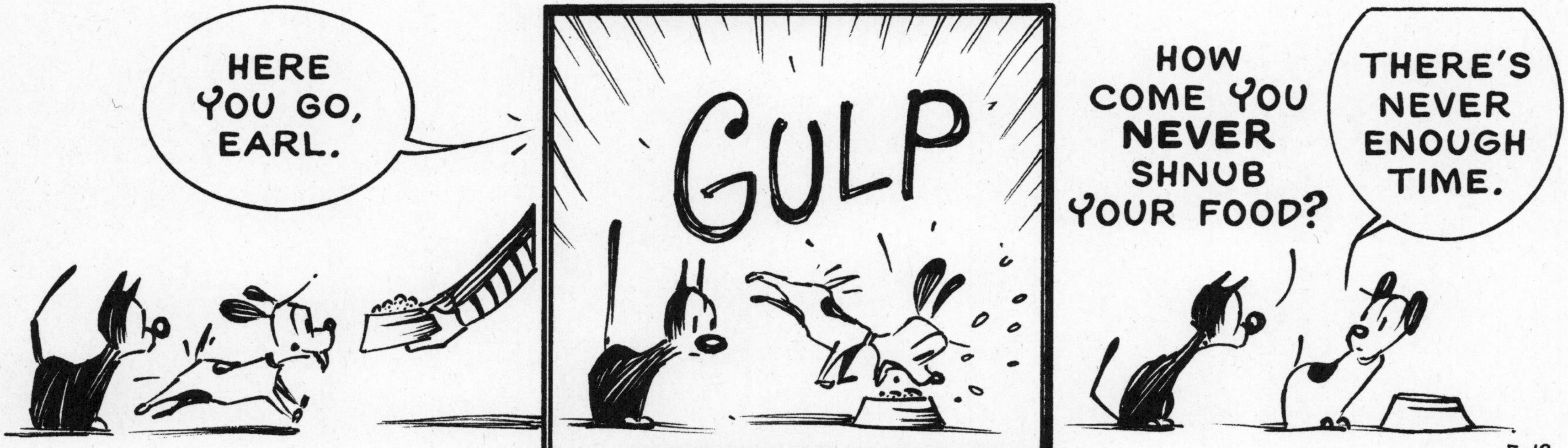
HERE YOU GO, EARL.
GULP
HOW COME YOU NEVER SHNUB YOUR FOOD?
THERE'S NEVER ENOUGH TIME.
5·19

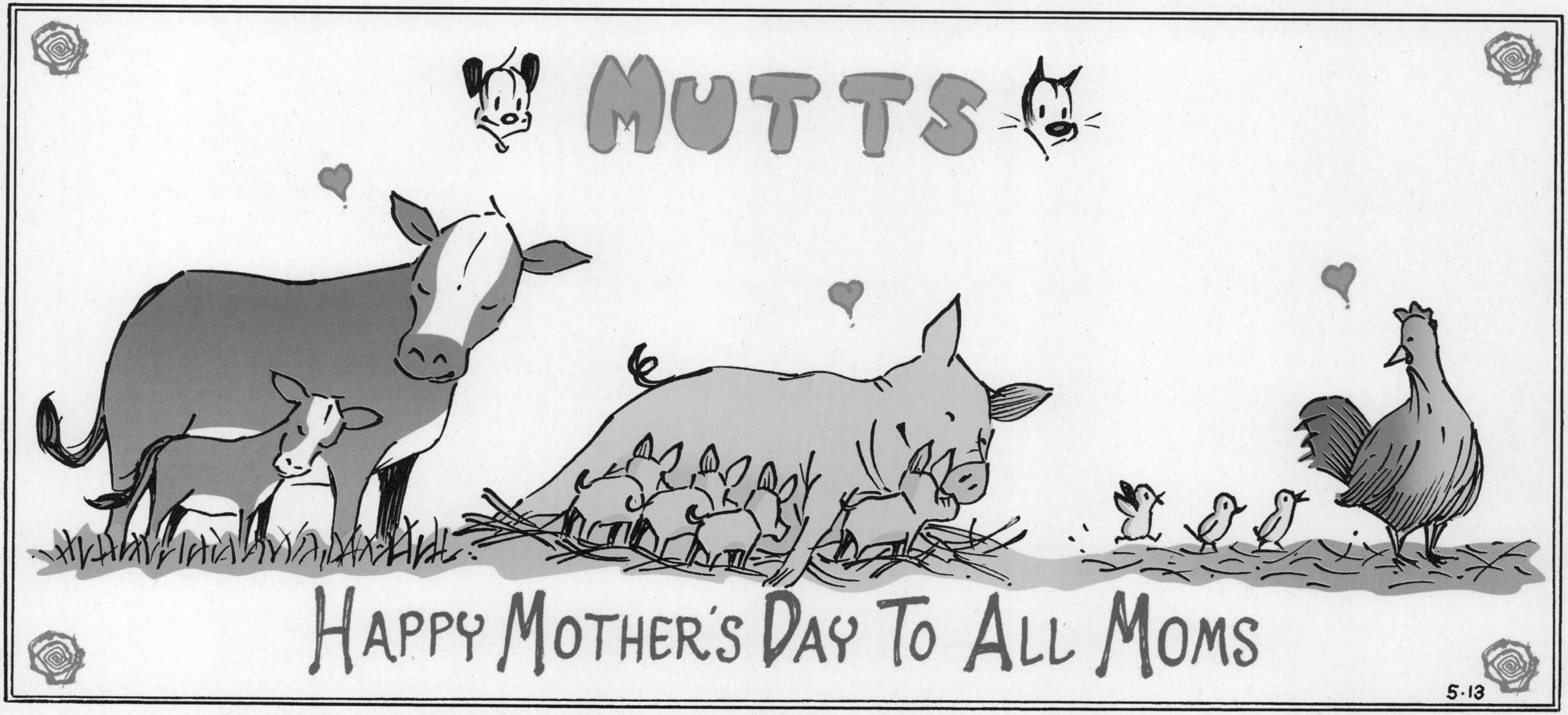
MUTTS
HAPPY MOTHER'S DAY TO ALL MOMS
5·13

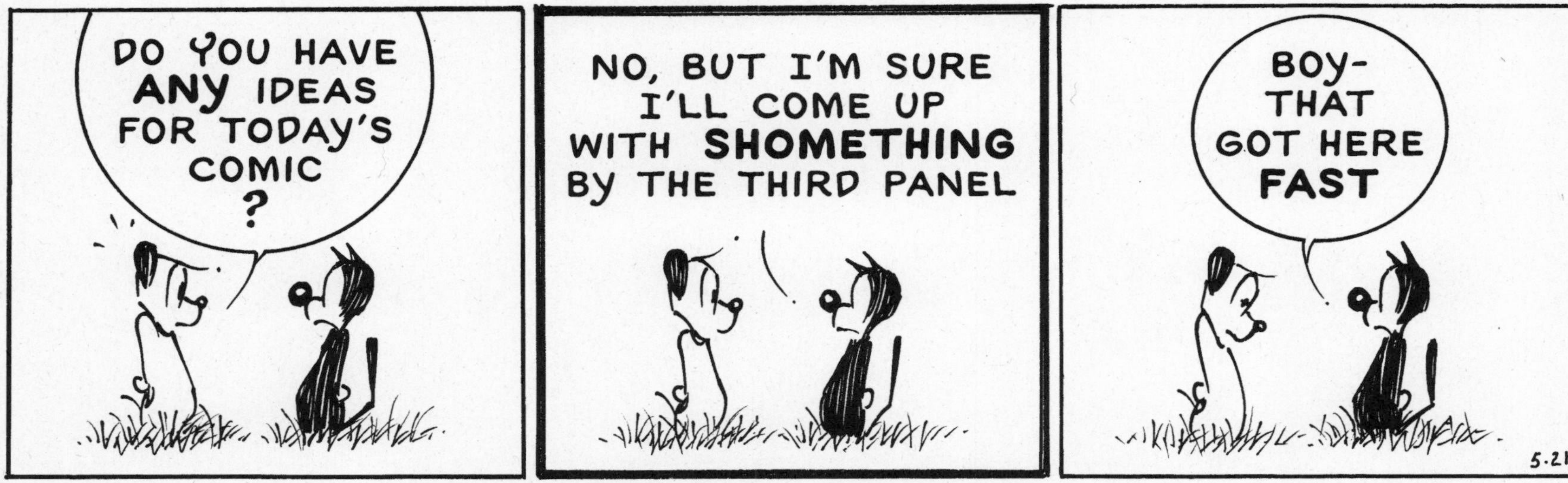
DO YOU HAVE ANY IDEAS FOR TODAY'S COMIC ?
NO, BUT I'M SURE I'LL COME UP WITH SHOMETHING BY THE THIRD PANEL
BOY- THAT GOT HERE FAST
5·21

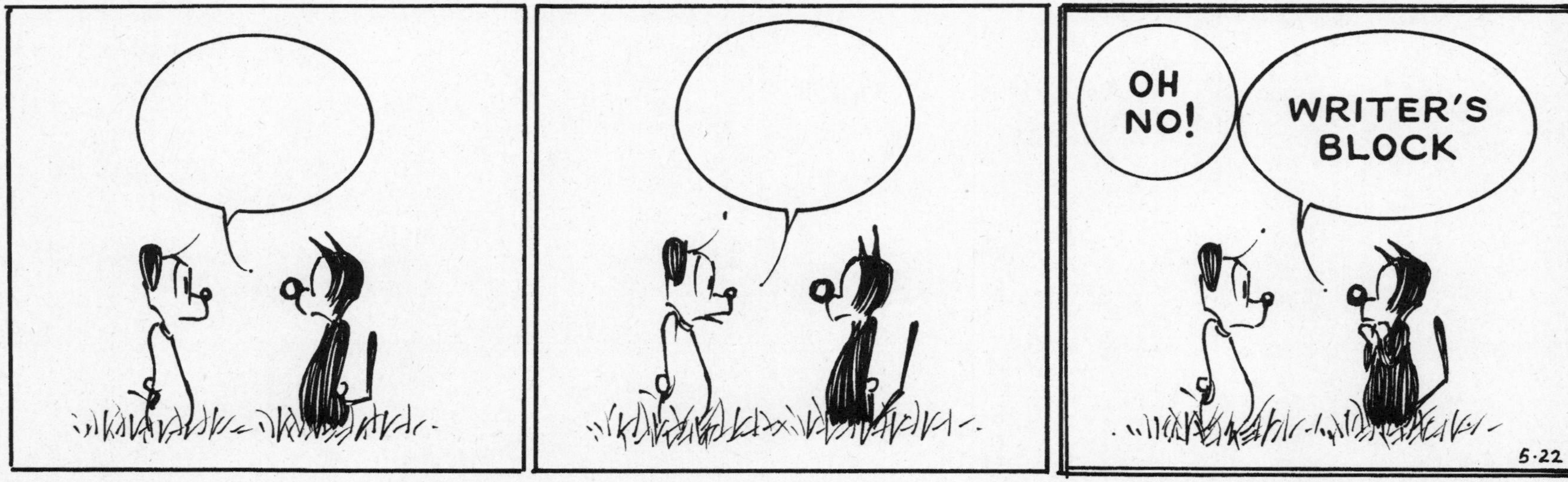
OH NO!
WRITER'S BLOCK
5·22

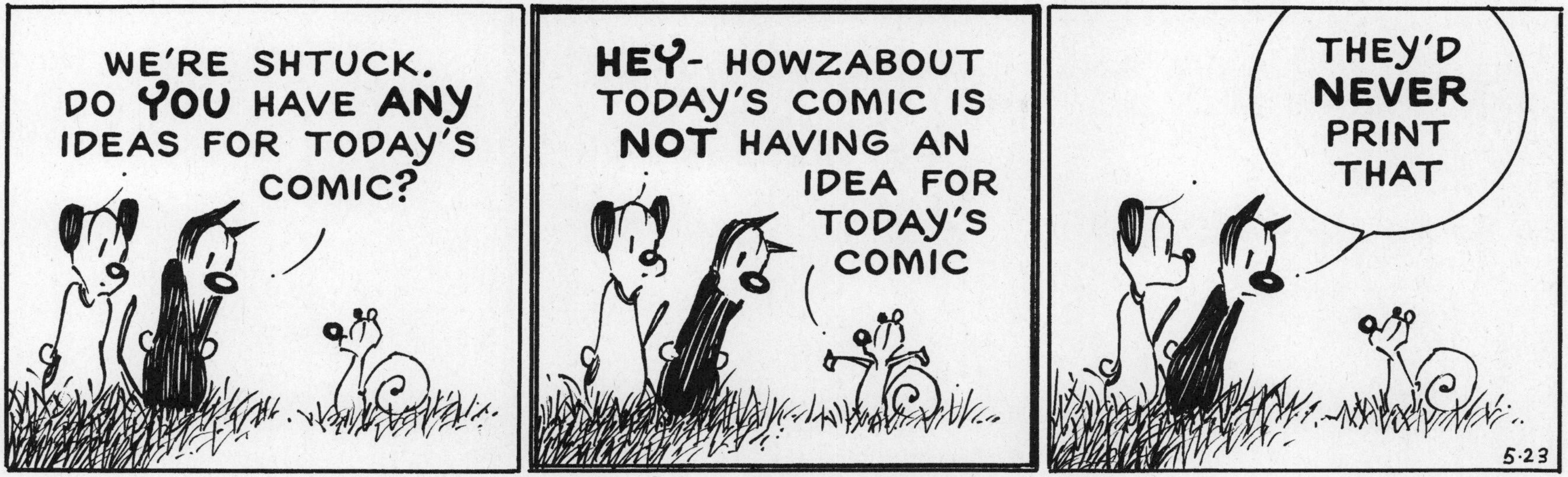
WE'RE SHTUCK. DO **YOU** HAVE **ANY** IDEAS FOR TODAY'S COMIC?
HEY- HOWZABOUT TODAY'S COMIC IS **NOT** HAVING AN IDEA FOR TODAY'S COMIC
THEY'D **NEVER** PRINT THAT
5·23

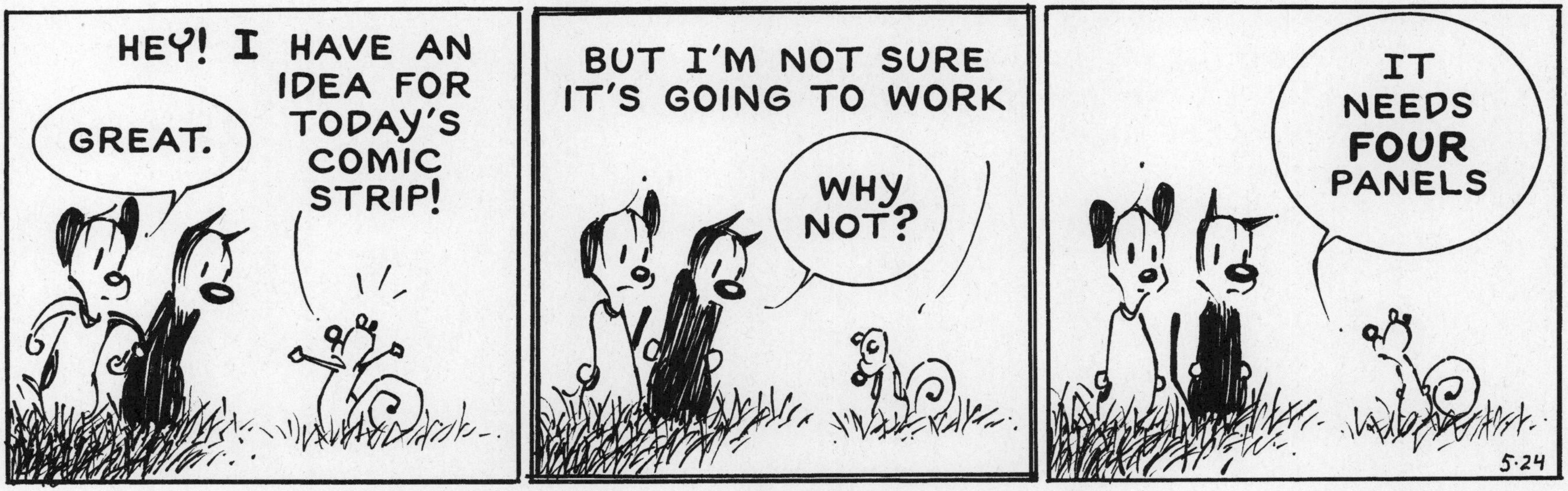
HEY! **I** HAVE AN IDEA FOR TODAY'S COMIC STRIP!
GREAT.
BUT I'M NOT SURE IT'S GOING TO WORK
WHY NOT?
IT NEEDS **FOUR** PANELS
5·24

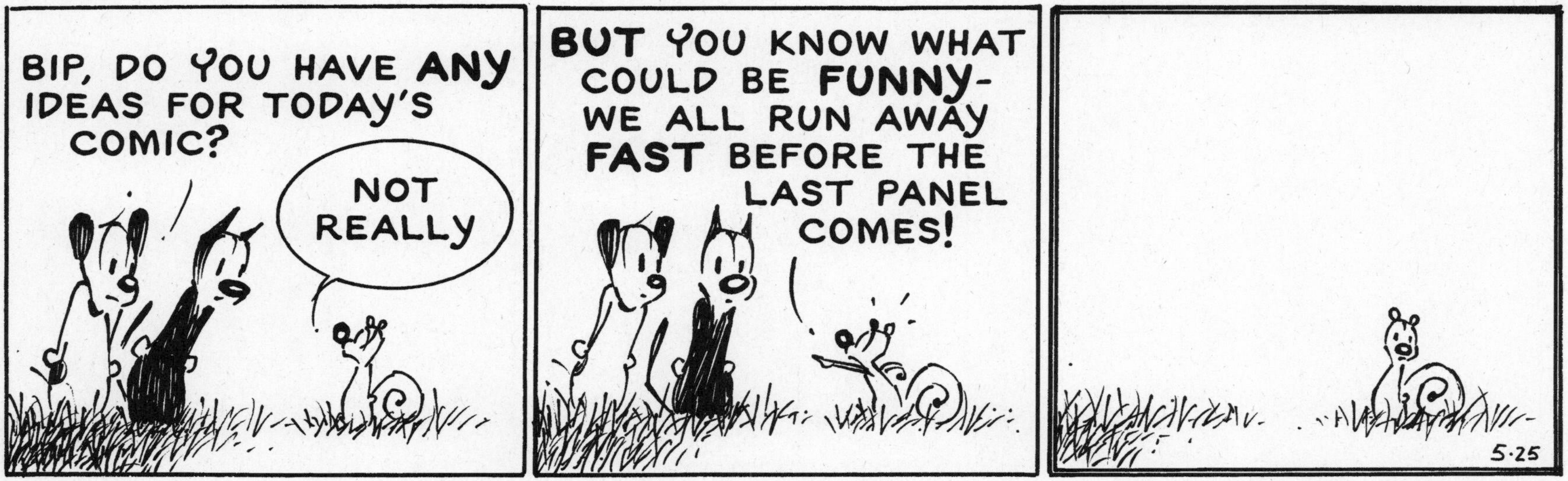
BIP, DO YOU HAVE ANY IDEAS FOR TODAY'S COMIC?
NOT REALLY
BUT YOU KNOW WHAT COULD BE FUNNY- WE ALL RUN AWAY FAST BEFORE THE LAST PANEL COMES!
5·25

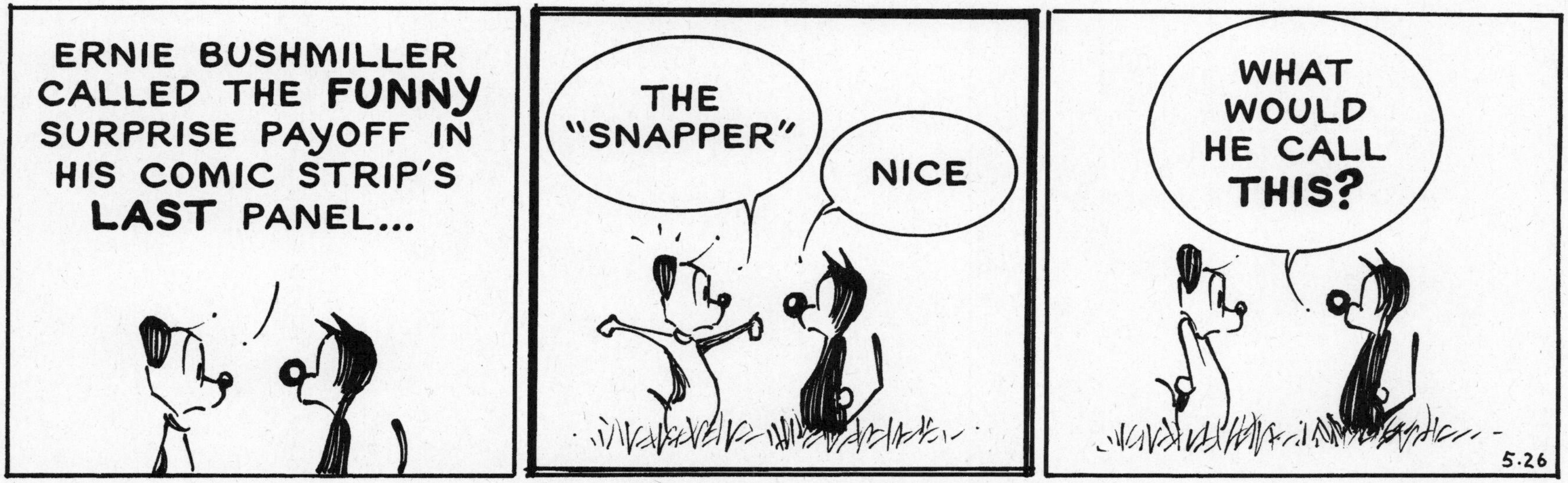
ERNIE BUSHMILLER CALLED THE FUNNY SURPRISE PAYOFF IN HIS COMIC STRIP'S LAST PANEL...
THE "SNAPPER"
NICE
WHAT WOULD HE CALL THIS?
5·26

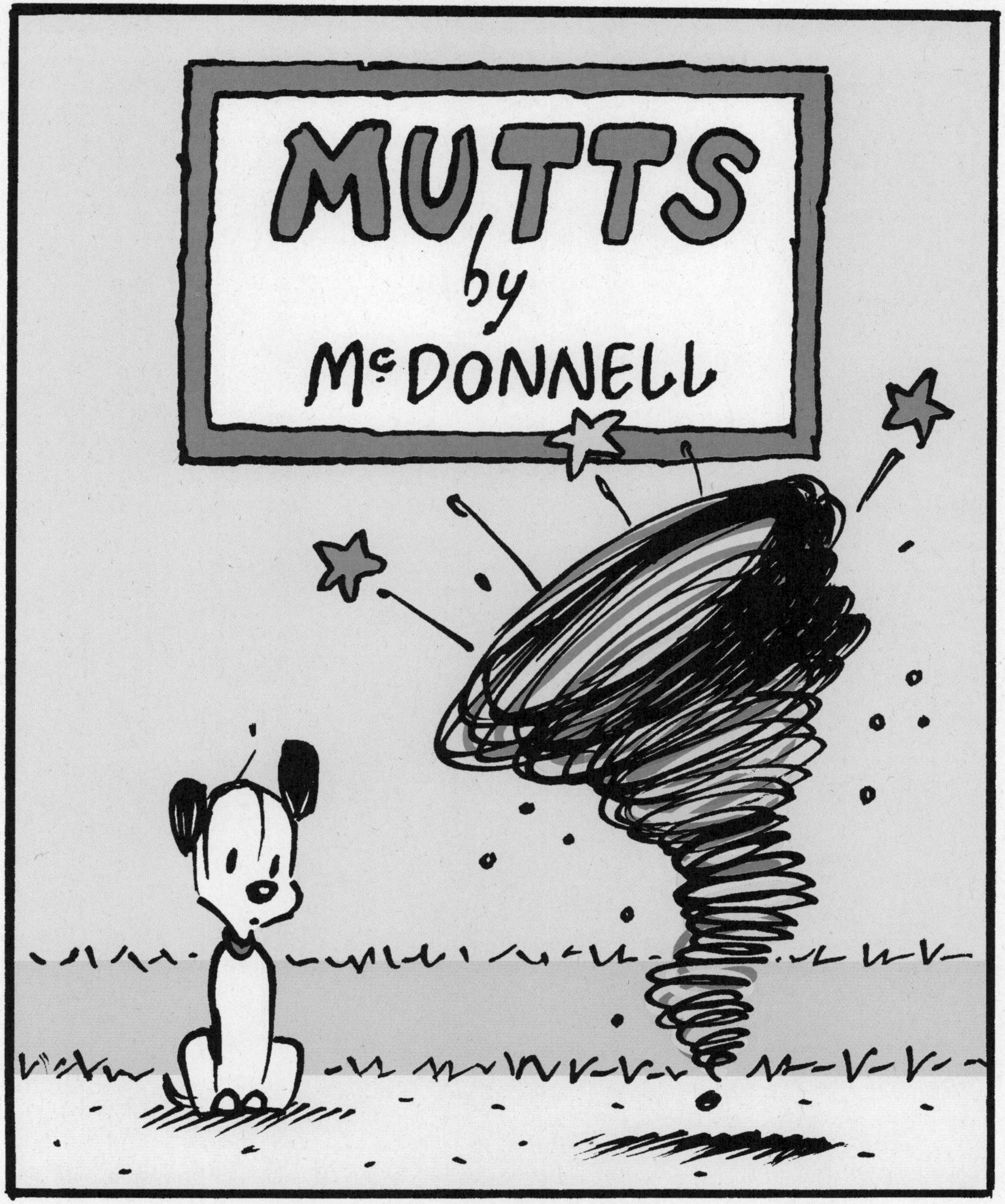
MUTTS
by
McDONNELL

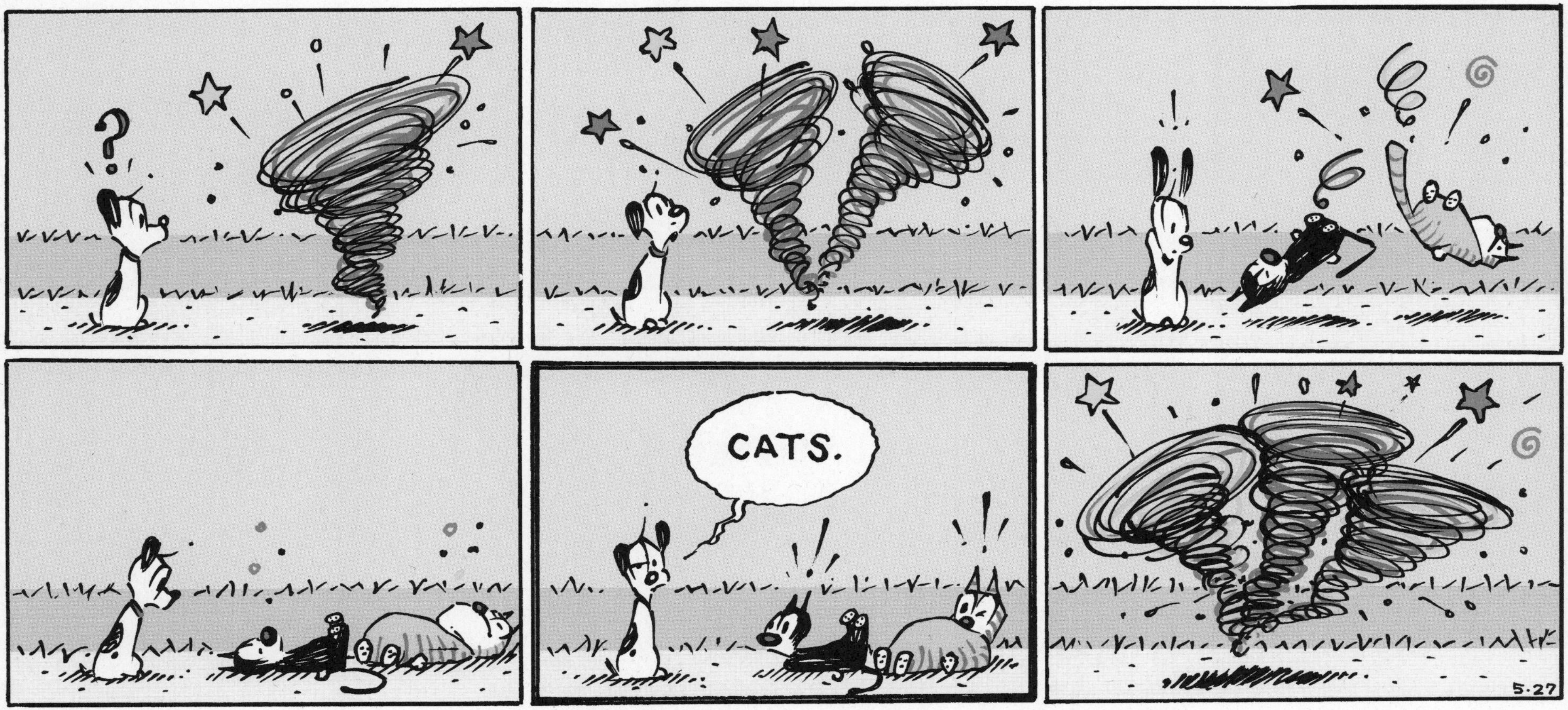
CATS.
5·27

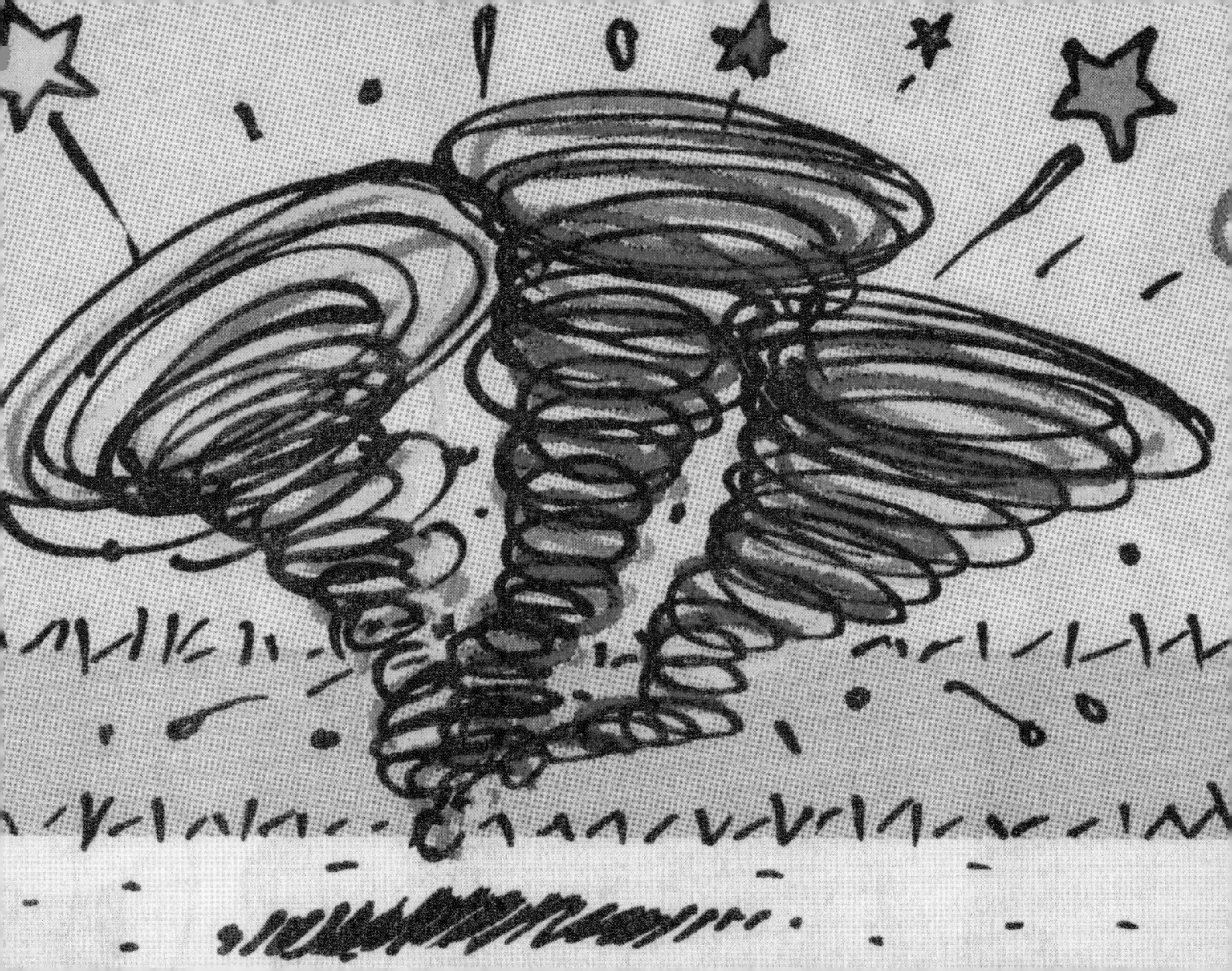

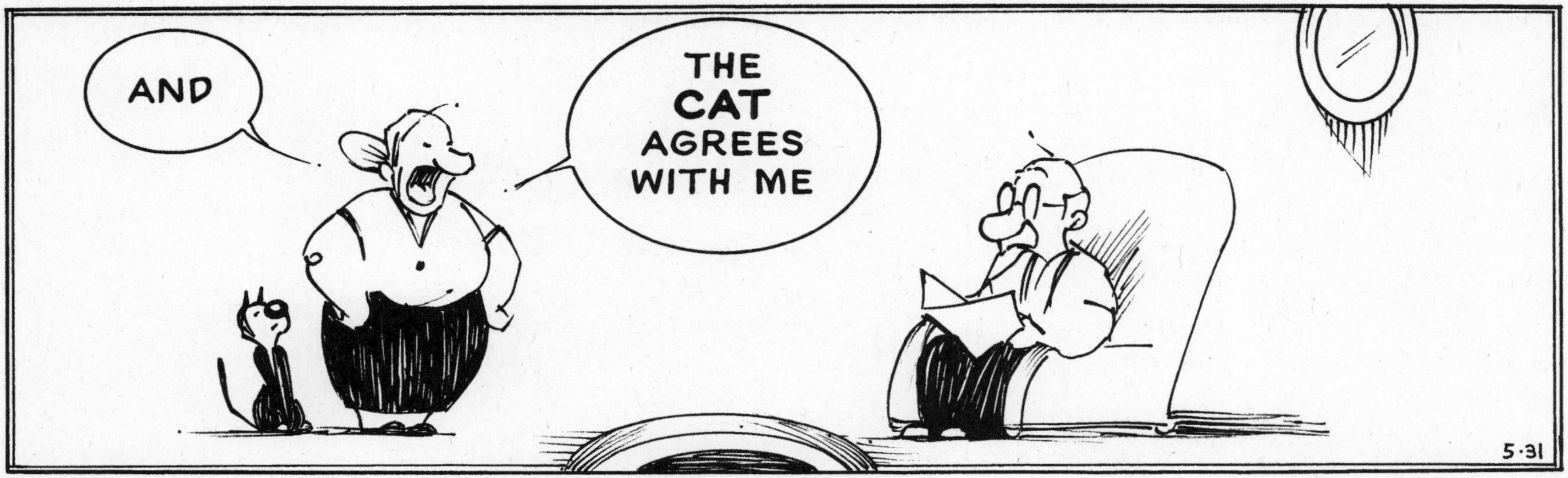
AND
THE CAT AGREES WITH ME
5·31

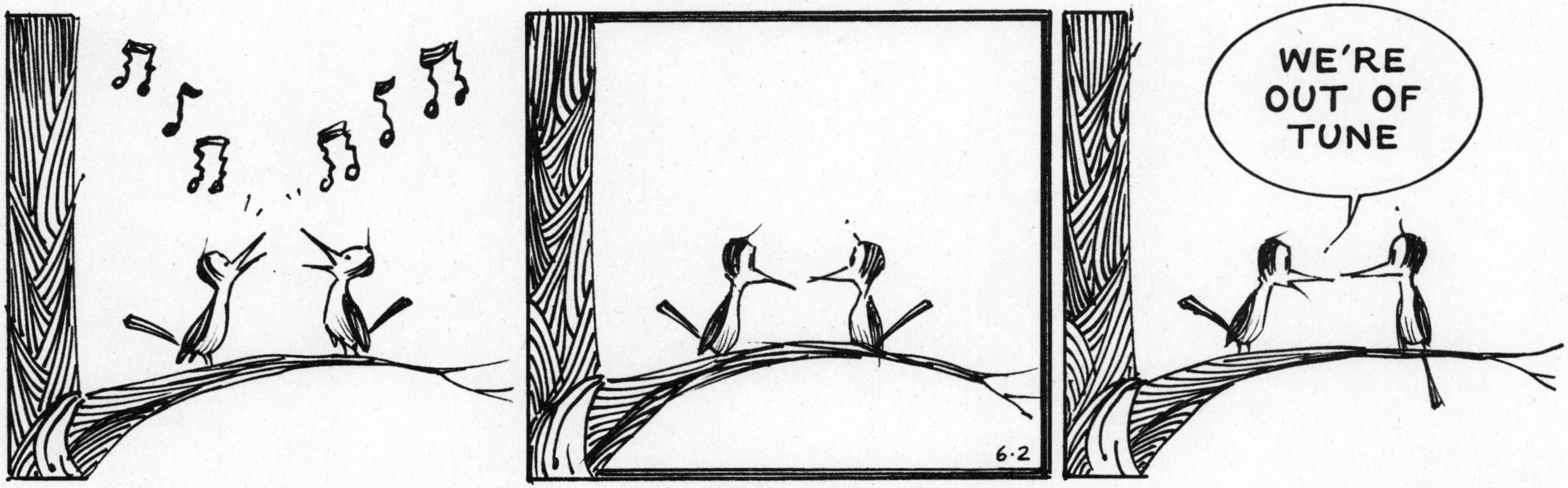
6·2
WE'RE OUT OF TUNE

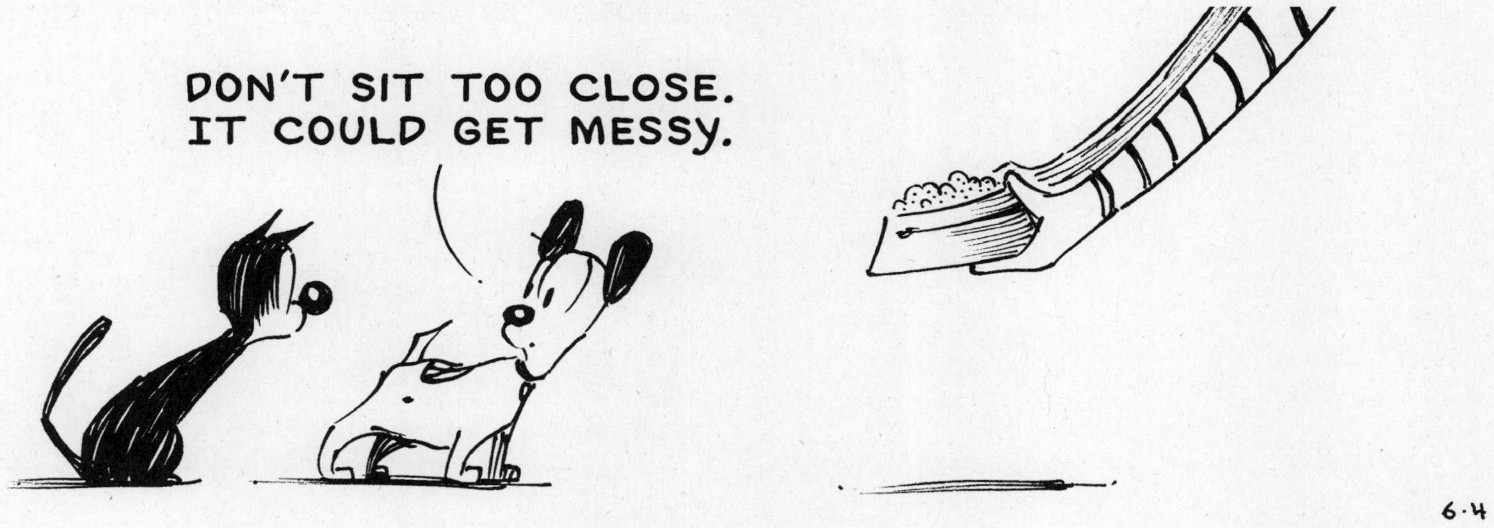
DON'T SIT TOO CLOSE. IT COULD GET MESSY.
6·4

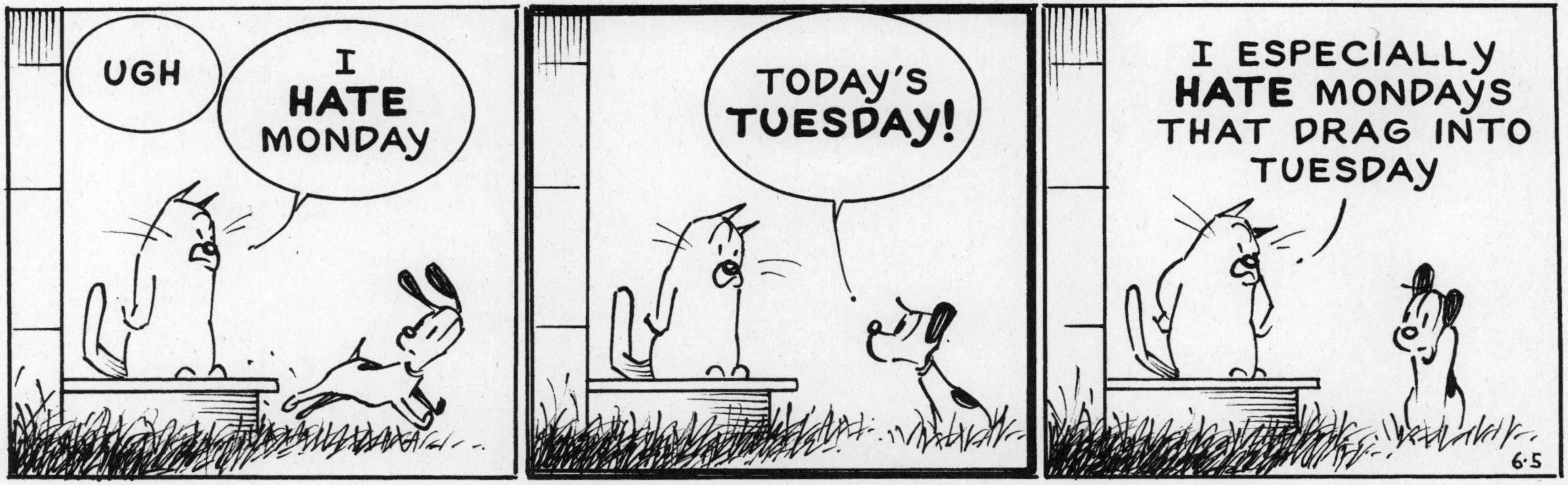
UGH
I HATE MONDAY
TODAY'S TUESDAY!
I ESPECIALLY HATE MONDAYS THAT DRAG INTO TUESDAY
6·5

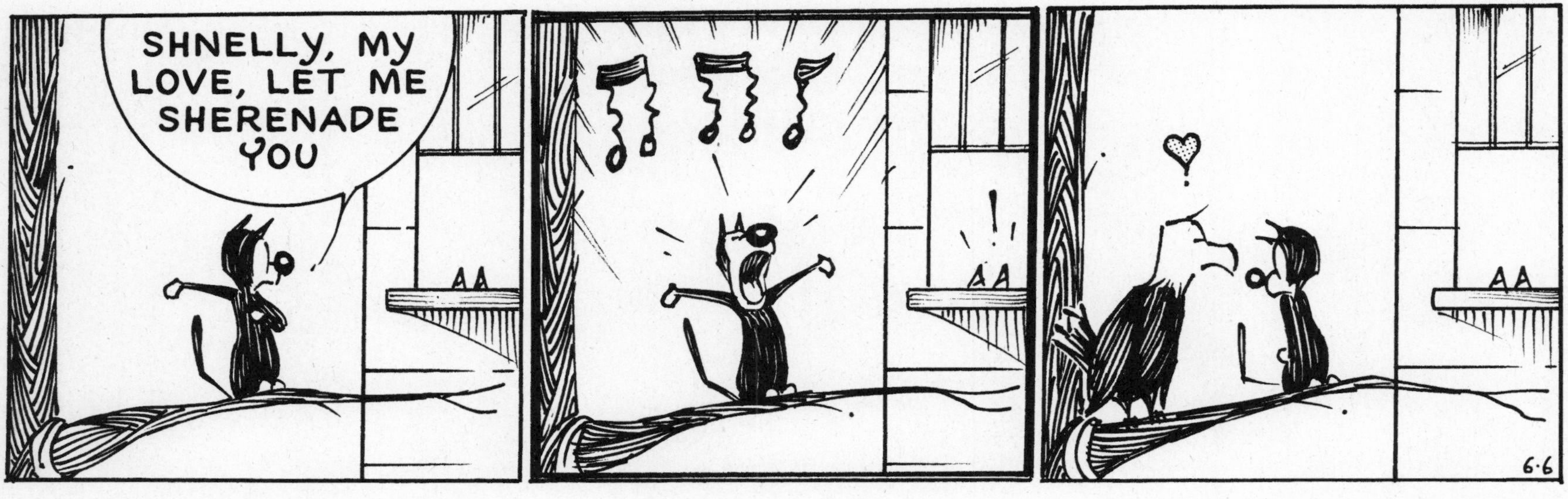
SHNELLY, MY LOVE, LET ME SHERENADE YOU
6·6

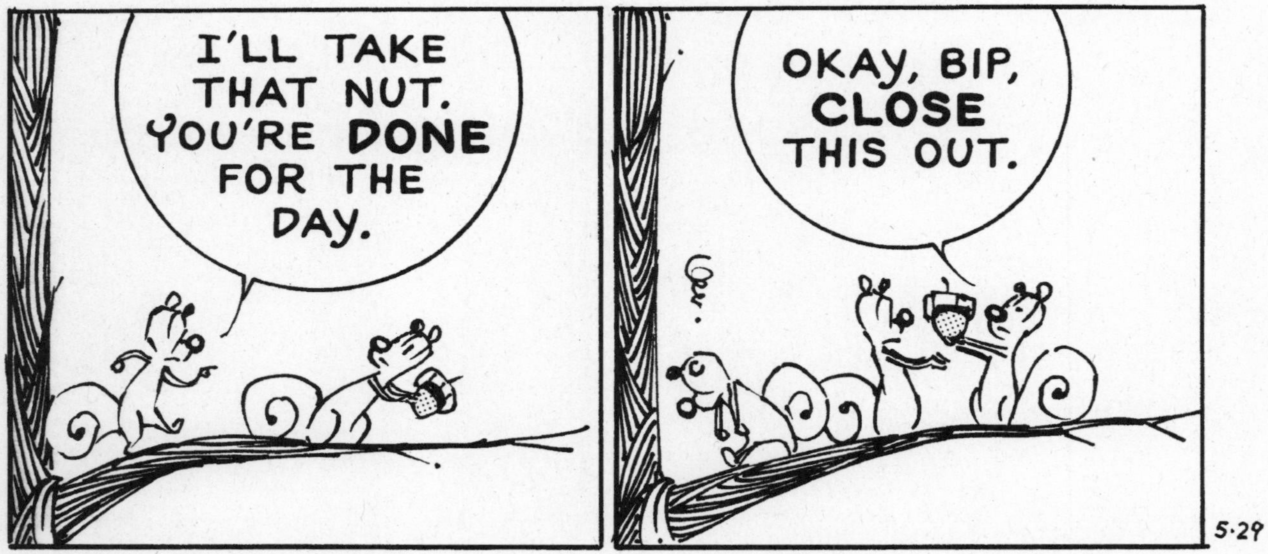
I'LL TAKE THAT NUT. YOU'RE **DONE** FOR THE DAY.
OKAY, BIP, **CLOSE** THIS OUT.
5·29

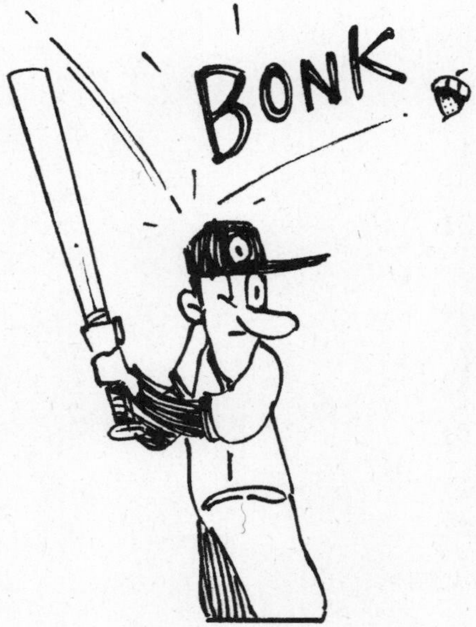
BONK

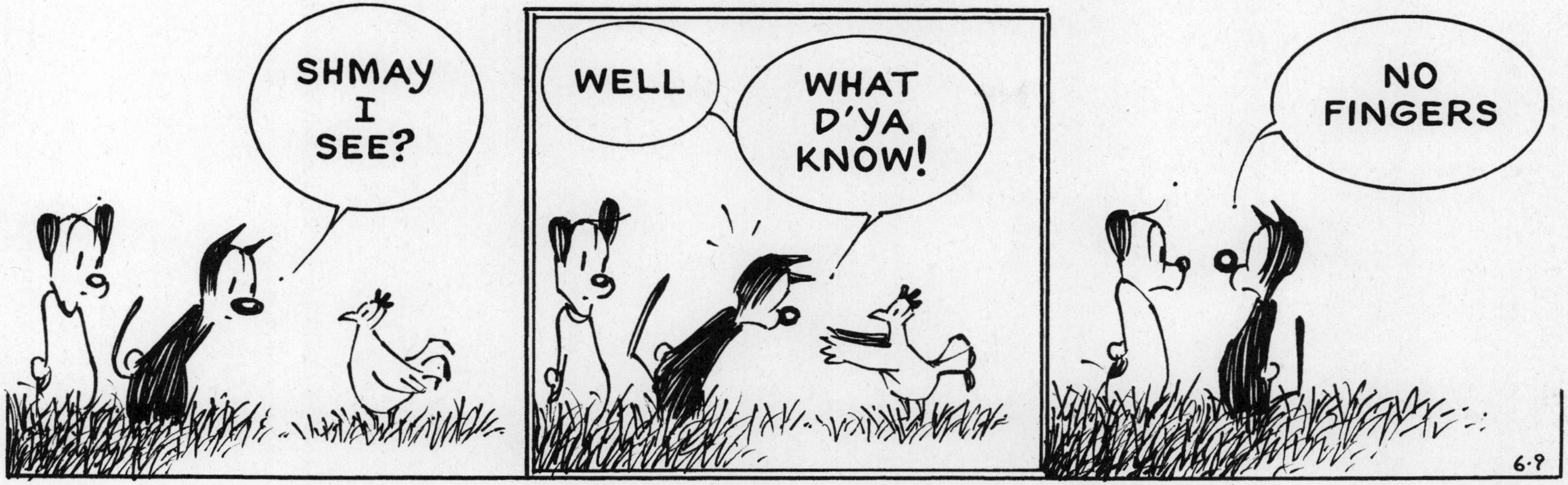
SHMAY I SEE?
WELL
WHAT D'YA KNOW!
NO FINGERS
6·9

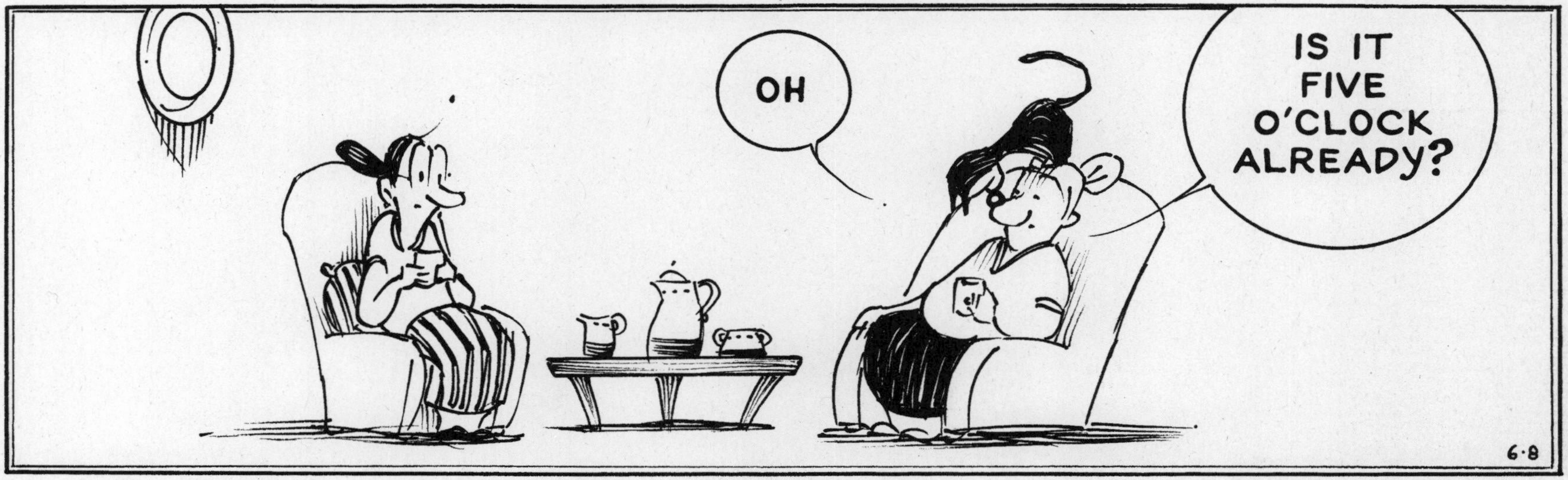
OH
IS IT FIVE O'CLOCK ALREADY?
6·8

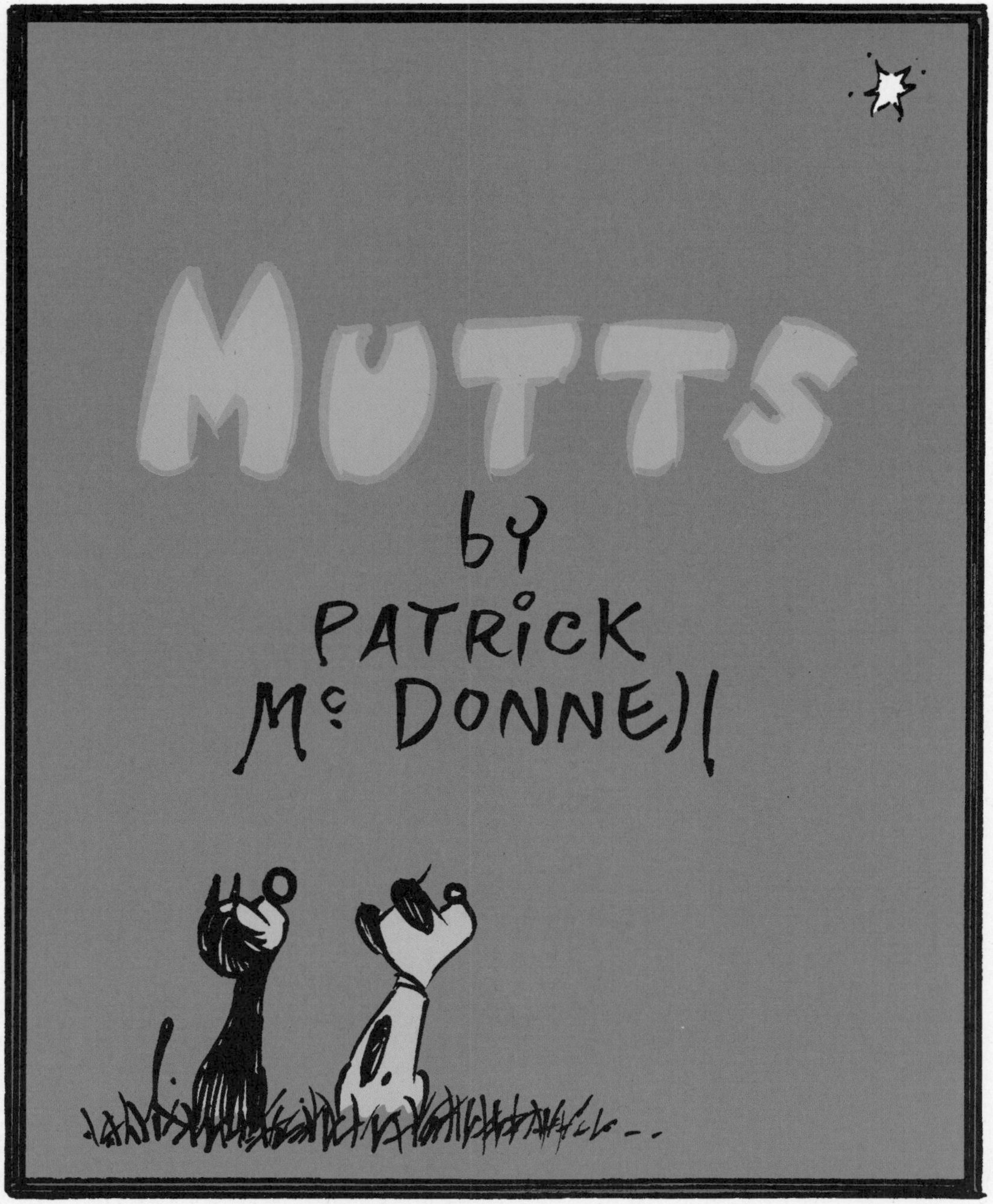
MUTTS
by
PATRICK
McDONNELL

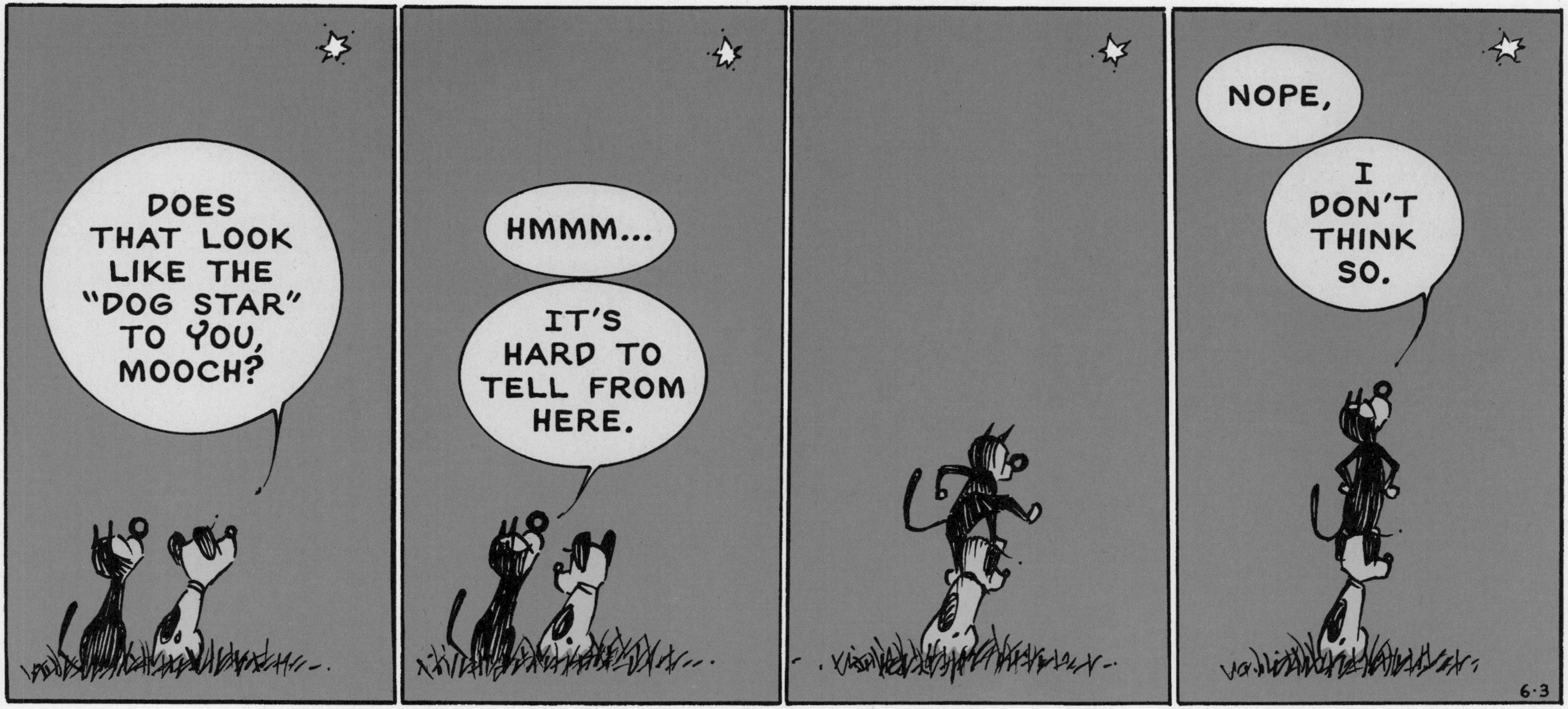
DOES THAT LOOK LIKE THE "DOG STAR" TO YOU, MOOCH?
HMMM...
IT'S HARD TO TELL FROM HERE.
NOPE,
I DON'T THINK SO.
6·3

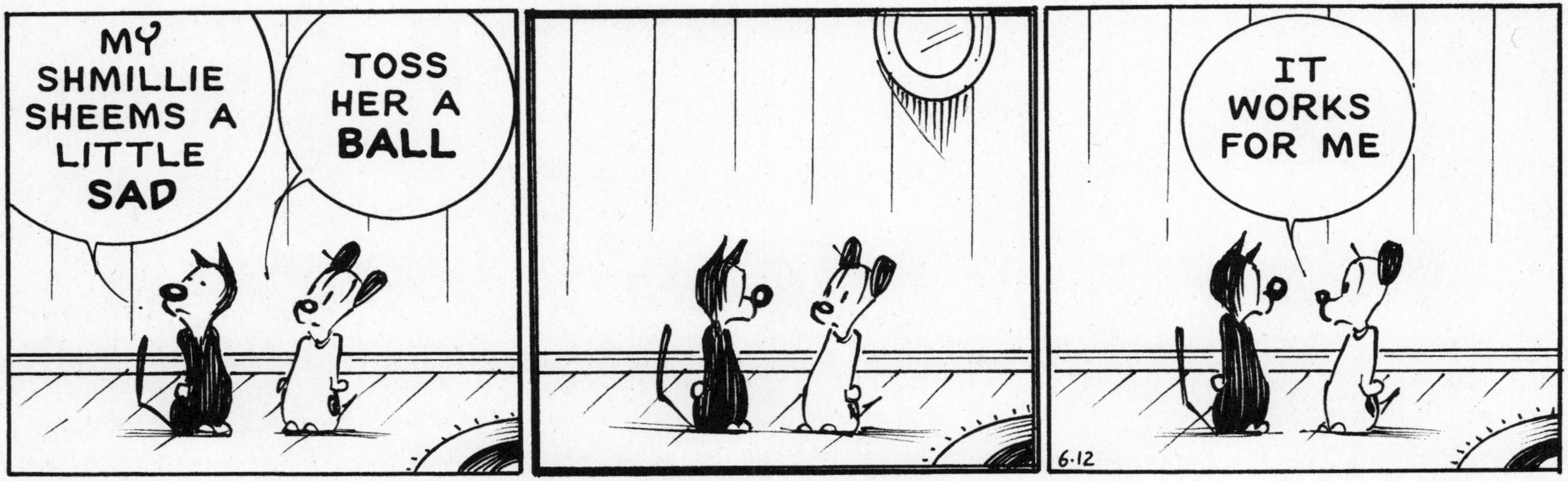
MY SHMILLIE SHEEMS A LITTLE SAD
TOSS HER A BALL
IT WORKS FOR ME
6·12

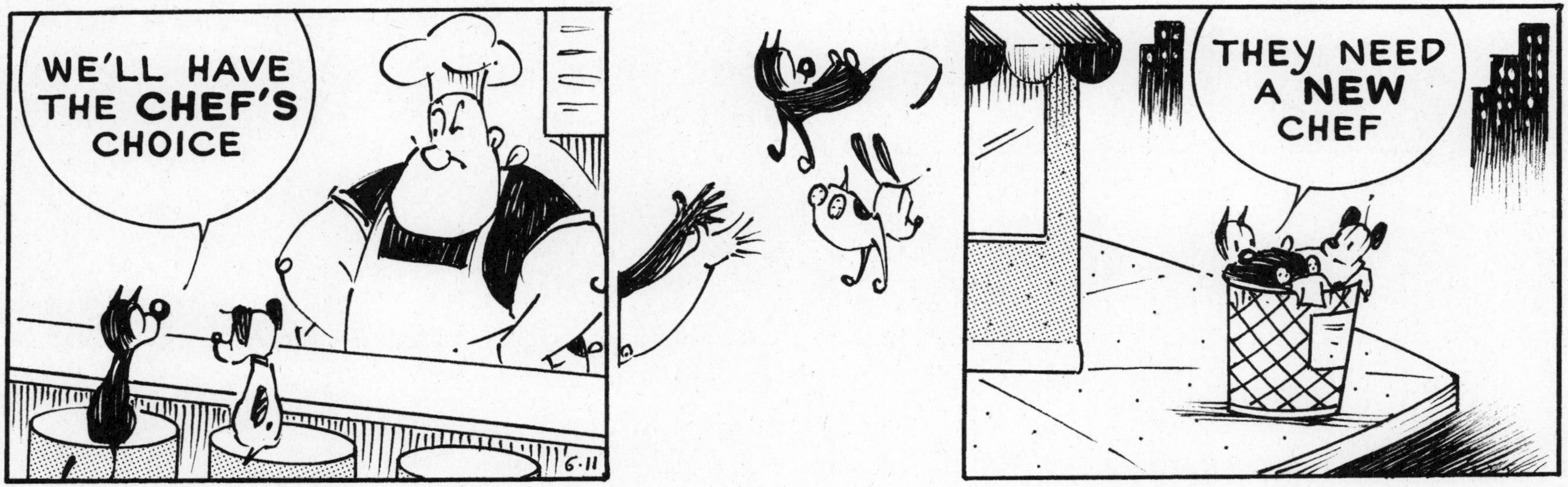
WE'LL HAVE THE CHEF'S CHOICE
6·11
THEY NEED A NEW CHEF

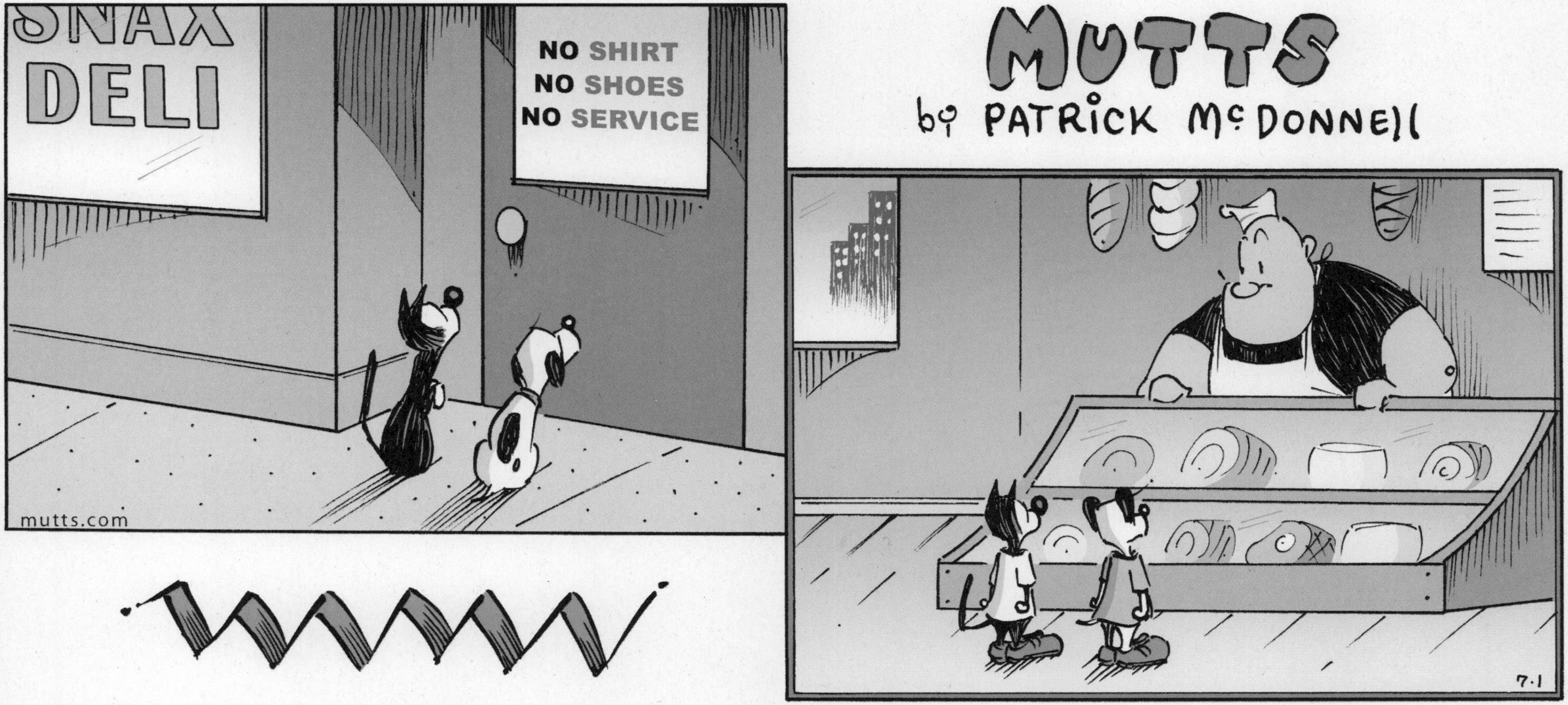
SNAX
DELI
NO SHIRT
NO SHOES
NO SERVICE
mutts.com
MUTTS
by PATRICK McDONNELL
7·1

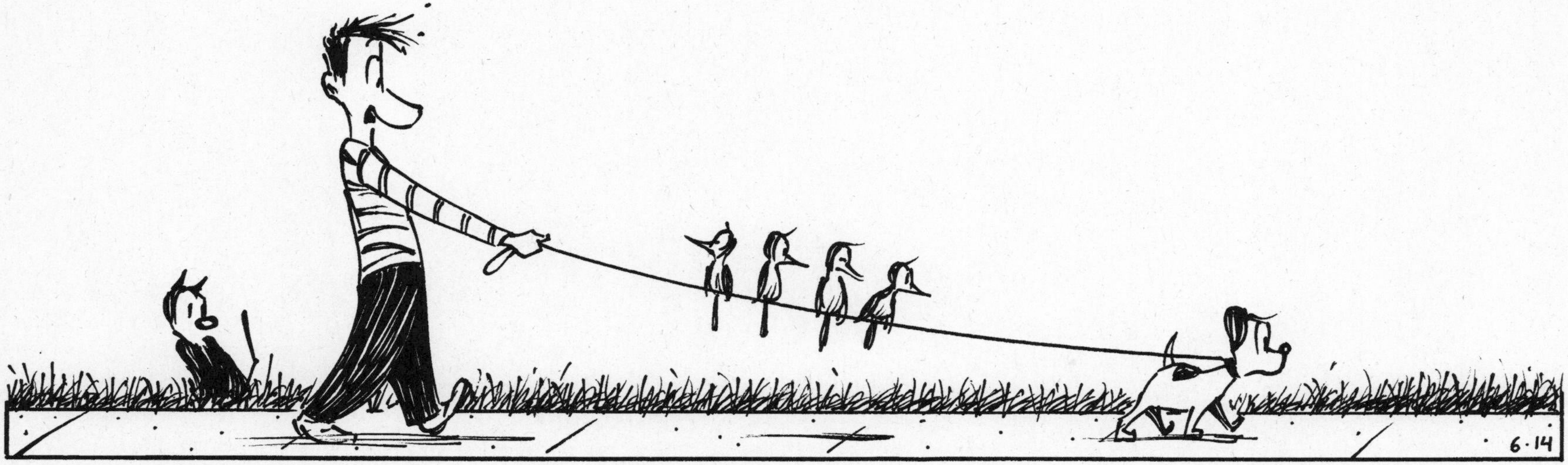
6·14

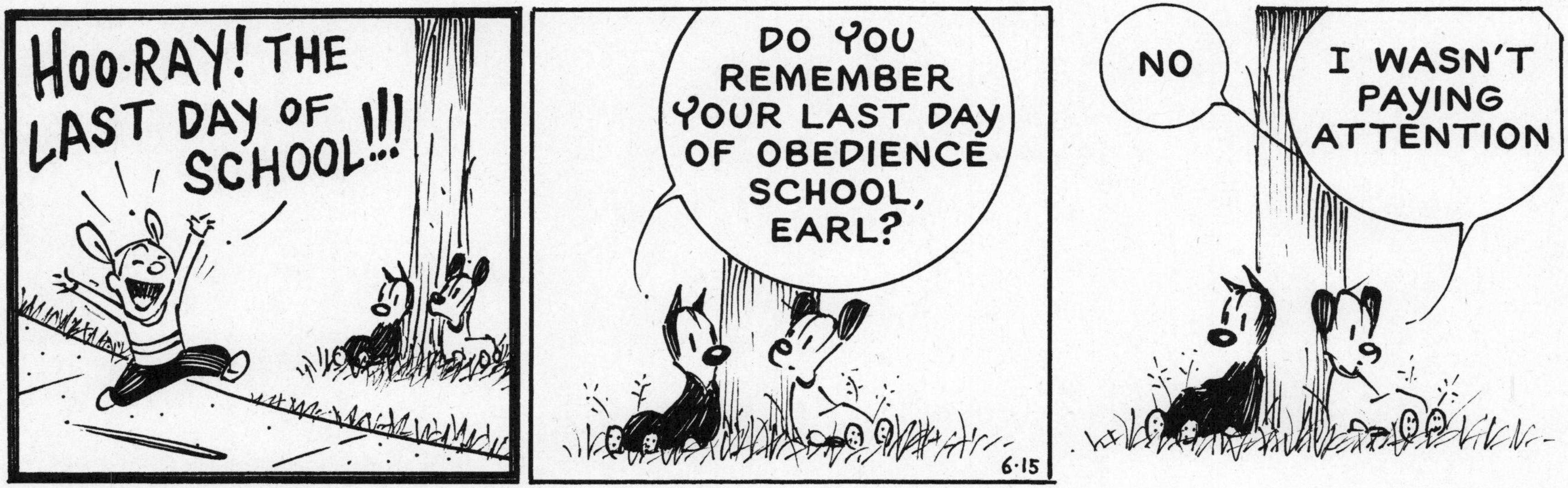
HOO·RAY! THE LAST DAY OF SCHOOL!!!
DO YOU REMEMBER YOUR LAST DAY OF OBEDIENCE SCHOOL, EARL?
6·15
NO
I WASN'T PAYING ATTENTION

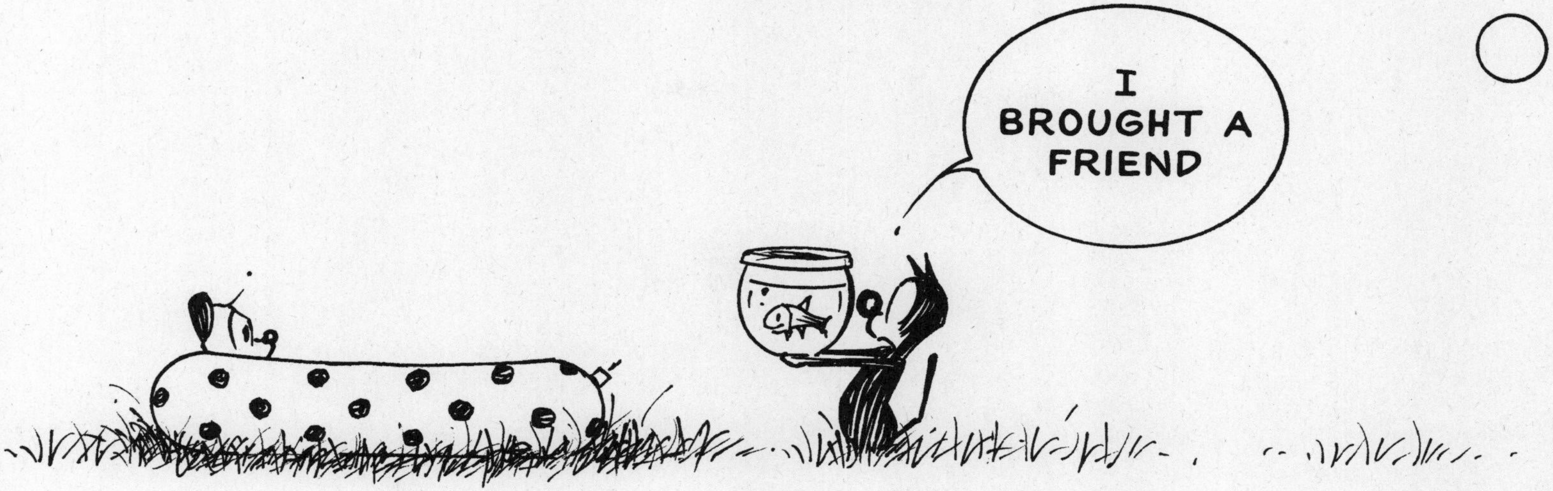
I BROUGHT A FRIEND

6.19

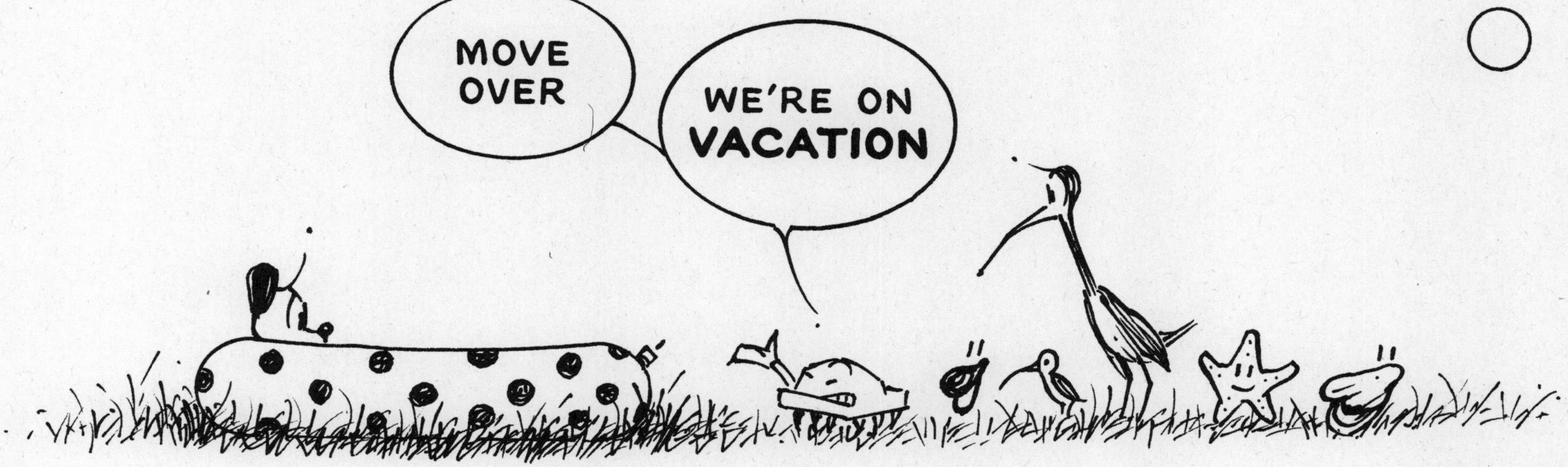
MOVE OVER
WE'RE ON VACATION

6.20

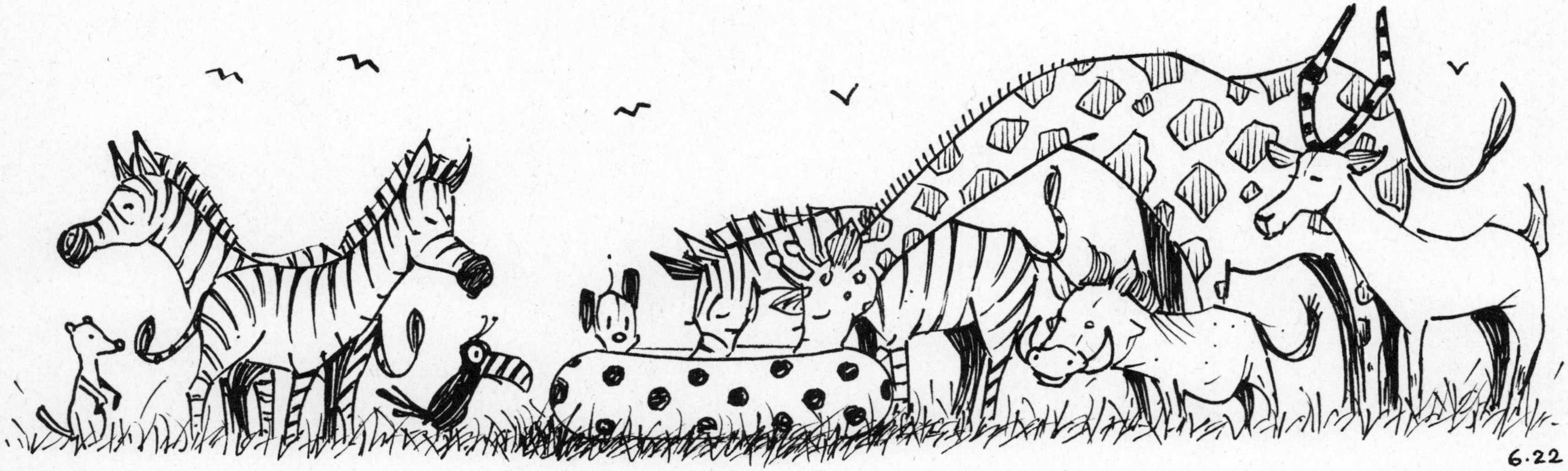

6.22

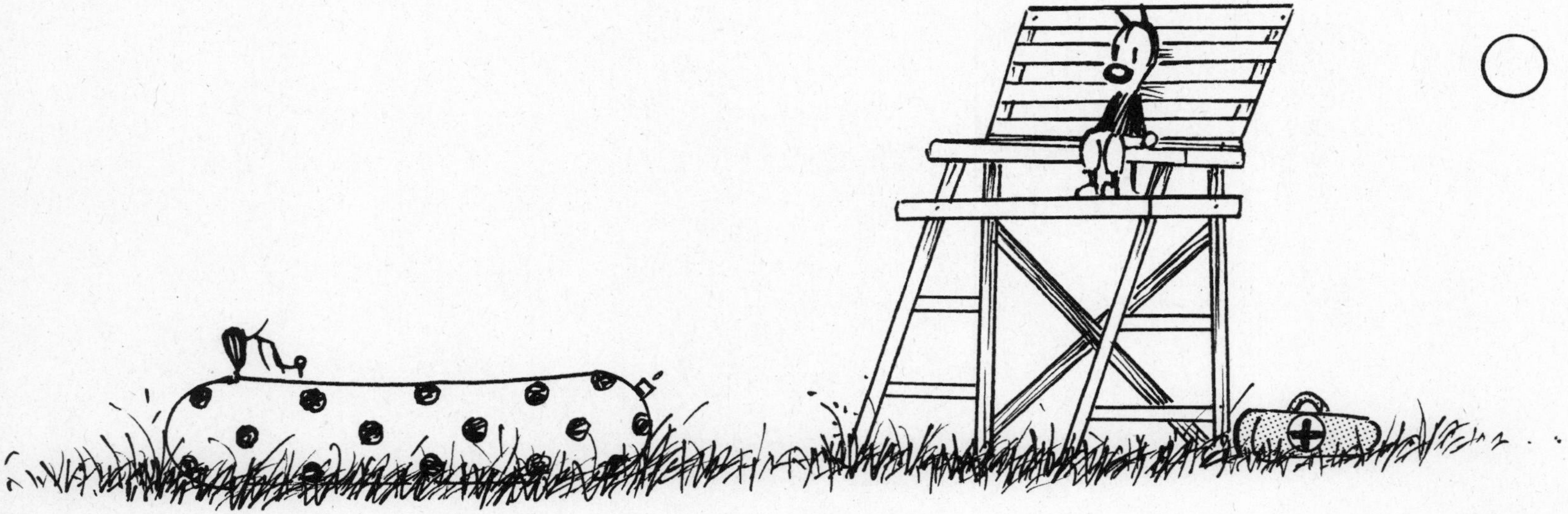

6.23

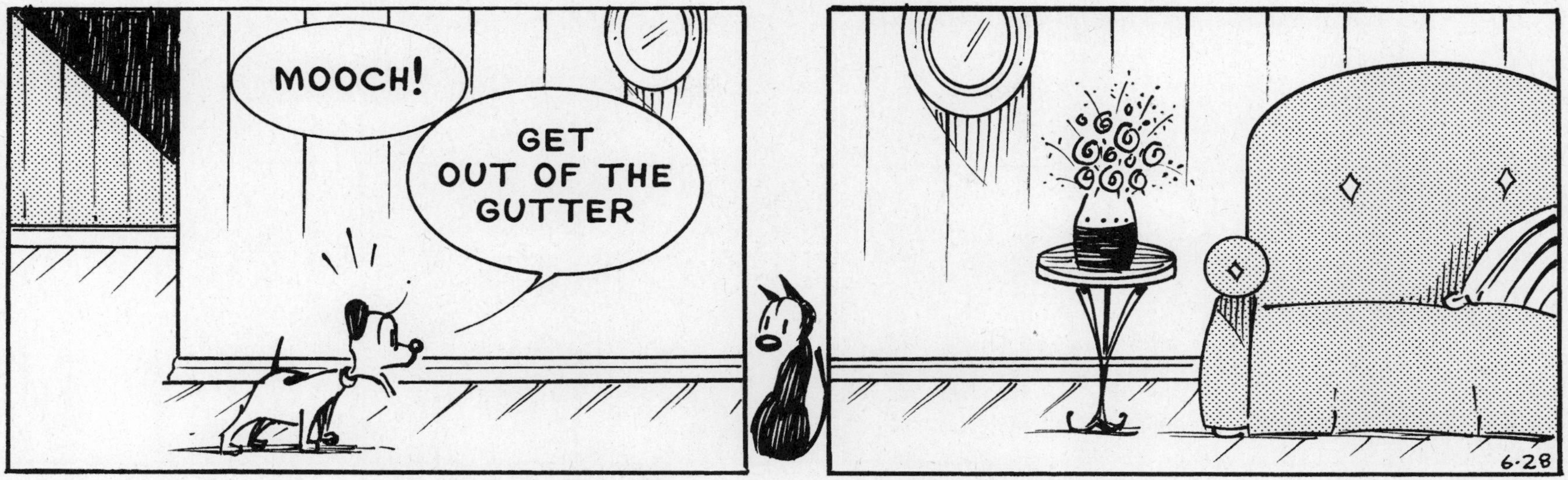
MOOCH!
GET OUT OF THE GUTTER
6-28

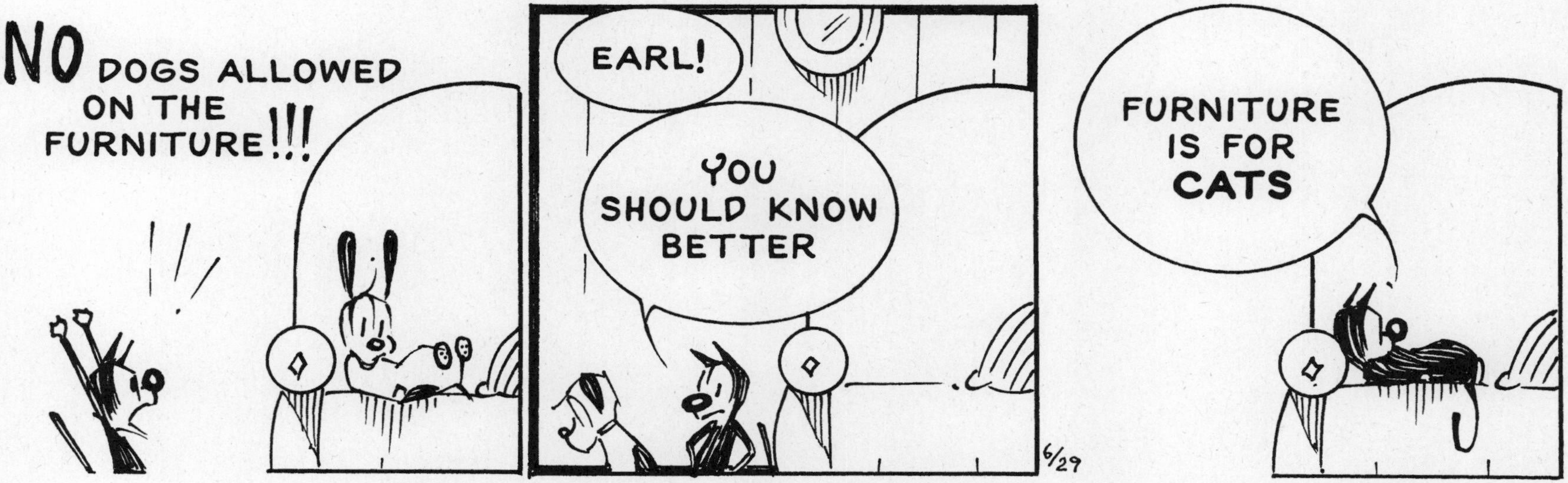
NO DOGS ALLOWED ON THE FURNITURE!!!
EARL!
YOU SHOULD KNOW BETTER
FURNITURE IS FOR CATS
6/29

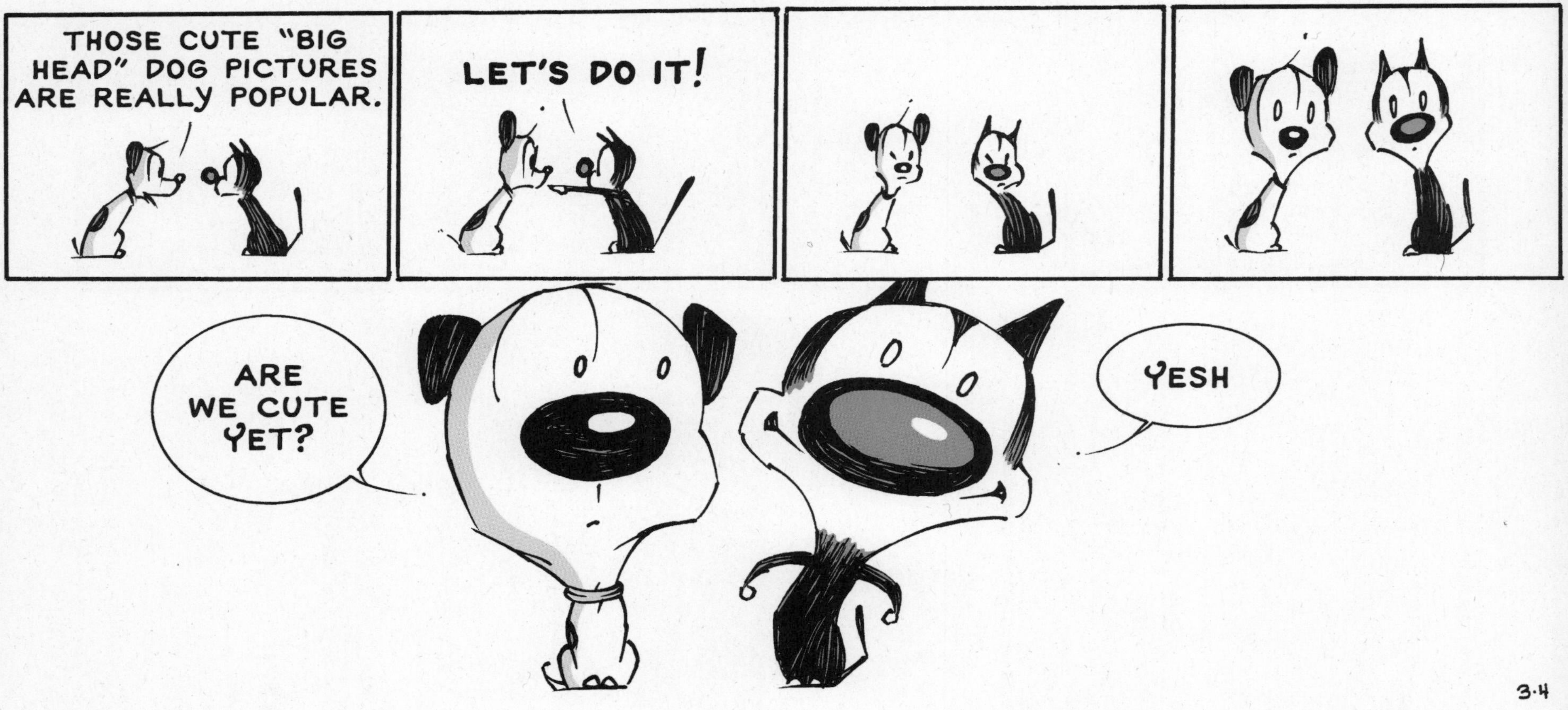
THOSE CUTE "BIG HEAD" DOG PICTURES ARE REALLY POPULAR.
LET'S DO IT!
ARE WE CUTE YET?
YESH
3·4

HOT DOGS

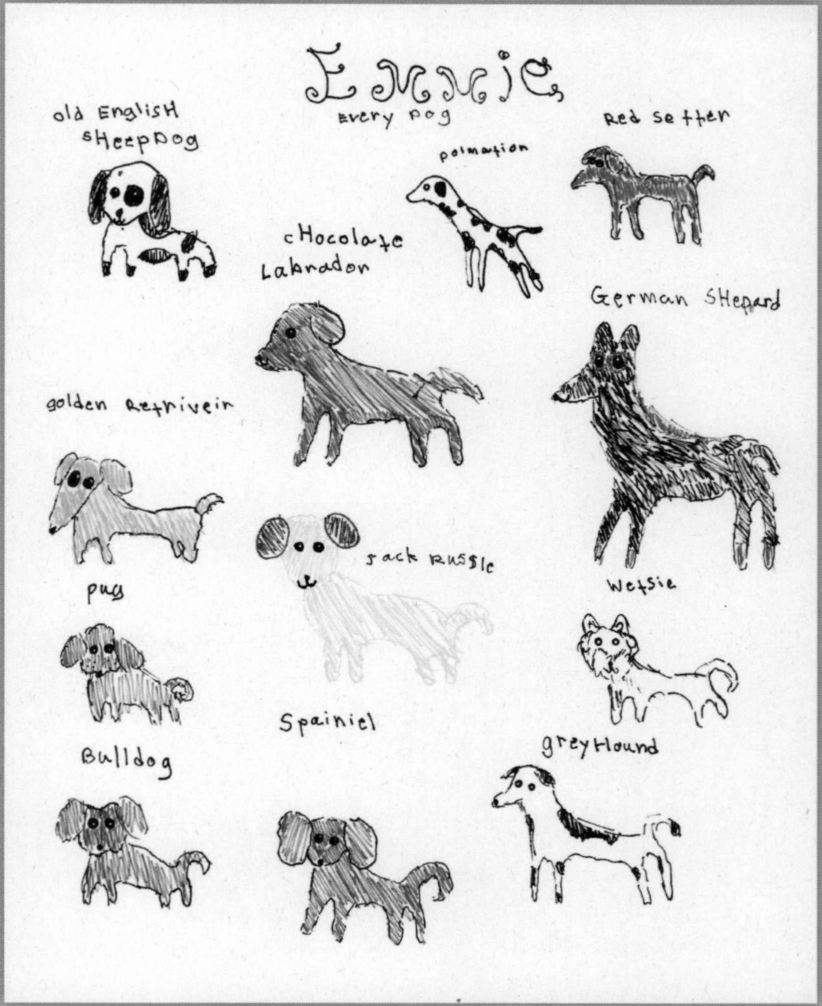

Emmie
every Dog
old English sHeepDog
Red se tter
cHocolate Labrador
German SHepard
golden Retrivein
Jack Russle
pug
Wetsie
Spainiel
Bulldog
greyHound

HOT CATS

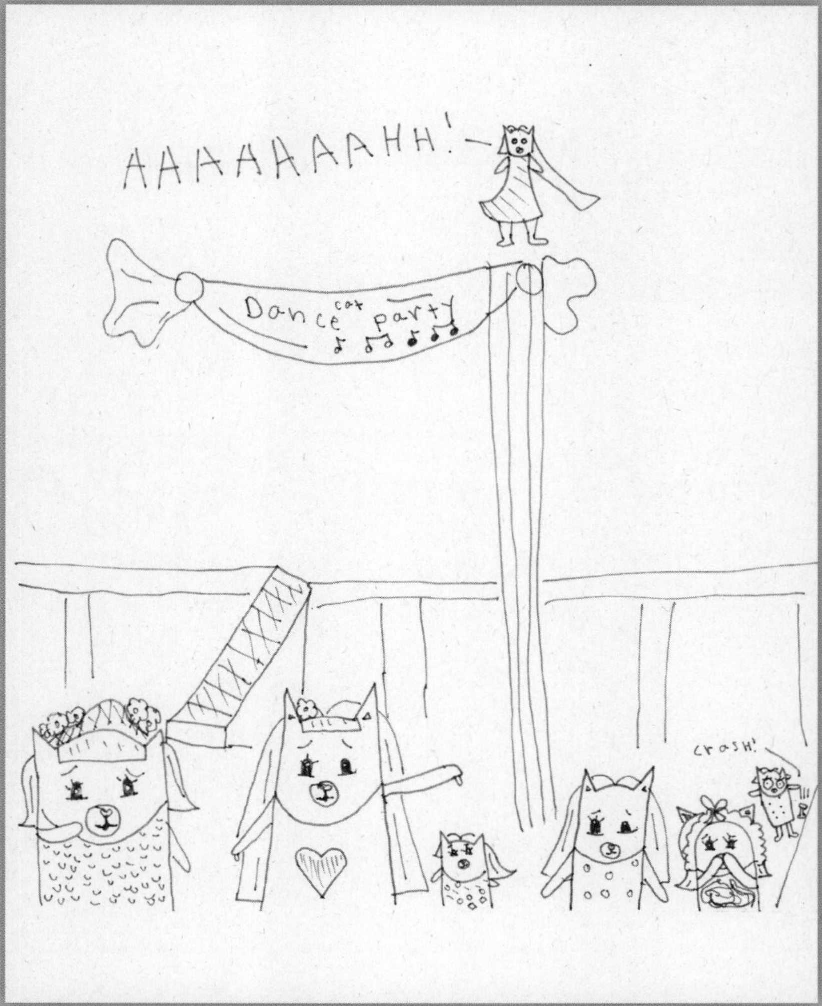

AAAAAAAHH!
Dance cat party
crash!

By Ruby Wetzel
(Our editor Lucas's seven-year-old daughter)

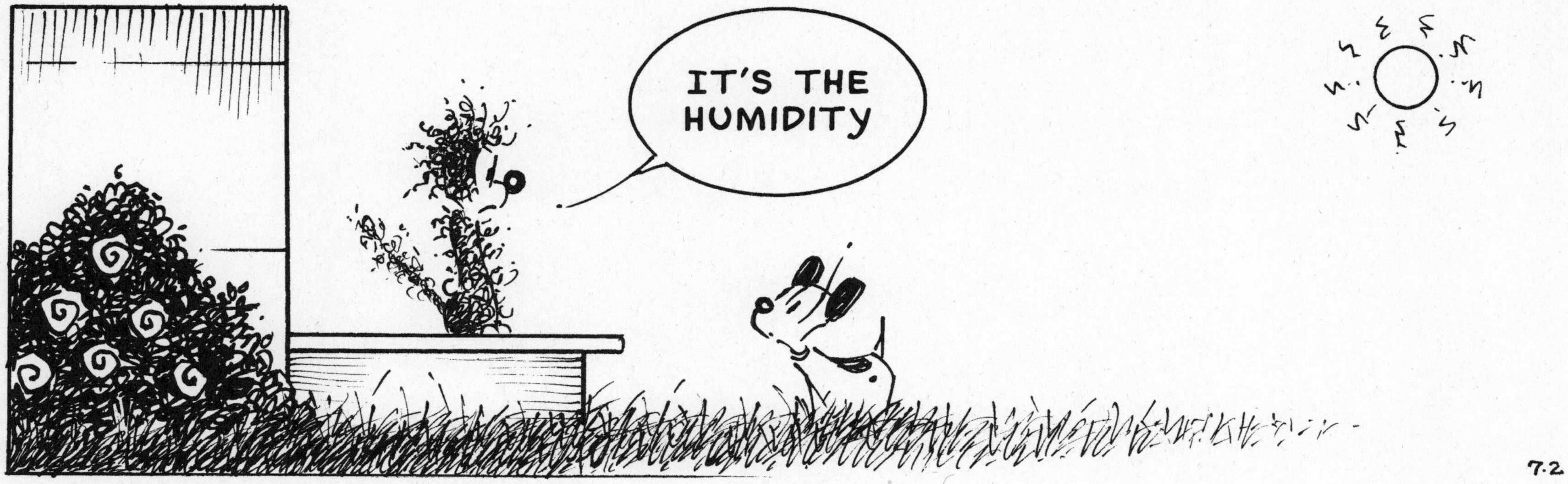
IT'S THE HUMIDITY
7.2

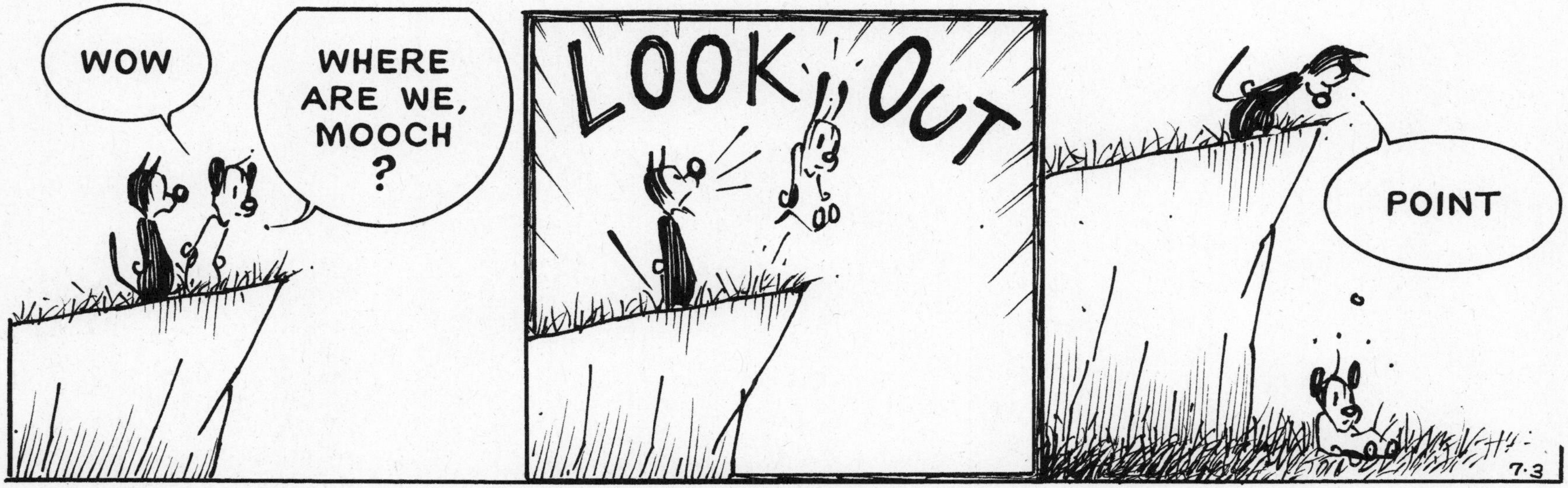
WOW
WHERE ARE WE, MOOCH ?
LOOK OUT
POINT
7.3

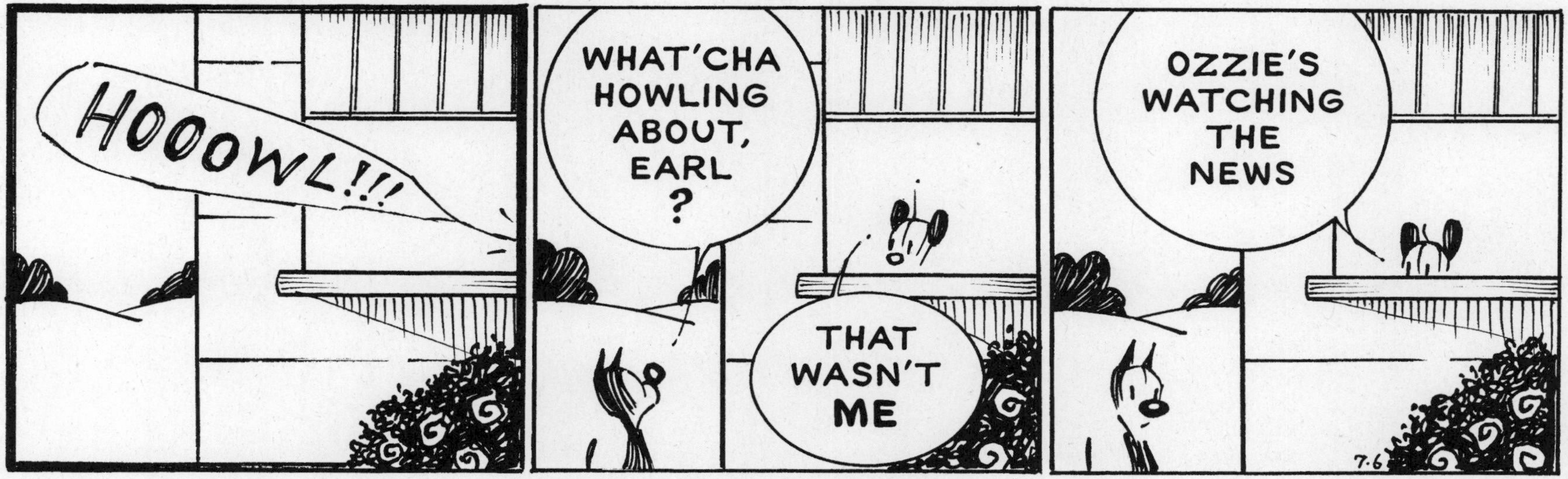
HOOOWL!!!
WHAT'CHA HOWLING ABOUT, EARL ?
THAT WASN'T ME
OZZIE'S WATCHING THE NEWS
7·6

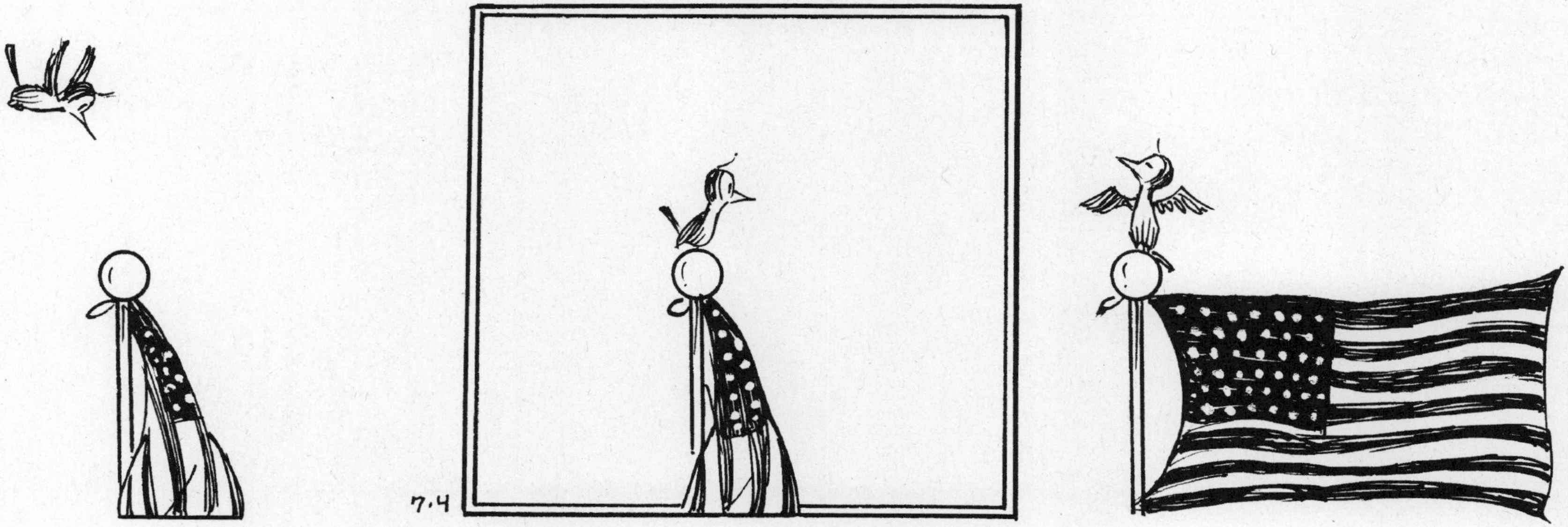
7·4

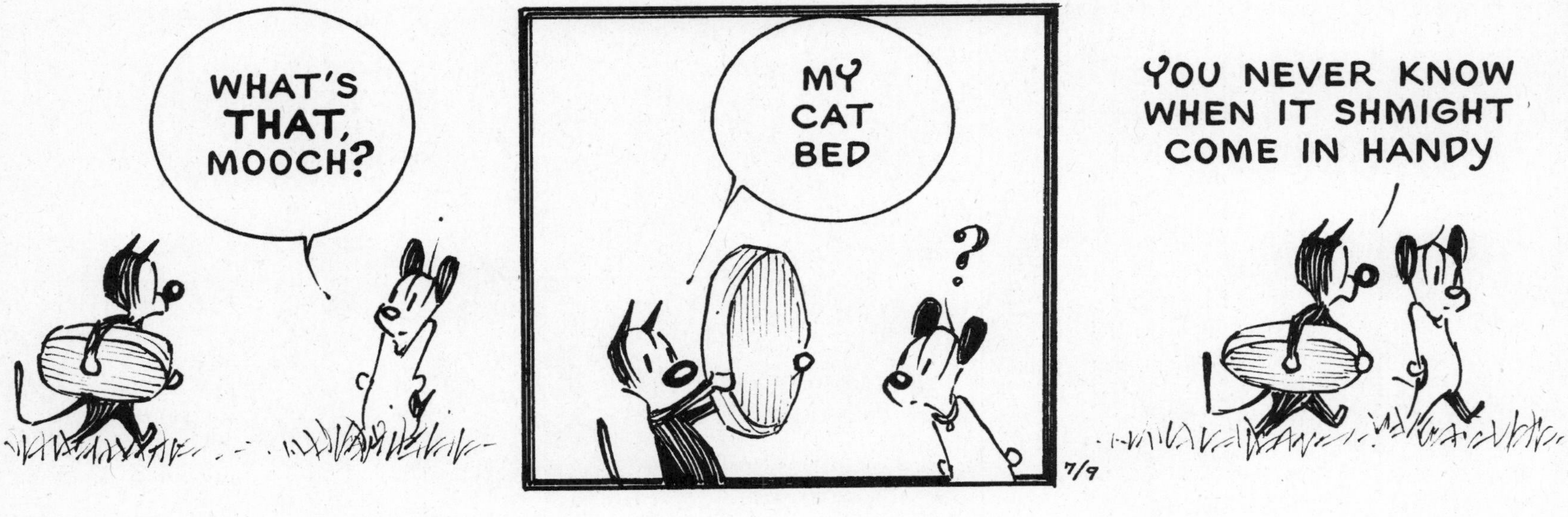
WHAT'S **THAT,** MOOCH?
MY CAT BED
?
YOU NEVER KNOW WHEN IT SHMIGHT COME IN HANDY
7/9

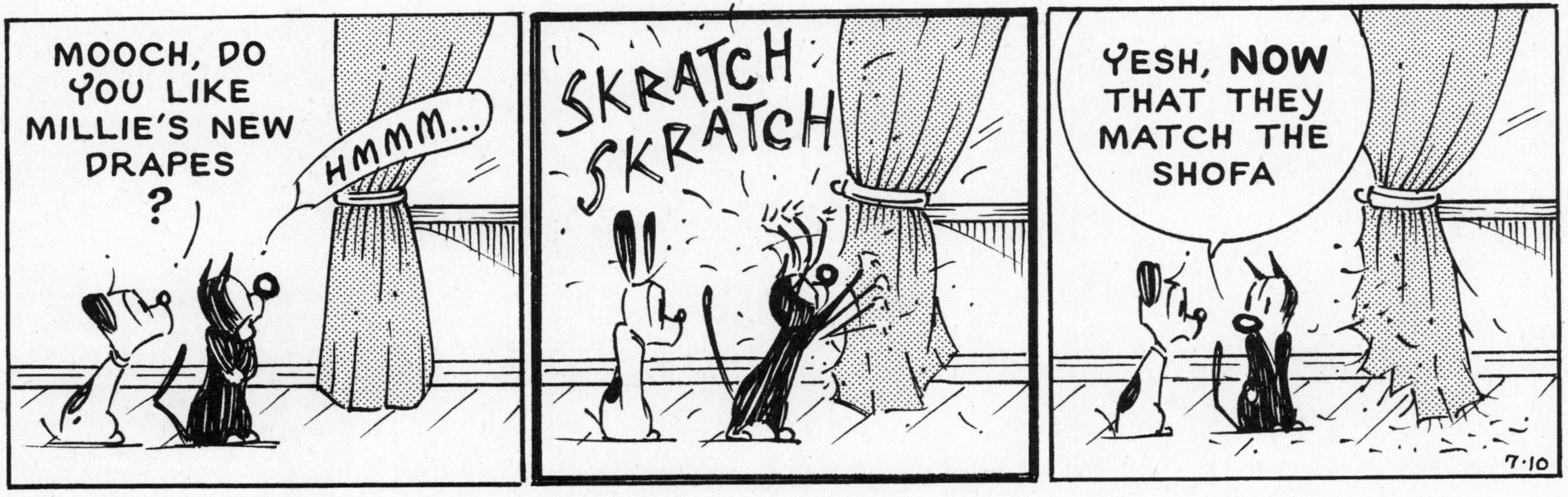
MOOCH, DO YOU LIKE MILLIE'S NEW DRAPES ?
HMMM...
SKRATCH SKRATCH
YESH, **NOW** THAT THEY MATCH THE SHOFA
7·10

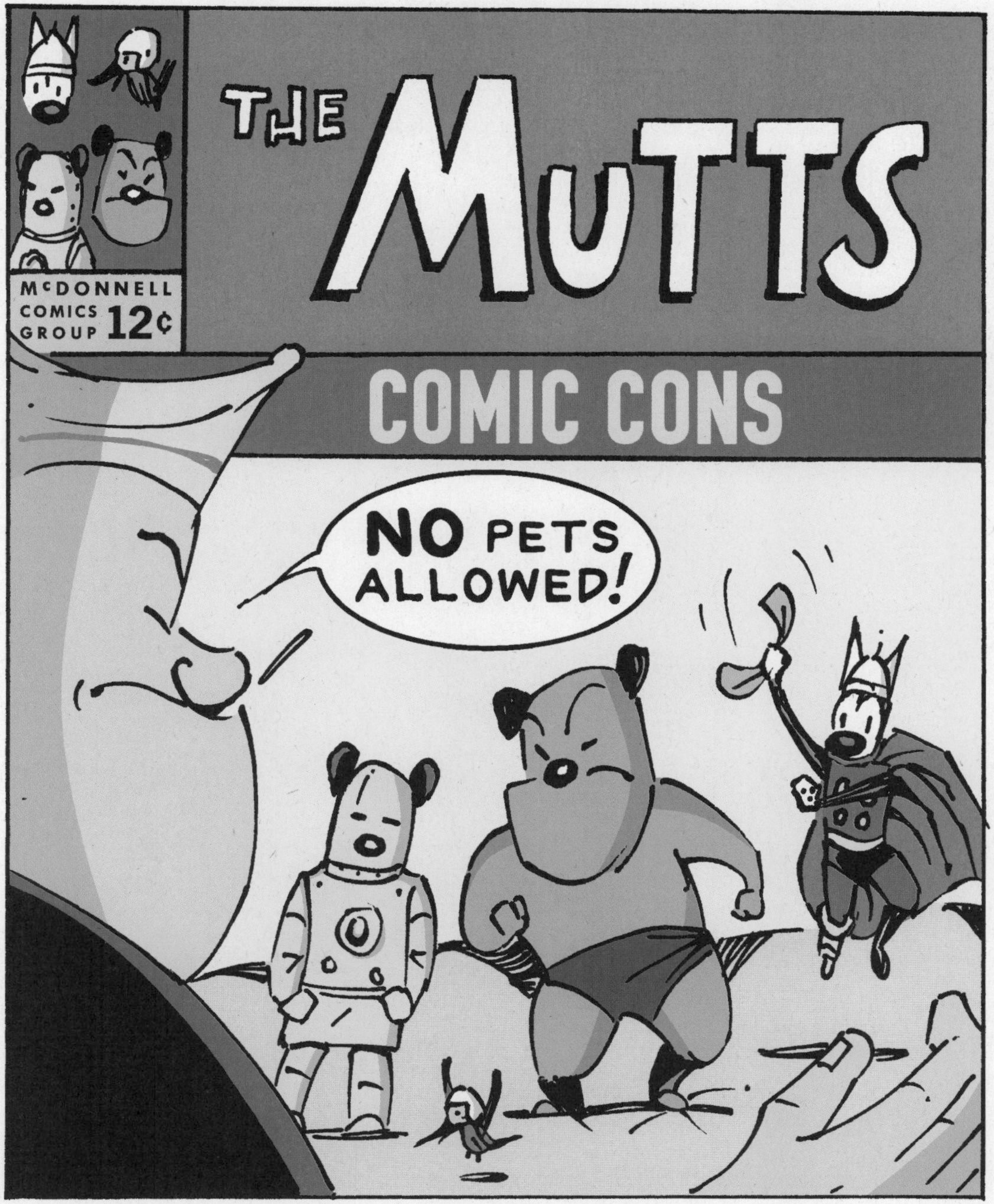
McDONNELL COMICS GROUP 12¢
THE MUTTS
COMIC CONS
NO PETS ALLOWED!

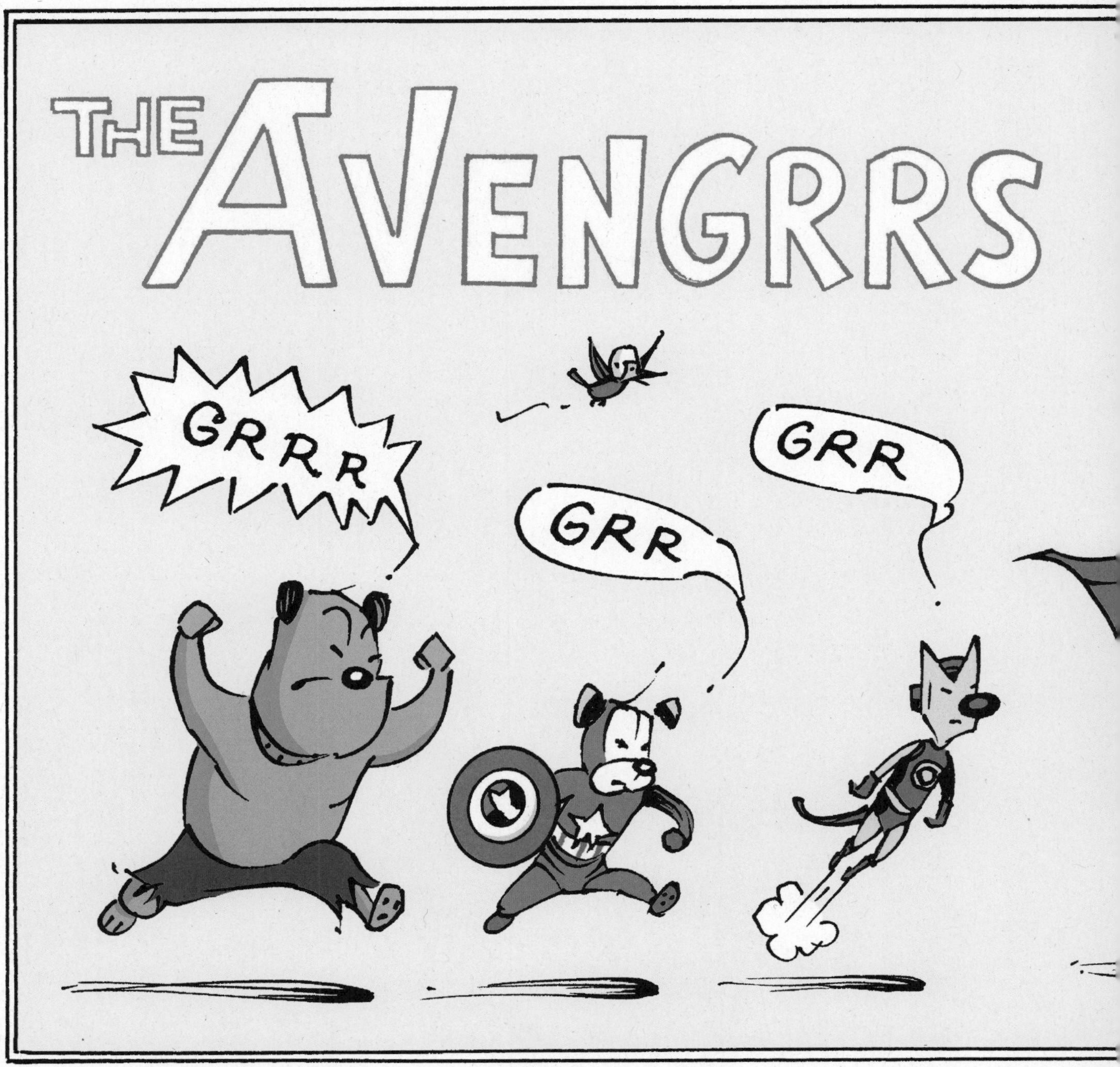
THE AVENGRRS
GRRRR
GRR
GRR

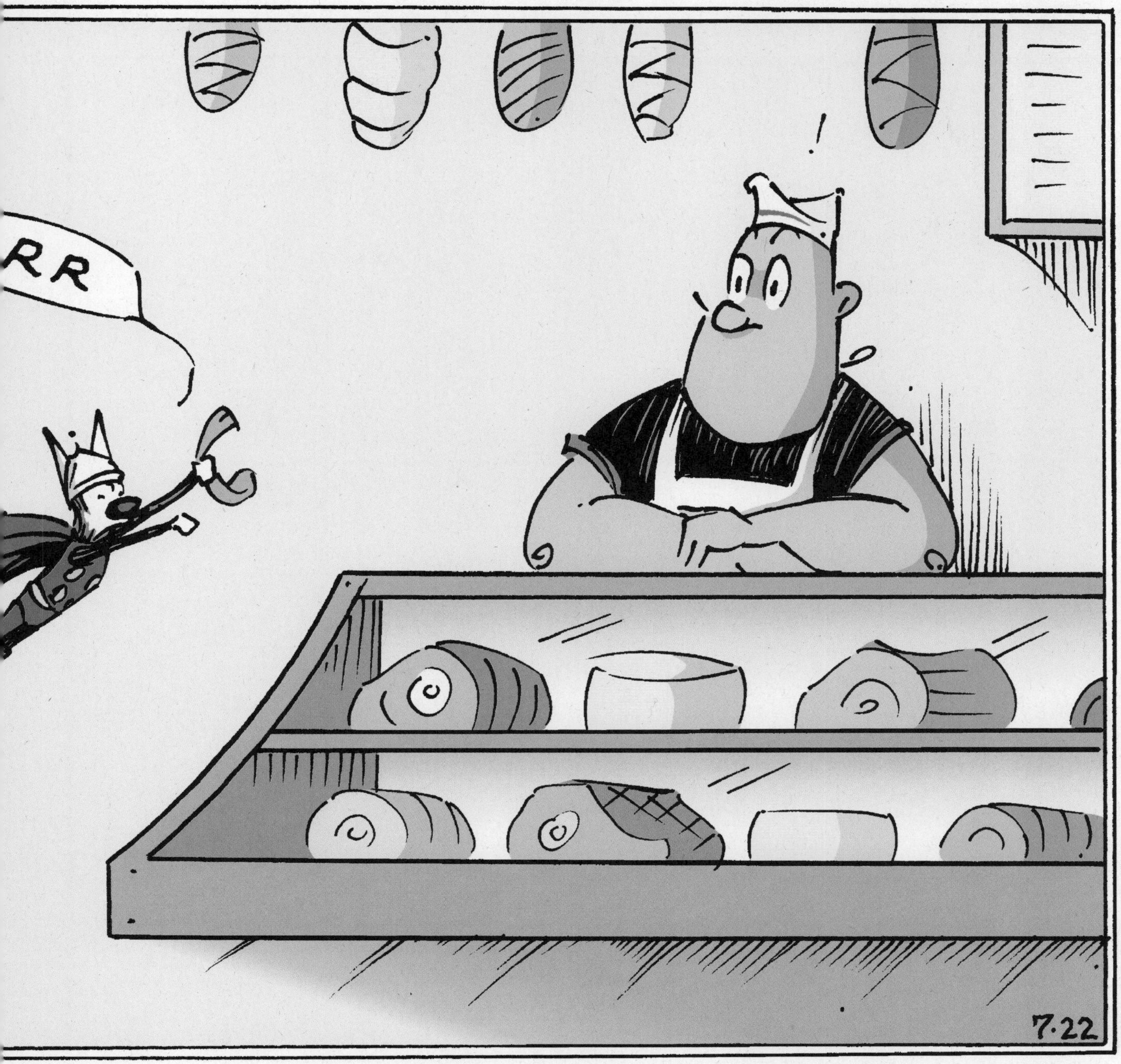
RR
!
7·22

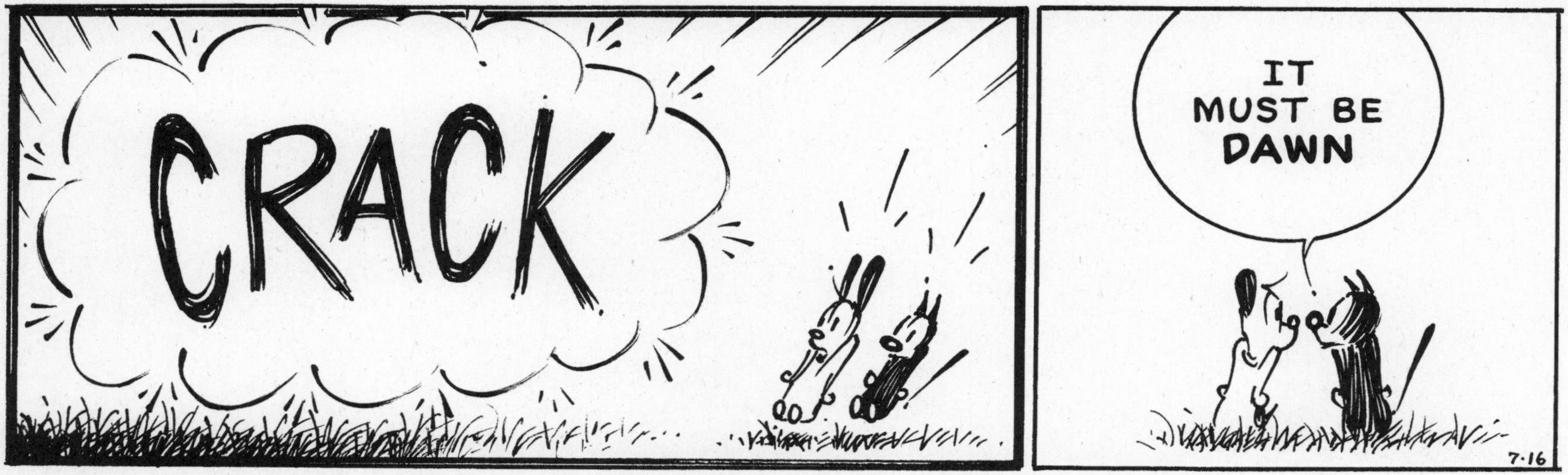
CRACK
IT MUST BE DAWN
7·16

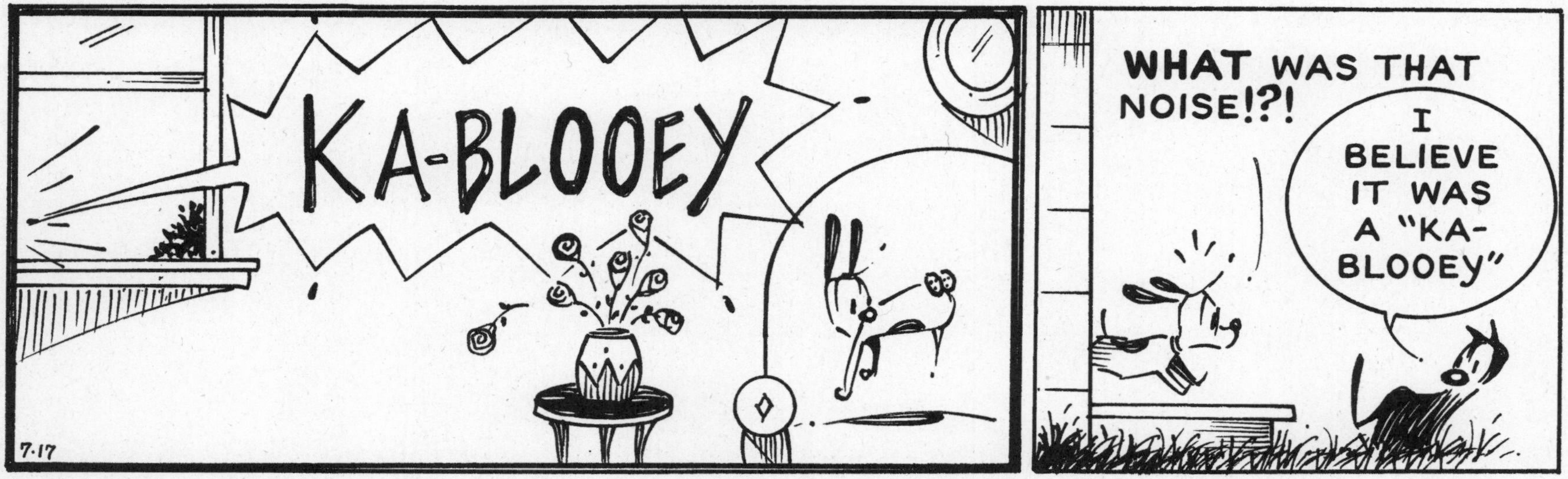
KA-BLOOEY
7·17
WHAT WAS THAT NOISE!?!
I BELIEVE IT WAS A "KA-BLOOEY"

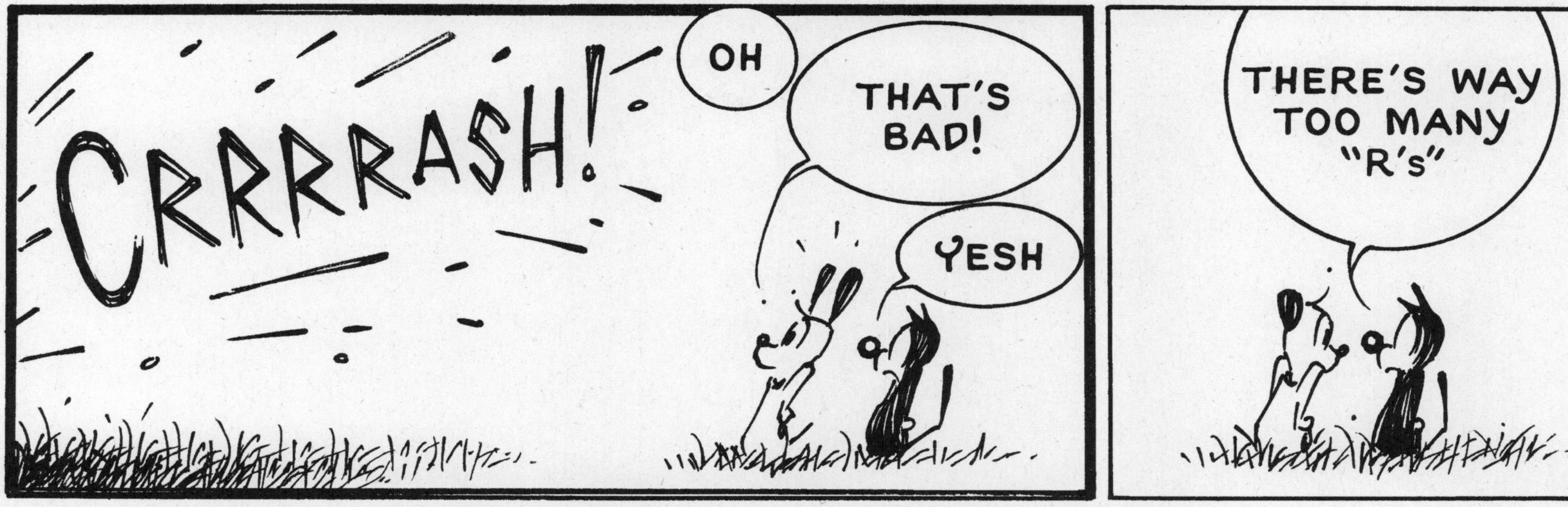
CRRRRASH!
OH
THAT'S BAD!
YESH
THERE'S WAY TOO MANY "R's"
7.18

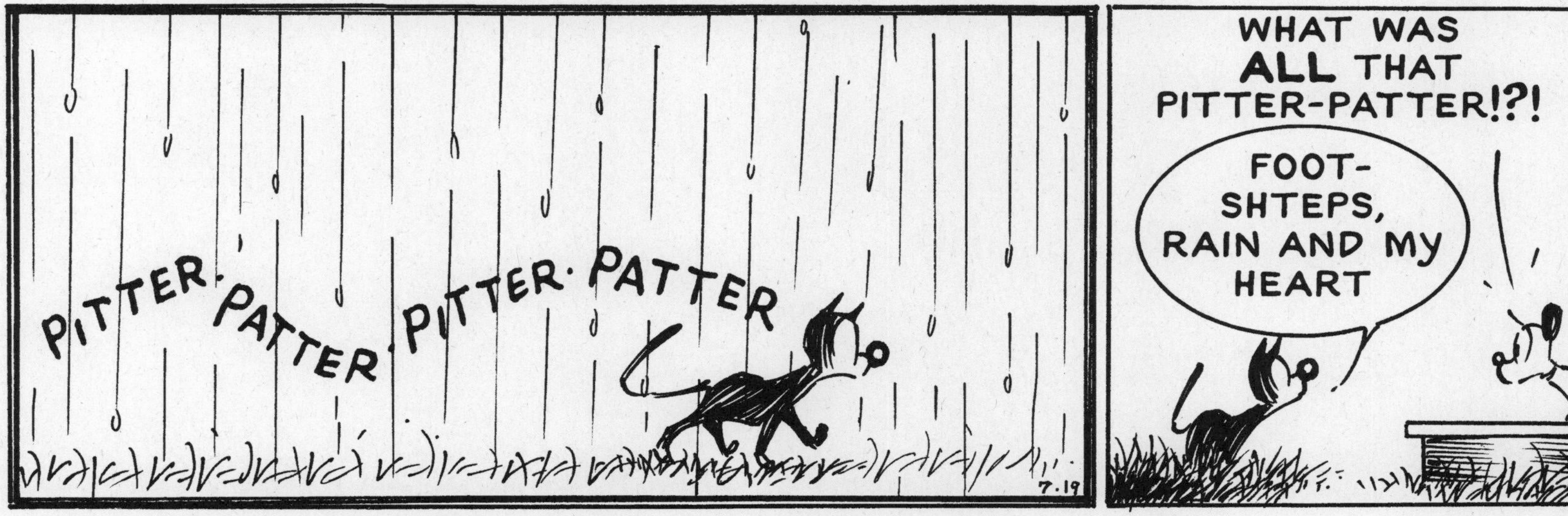
PITTER-PATTER-PITTER-PATTER
7.19
WHAT WAS ALL THAT PITTER-PATTER!?!
FOOT-SHTEPS, RAIN AND MY HEART

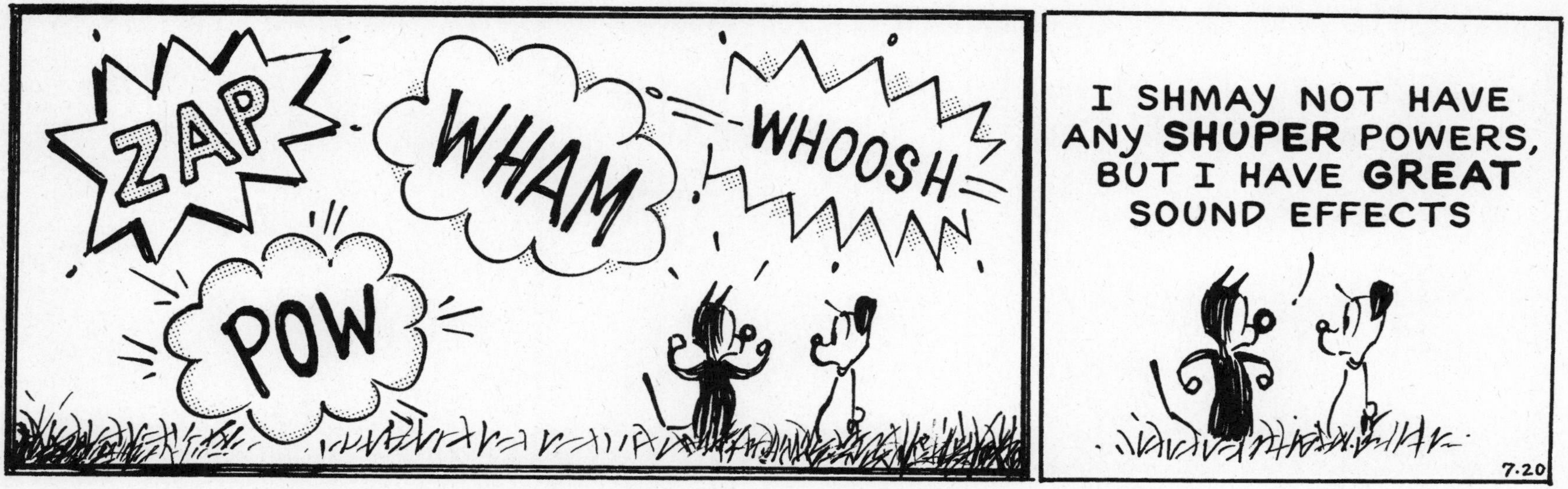
ZAP
WHAM
WHOOSH
POW
I SHMAY NOT HAVE ANY **SHUPER** POWERS, BUT I HAVE **GREAT** SOUND EFFECTS
7.20

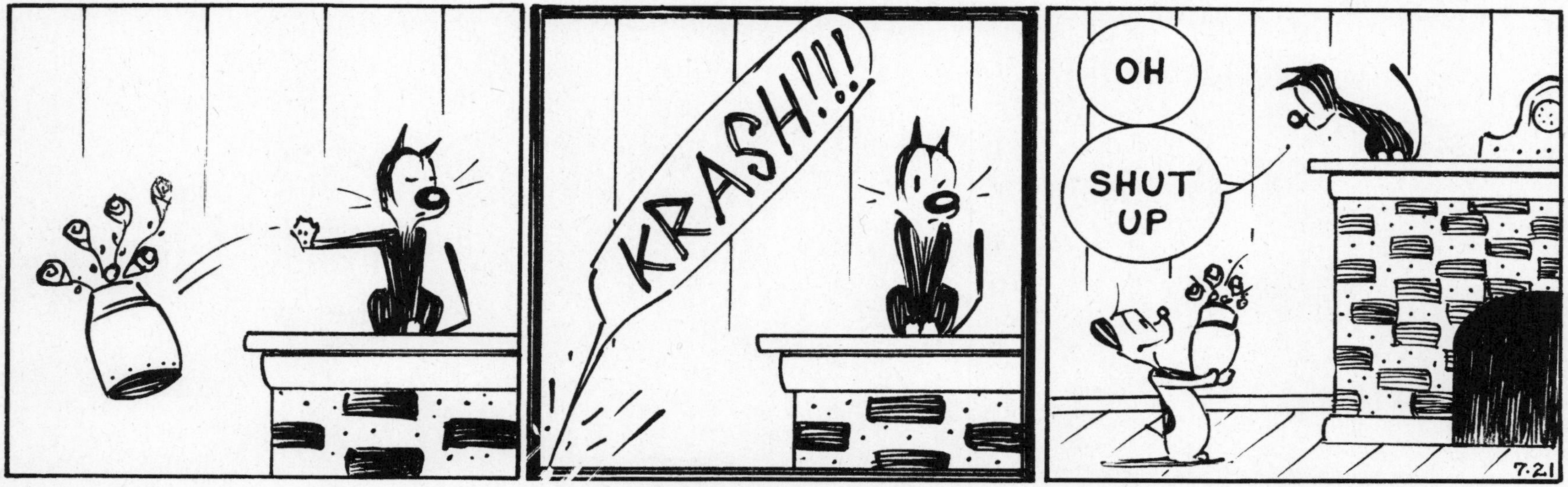
KRASH!!!
OH
SHUT UP
7.21

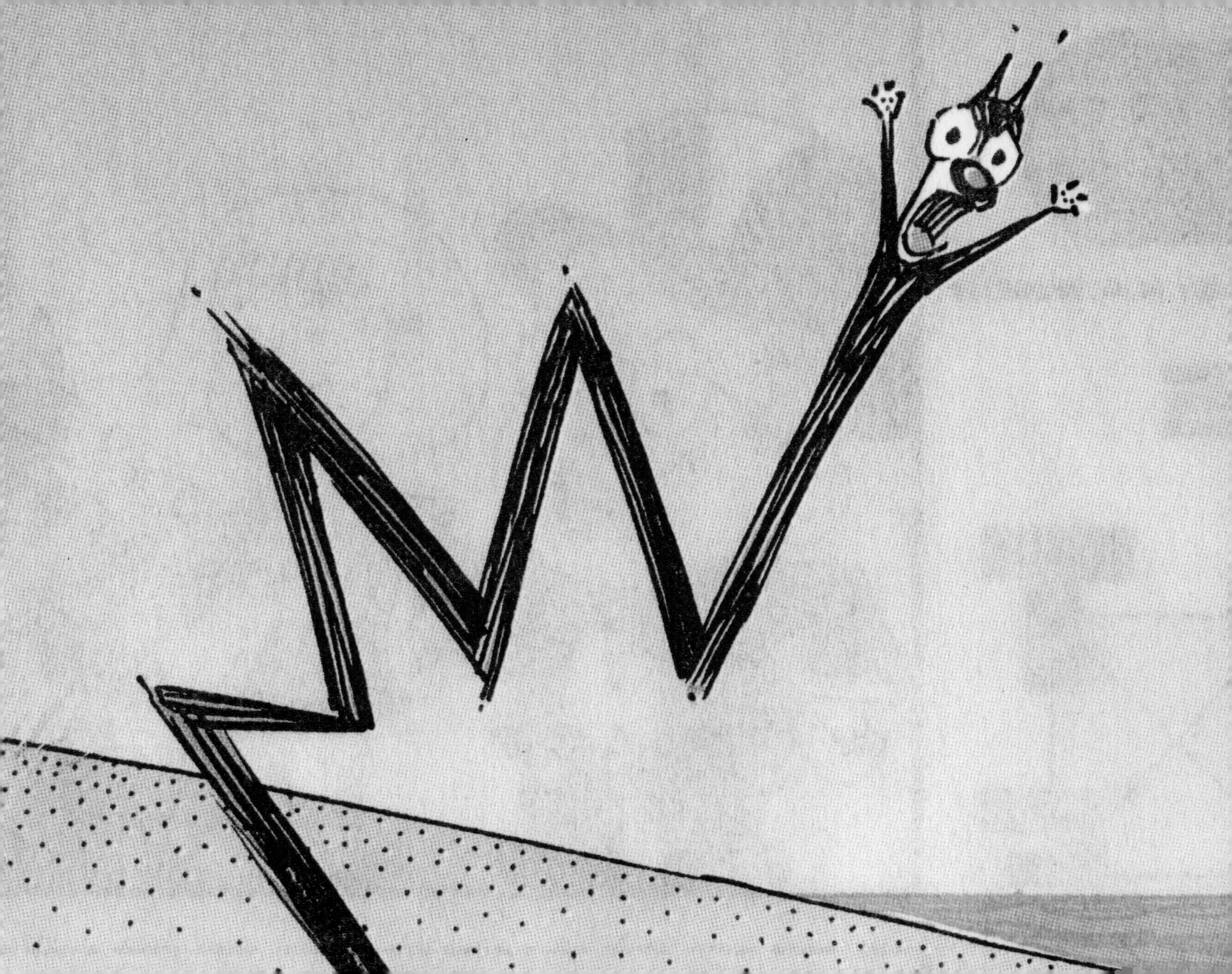

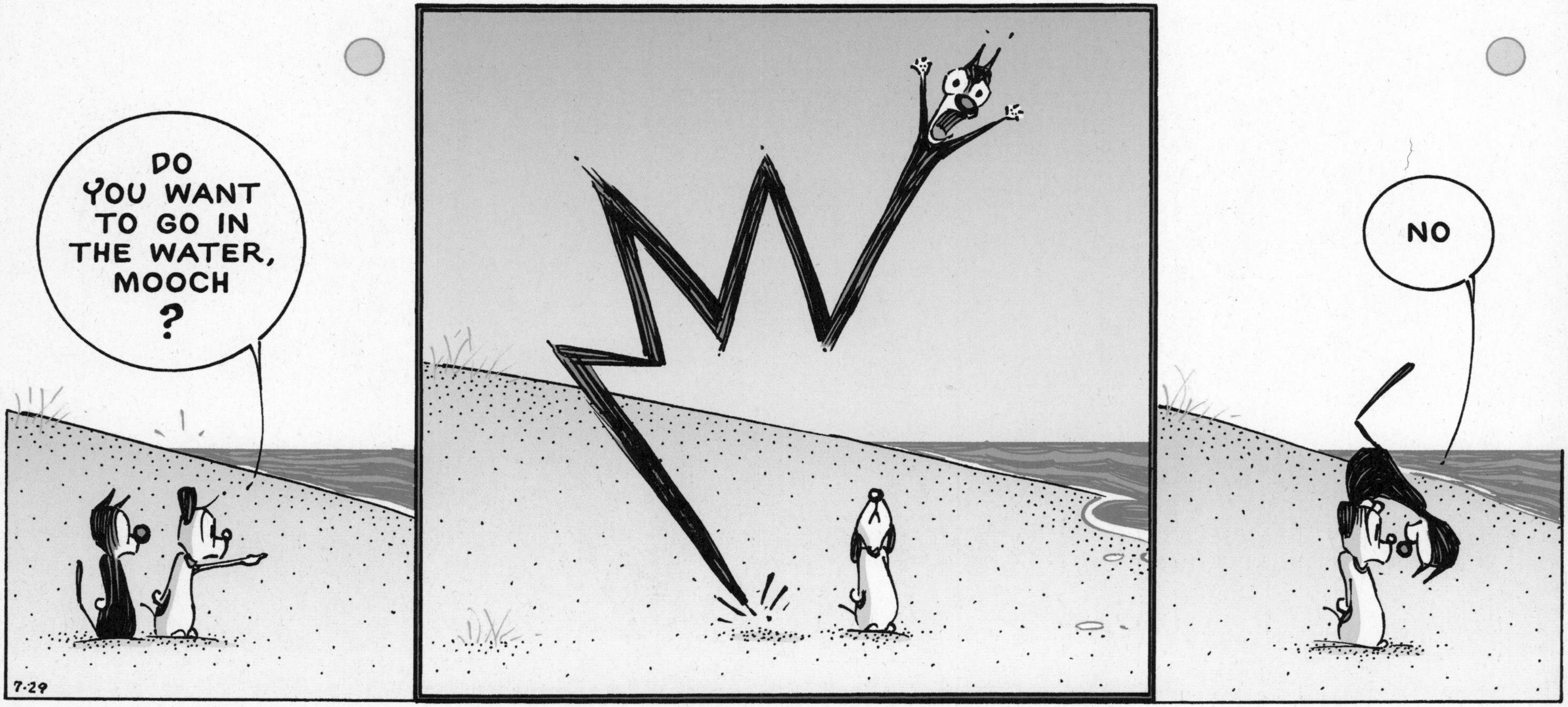
DO YOU WANT TO GO IN THE WATER, MOOCH ?
7-29
NO

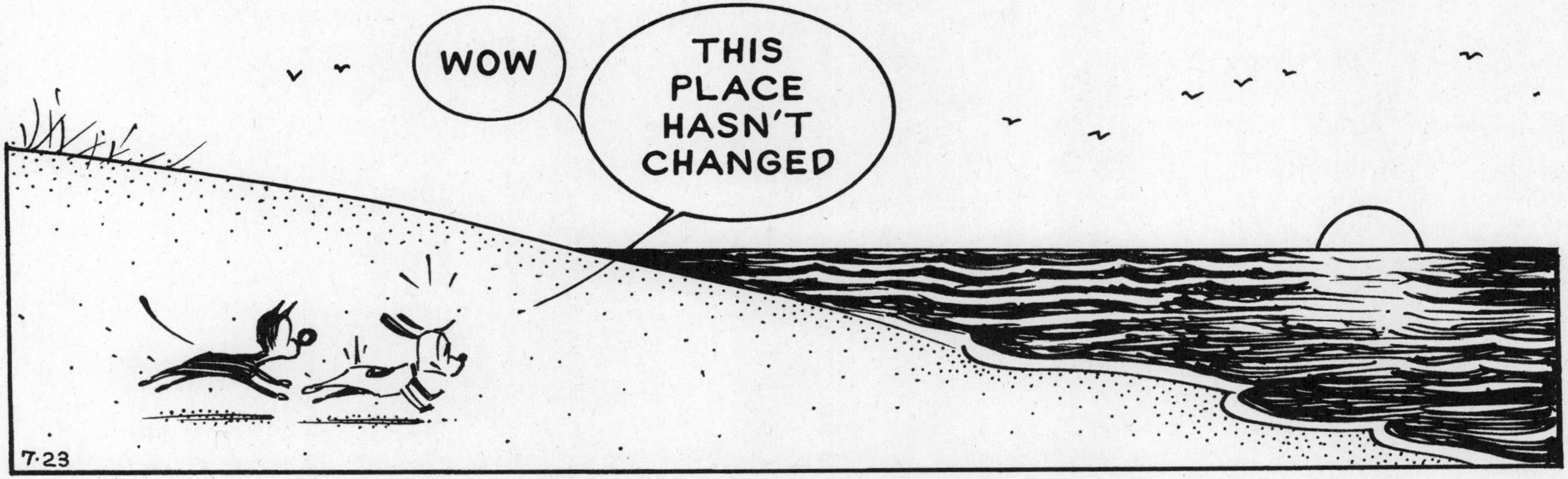
WOW
THIS PLACE HASN'T CHANGED
7·23

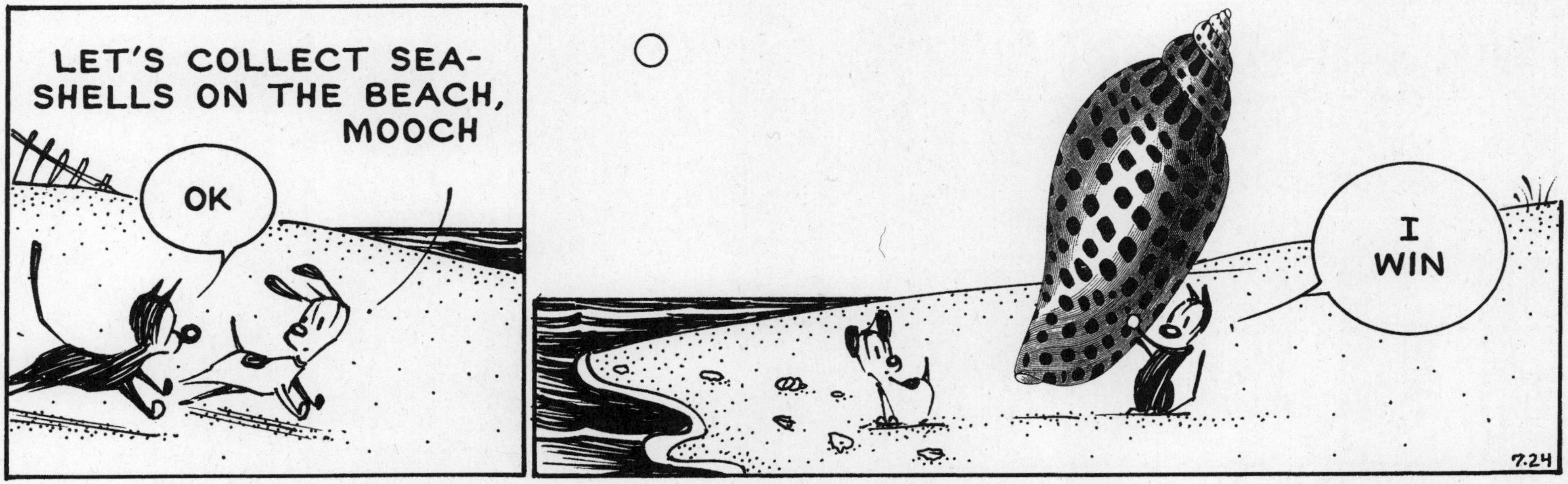
LET'S COLLECT SEA-SHELLS ON THE BEACH, MOOCH
OK
I WIN
7·24

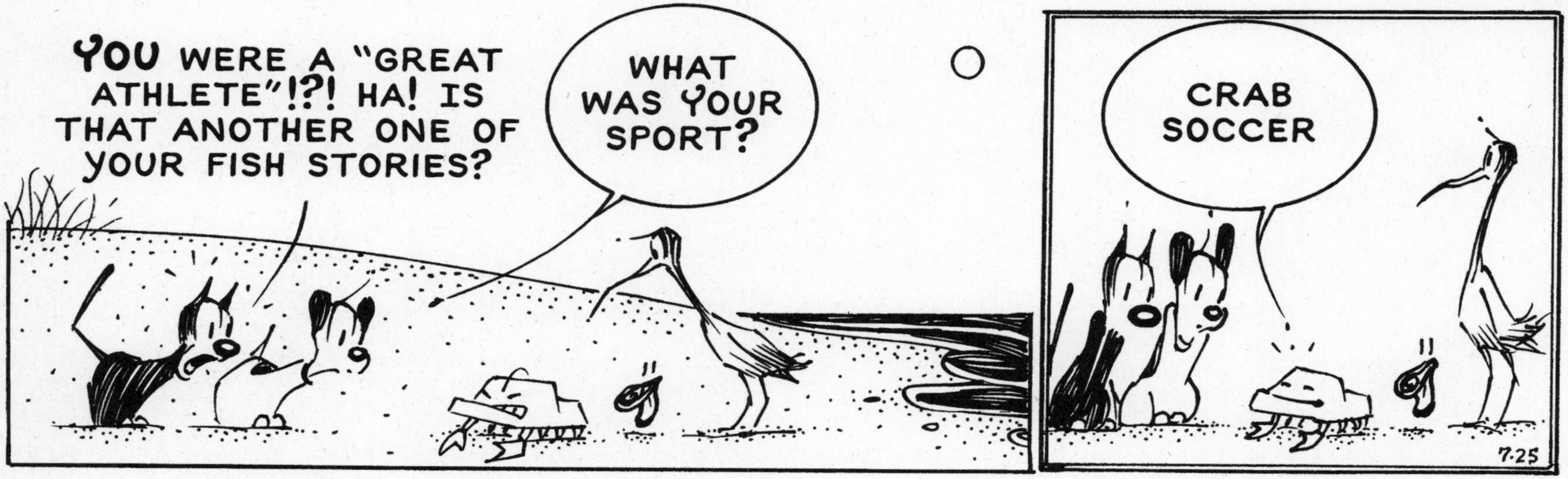
YOU WERE A "GREAT ATHLETE"!?! HA! IS THAT ANOTHER ONE OF YOUR FISH STORIES?
WHAT WAS YOUR SPORT?
CRAB SOCCER
7·25

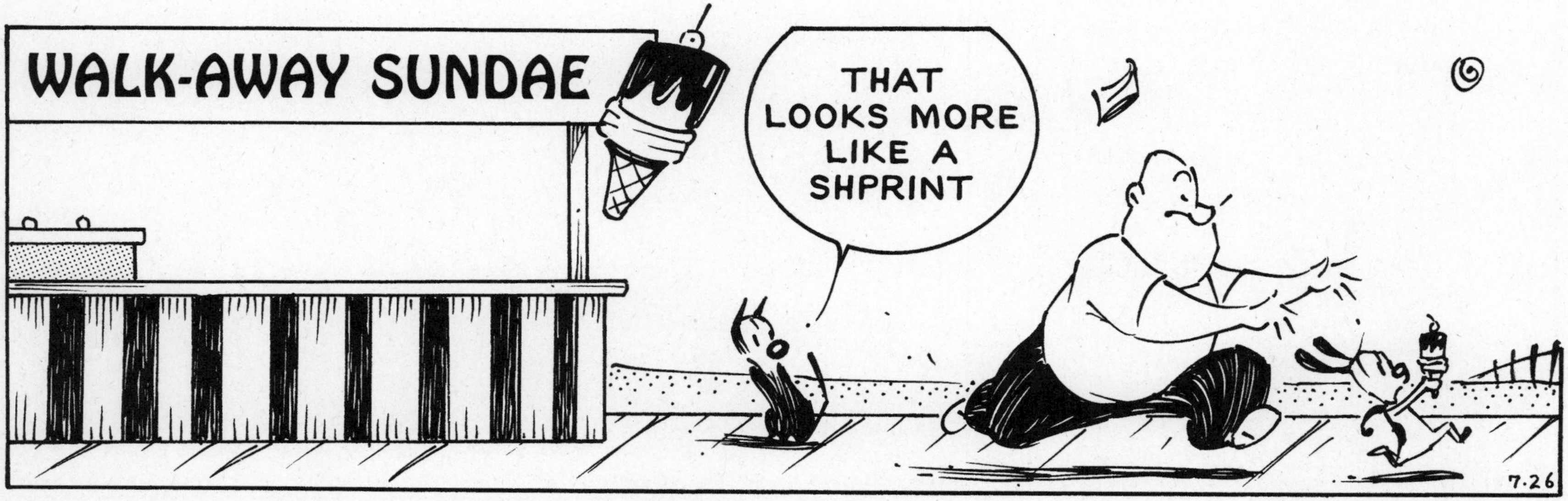
WALK-AWAY SUNDAE
THAT LOOKS MORE LIKE A SHPRINT
7·26

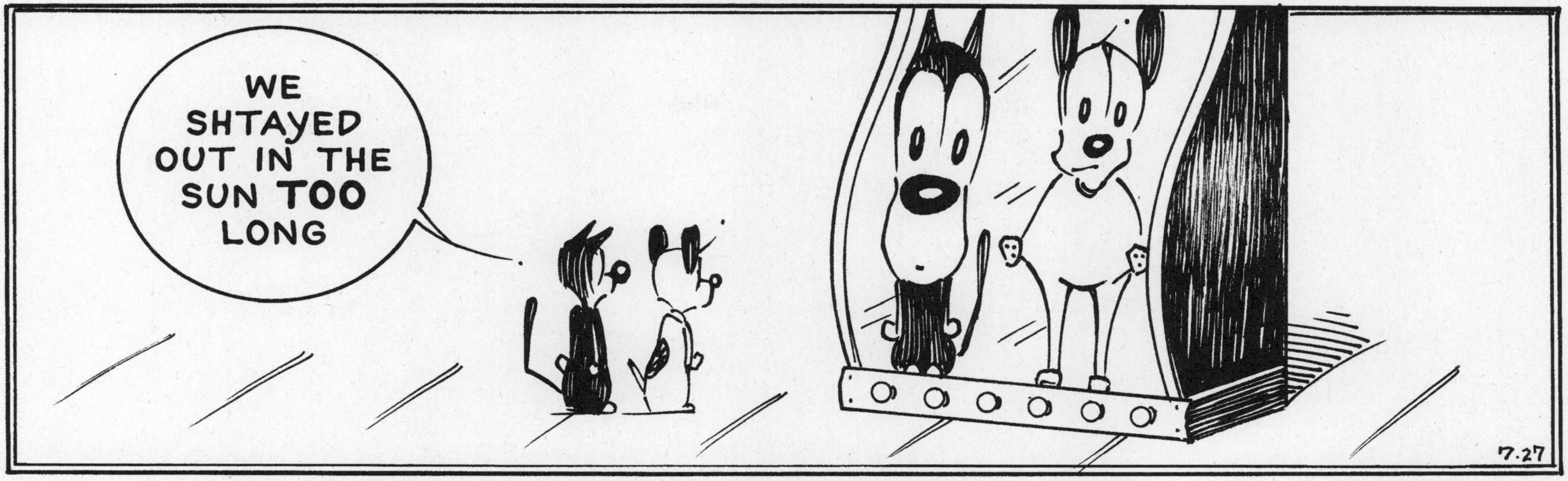
WE SHTAYED OUT IN THE SUN TOO LONG
7.27

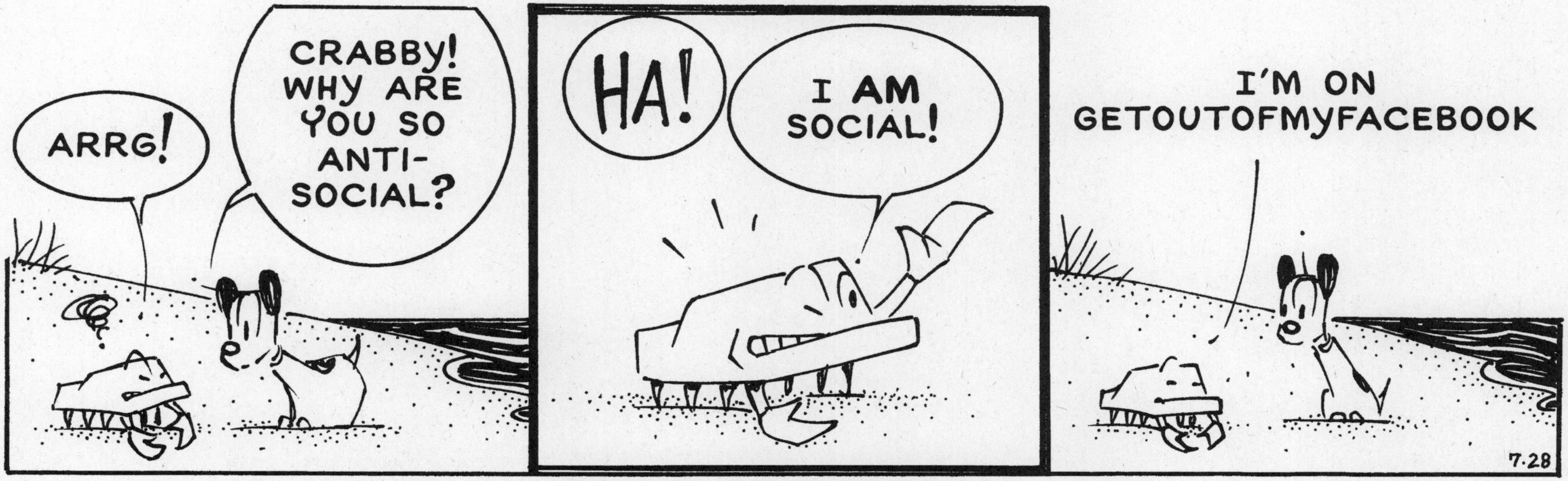
ARRG!
CRABBY! WHY ARE YOU SO ANTI-SOCIAL?
HA!
I AM SOCIAL!
I'M ON GETOUTOFMYFACEBOOK
7.28

MUTTS
Patrick McDonnell

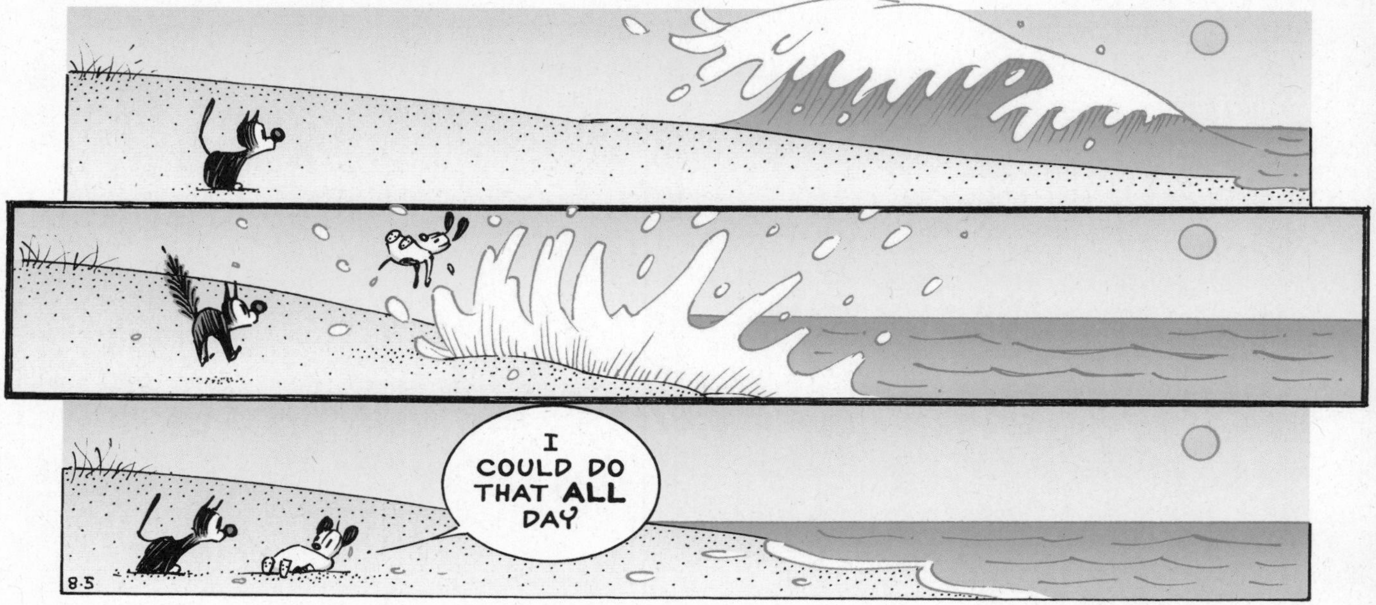
I COULD DO THAT ALL DAY
8.5

MUTTS
Patrick McDonnell

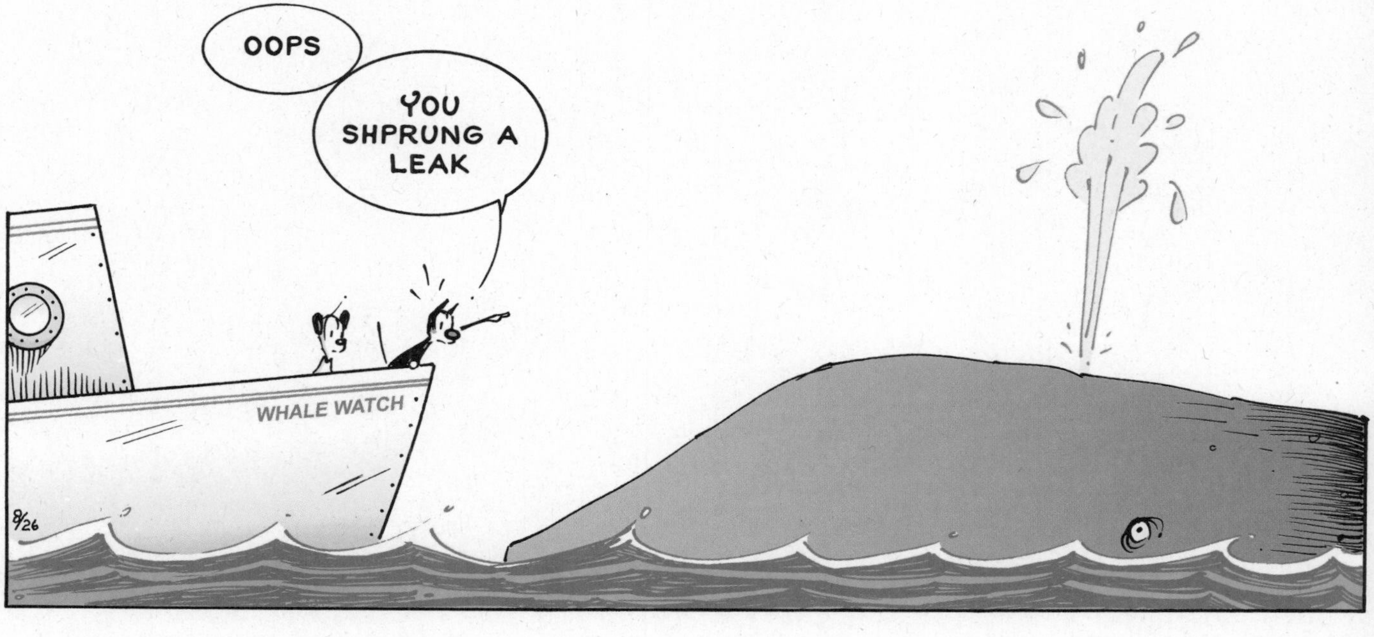
OOPS
YOU SHPRUNG A LEAK
WHALE WATCH
8/26

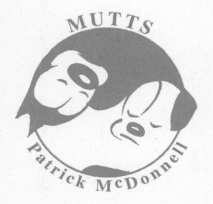

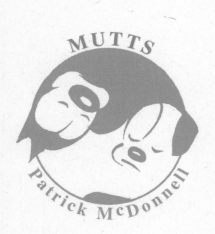

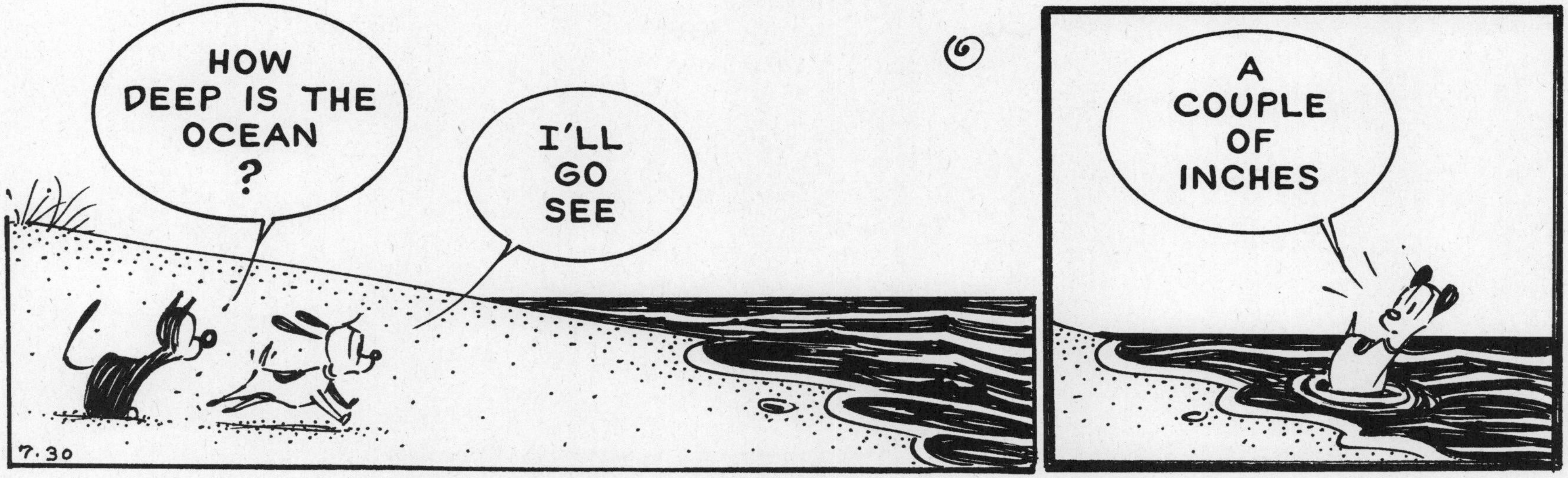
HOW DEEP IS THE OCEAN ?
I'LL GO SEE
A COUPLE OF INCHES
7.30

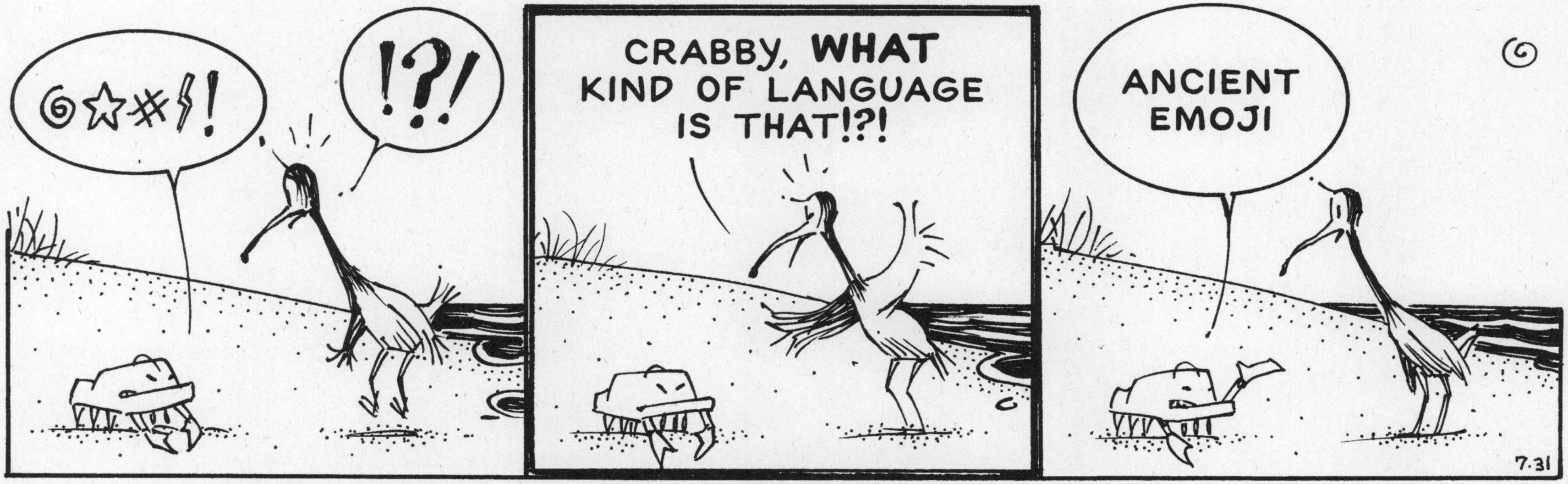
!?!
CRABBY, WHAT KIND OF LANGUAGE IS THAT!?!
ANCIENT EMOJI
7.31

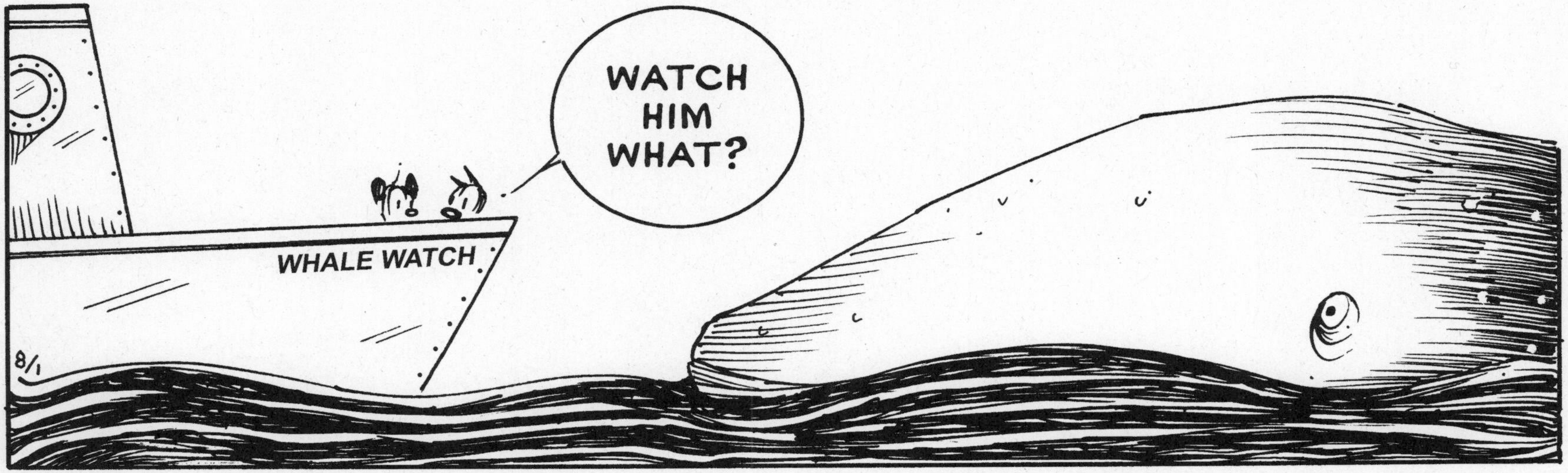
WATCH HIM WHAT?
WHALE WATCH
8/1

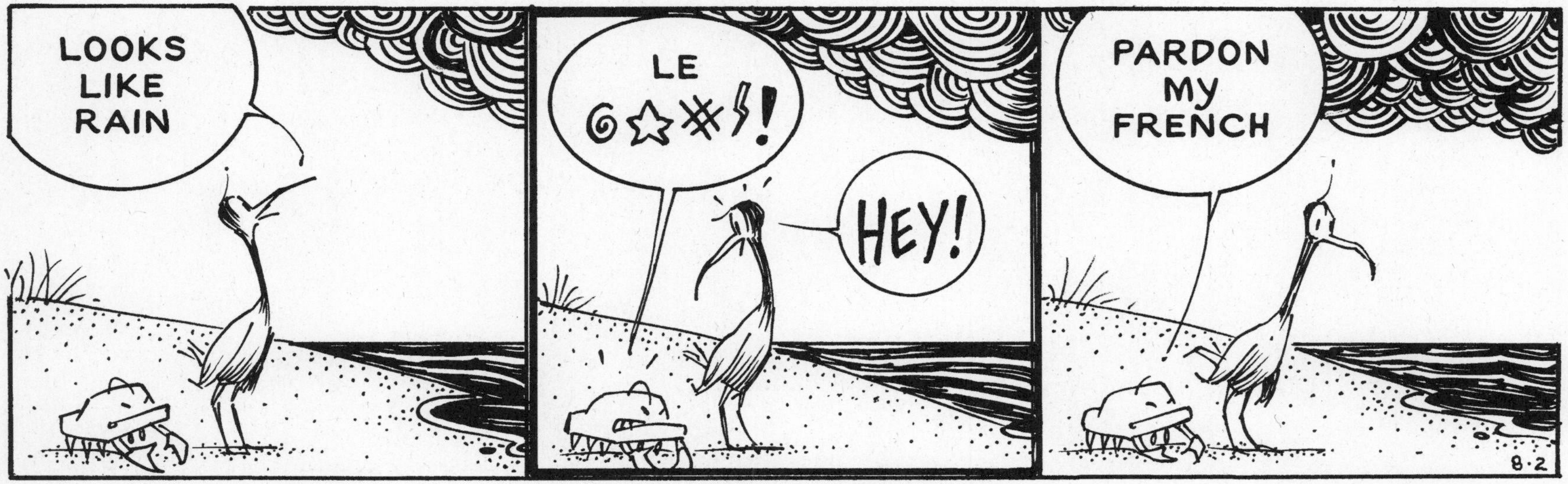
LOOKS LIKE RAIN
LE @☆#$!
HEY!
PARDON MY FRENCH
8·2

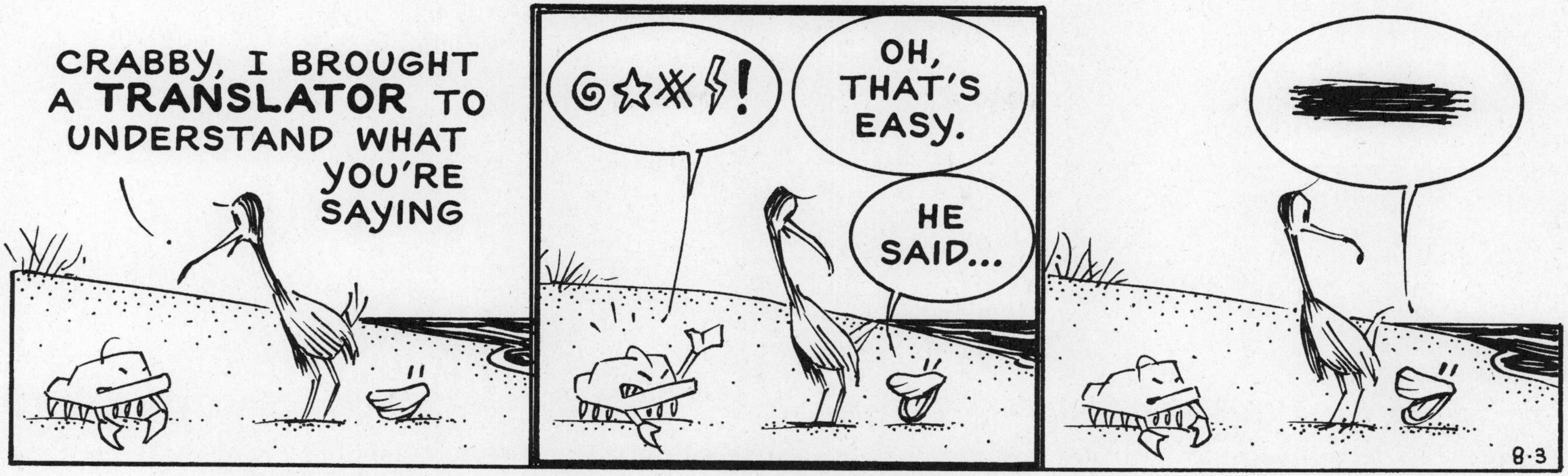
CRABBY, I BROUGHT A TRANSLATOR TO UNDERSTAND WHAT YOU'RE SAYING
OH, THAT'S EASY.
HE SAID...
8·3

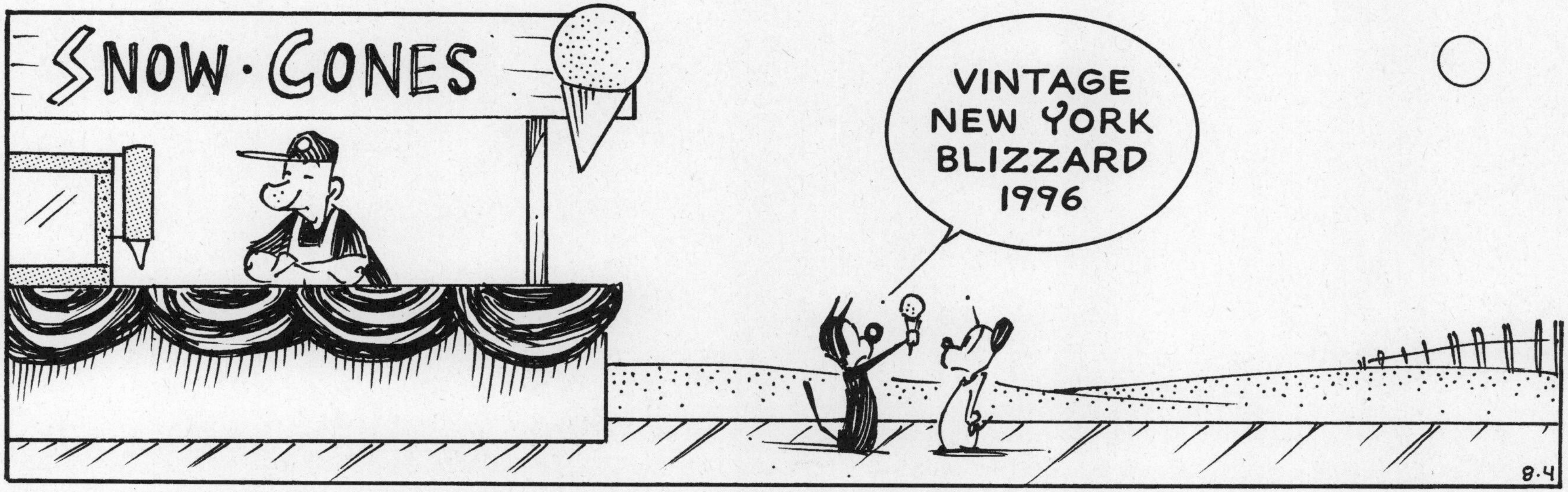
SNOW · CONES
VINTAGE NEW YORK BLIZZARD 1996
8·4

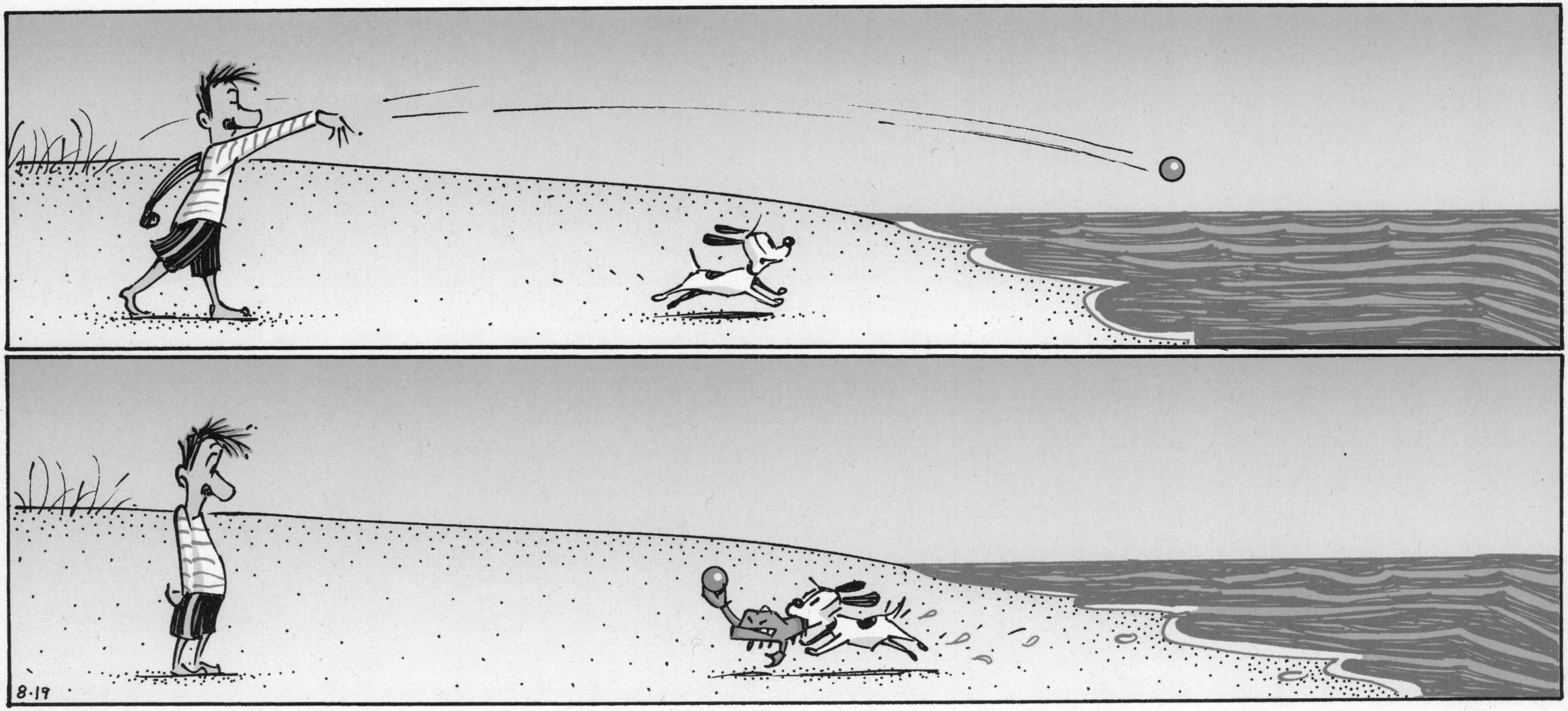
8·19

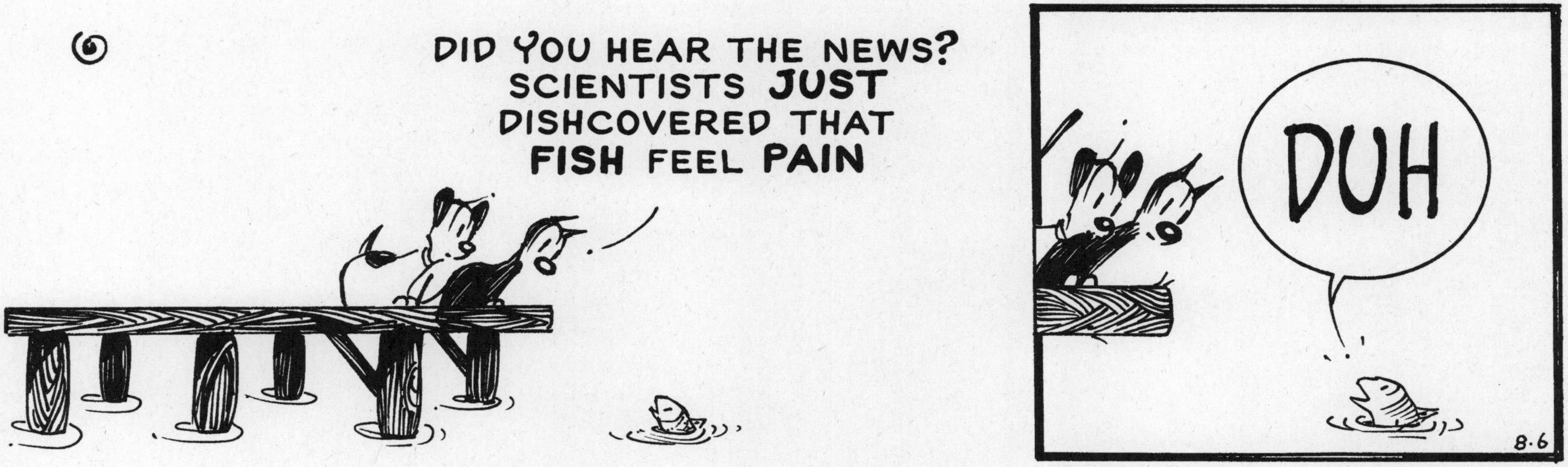
DID YOU HEAR THE NEWS? SCIENTISTS JUST DISHCOVERED THAT FISH FEEL PAIN
DUH
8·6

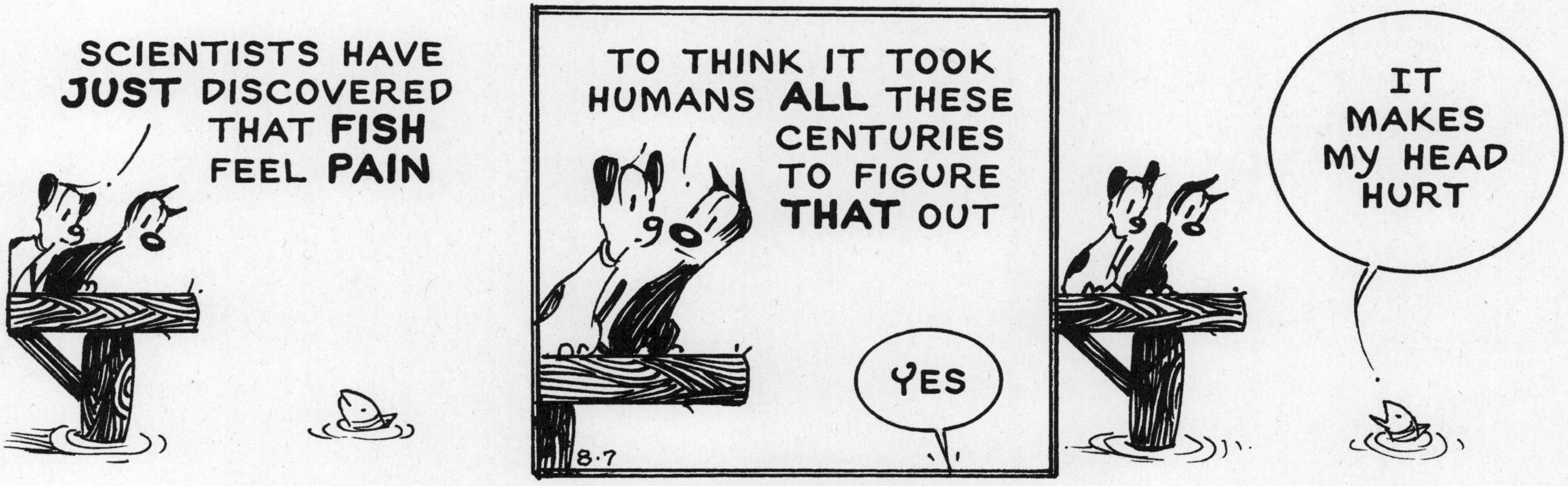
SCIENTISTS HAVE JUST DISCOVERED THAT FISH FEEL PAIN
TO THINK IT TOOK HUMANS ALL THESE CENTURIES TO FIGURE THAT OUT
YES
8·7
IT MAKES MY HEAD HURT

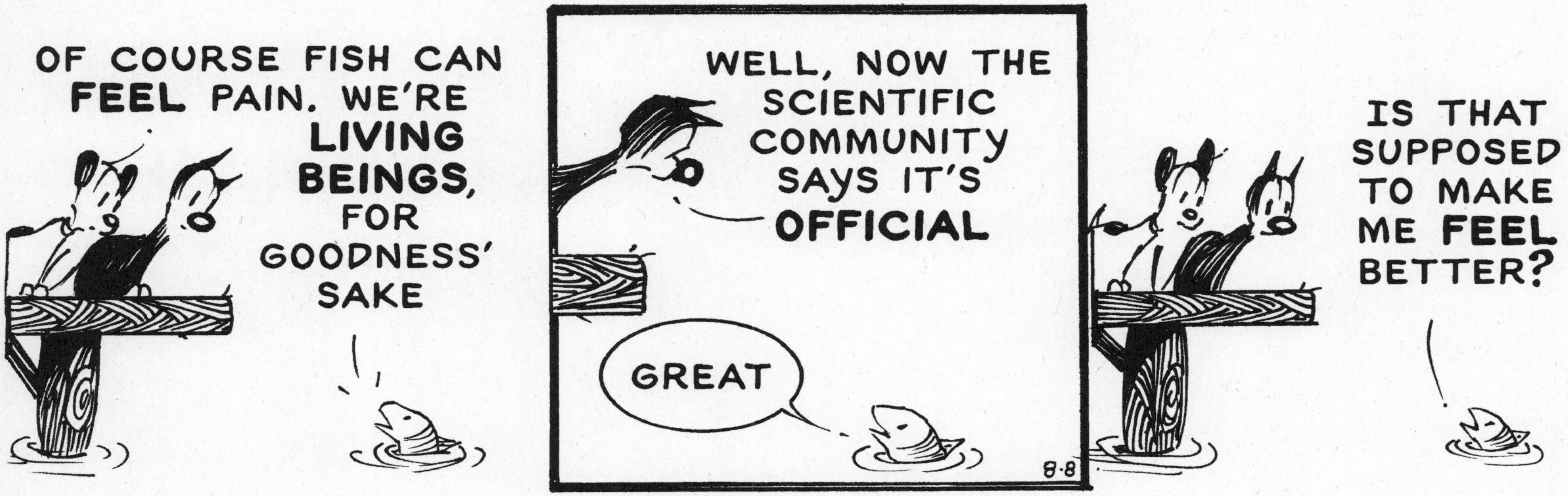
OF COURSE FISH CAN FEEL PAIN. WE'RE LIVING BEINGS, FOR GOODNESS' SAKE
WELL, NOW THE SCIENTIFIC COMMUNITY SAYS IT'S OFFICIAL
GREAT
IS THAT SUPPOSED TO MAKE ME FEEL BETTER?
8·8

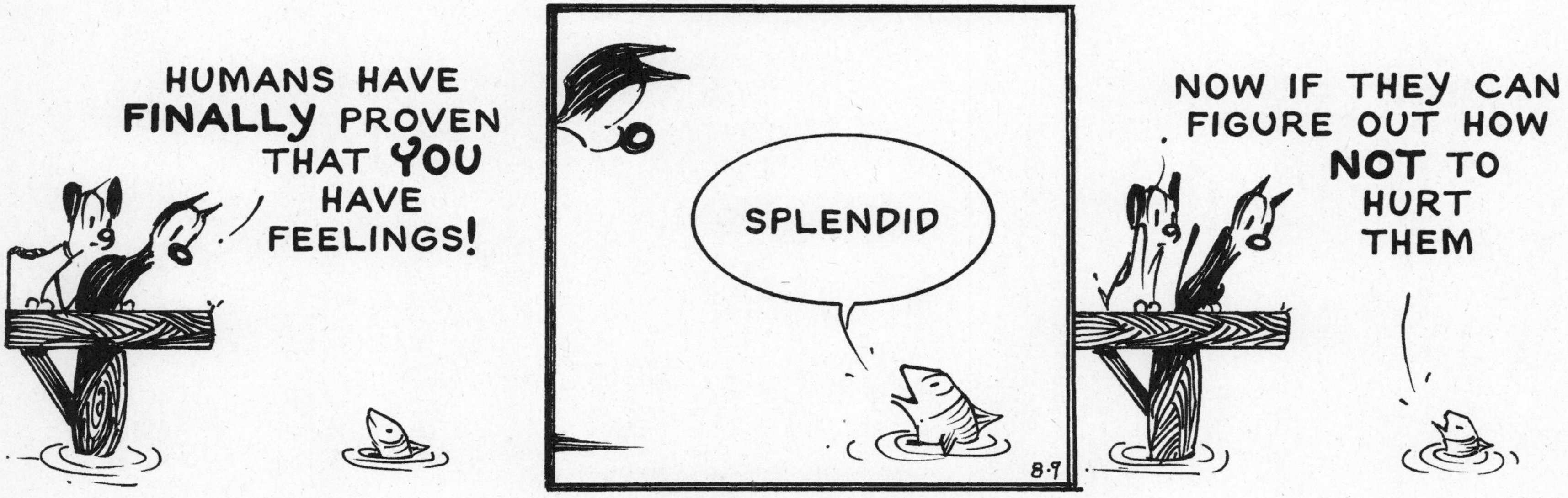
HUMANS HAVE FINALLY PROVEN THAT YOU HAVE FEELINGS!
SPLENDID
NOW IF THEY CAN FIGURE OUT HOW NOT TO HURT THEM
8·9

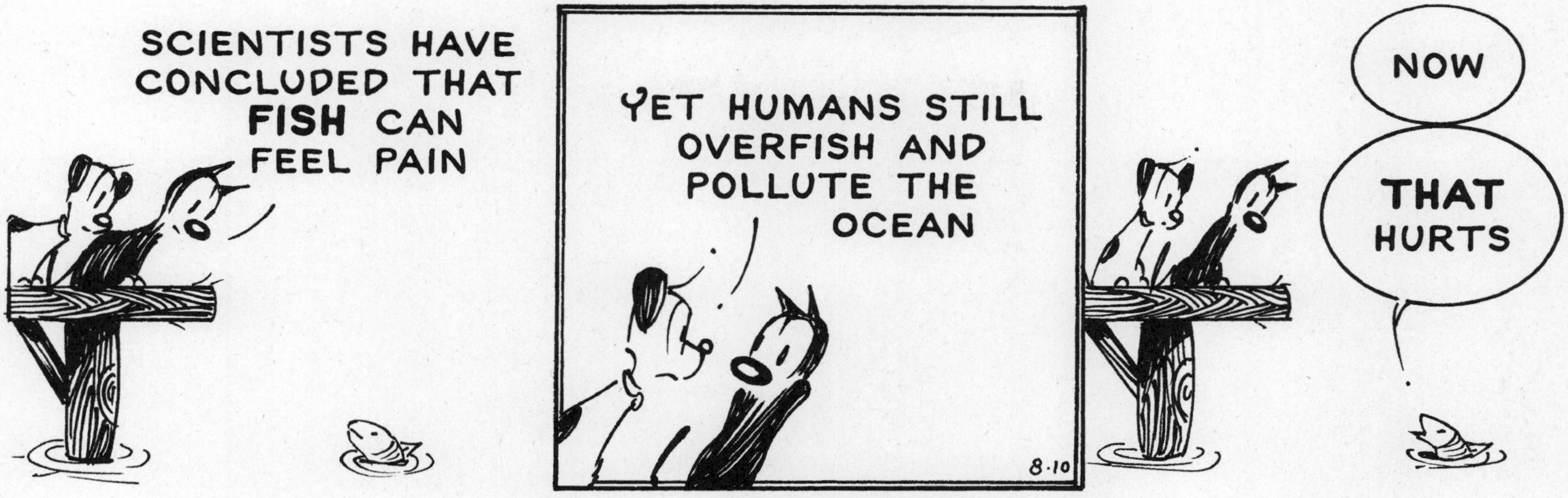
SCIENTISTS HAVE CONCLUDED THAT FISH CAN FEEL PAIN
YET HUMANS STILL OVERFISH AND POLLUTE THE OCEAN
8.10
NOW
THAT HURTS

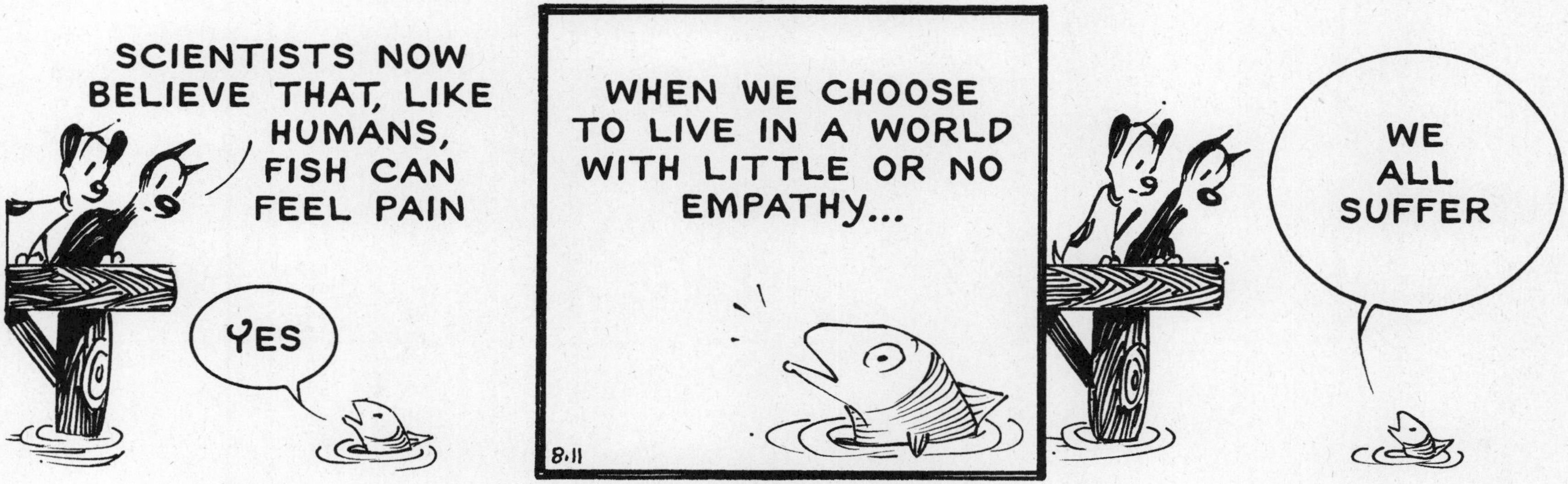
SCIENTISTS NOW BELIEVE THAT, LIKE HUMANS, FISH CAN FEEL PAIN
YES
WHEN WE CHOOSE TO LIVE IN A WORLD WITH LITTLE OR NO EMPATHY...
8.11
WE ALL SUFFER

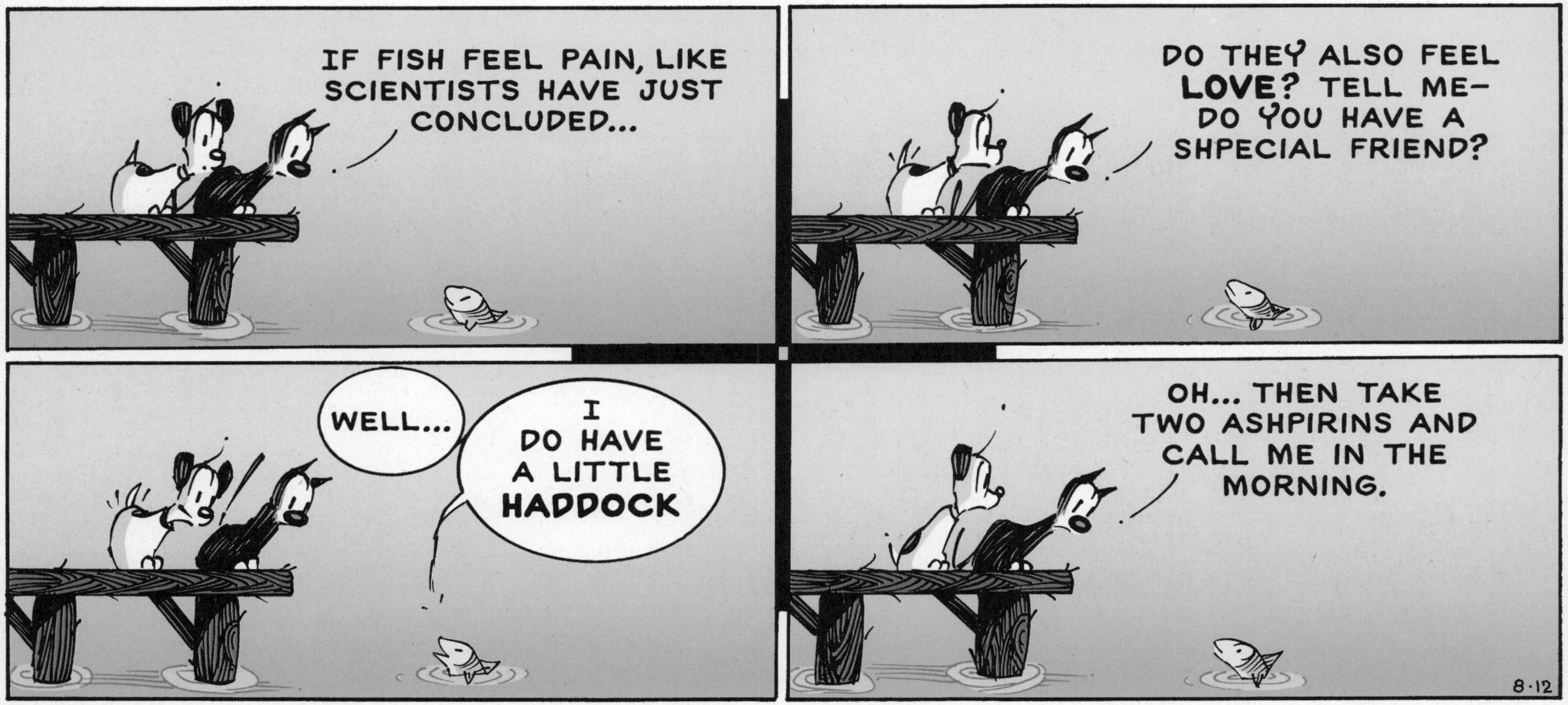
IF FISH FEEL PAIN, LIKE SCIENTISTS HAVE JUST CONCLUDED...
DO THEY ALSO FEEL LOVE? TELL ME– DO YOU HAVE A SHPECIAL FRIEND?
WELL...
I DO HAVE A LITTLE HADDOCK
OH... THEN TAKE TWO ASHPIRINS AND CALL ME IN THE MORNING.
8·12

. . . it is easier to do nothing
by the sea than anywhere else . . .

~ E.F. Benson

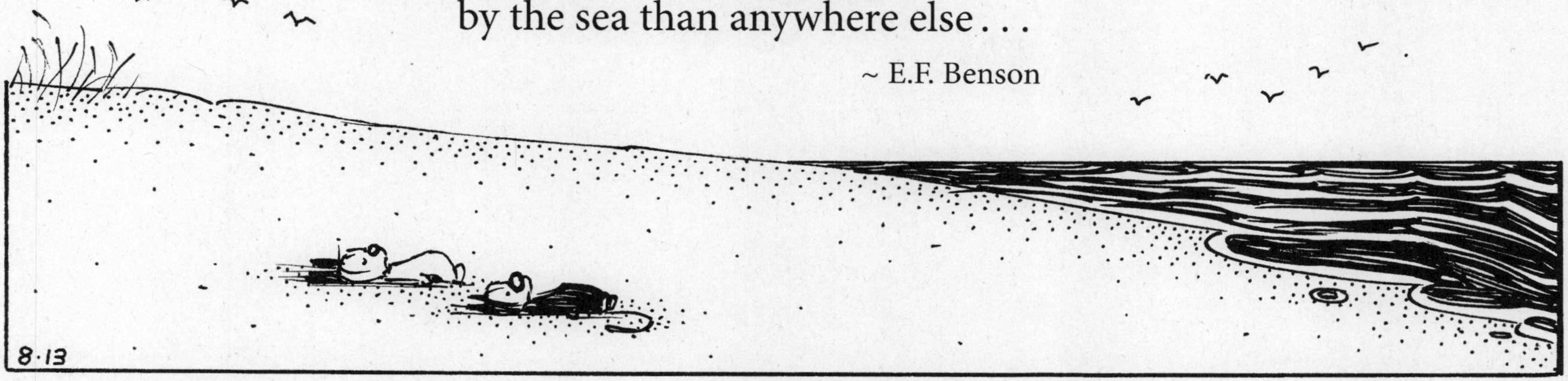
8·13

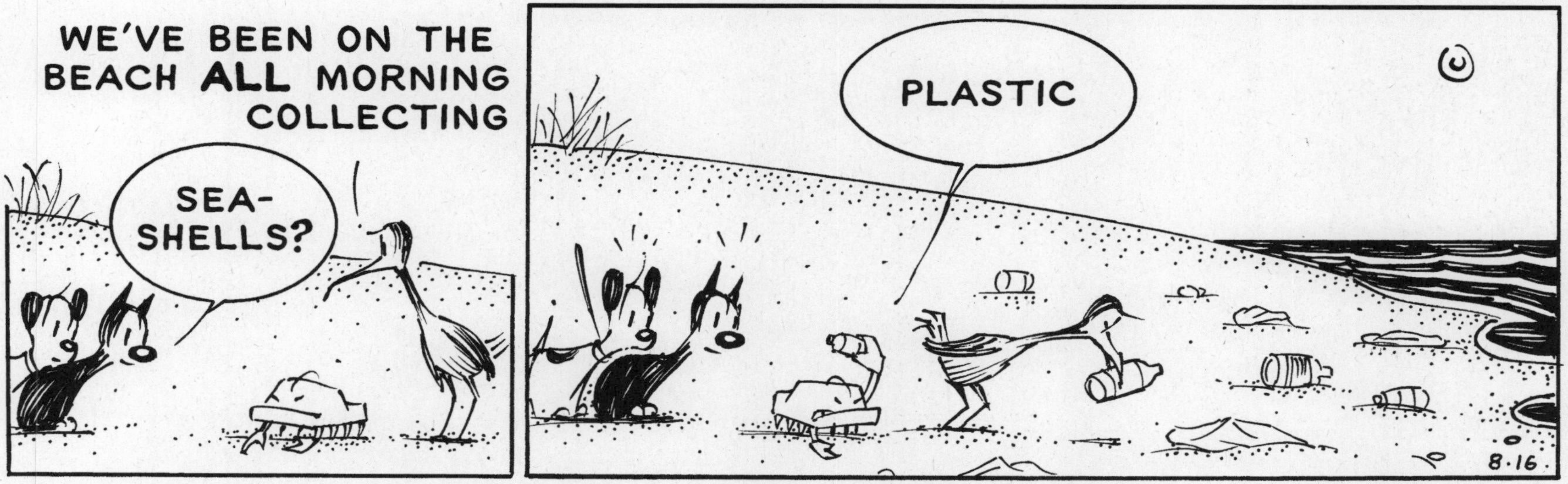
WE'VE BEEN ON THE BEACH ALL MORNING COLLECTING
SEA-SHELLS?
PLASTIC
8·16

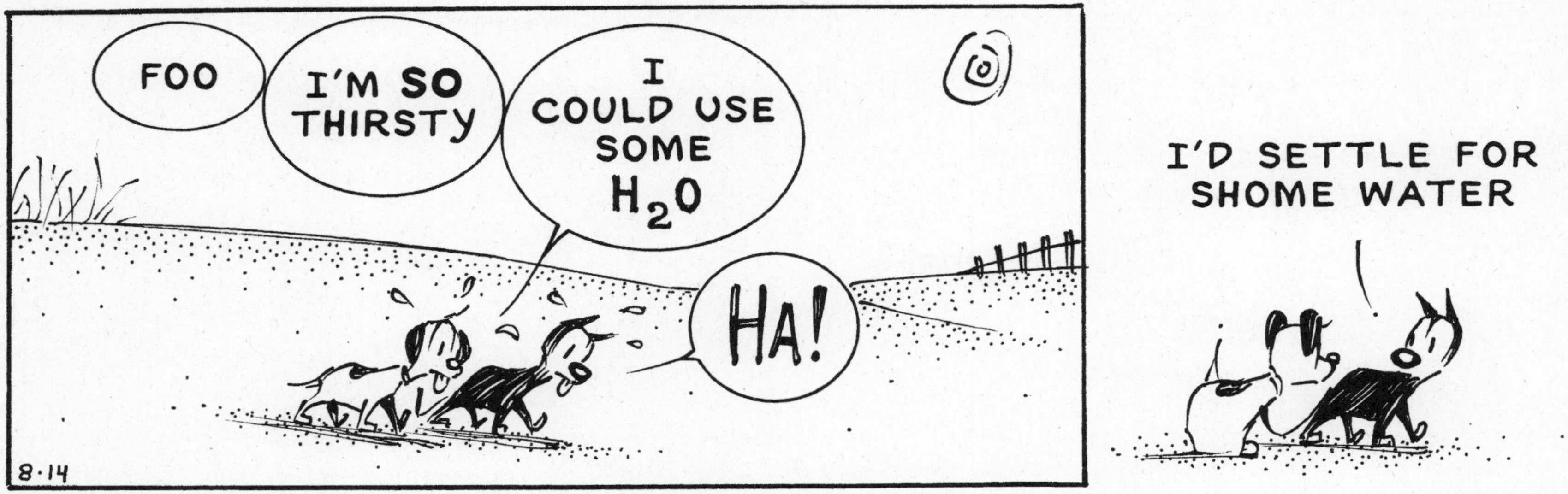
FOO
I'M SO THIRSTY
I COULD USE SOME H_2O
HA!
I'D SETTLE FOR SHOME WATER
8·14

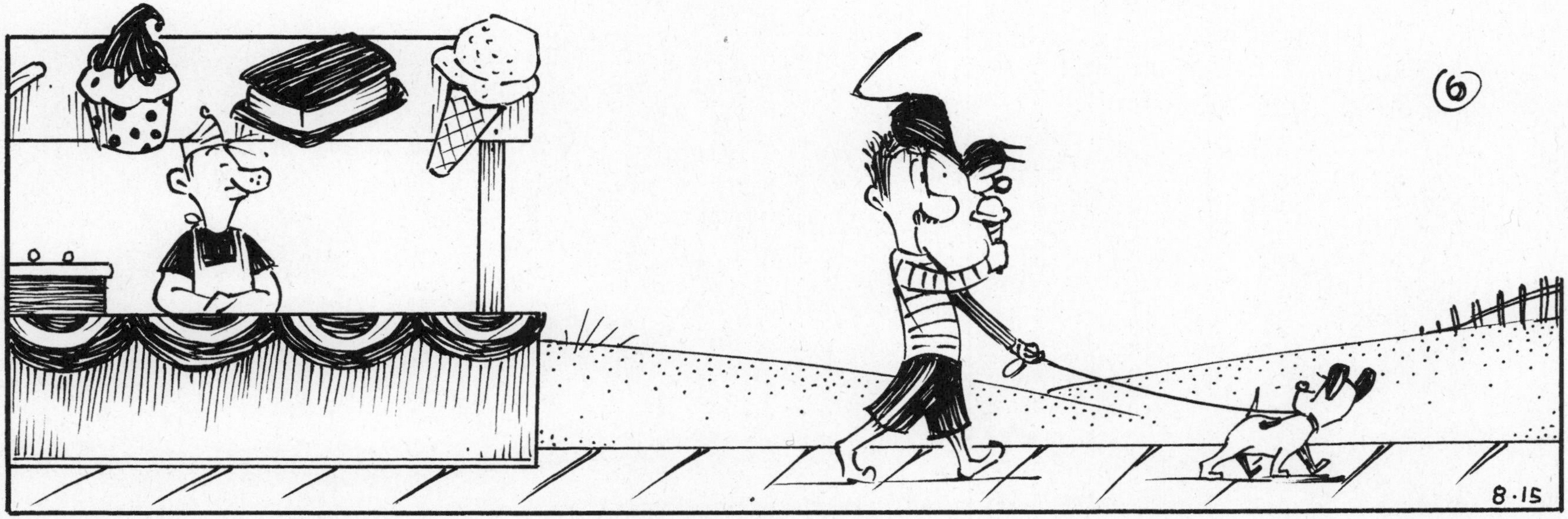
8·15

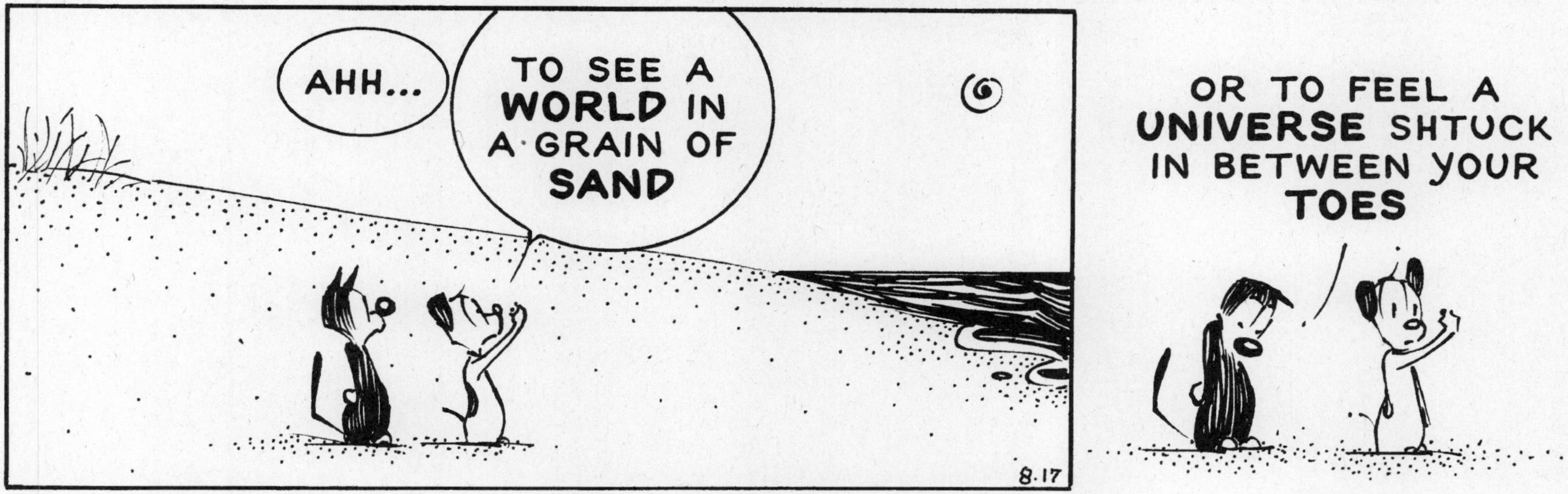
AHH...
TO SEE A WORLD IN A GRAIN OF SAND
OR TO FEEL A UNIVERSE SHTUCK IN BETWEEN YOUR TOES
8.17

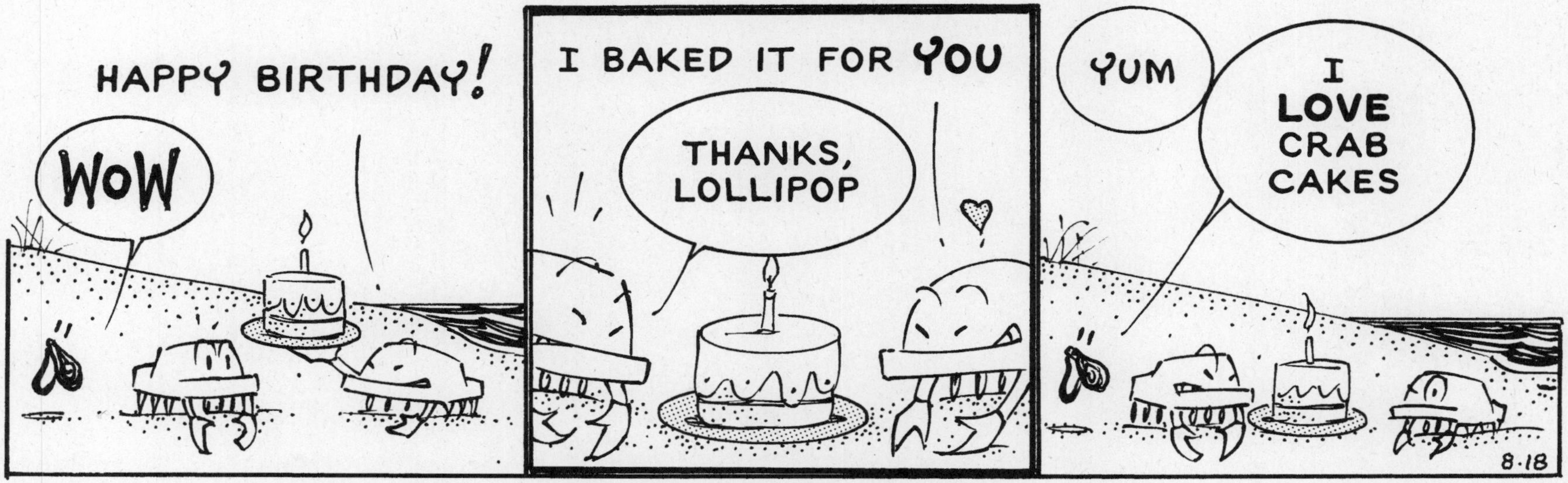
HAPPY BIRTHDAY!
WOW
I BAKED IT FOR YOU
THANKS, LOLLIPOP
YUM
I LOVE CRAB CAKES
8.18

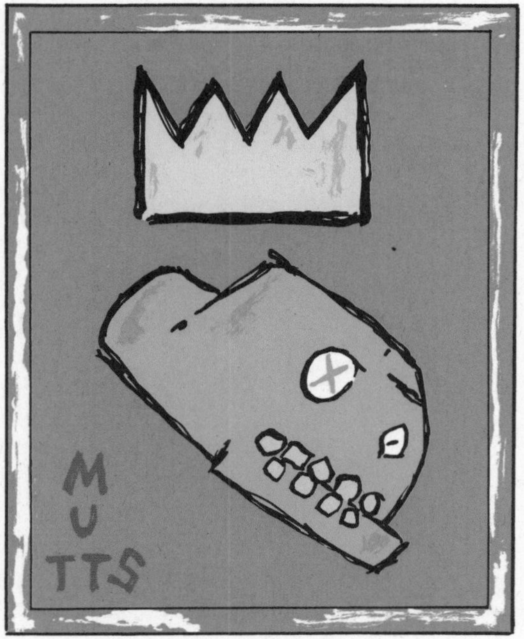
MUTTS

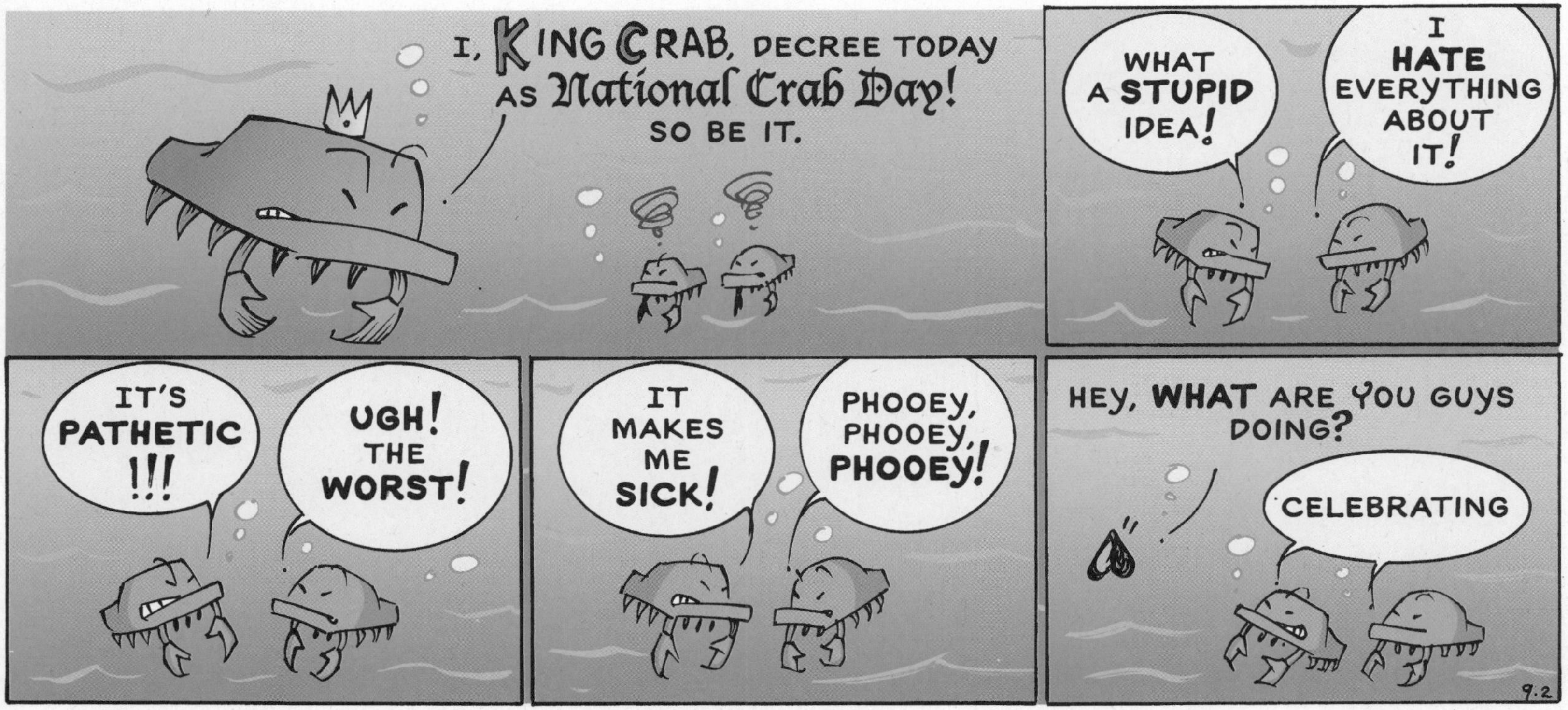
I, KING CRAB, DECREE TODAY AS National Crab Day! SO BE IT.
WHAT A STUPID IDEA!
I HATE EVERYTHING ABOUT IT!
IT'S PATHETIC !!!
UGH! THE WORST!
IT MAKES ME SICK!
PHOOEY, PHOOEY, PHOOEY!
HEY, WHAT ARE YOU GUYS DOING?
CELEBRATING
9.2

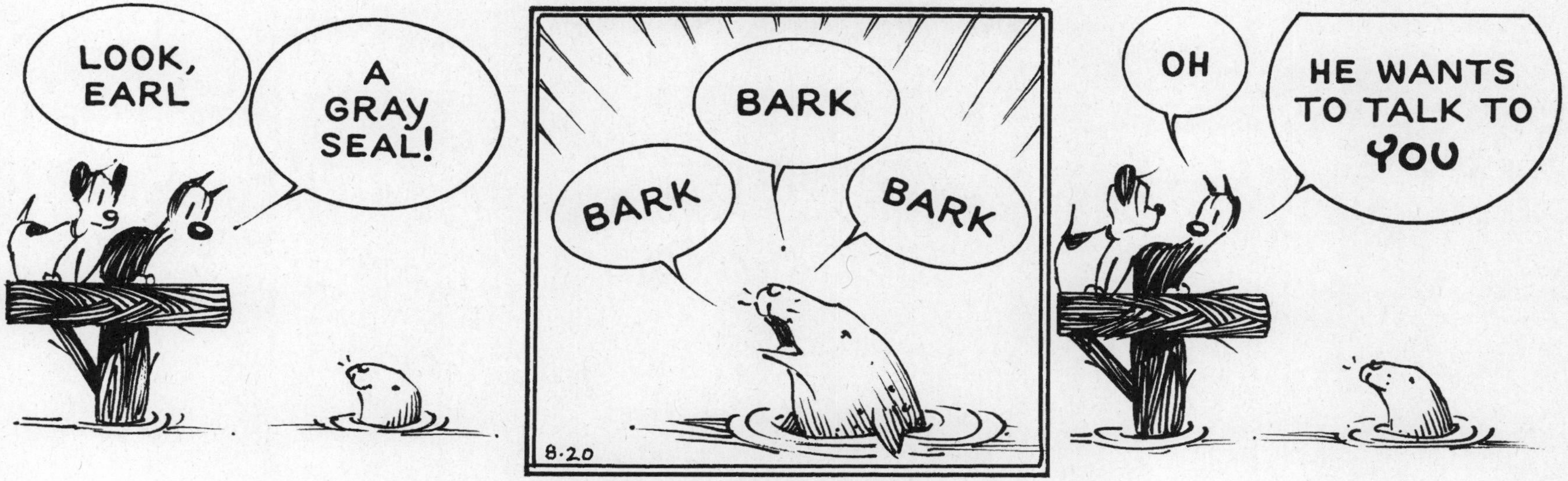
LOOK, EARL
A GRAY SEAL!
BARK
BARK
BARK
8·20
OH
HE WANTS TO TALK TO YOU

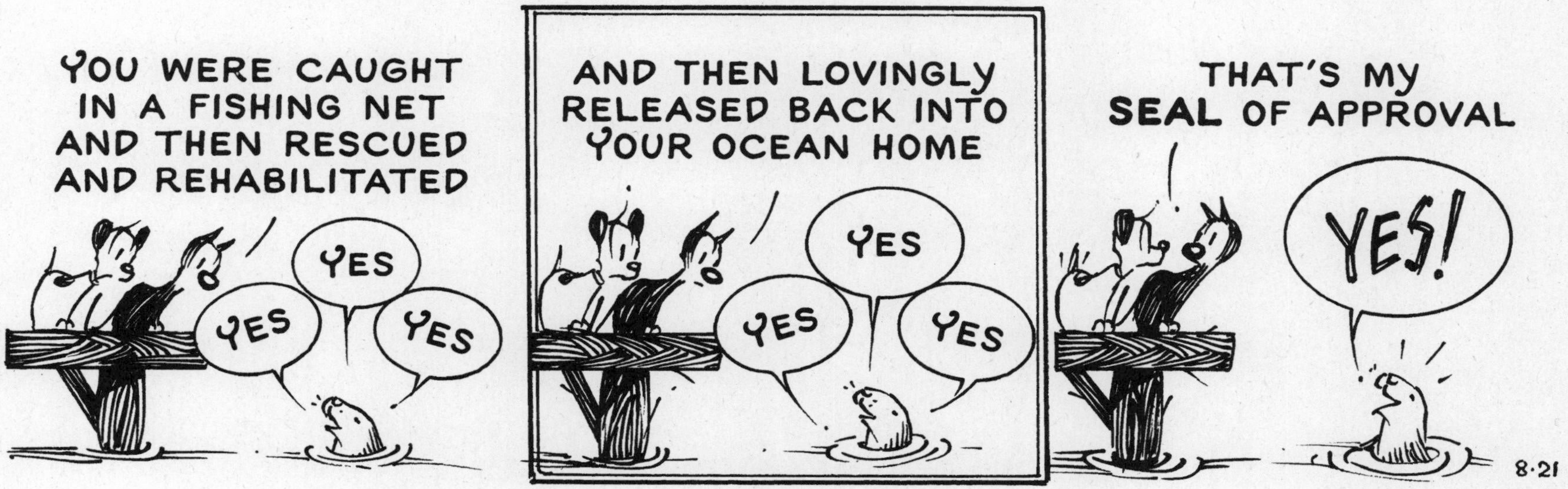
YOU WERE CAUGHT IN A FISHING NET AND THEN RESCUED AND REHABILITATED
YES
YES
YES
AND THEN LOVINGLY RELEASED BACK INTO YOUR OCEAN HOME
YES
YES
YES
THAT'S MY SEAL OF APPROVAL
YES!
8·21

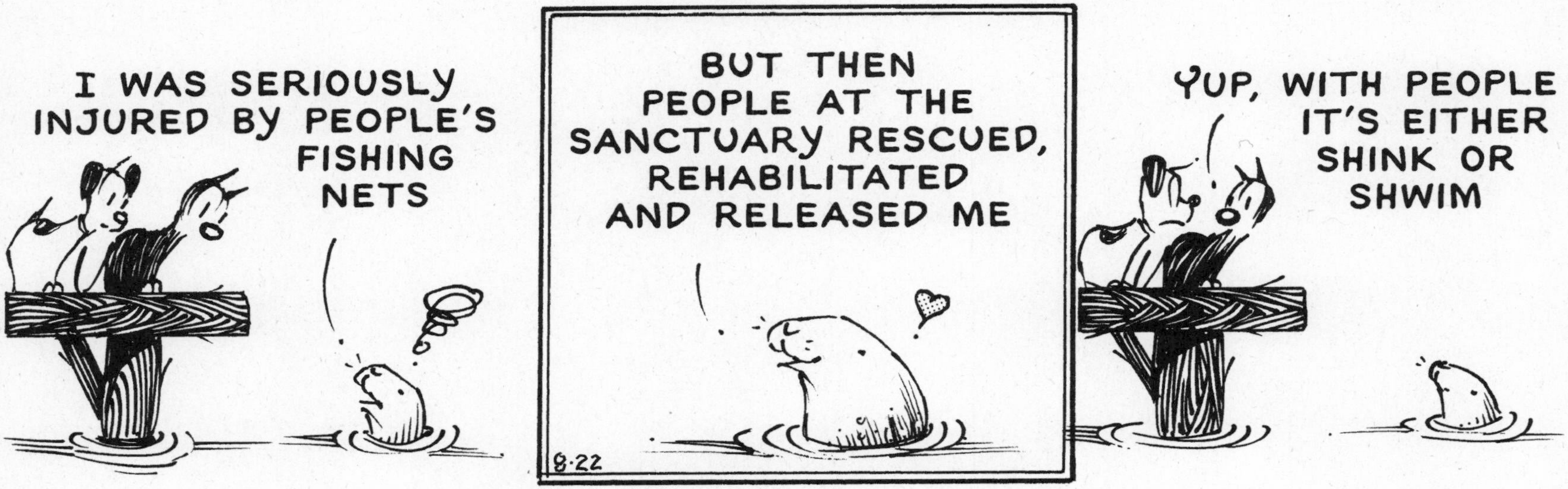
I WAS SERIOUSLY INJURED BY PEOPLE'S FISHING NETS
BUT THEN PEOPLE AT THE SANCTUARY RESCUED, REHABILITATED AND RELEASED ME
YUP, WITH PEOPLE IT'S EITHER SHINK OR SHWIM
8·22

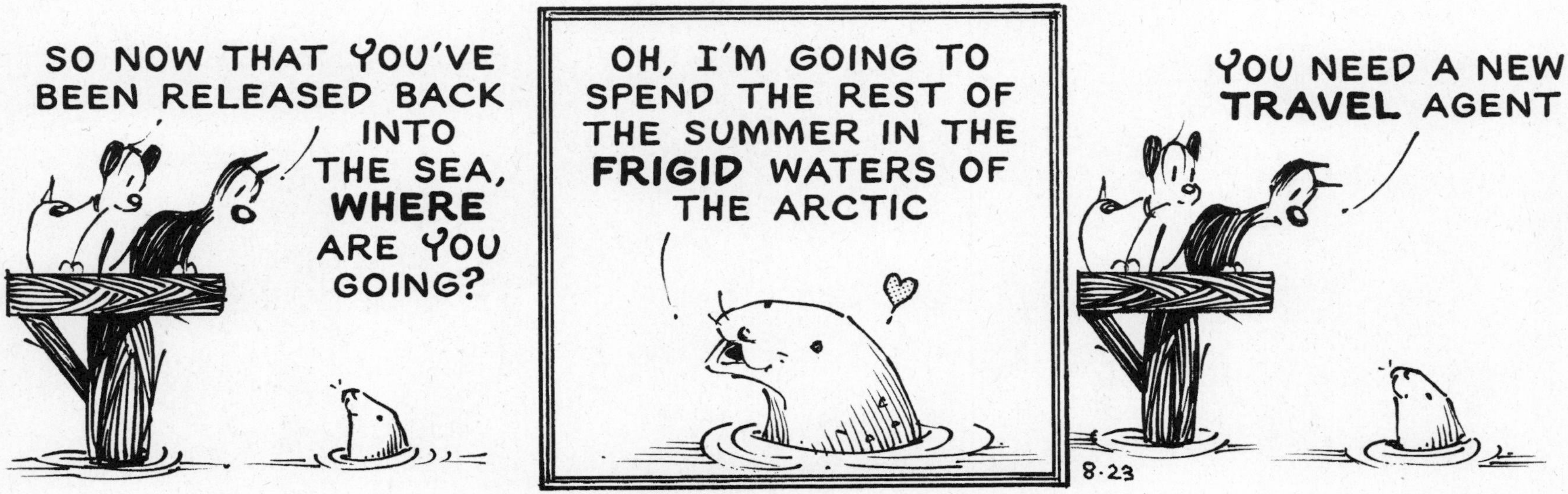
SO NOW THAT YOU'VE BEEN RELEASED BACK INTO THE SEA, **WHERE** ARE YOU GOING?
OH, I'M GOING TO SPEND THE REST OF THE SUMMER IN THE **FRIGID** WATERS OF THE ARCTIC
YOU NEED A NEW **TRAVEL** AGENT
8·23

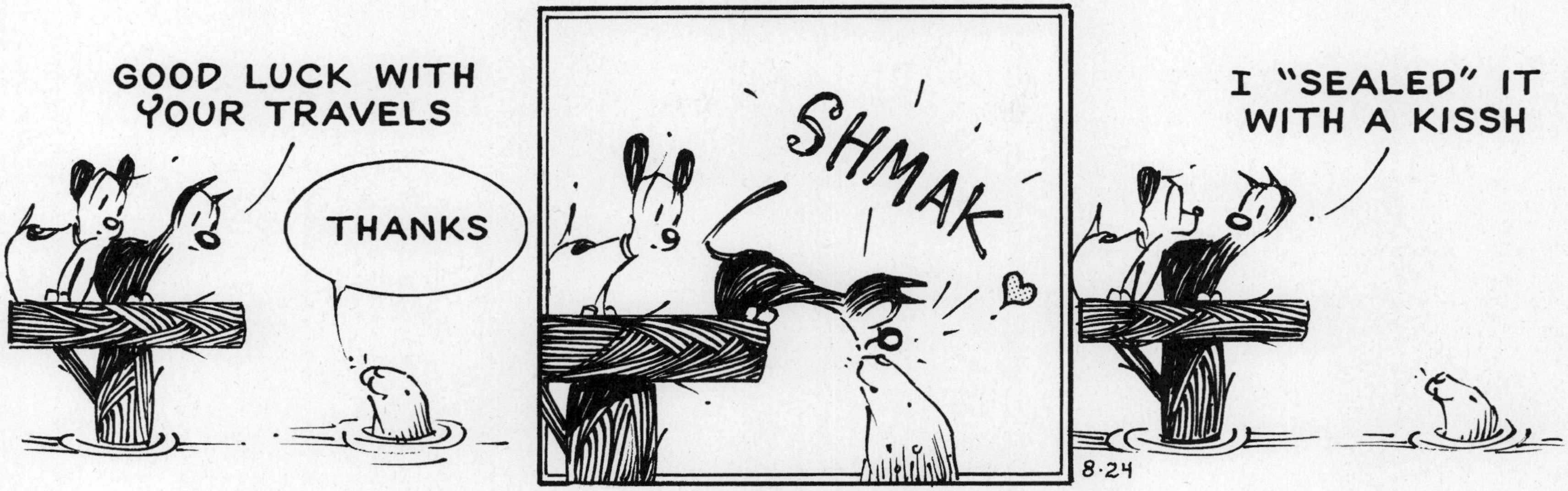
GOOD LUCK WITH YOUR TRAVELS
THANKS
SHMAK
I "SEALED" IT WITH A KISSH
8·24

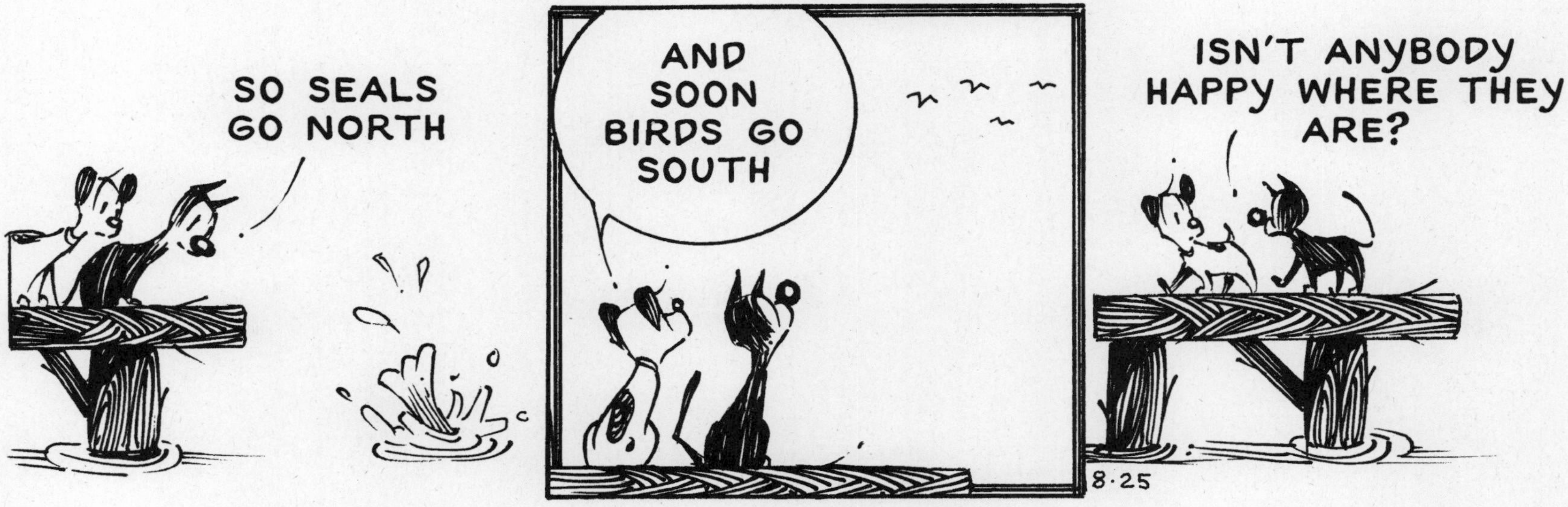
SO SEALS GO NORTH
AND SOON BIRDS GO SOUTH
ISN'T ANYBODY HAPPY WHERE THEY ARE?
8·25

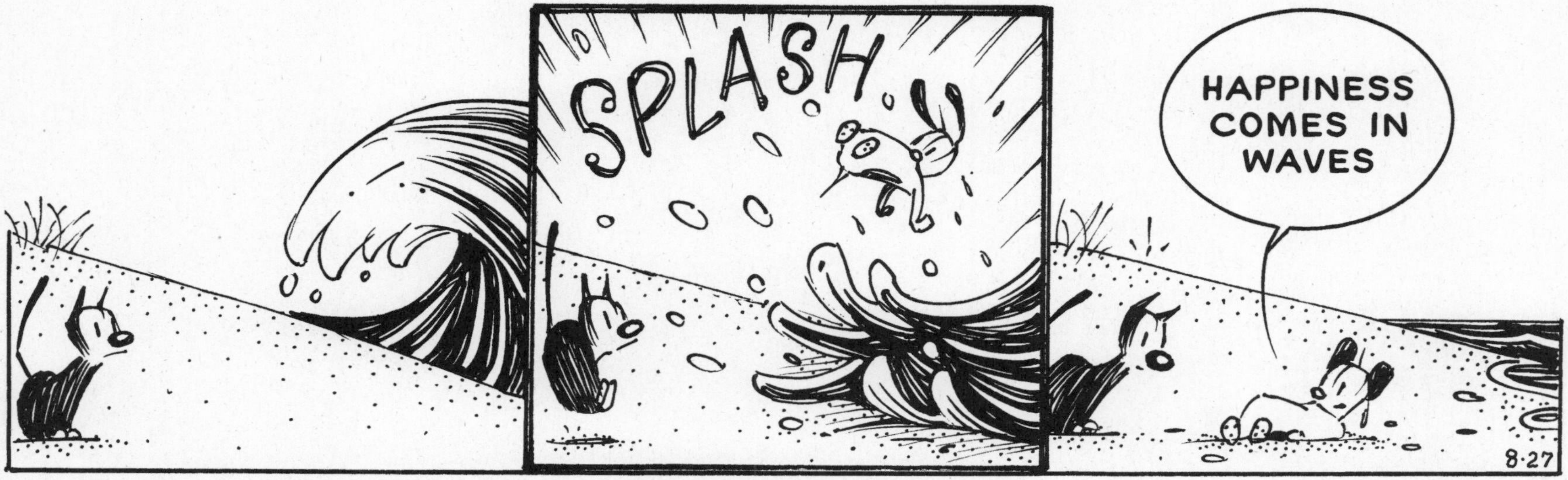
SPLASH
HAPPINESS COMES IN WAVES
8·27

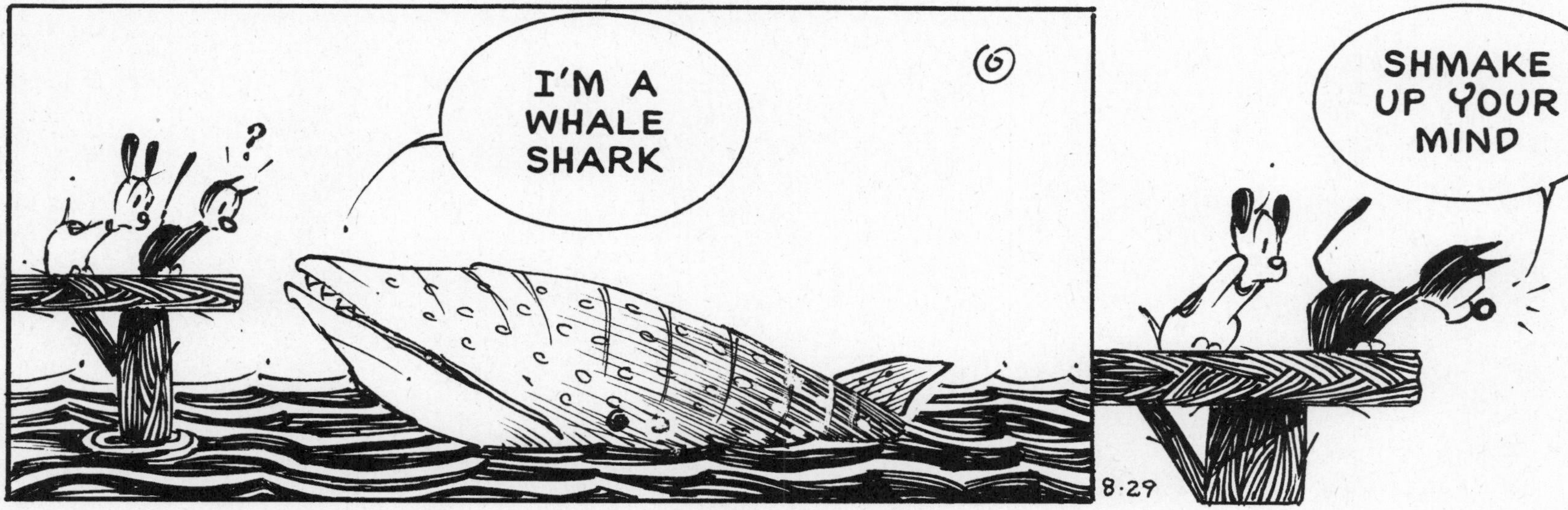
I'M A WHALE SHARK
SHMAKE UP YOUR MIND
8·29

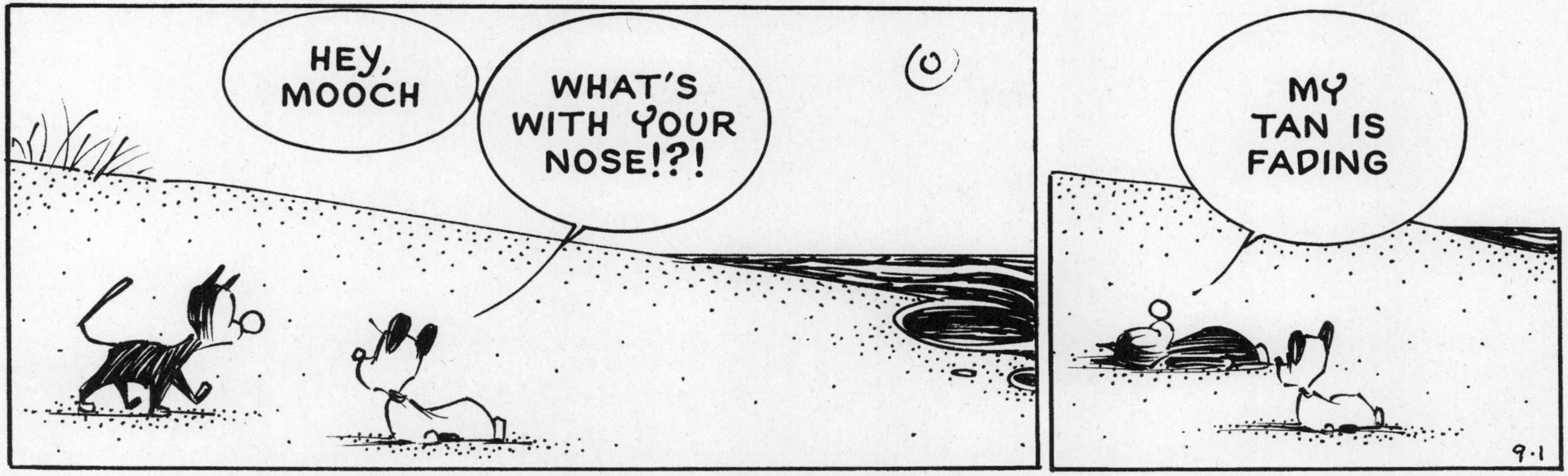
HEY, MOOCH
WHAT'S WITH YOUR NOSE!?!
MY TAN IS FADING
9·1

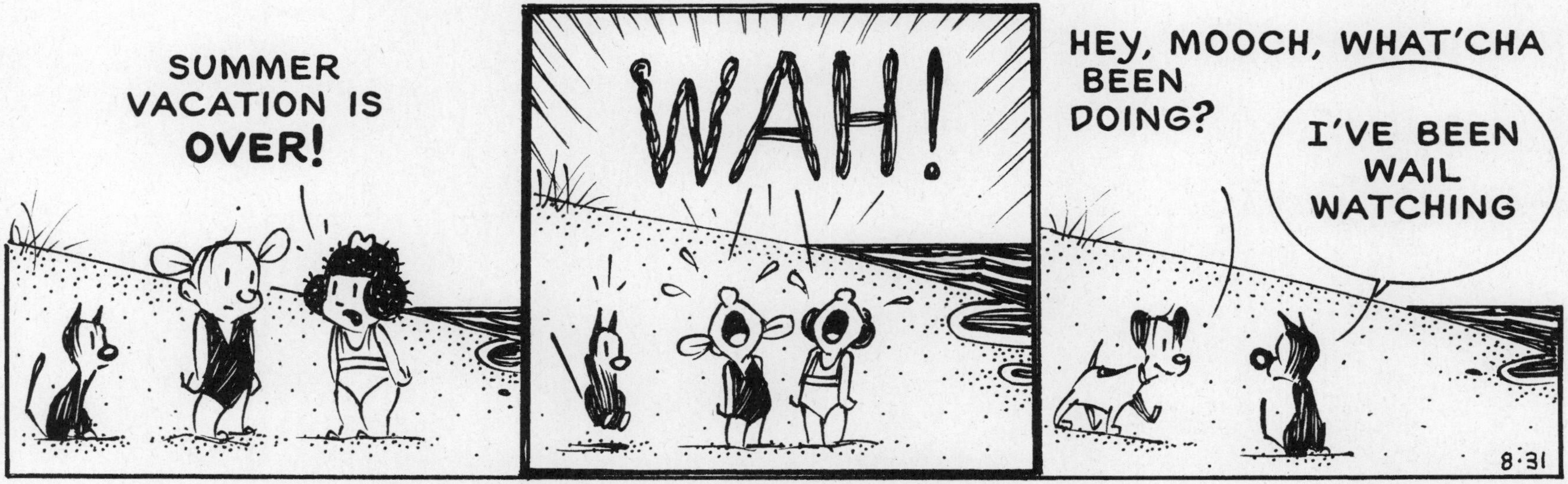
SUMMER VACATION IS OVER!
WAH!
HEY, MOOCH, WHAT'CHA BEEN DOING?
I'VE BEEN WAIL WATCHING
8·31

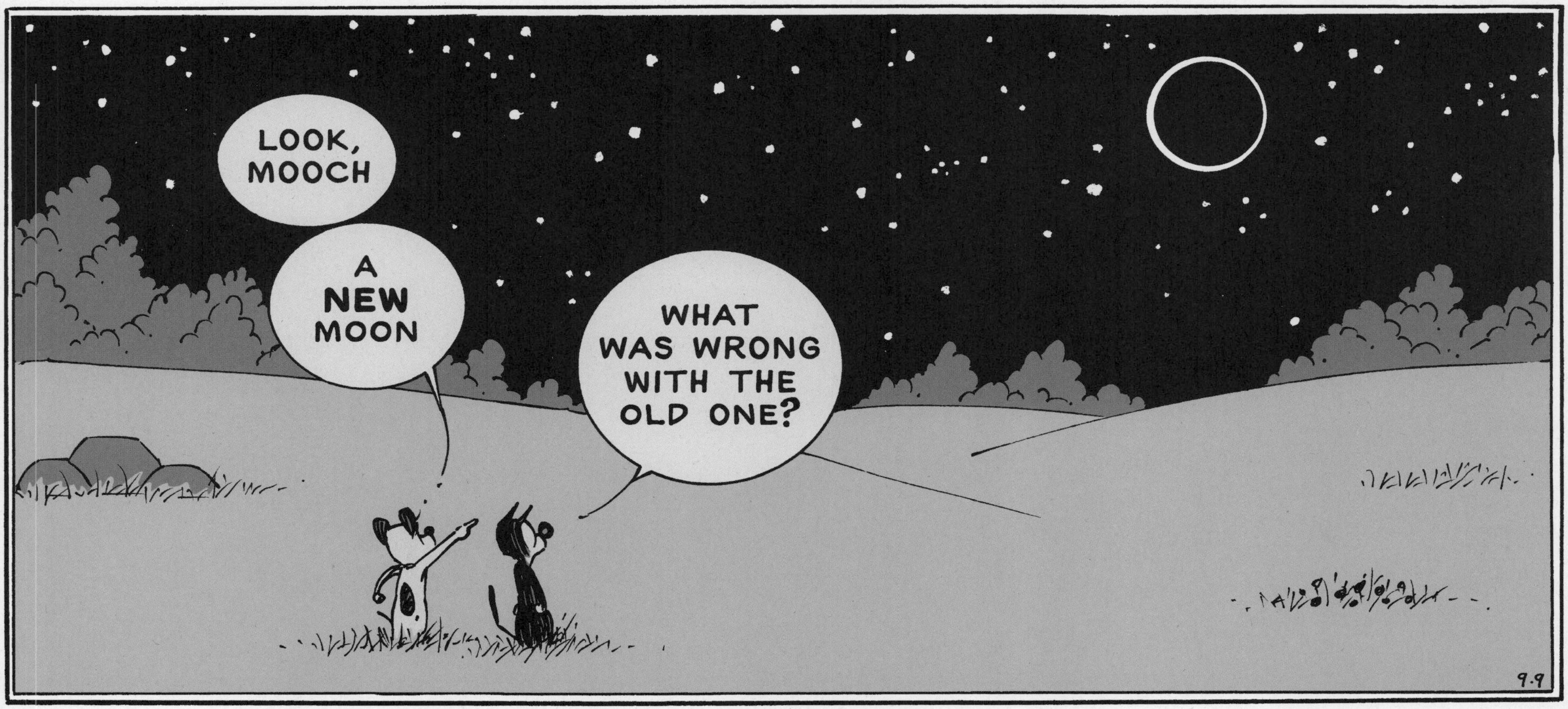
LOOK, MOOCH
A NEW MOON
WHAT WAS WRONG WITH THE OLD ONE?
9.9

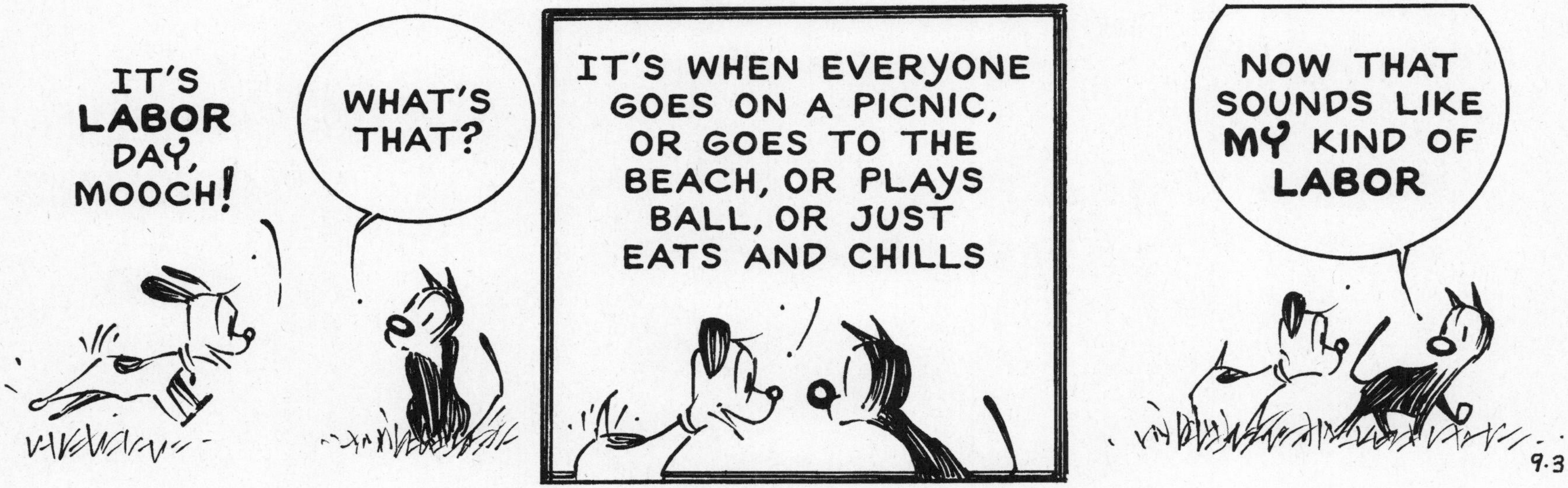
IT'S LABOR DAY, MOOCH!
WHAT'S THAT?
IT'S WHEN EVERYONE GOES ON A PICNIC, OR GOES TO THE BEACH, OR PLAYS BALL, OR JUST EATS AND CHILLS
NOW THAT SOUNDS LIKE MY KIND OF LABOR
9.3

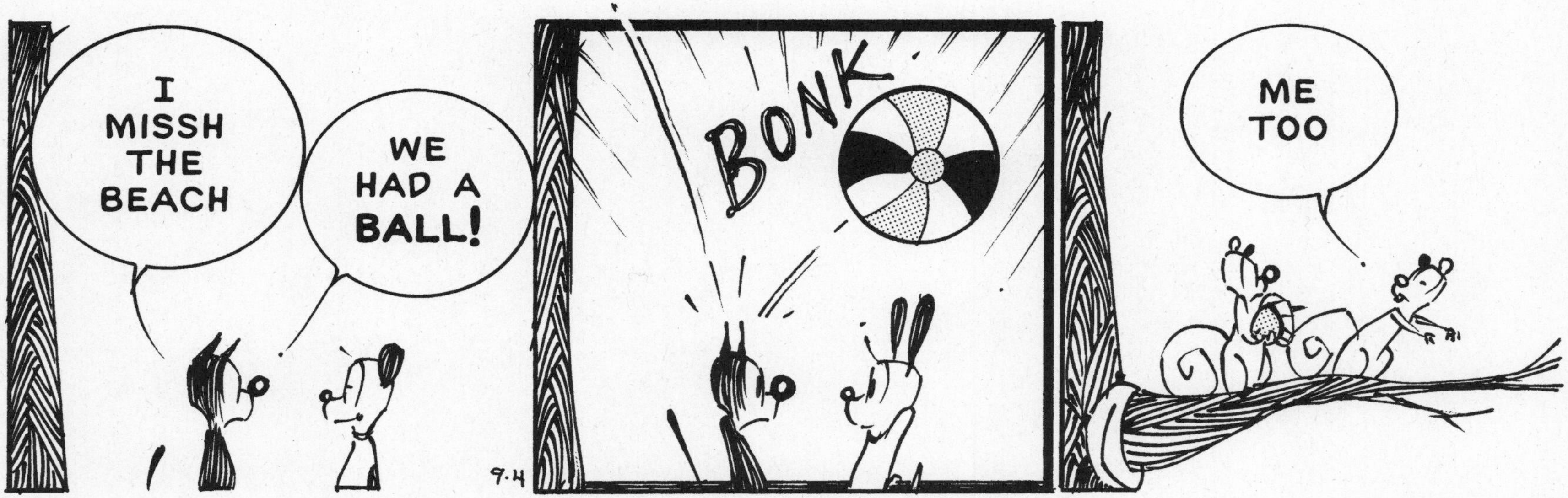
I MISSH THE BEACH
WE HAD A BALL!
9.4
BONK
ME TOO

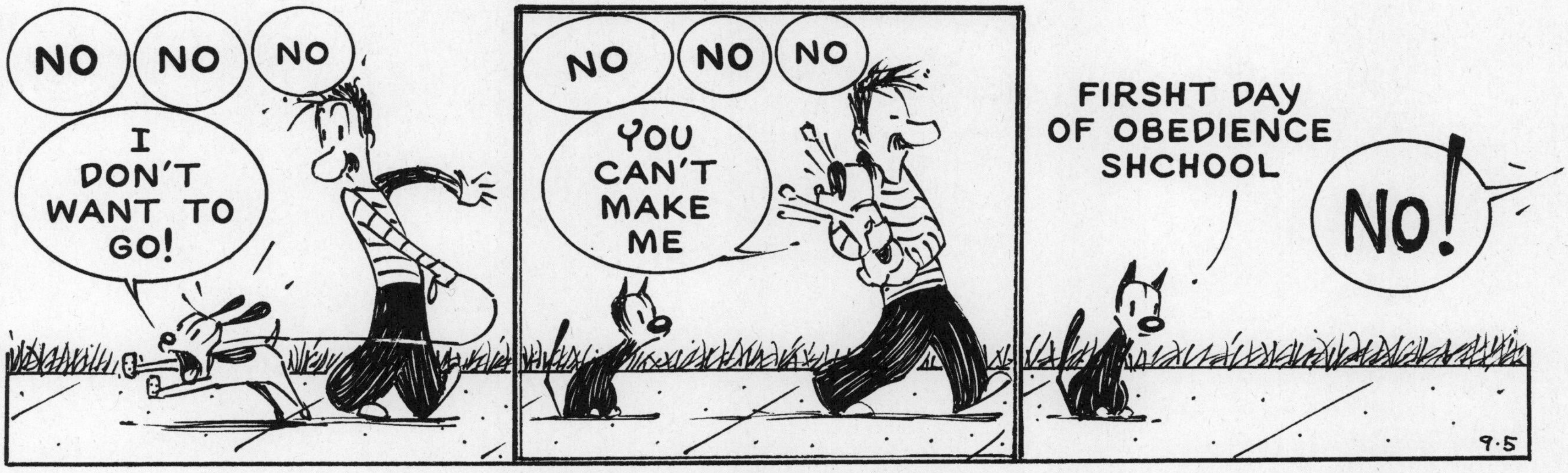
NO
NO
NO
I DON'T WANT TO GO!
NO
NO
NO
YOU CAN'T MAKE ME
FIRSHT DAY OF OBEDIENCE SHCHOOL
NO!
9·5

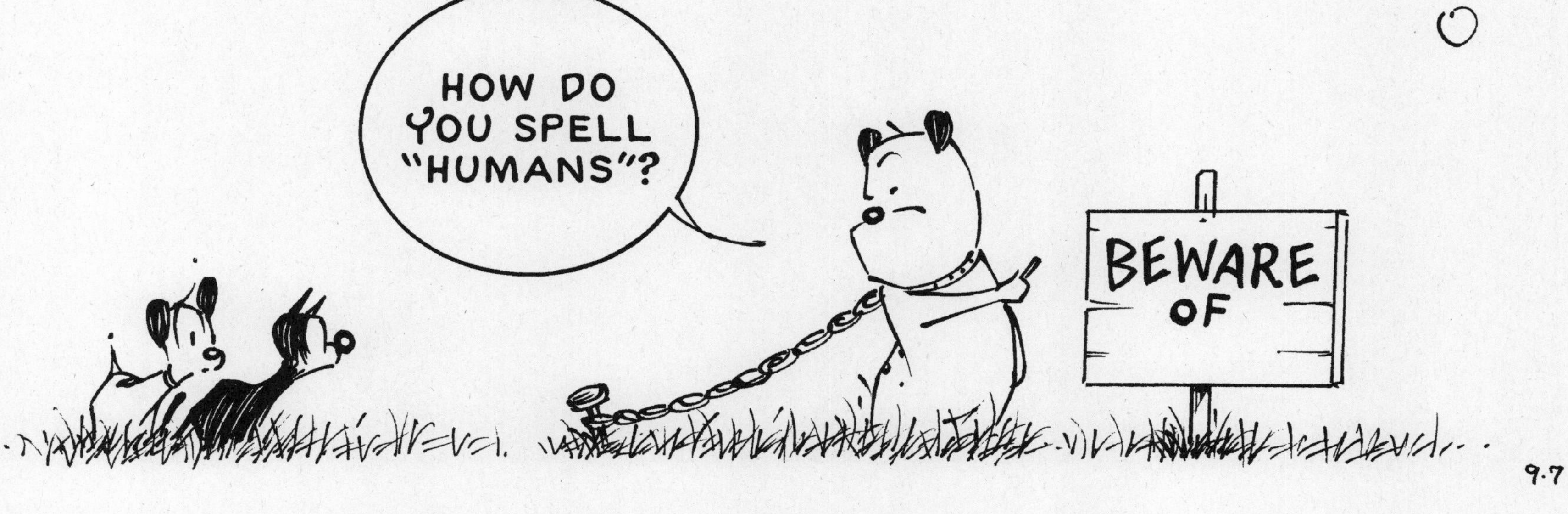
HOW DO YOU SPELL "HUMANS"?
BEWARE OF
9·7

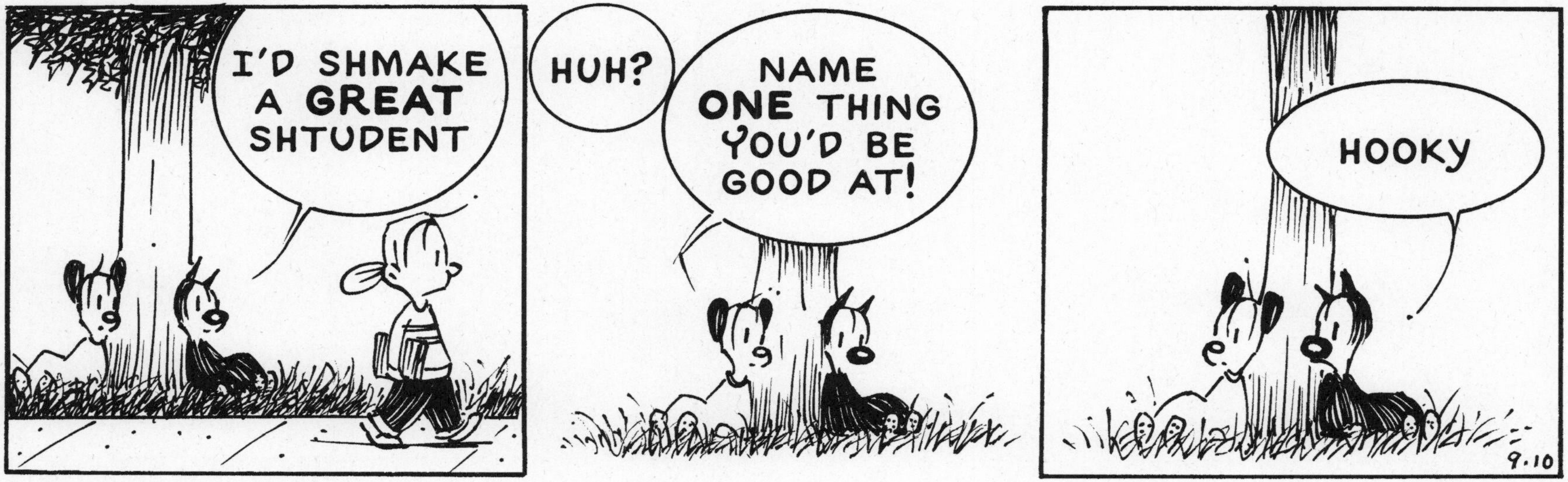
I'D SHMAKE A GREAT SHTUDENT
HUH?
NAME ONE THING YOU'D BE GOOD AT!
HOOKY
9.10

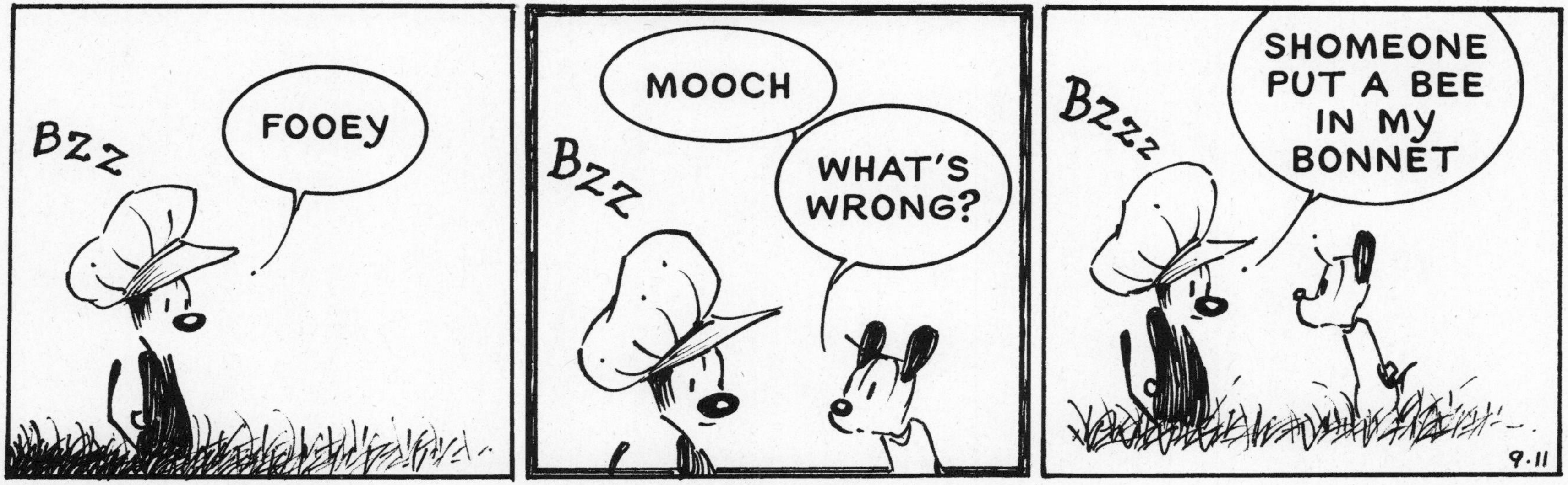
BZZ
FOOEY
MOOCH
BZZ
WHAT'S WRONG?
BZZZZ
SHOMEONE PUT A BEE IN MY BONNET
9.11

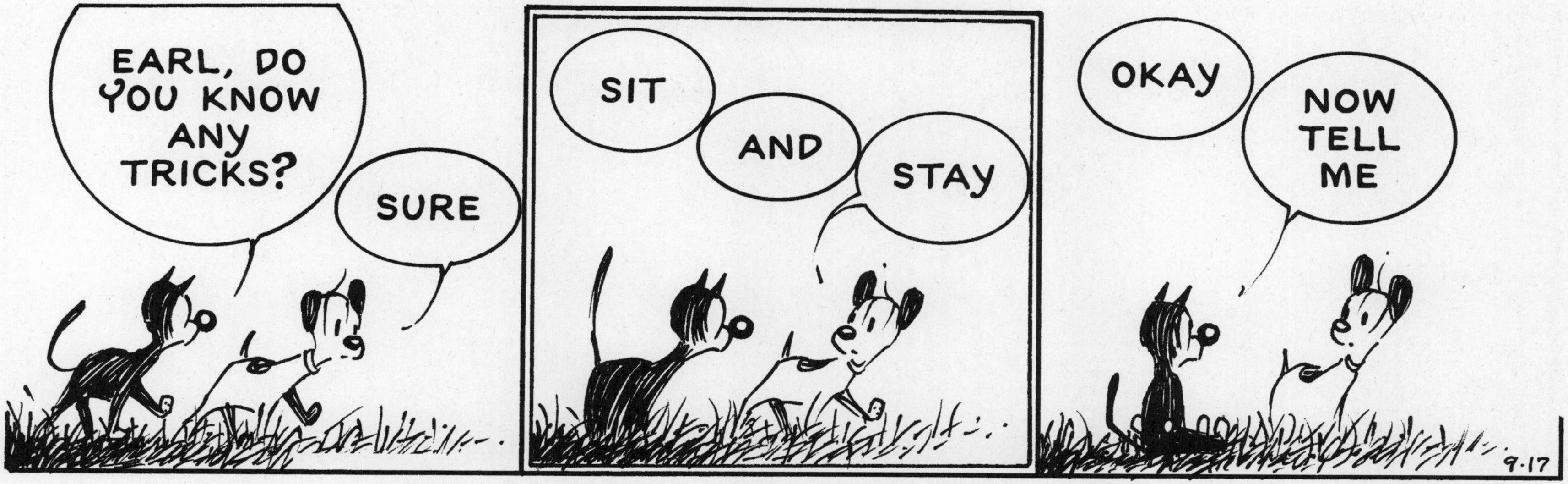
EARL, DO YOU KNOW ANY TRICKS?
SURE
SIT
AND
STAY
OKAY
NOW TELL ME
9·17

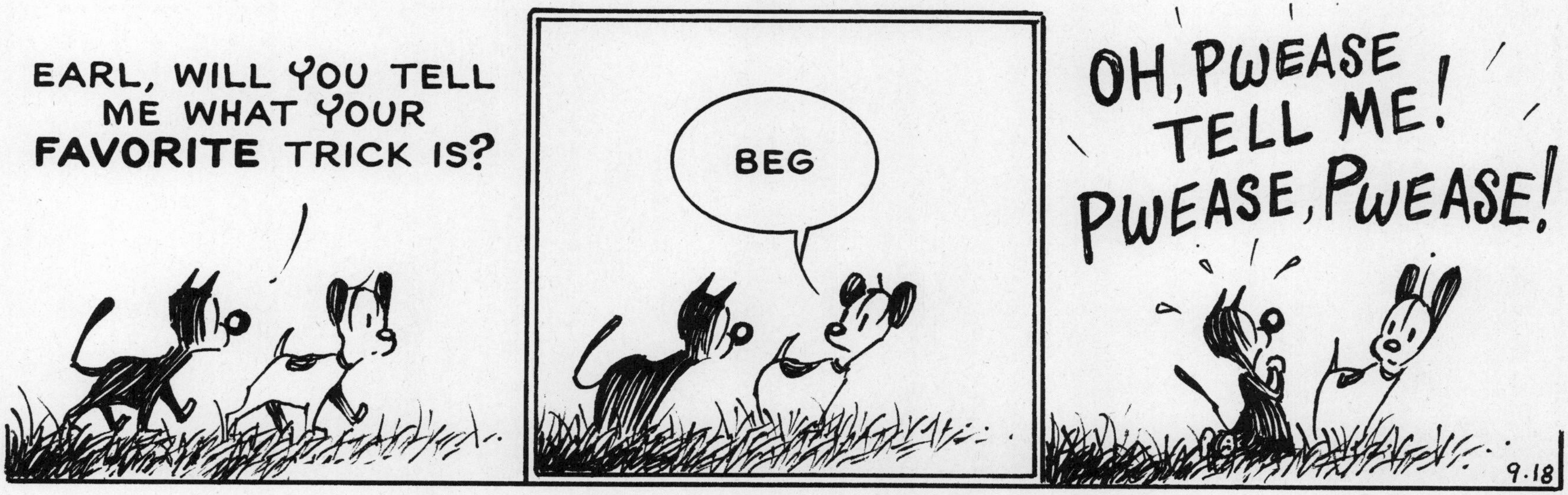
EARL, WILL YOU TELL ME WHAT YOUR FAVORITE TRICK IS?
BEG
OH, PWEASE TELL ME! PWEASE, PWEASE!
9·18

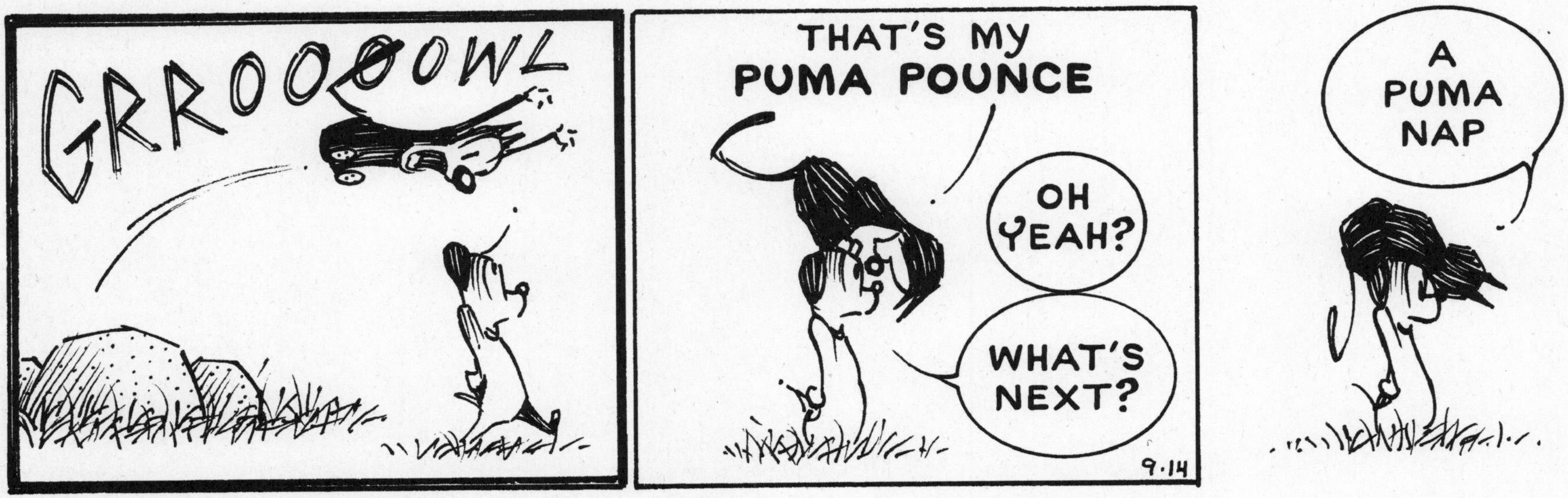
GRROOOOWL
THAT'S MY PUMA POUNCE
OH YEAH?
WHAT'S NEXT?
A PUMA NAP
9.14

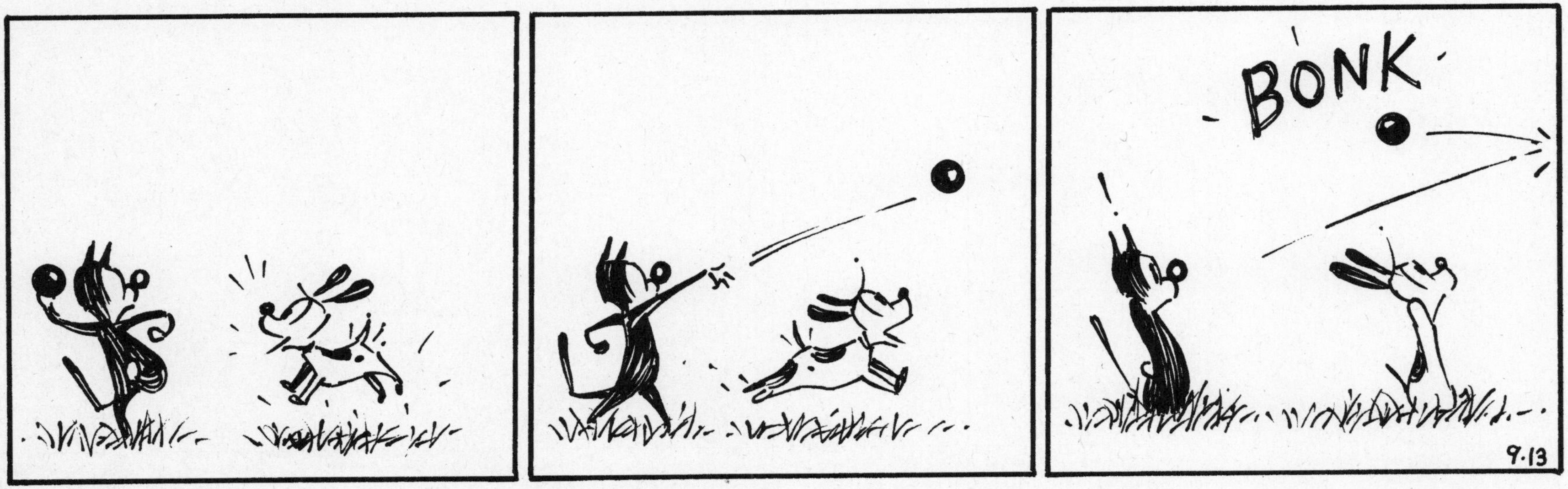
BONK
9.13

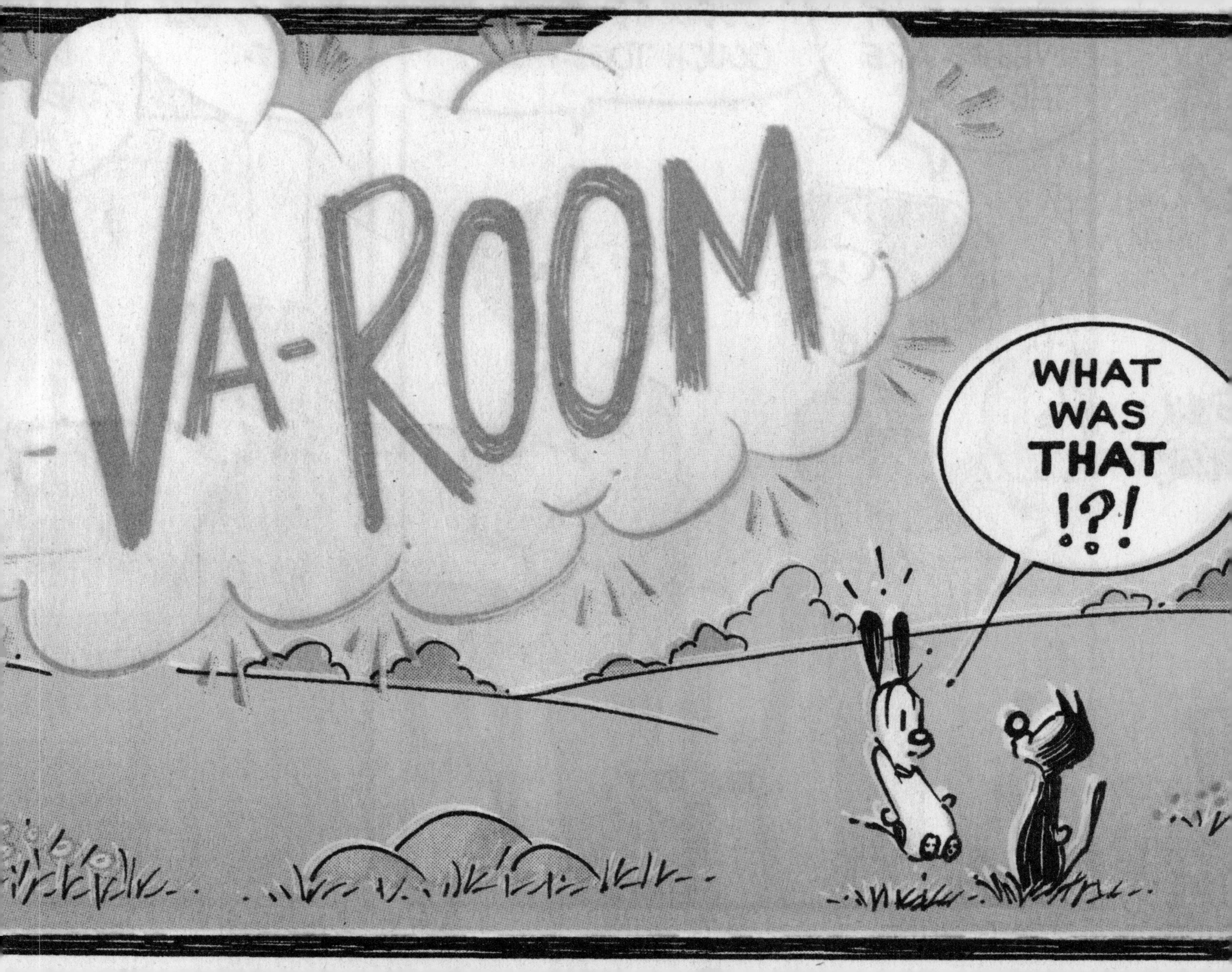
VA-ROOM
WHAT WAS THAT !?!

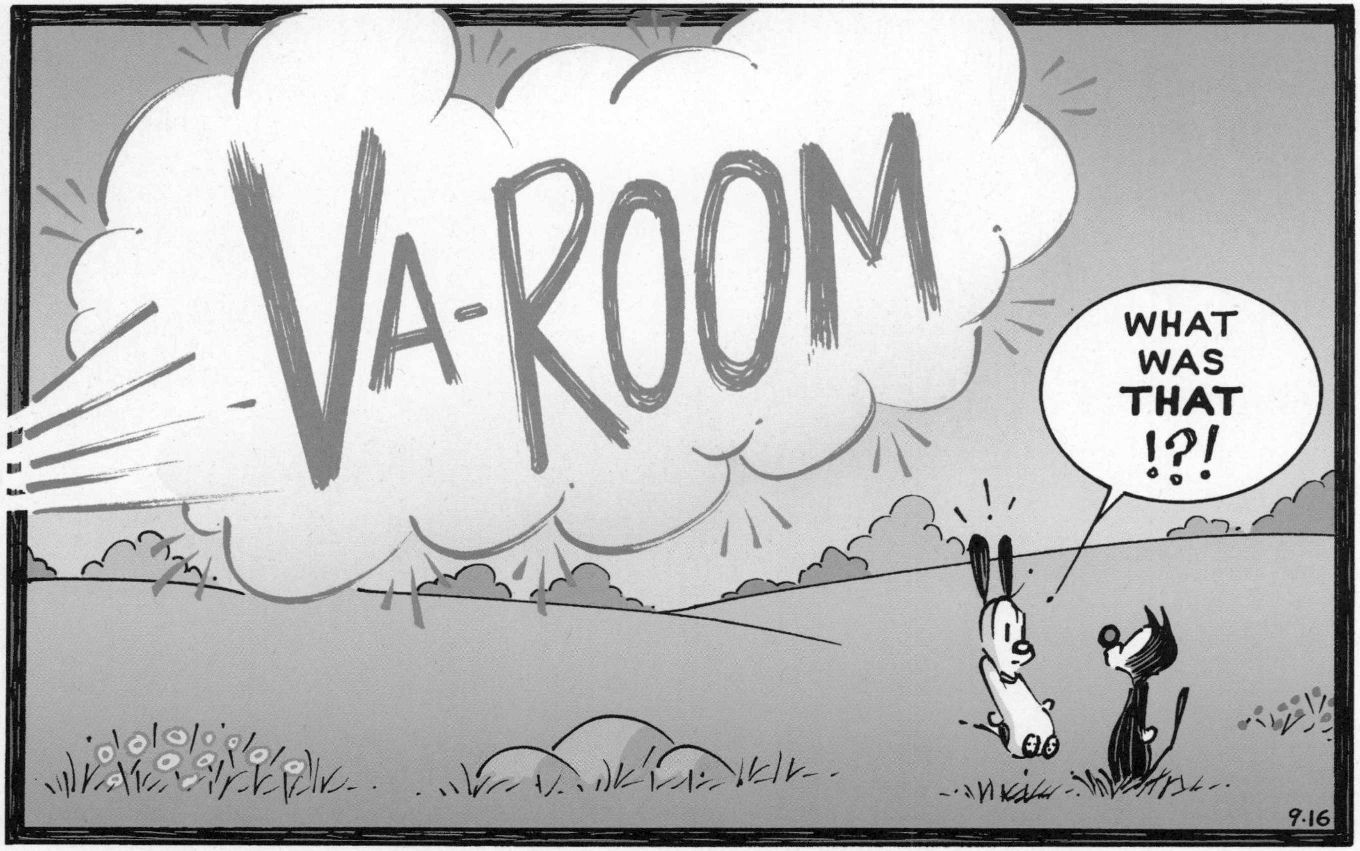
VA-ROOM
WHAT WAS THAT !?!
9.16

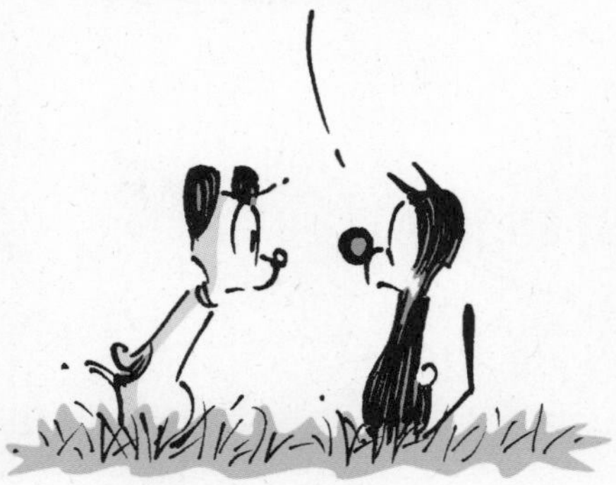
ONOMATOPOEIA

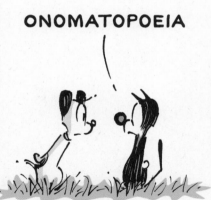

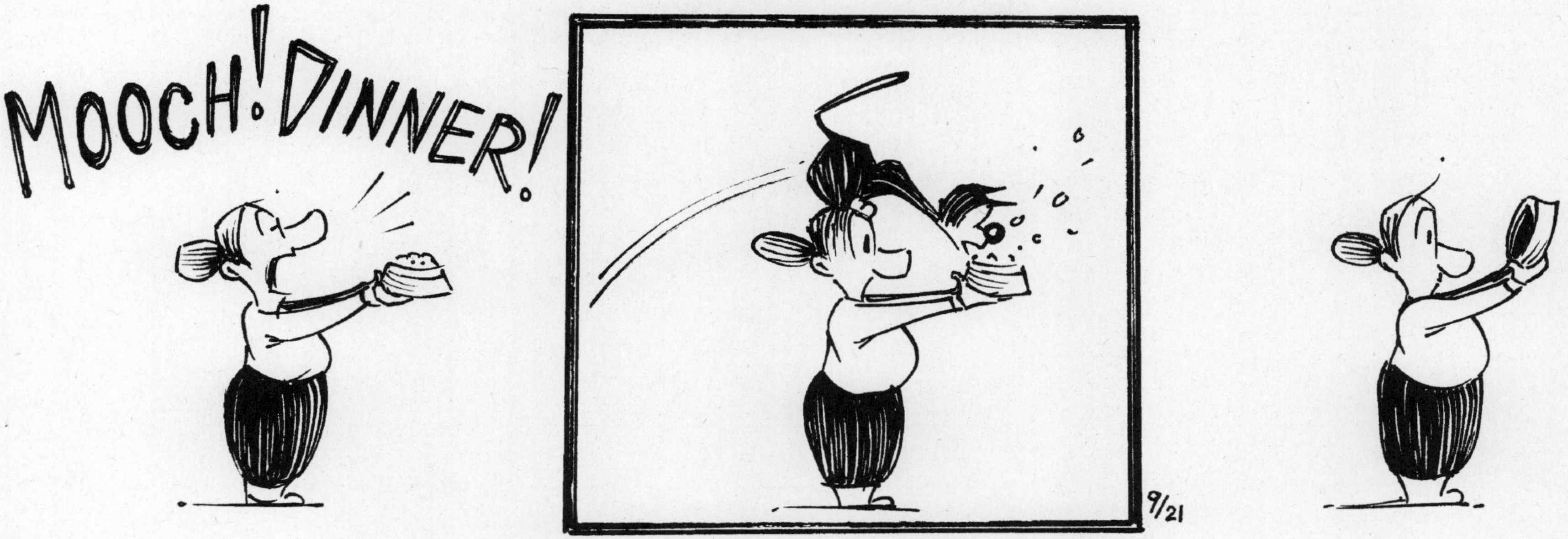
MOOCH! DINNER!
9/21

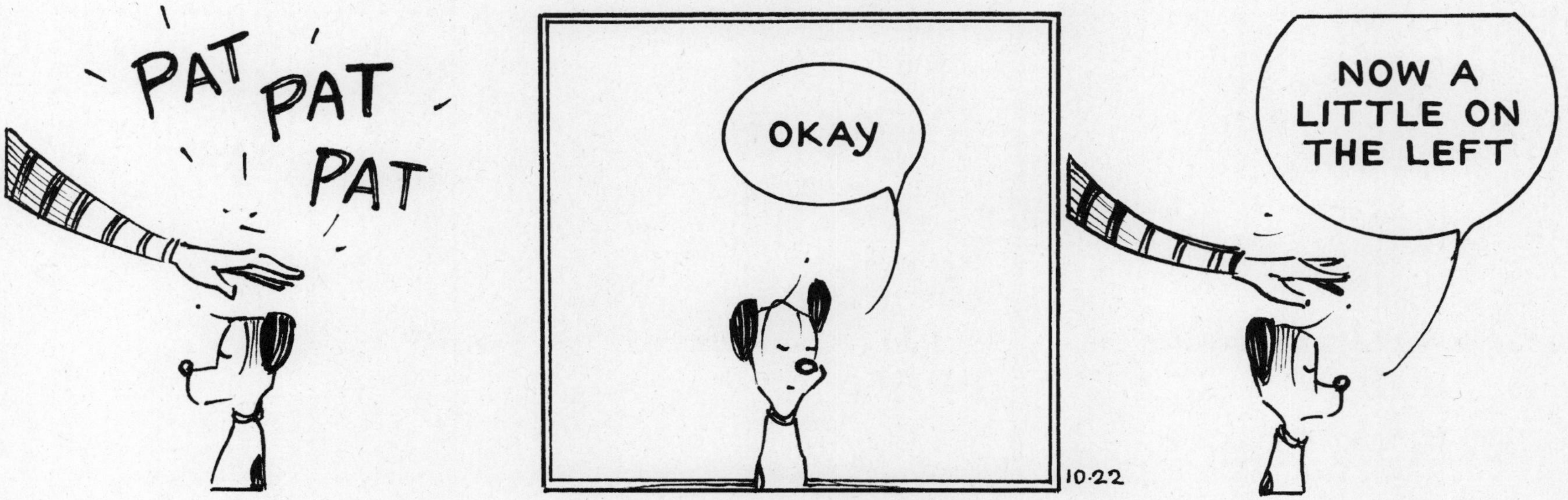
PAT PAT PAT
OKAY
NOW A LITTLE ON THE LEFT
10.22

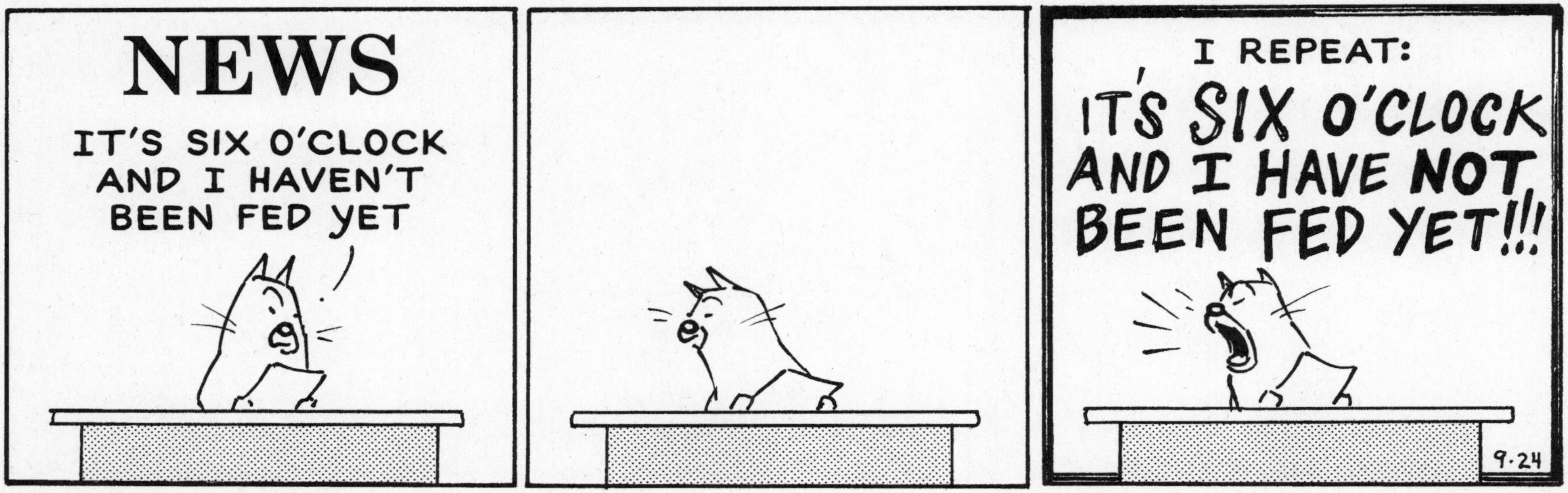
NEWS
IT'S SIX O'CLOCK AND I HAVEN'T BEEN FED YET
I REPEAT:
IT'S SIX O'CLOCK AND I HAVE NOT BEEN FED YET!!!
9·24

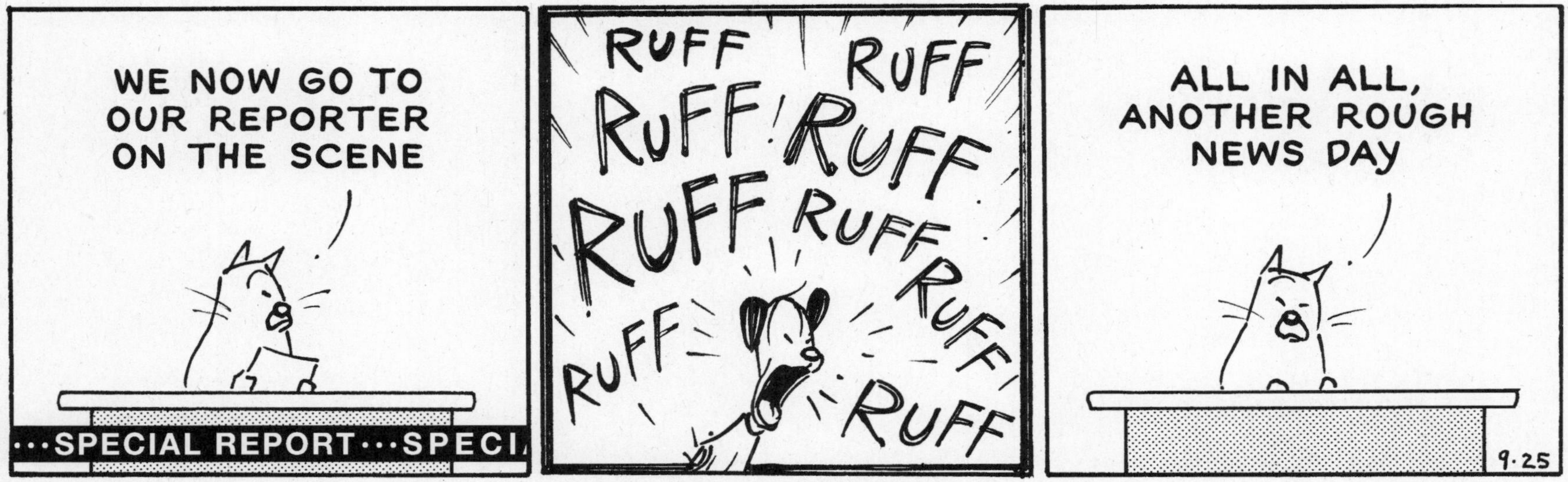
WE NOW GO TO OUR REPORTER ON THE SCENE
···SPECIAL REPORT···SPECI
RUFF
RUFF
RUFF!
RUFF
RUFF
RUFF
RUFF
RUFF
RUFF
RUFF
ALL IN ALL, ANOTHER ROUGH NEWS DAY
9·25

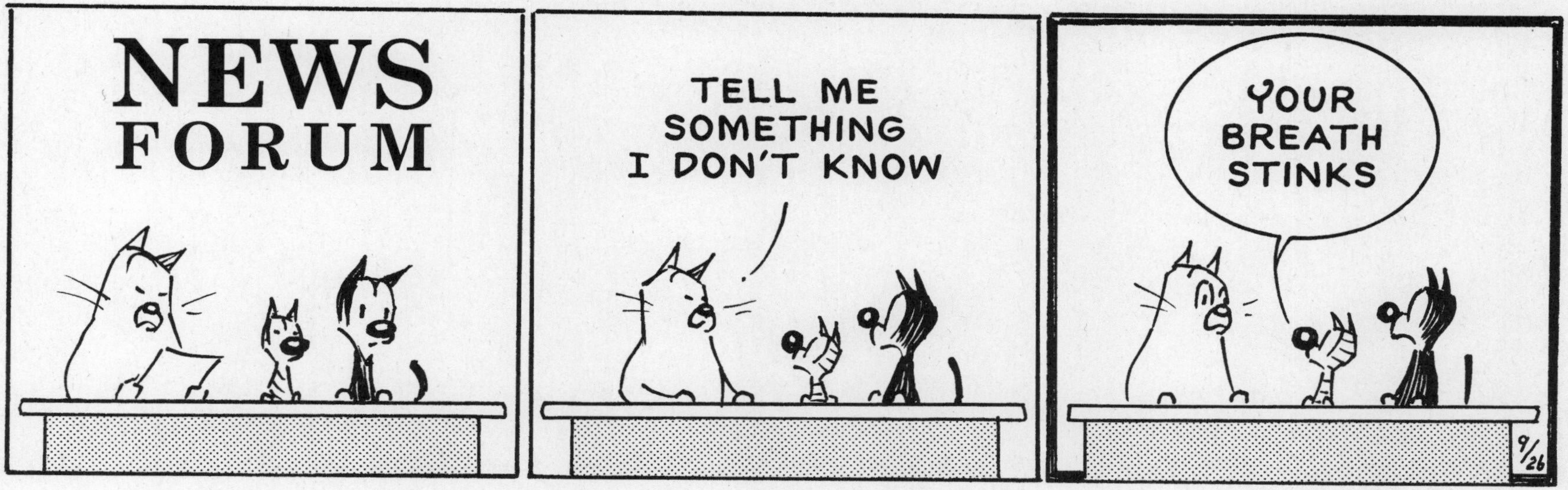
NEWS FORUM
TELL ME SOMETHING I DON'T KNOW
YOUR BREATH STINKS
9/26

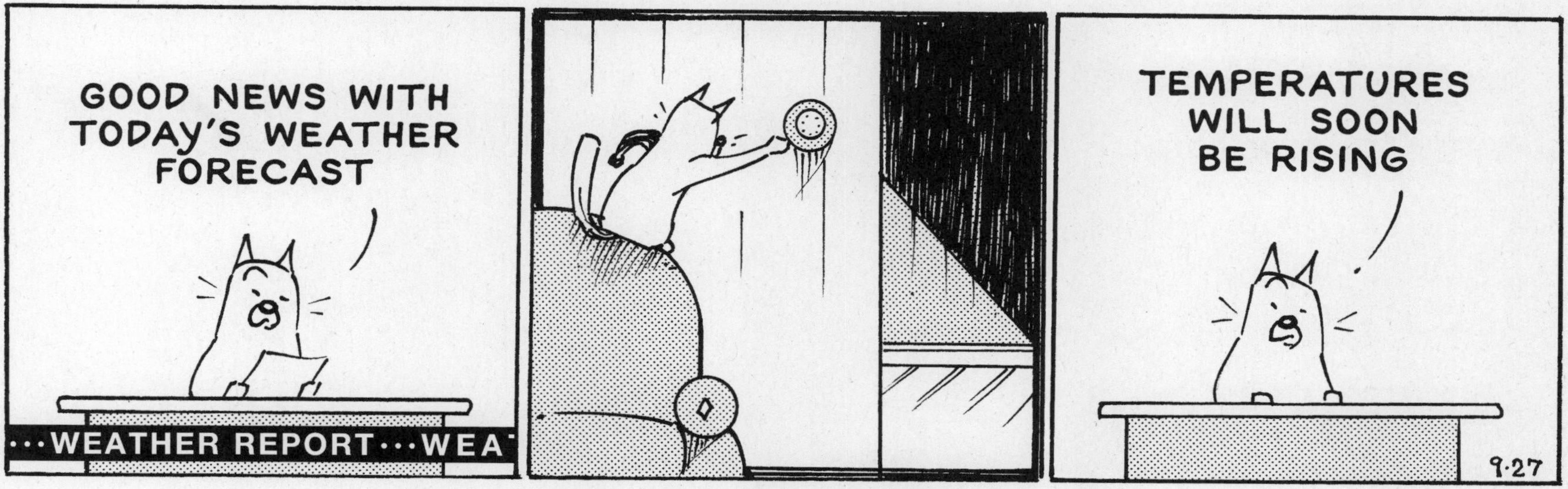
GOOD NEWS WITH TODAY'S WEATHER FORECAST
···WEATHER REPORT···WEA
TEMPERATURES WILL SOON BE RISING
9·27

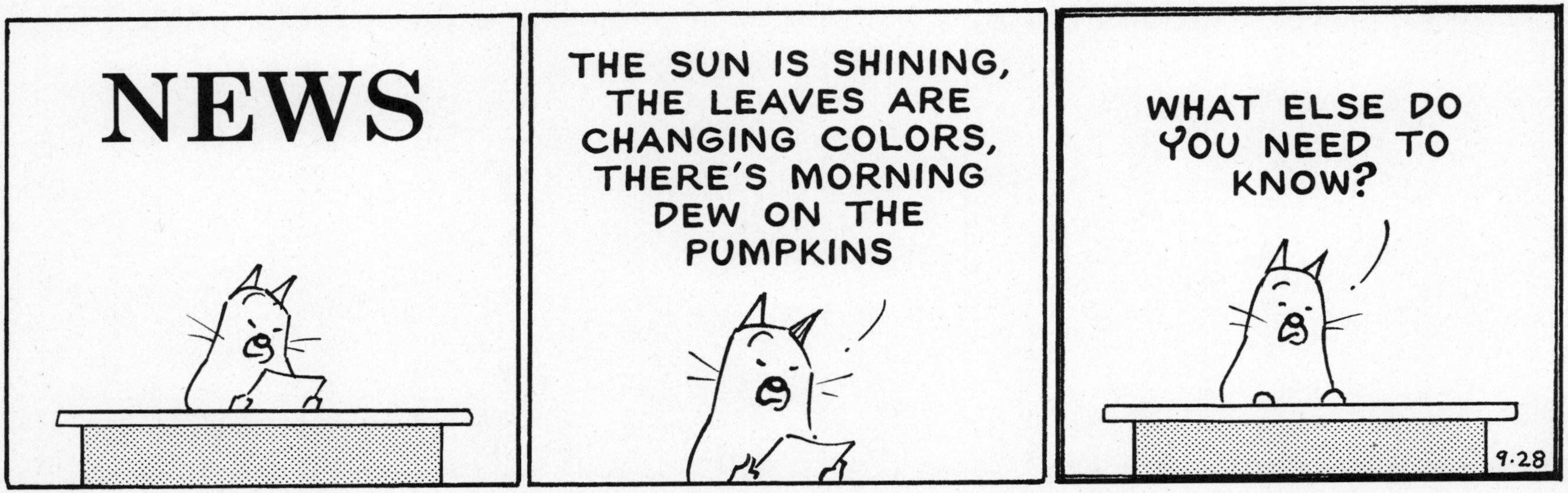
NEWS
THE SUN IS SHINING, THE LEAVES ARE CHANGING COLORS, THERE'S MORNING DEW ON THE PUMPKINS
WHAT ELSE DO YOU NEED TO KNOW?
9·28

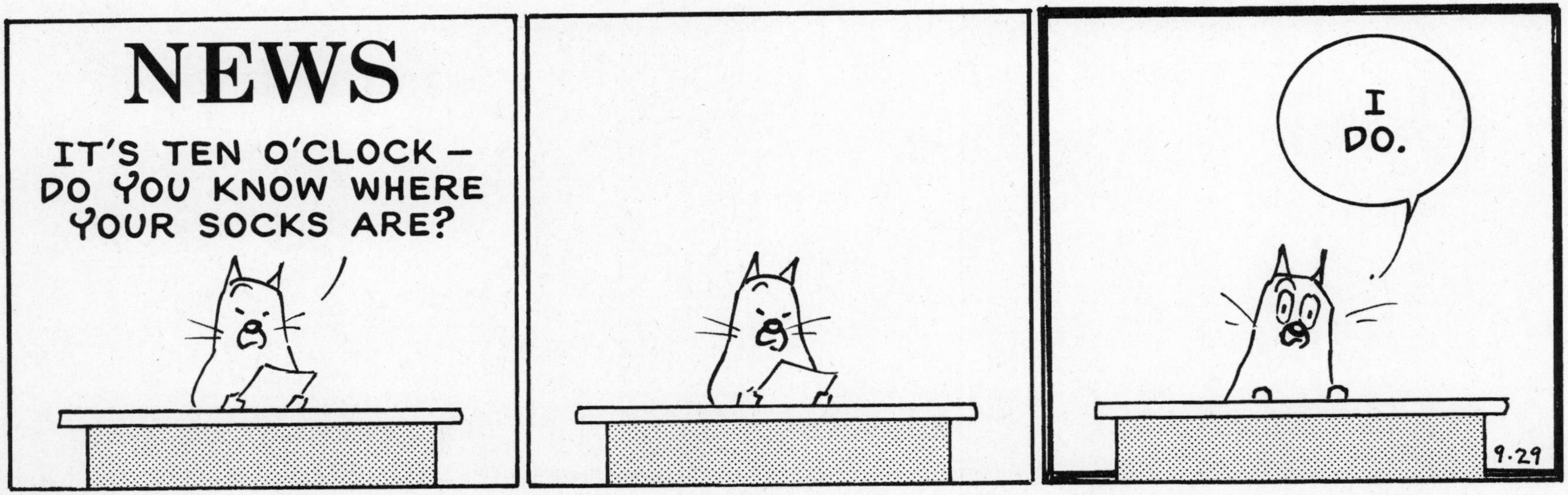
NEWS
IT'S TEN O'CLOCK – DO YOU KNOW WHERE YOUR SOCKS ARE?
I DO.
9·29

MUTTS

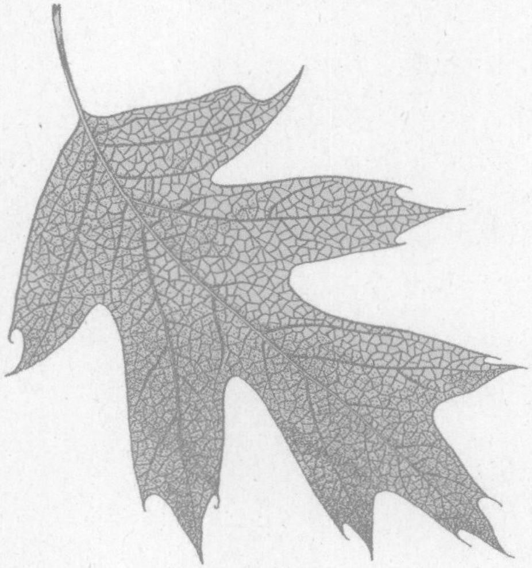

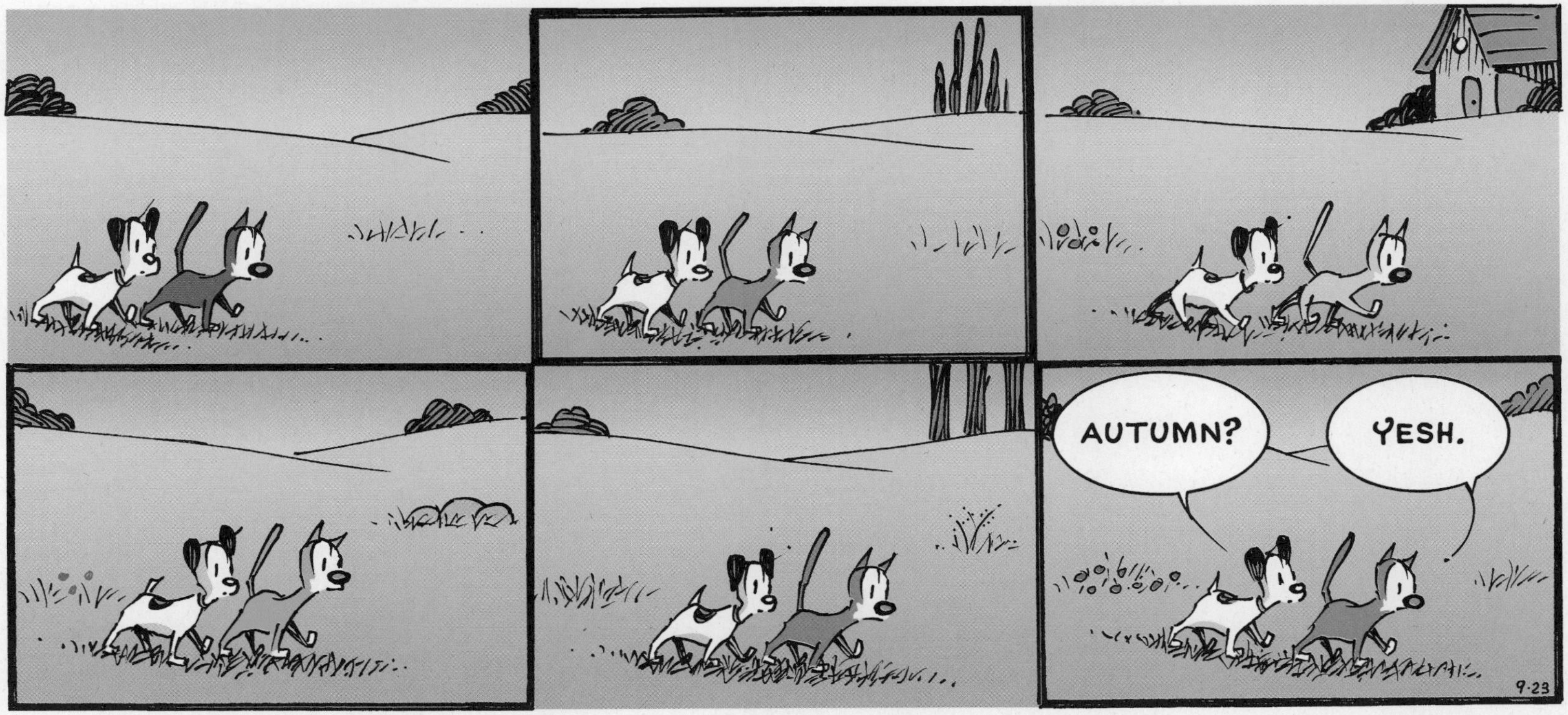
AUTUMN?
YESH.
9·23

MUTTS
Patrick
McDonnell

HELLO, EARL
MOOCH?
IS THAT YOU!?!
YESH
I'M DOING THE OL' CHESHIRE CAT BIT
HOW?
OH, IT'S EASY
EXCEPT MY CHEEKS ARE KILLING ME WITH ALL THIS SHMILING
9.30

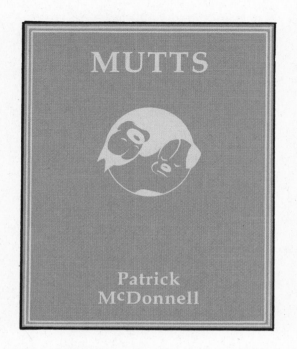

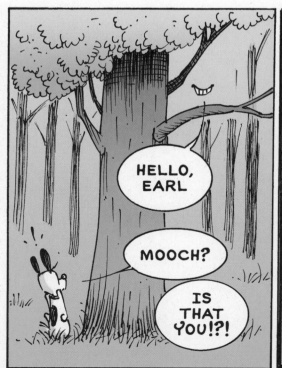

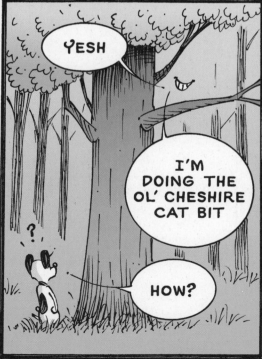

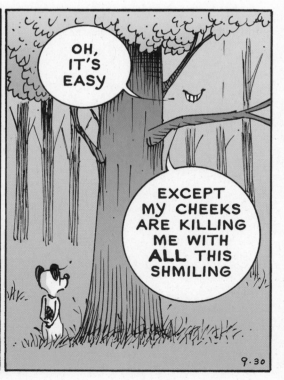

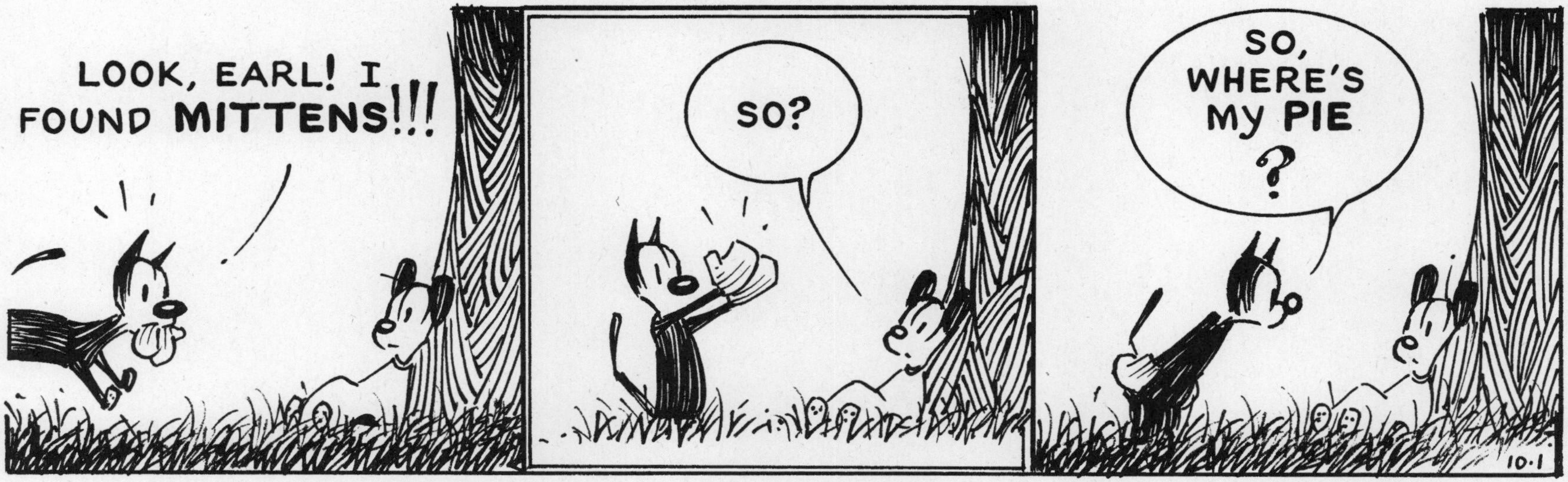
LOOK, EARL! I FOUND MITTENS!!!
SO?
SO, WHERE'S MY PIE ?
10·1

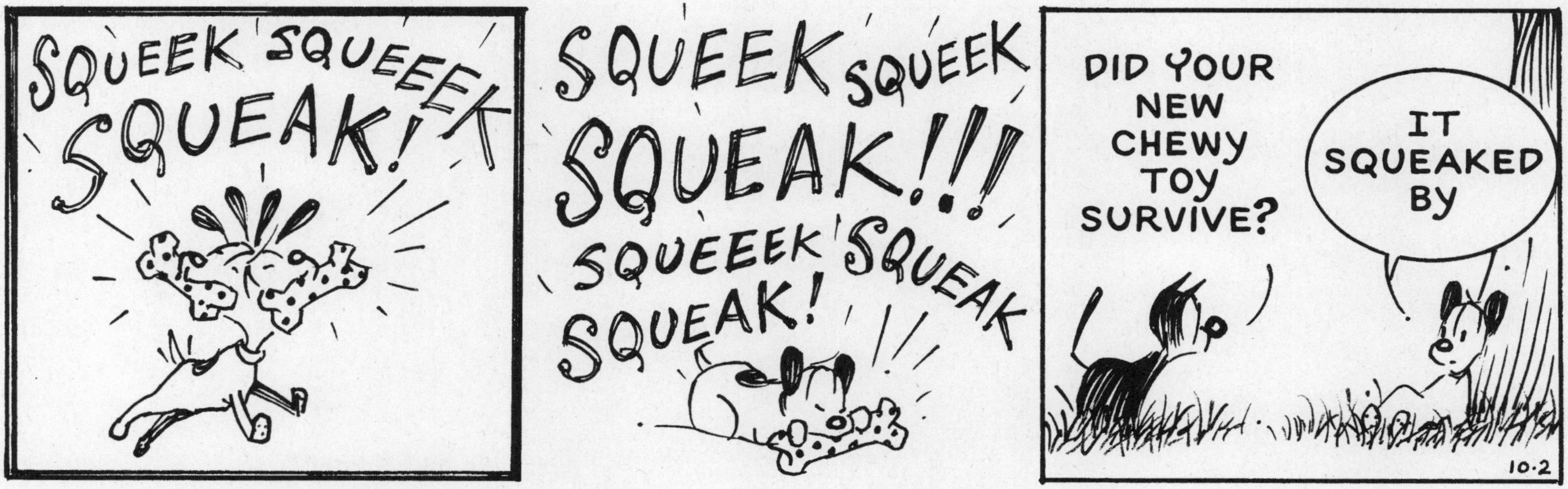
SQUEEK SQUEEEEK
SQUEAK!
SQUEEK SQUEEK
SQUEAK!!!
SQUEEEK
SQUEAK
SQUEAK!
DID YOUR NEW CHEWY TOY SURVIVE?
IT SQUEAKED BY
10·2

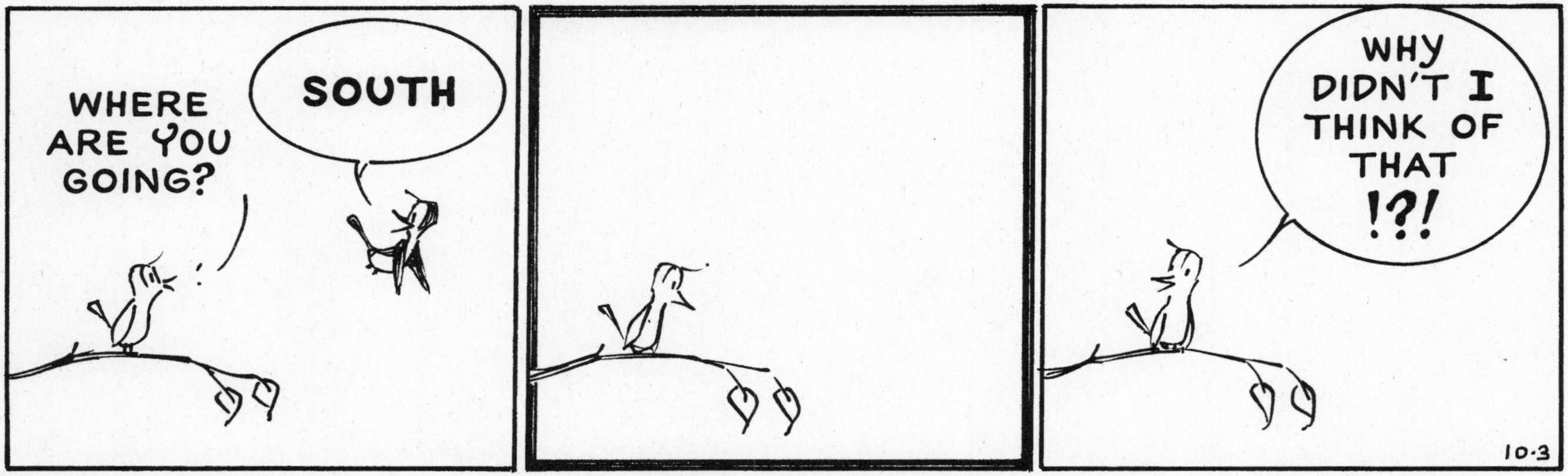
WHERE ARE YOU GOING?
SOUTH
WHY DIDN'T I THINK OF THAT !?!
10·3

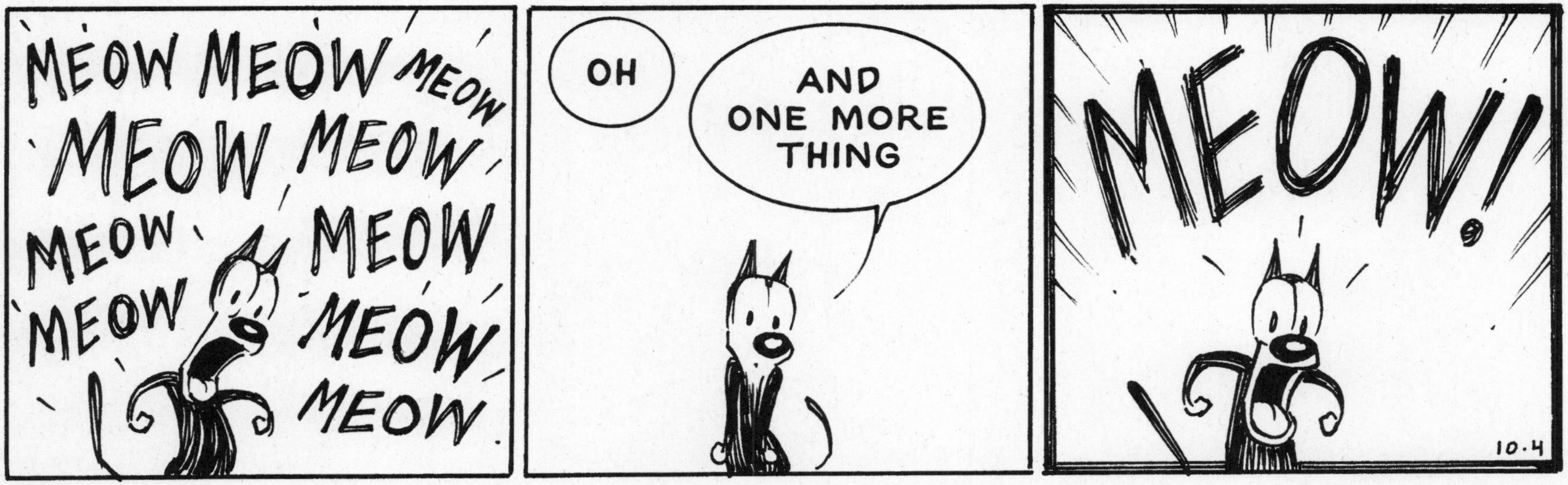
MEOW MEOW MEOW
MEOW MEOW
MEOW
MEOW
MEOW
MEOW
MEOW
OH
AND ONE MORE THING
MEOW!
10·4

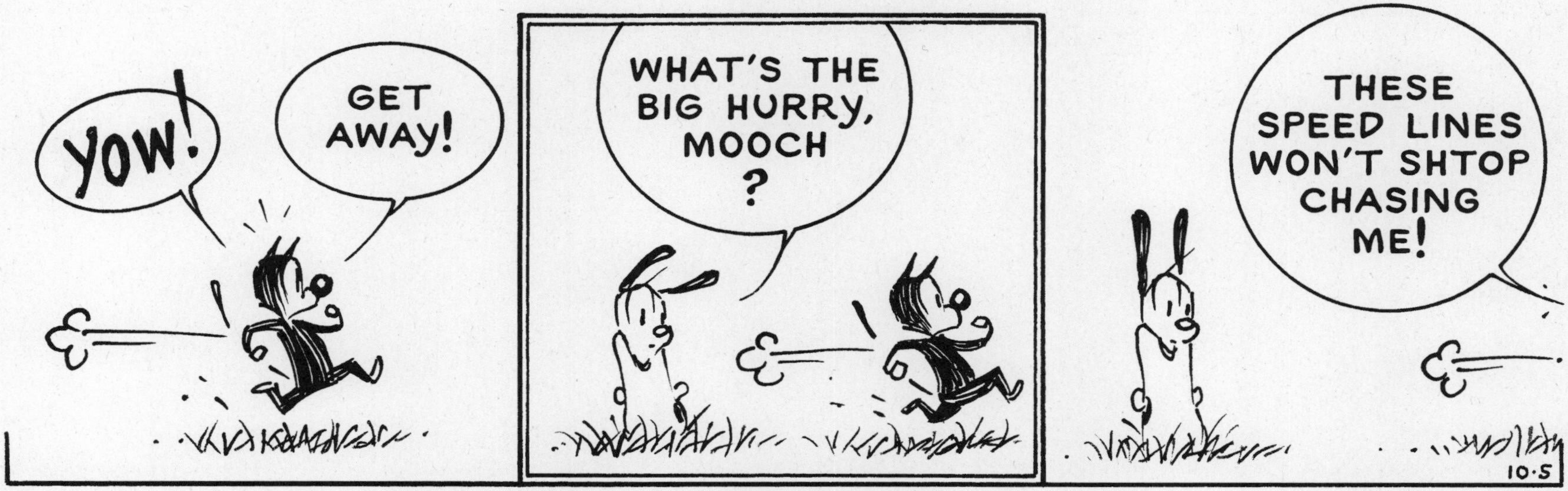
YOW!
GET AWAY!
WHAT'S THE BIG HURRY, MOOCH ?
THESE SPEED LINES WON'T SHTOP CHASING ME!
10·5

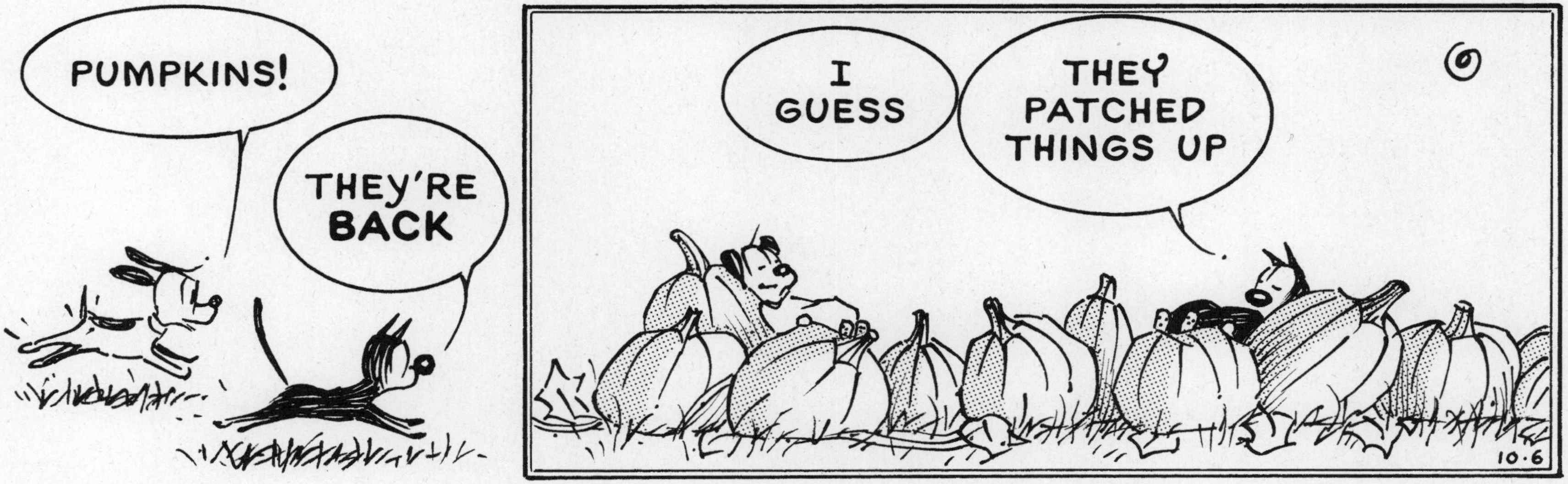
PUMPKINS!
THEY'RE BACK
I GUESS
THEY PATCHED THINGS UP
10·6

mutts

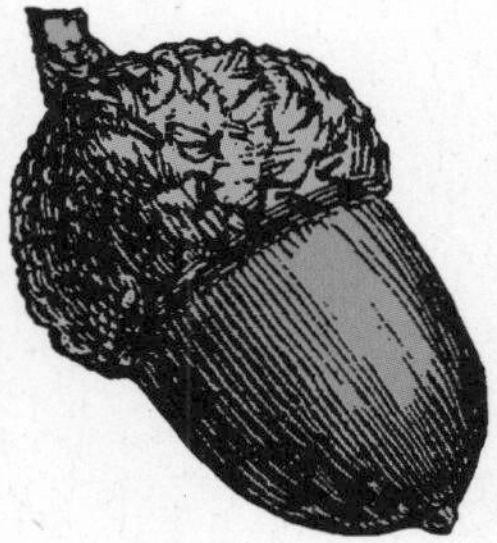

Patrick McDonnell

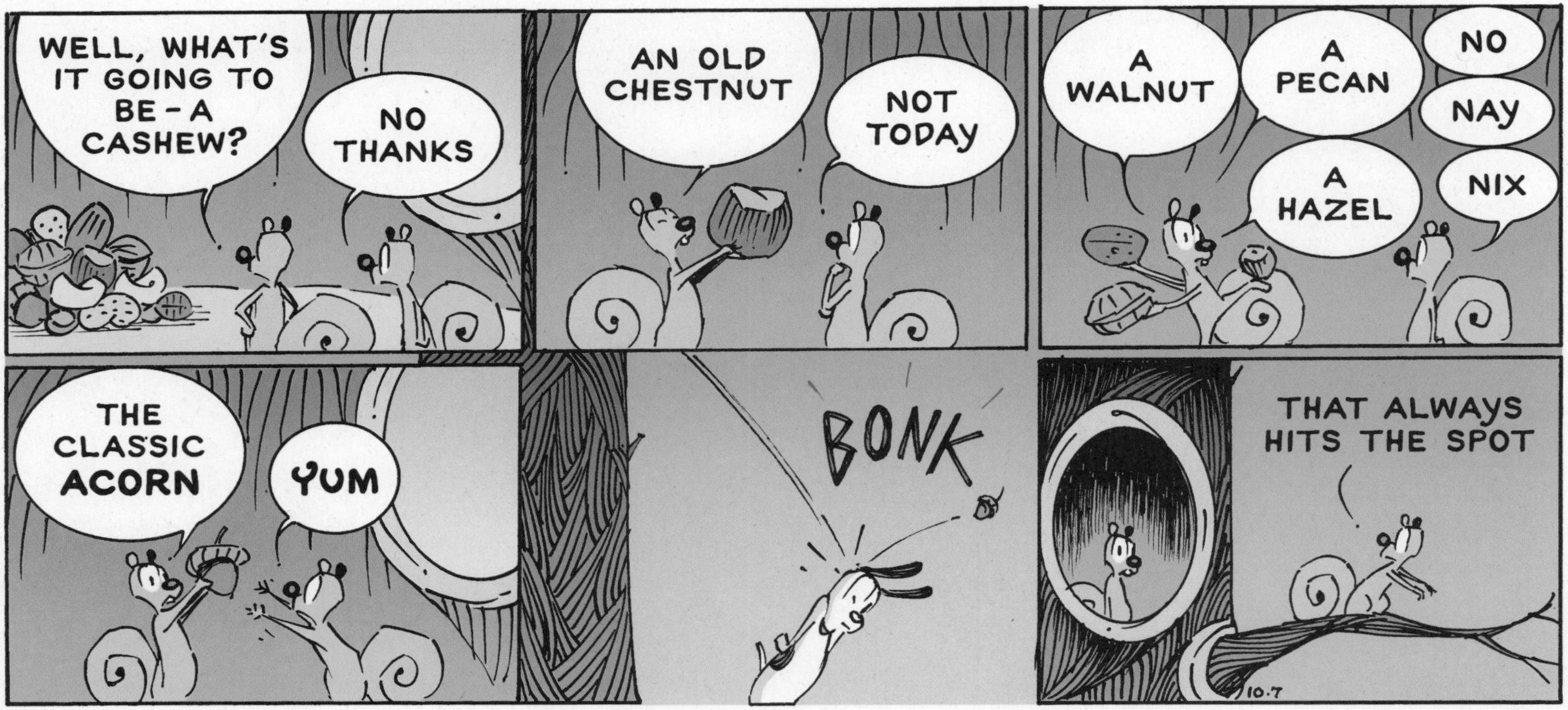
WELL, WHAT'S IT GOING TO BE - A CASHEW?
NO THANKS
AN OLD CHESTNUT
NOT TODAY
A WALNUT
A PECAN
NO
NAY
A HAZEL
NIX
THE CLASSIC ACORN
YUM
BONK
THAT ALWAYS HITS THE SPOT
10.7

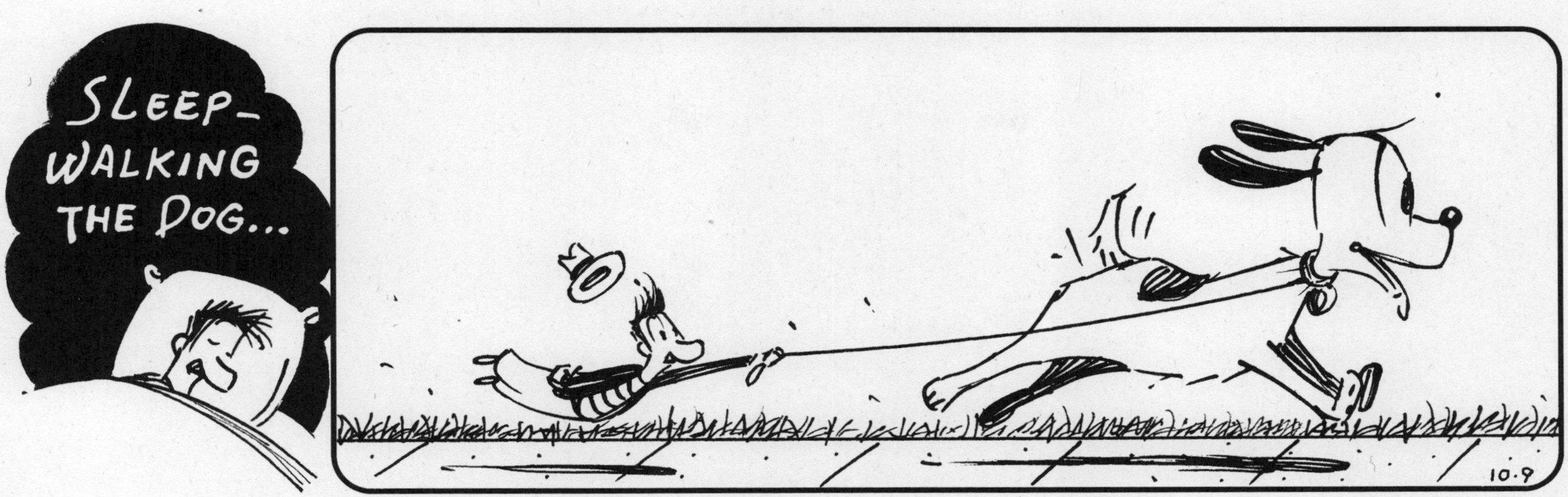
SLEEP-
WALKING
THE DOG...
10·9

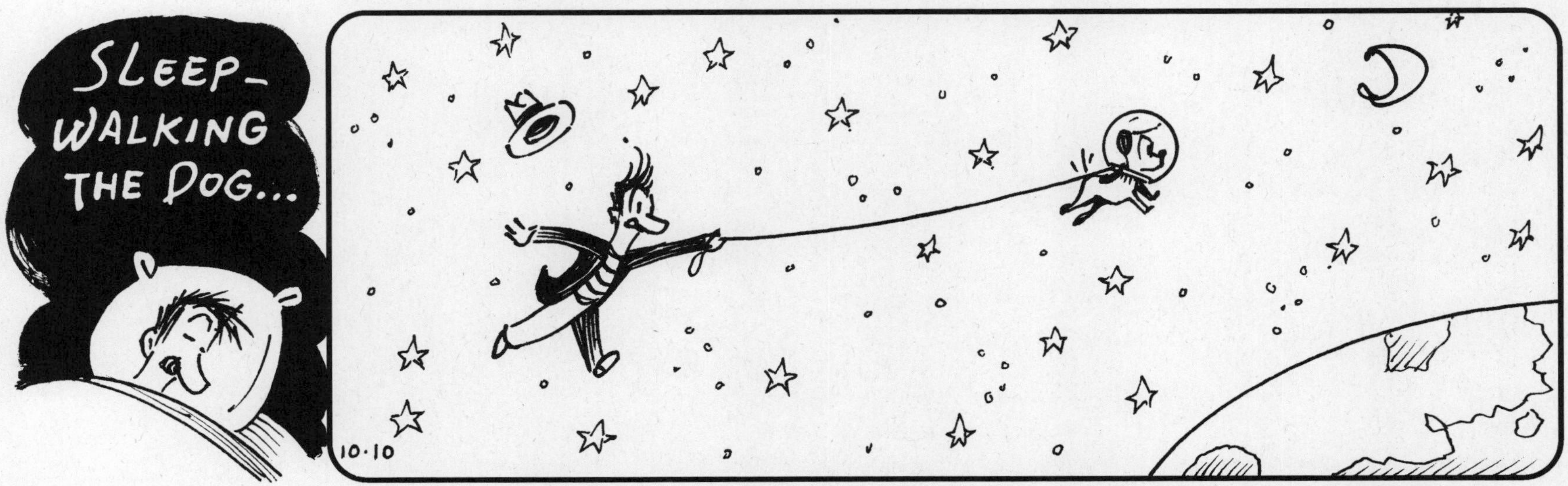
SLEEP-
WALKING
THE DOG...
10·10

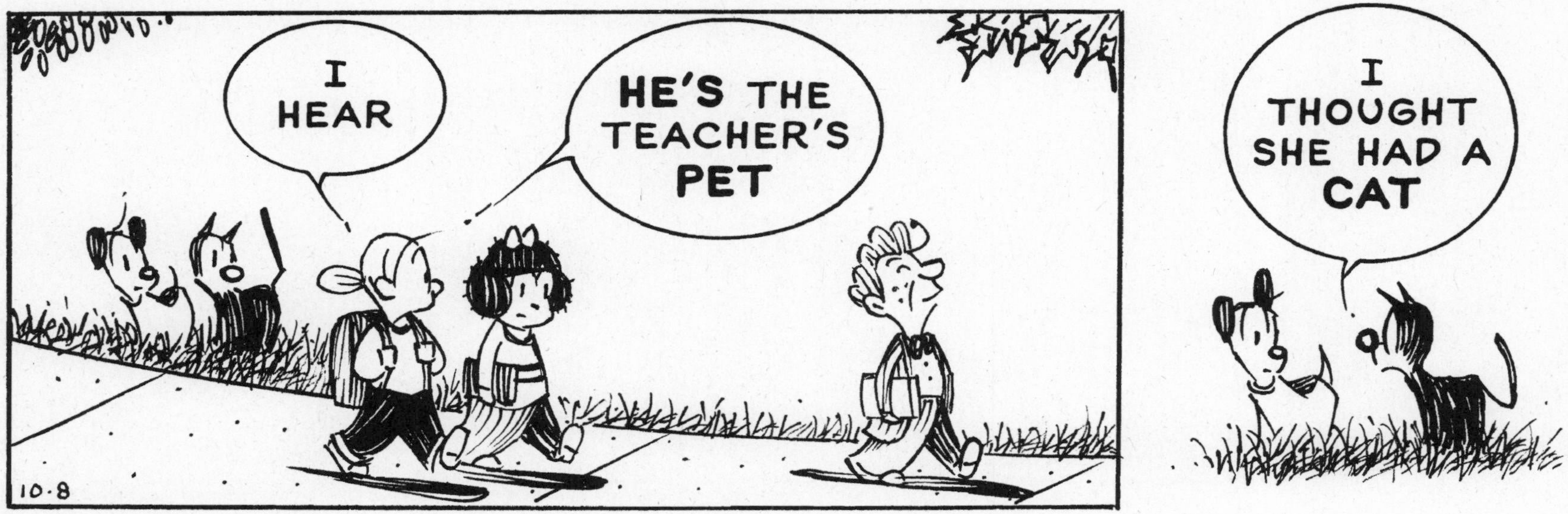
I HEAR
HE'S THE TEACHER'S PET
I THOUGHT SHE HAD A CAT
10·8

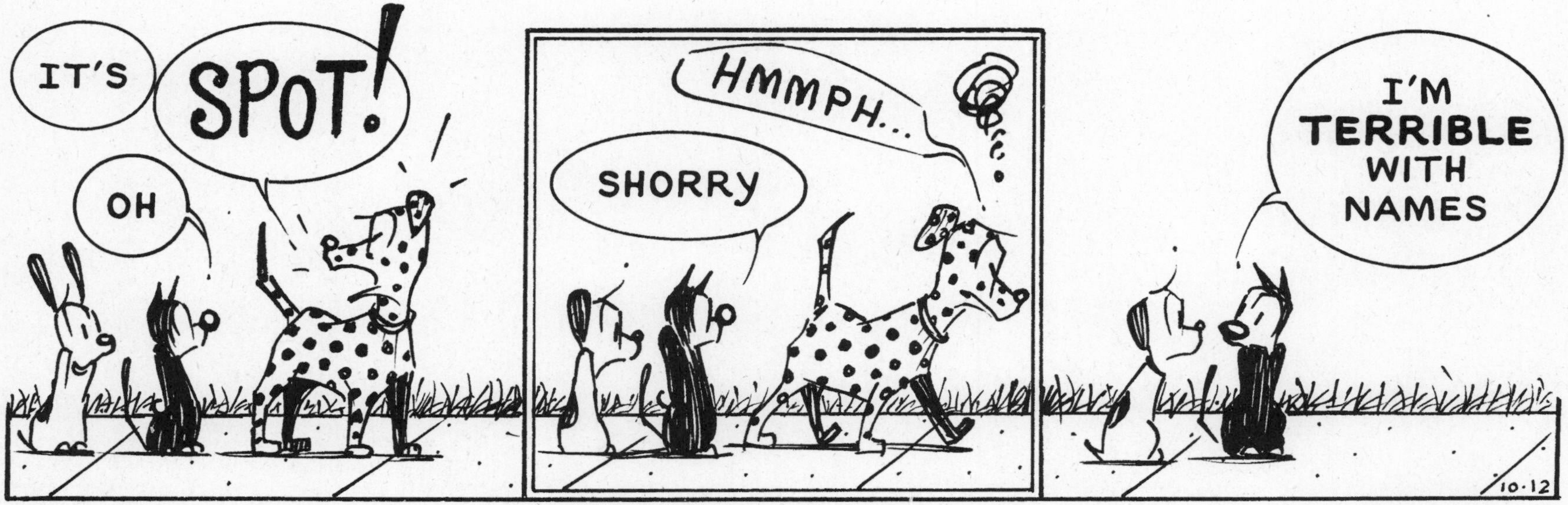
IT'S
SPOT!
OH
HMMPH...
SHORRY
I'M TERRIBLE WITH NAMES
10·12

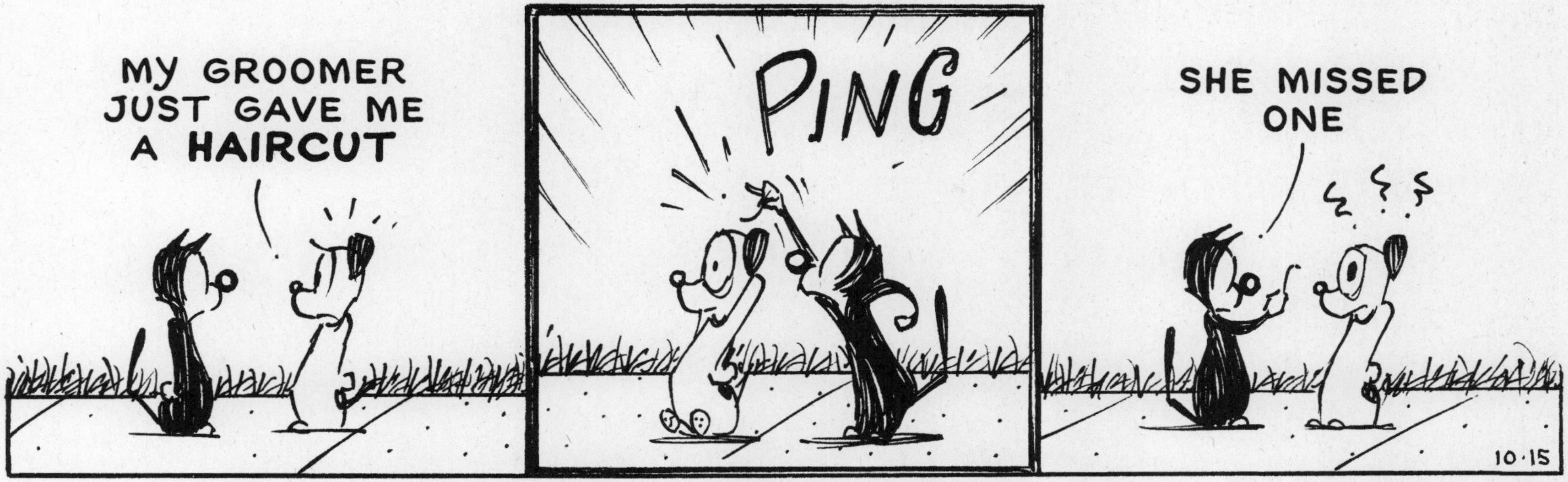
MY GROOMER JUST GAVE ME A **HAIRCUT**
PING
SHE MISSED ONE
10·15

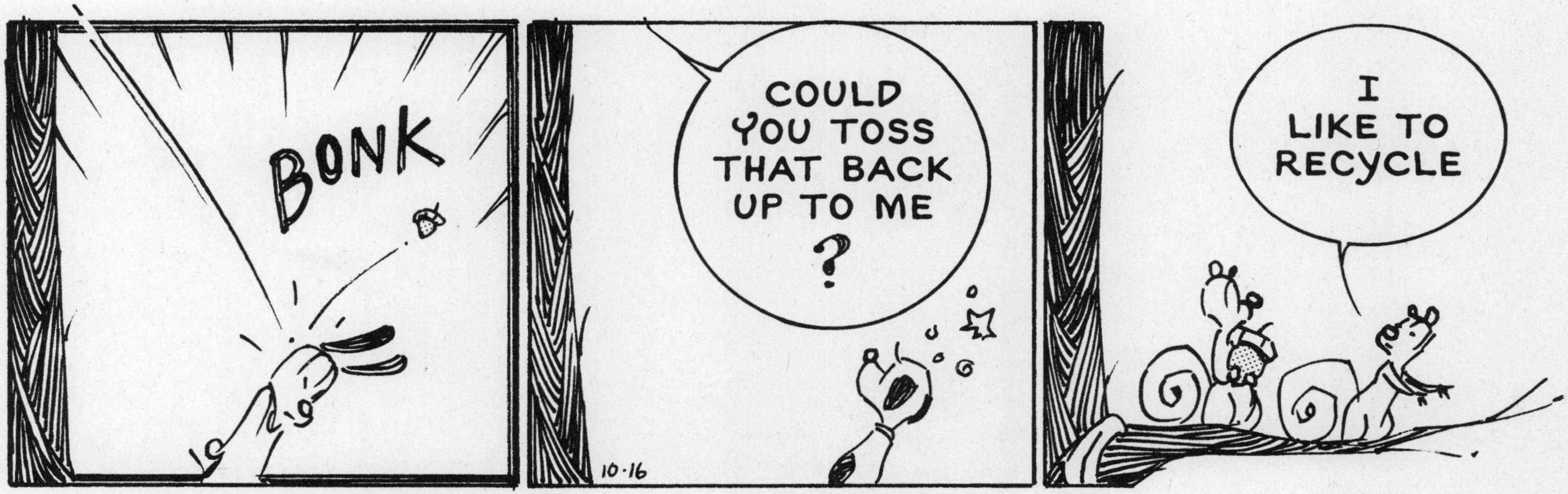
BONK
COULD YOU TOSS THAT BACK UP TO ME ?
10·16
I LIKE TO RECYCLE

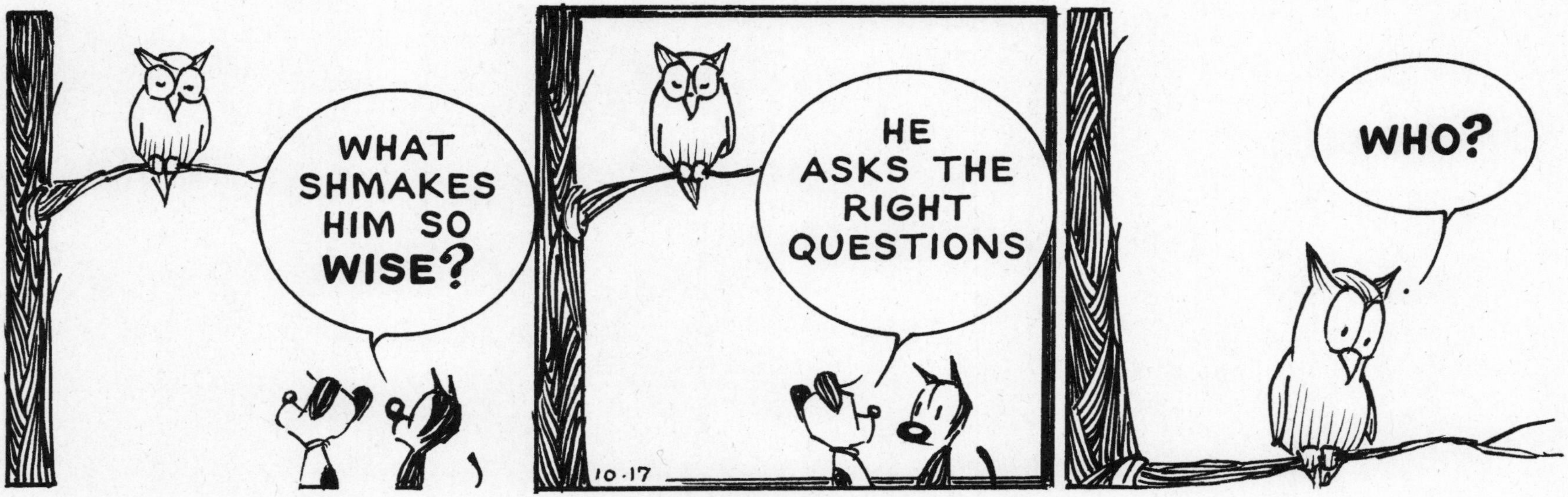
WHAT SHMAKES HIM SO WISE?
HE ASKS THE RIGHT QUESTIONS
10.17
WHO?

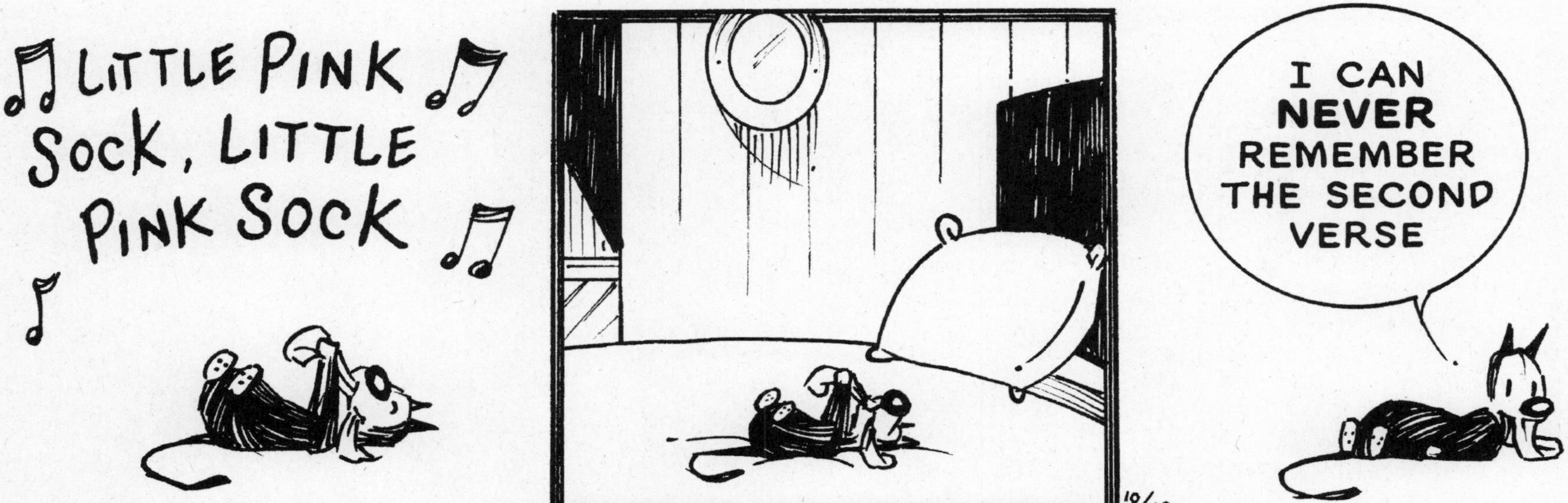
LITTLE PINK SOCK, LITTLE PINK SOCK
10/18
I CAN NEVER REMEMBER THE SECOND VERSE

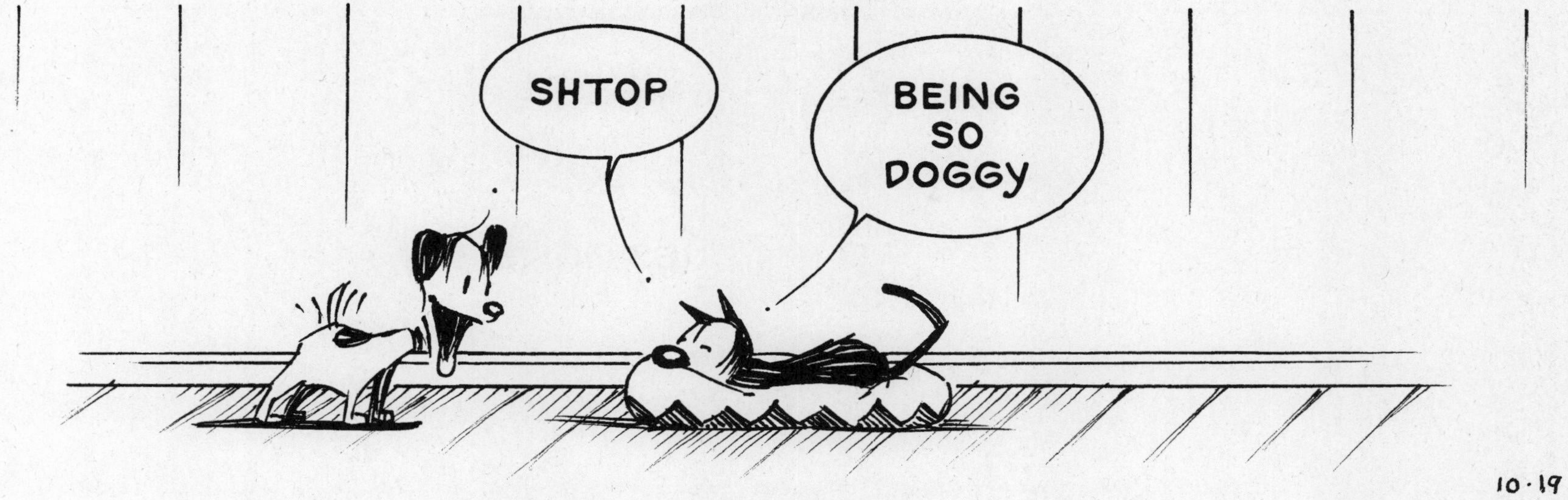
SHTOP
BEING SO DOGGY
10·19

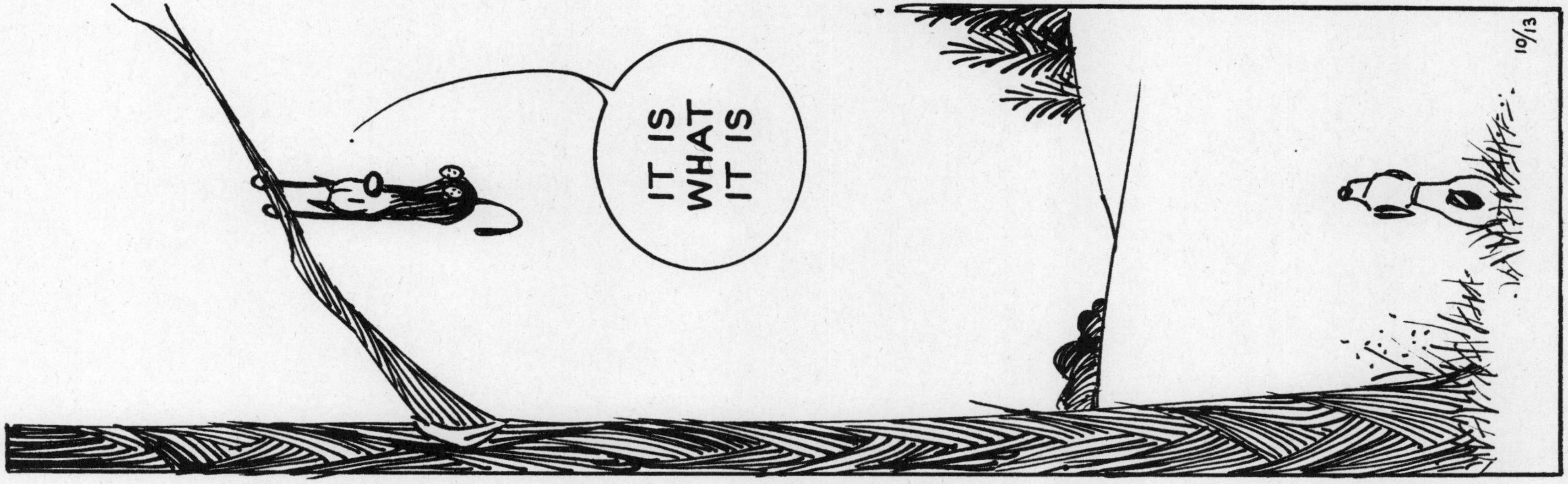
IT IS WHAT IT IS
10/13

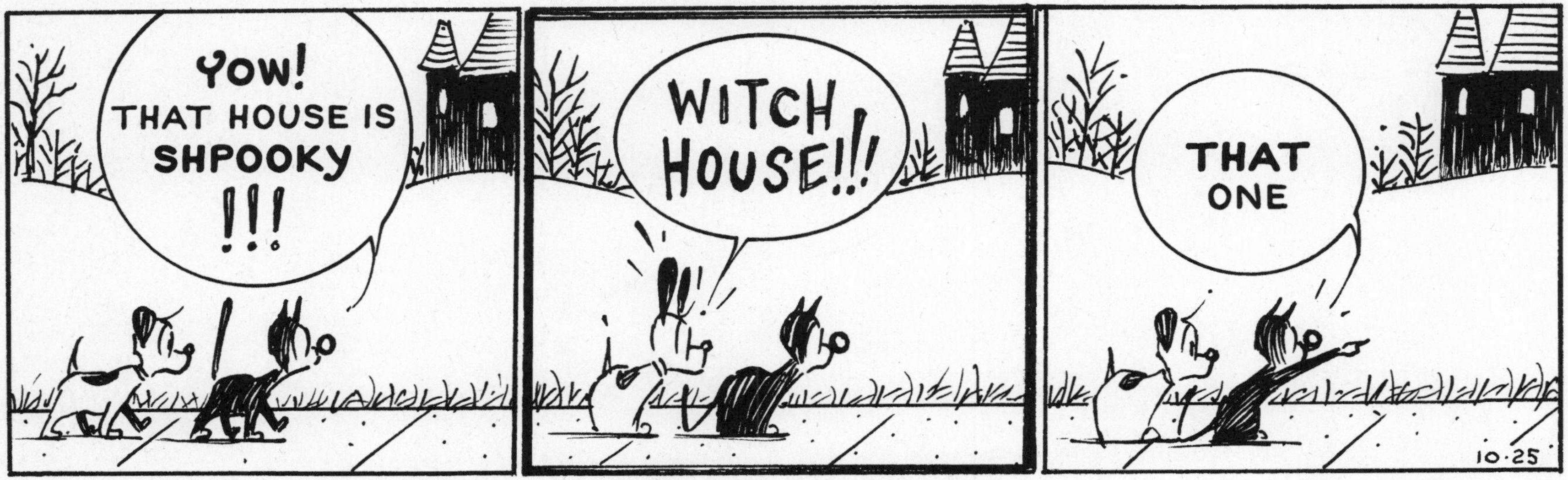
YOW!
THAT HOUSE IS
SHPOOKY
!!!
WITCH
HOUSE!!!
THAT
ONE
10·25

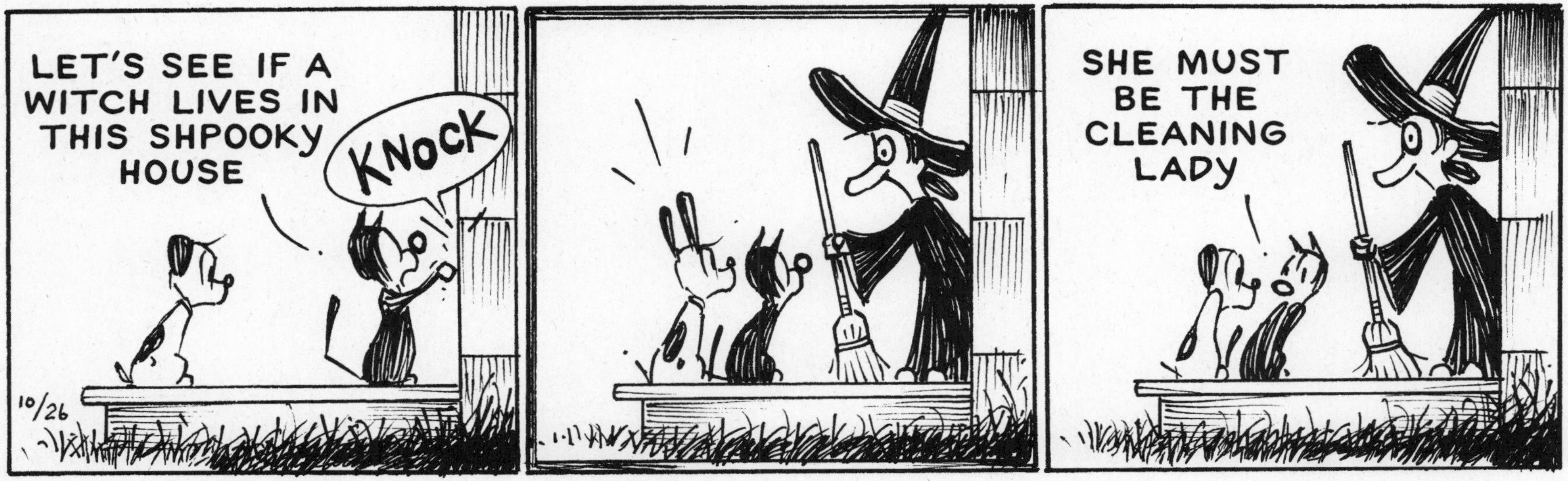
LET'S SEE IF A
WITCH LIVES IN
THIS SHPOOKY
HOUSE
KNOCK
SHE MUST
BE THE
CLEANING
LADY
10/26

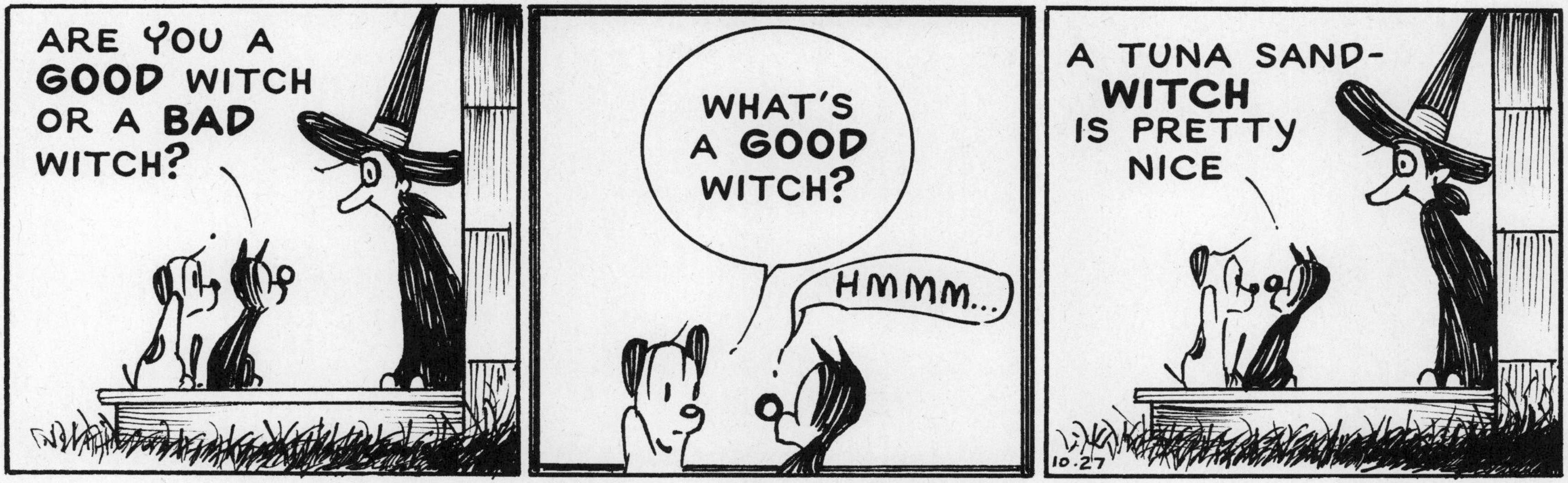
ARE YOU A GOOD WITCH OR A BAD WITCH?
WHAT'S A GOOD WITCH?
HMMM...
A TUNA SAND-WITCH IS PRETTY NICE
10·27

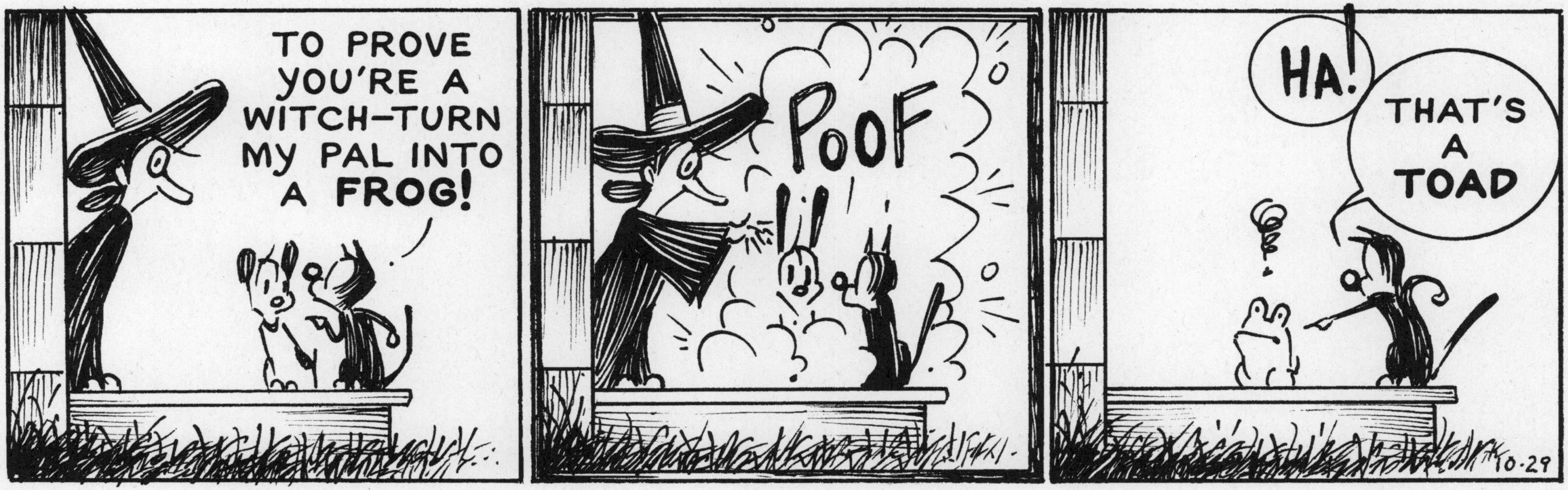
TO PROVE YOU'RE A WITCH–TURN MY PAL INTO A FROG!
POOF
!!
HA!
THAT'S A TOAD
10·29

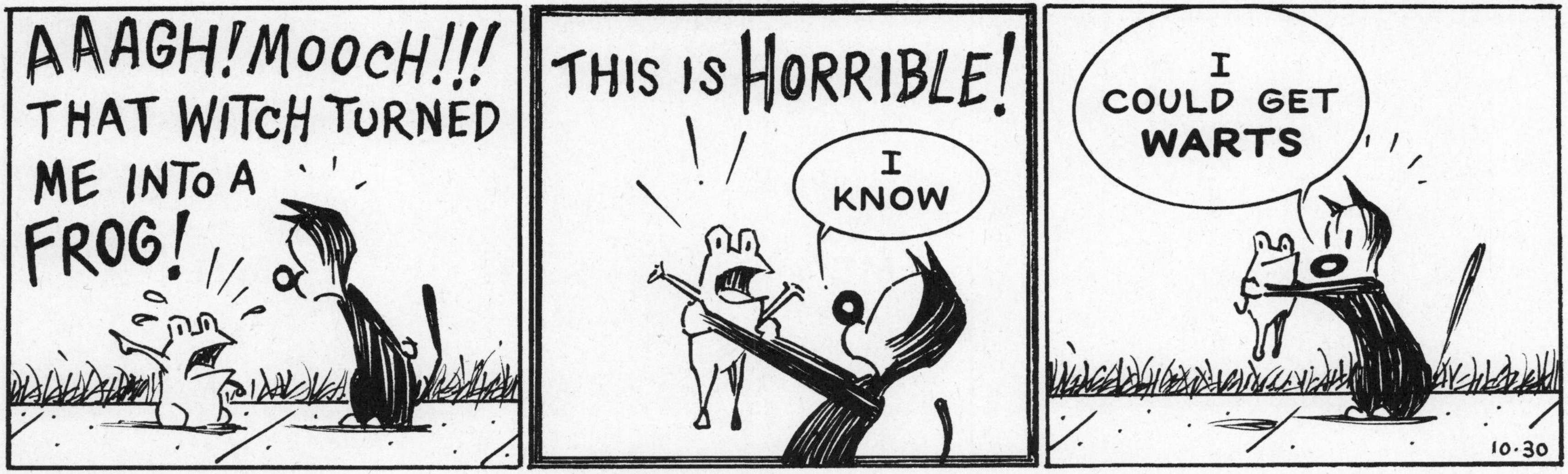
AAAGH! MOOCH!!! THAT WITCH TURNED ME INTO A FROG!
THIS IS HORRIBLE!
I KNOW
I COULD GET WARTS
10·30

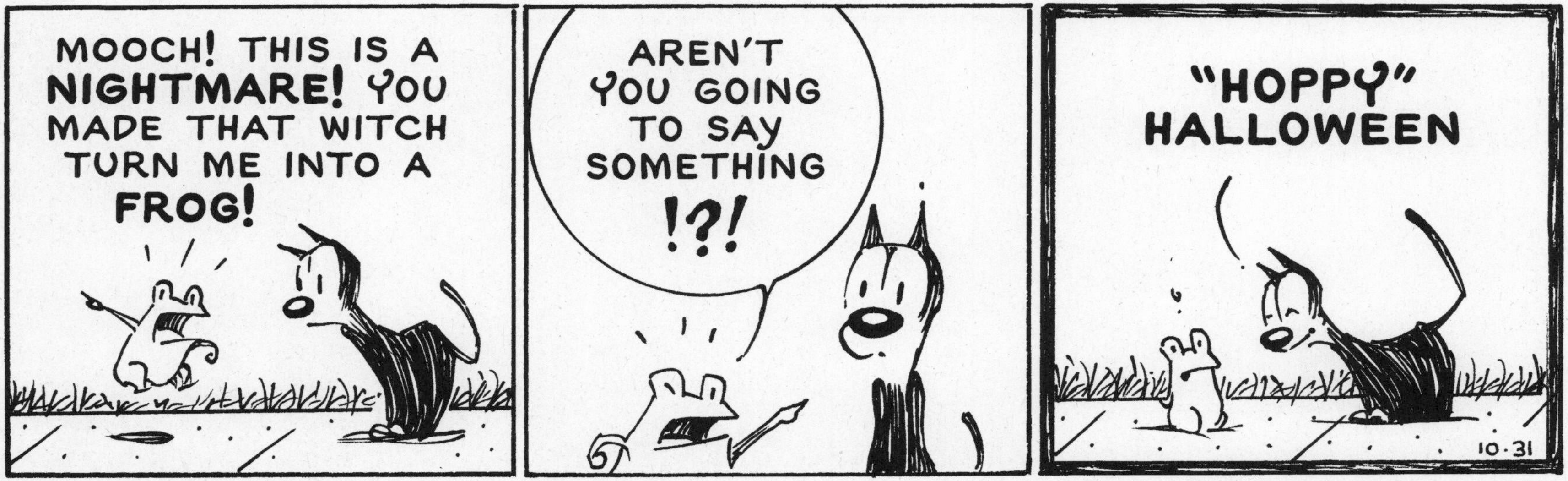
MOOCH! THIS IS A NIGHTMARE! YOU MADE THAT WITCH TURN ME INTO A FROG!
AREN'T YOU GOING TO SAY SOMETHING !?!
"HOPPY" HALLOWEEN
10·31

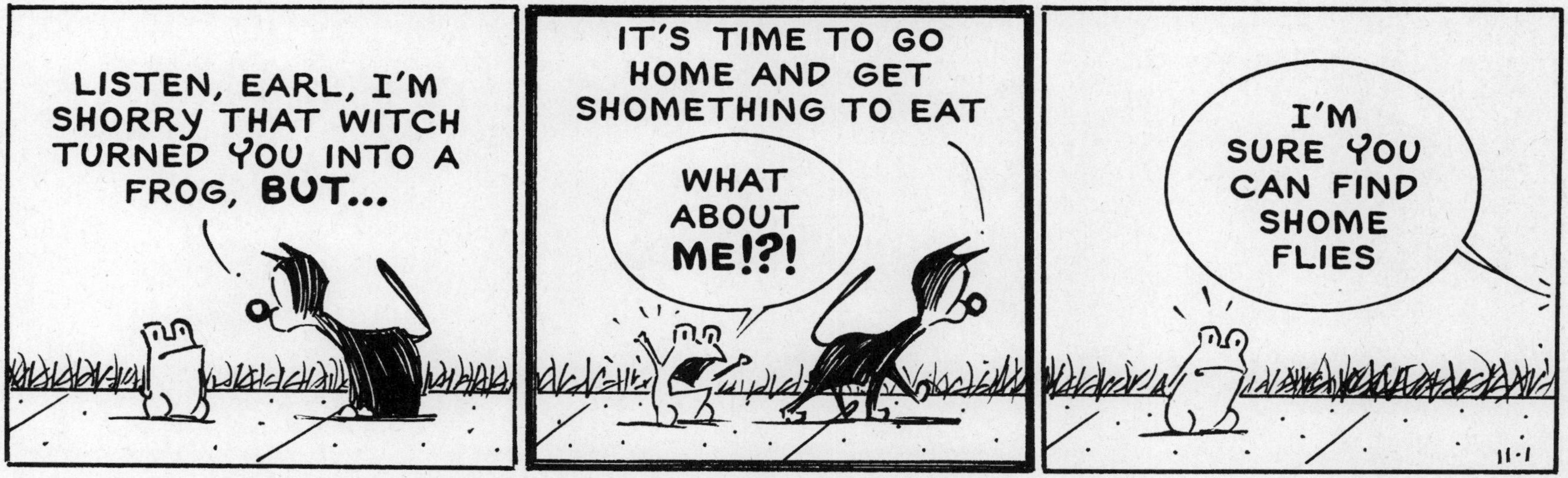
LISTEN, EARL, I'M SHORRY THAT WITCH TURNED YOU INTO A FROG, BUT...
IT'S TIME TO GO HOME AND GET SHOMETHING TO EAT
WHAT ABOUT ME!?!
I'M SURE YOU CAN FIND SHOME FLIES
11·1

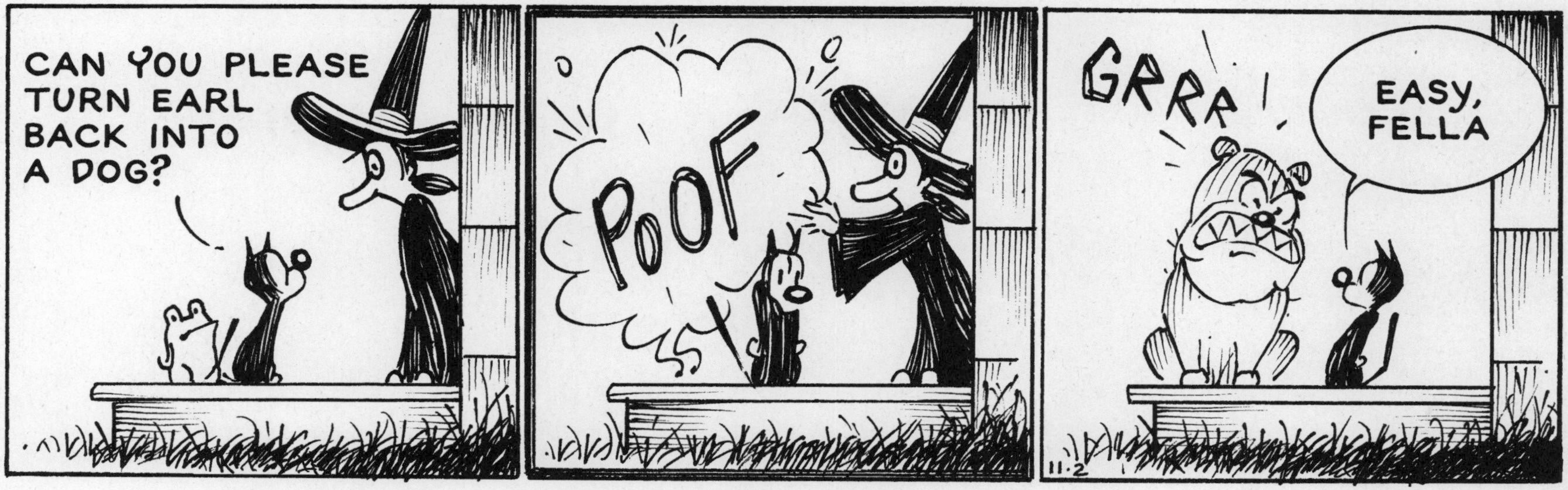
CAN YOU PLEASE TURN EARL BACK INTO A DOG?
POOF
GRRR
EASY, FELLA
11·2

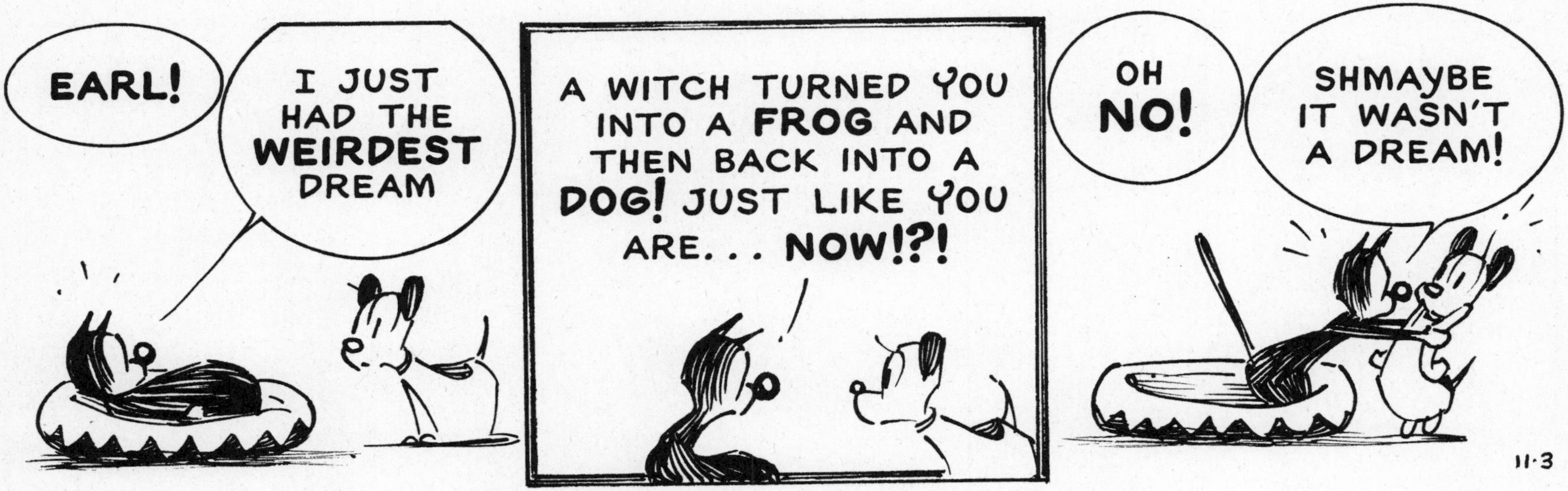
EARL!
I JUST HAD THE WEIRDEST DREAM
A WITCH TURNED YOU INTO A FROG AND THEN BACK INTO A DOG! JUST LIKE YOU ARE... NOW!?!
OH NO!
SHMAYBE IT WASN'T A DREAM!
11·3

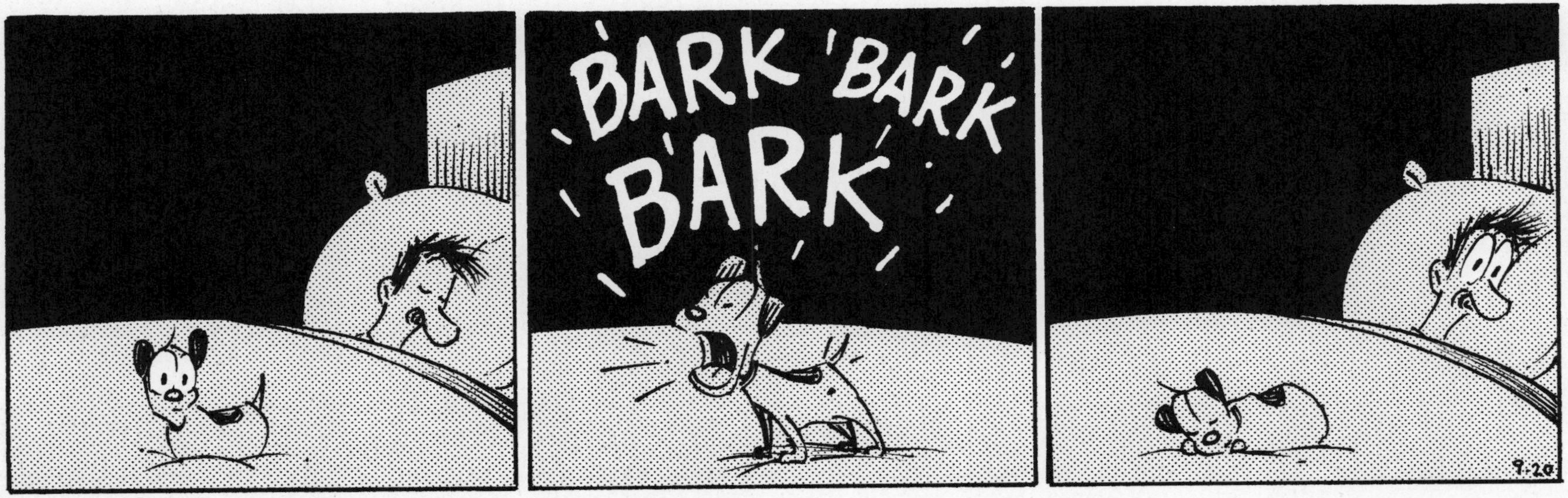
BARK BARK BARK
9·20

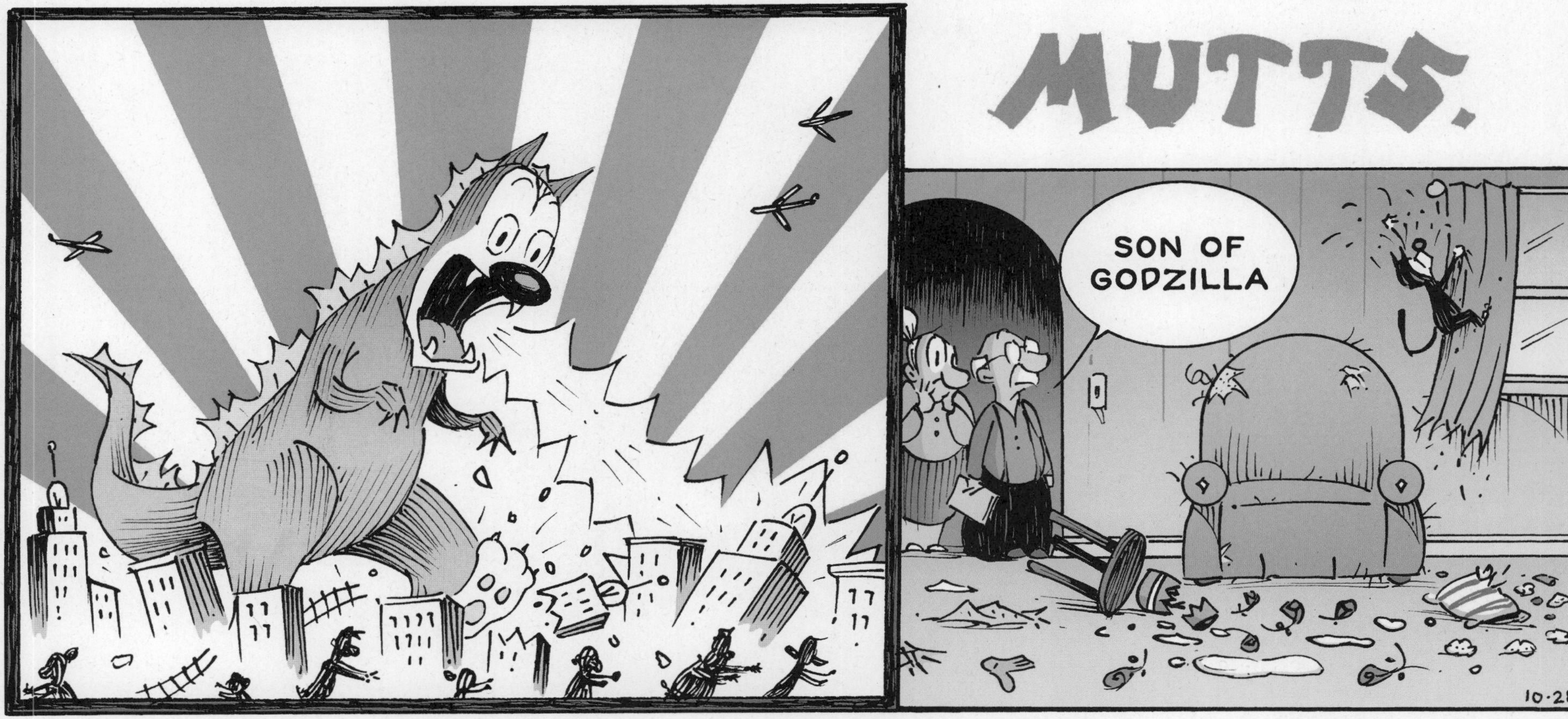
MUTTS.
SON OF GODZILLA
10·28

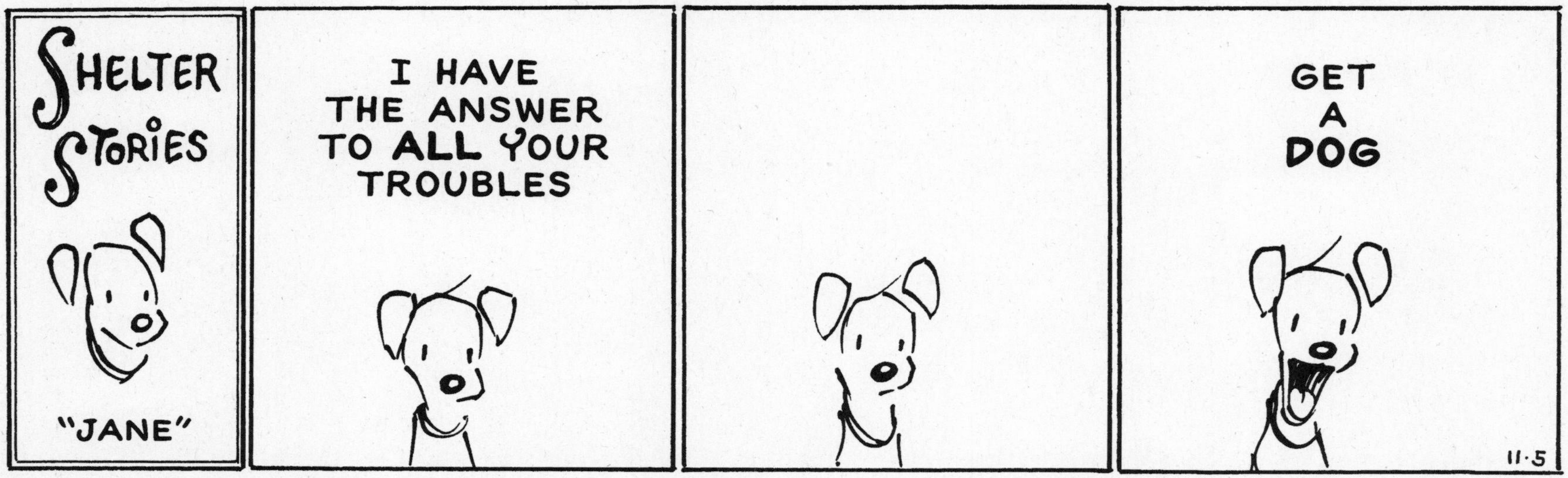
SHELTER STORIES
"JANE"
I HAVE THE ANSWER TO **ALL** YOUR TROUBLES
GET A **DOG**
11·5

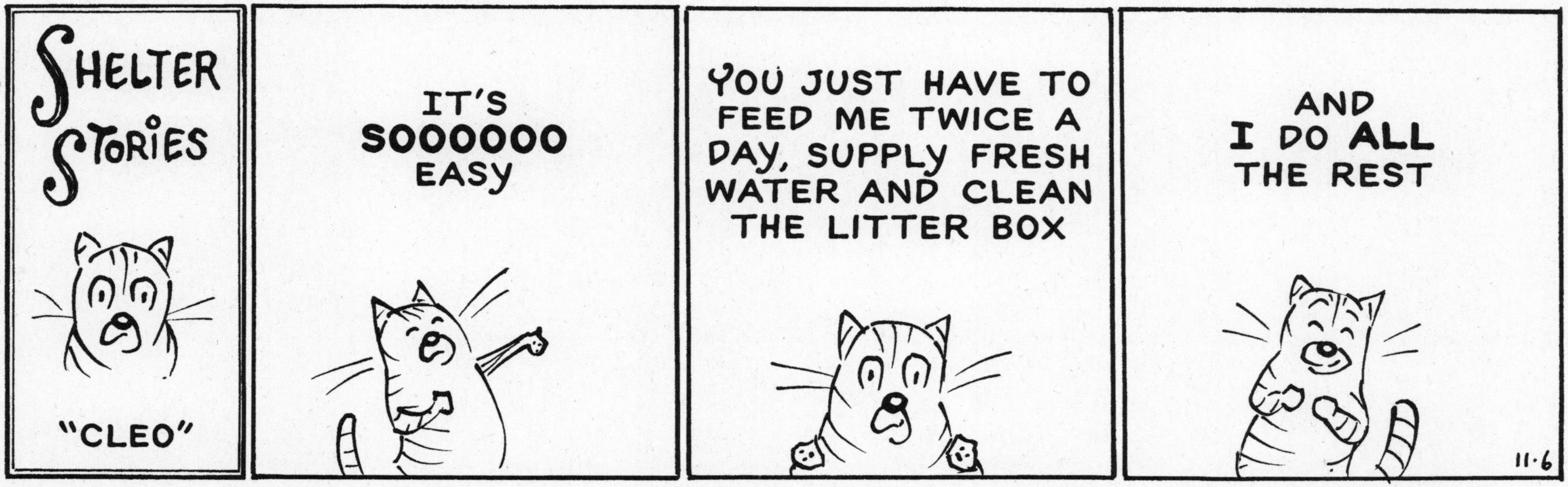
SHELTER STORIES
"CLEO"
IT'S **SOOOOOO** EASY
YOU JUST HAVE TO FEED ME TWICE A DAY, SUPPLY FRESH WATER AND CLEAN THE LITTER BOX
AND **I** DO **ALL** THE REST
11·6

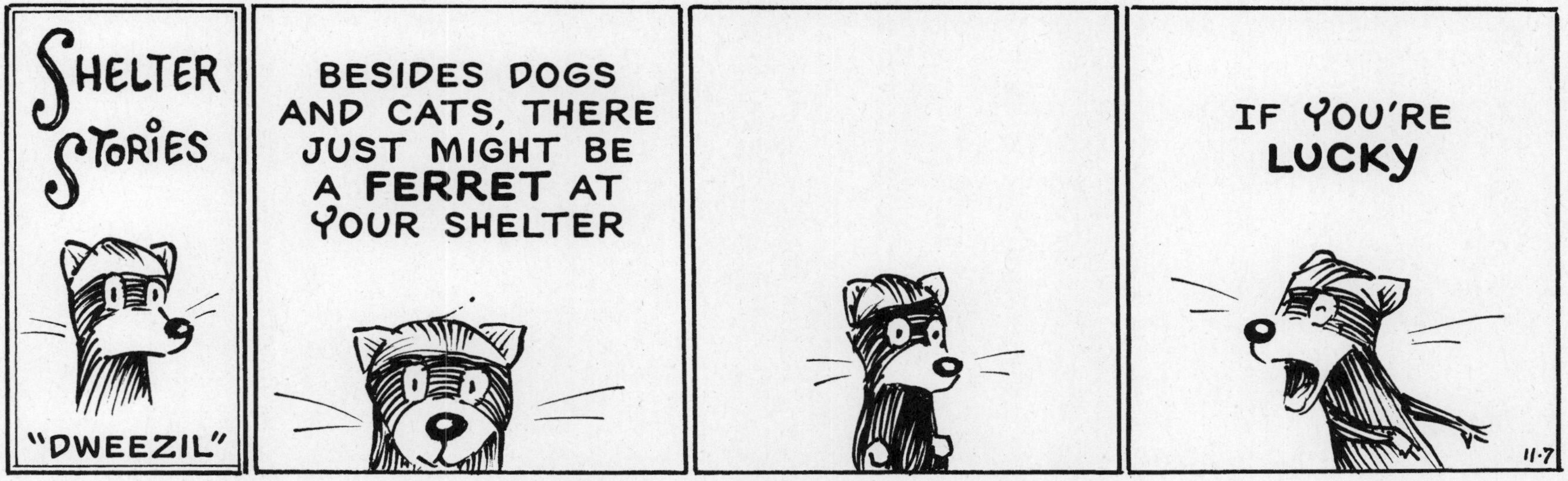
SHELTER STORIES
"DWEEZIL"
BESIDES DOGS AND CATS, THERE JUST MIGHT BE A **FERRET** AT YOUR SHELTER
IF YOU'RE **LUCKY**
11·7

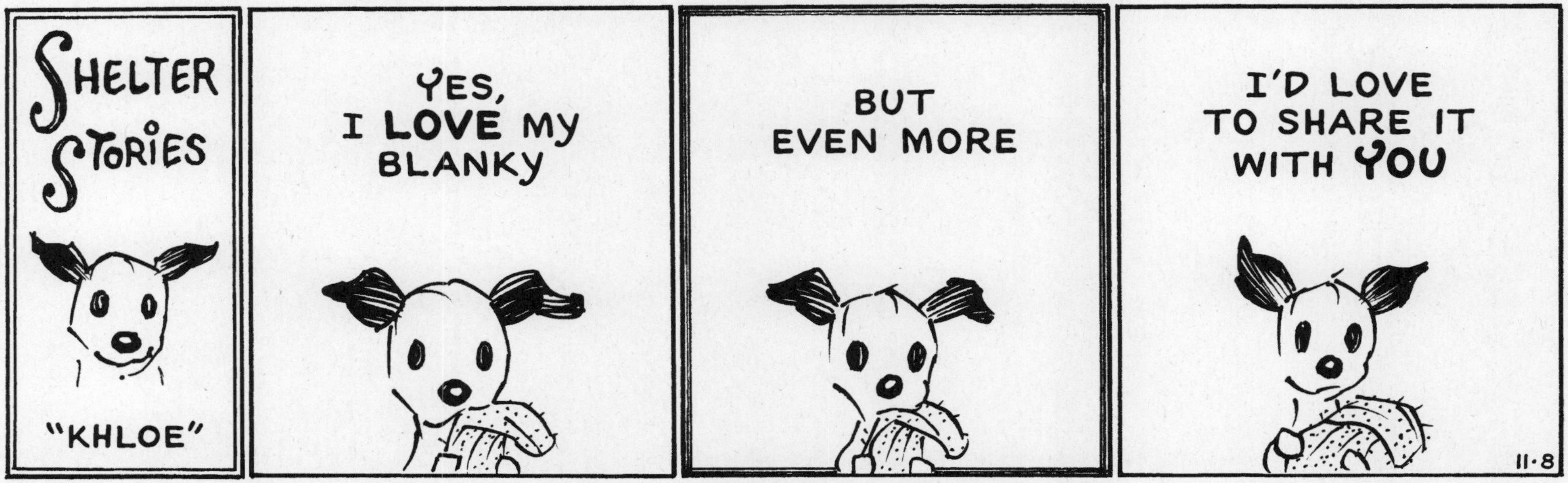
SHELTER STORIES
"KHLOE"
YES, I **LOVE** MY BLANKY
BUT EVEN MORE
I'D LOVE TO SHARE IT WITH **YOU**
11·8

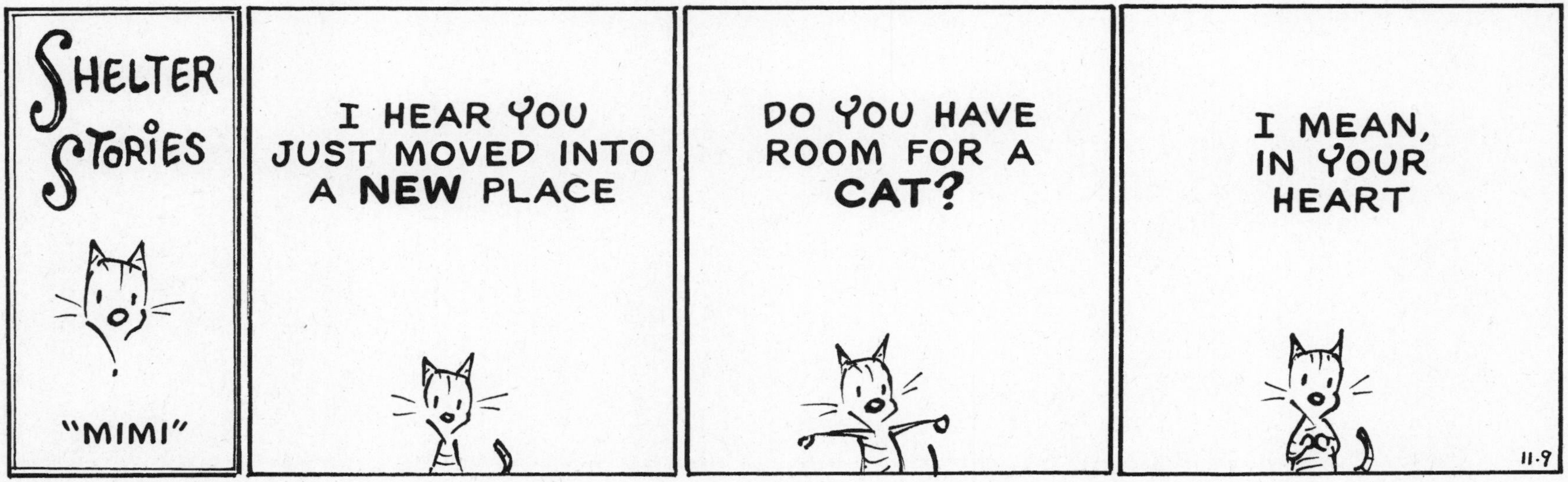
SHELTER STORIES
"MIMI"
I HEAR YOU JUST MOVED INTO A **NEW** PLACE
DO YOU HAVE ROOM FOR A **CAT?**
I MEAN, IN YOUR HEART
11·9

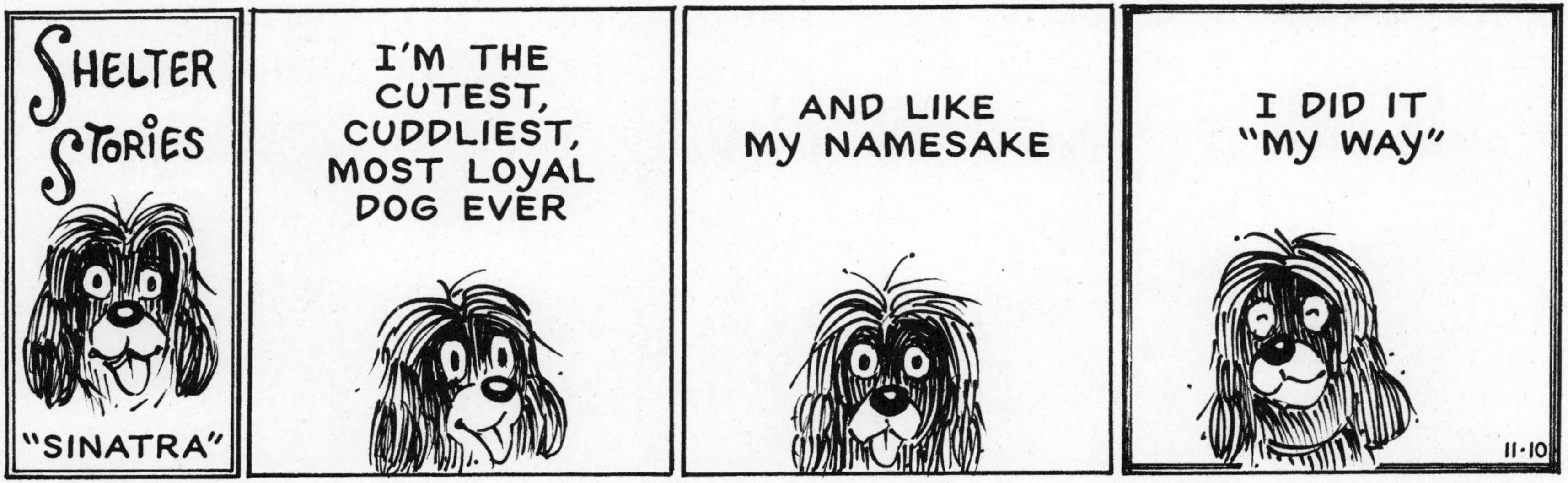
SHELTER STORIES
"SINATRA"
I'M THE CUTEST, CUDDLIEST, MOST LOYAL DOG EVER
AND LIKE MY NAMESAKE
I DID IT "MY WAY"
11·10

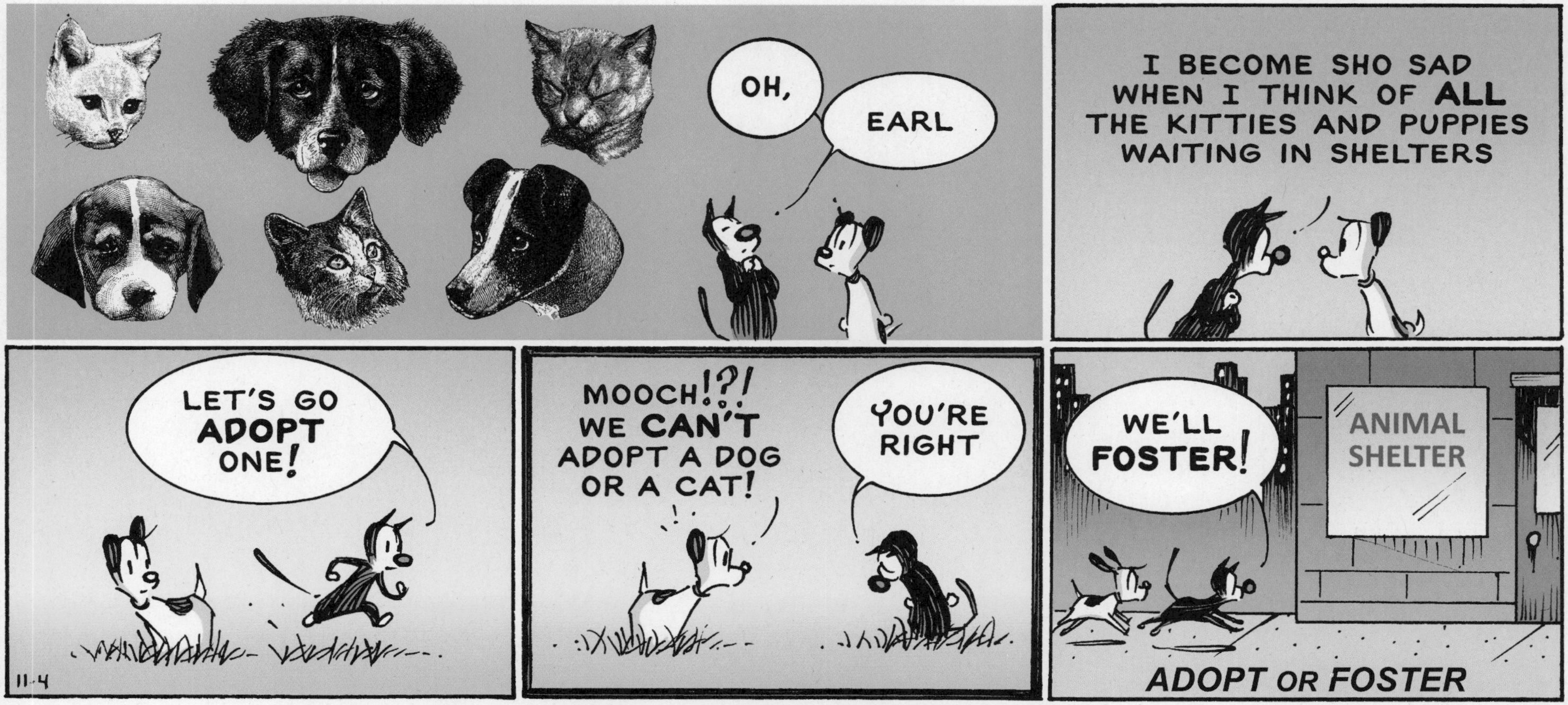
OH,
EARL
I BECOME SHO SAD WHEN I THINK OF ALL THE KITTIES AND PUPPIES WAITING IN SHELTERS
LET'S GO ADOPT ONE!
11-4
MOOCH!?! WE CAN'T ADOPT A DOG OR A CAT!
YOU'RE RIGHT
WE'LL FOSTER!
ANIMAL SHELTER
ADOPT OR FOSTER

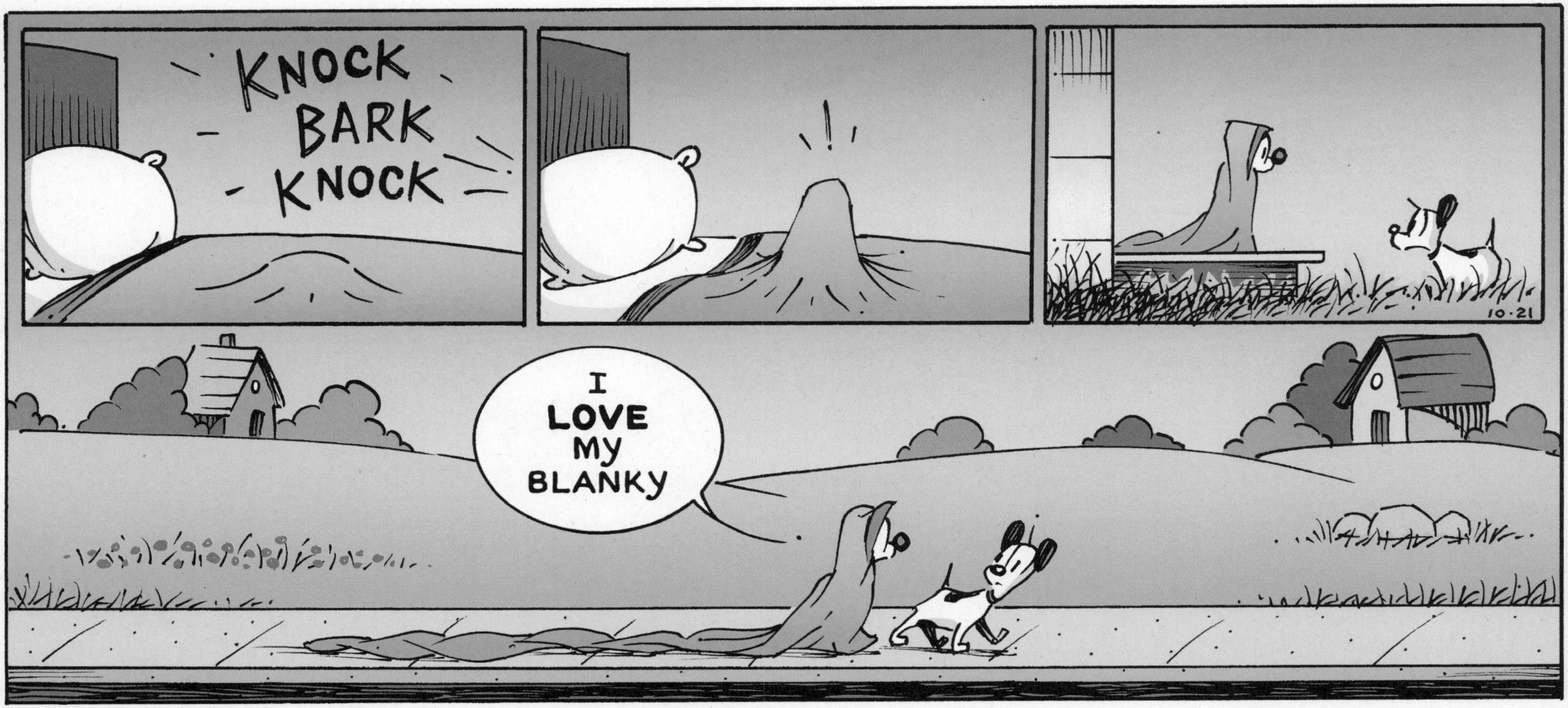
KNOCK
BARK
KNOCK
!
10·21
I LOVE MY BLANKY

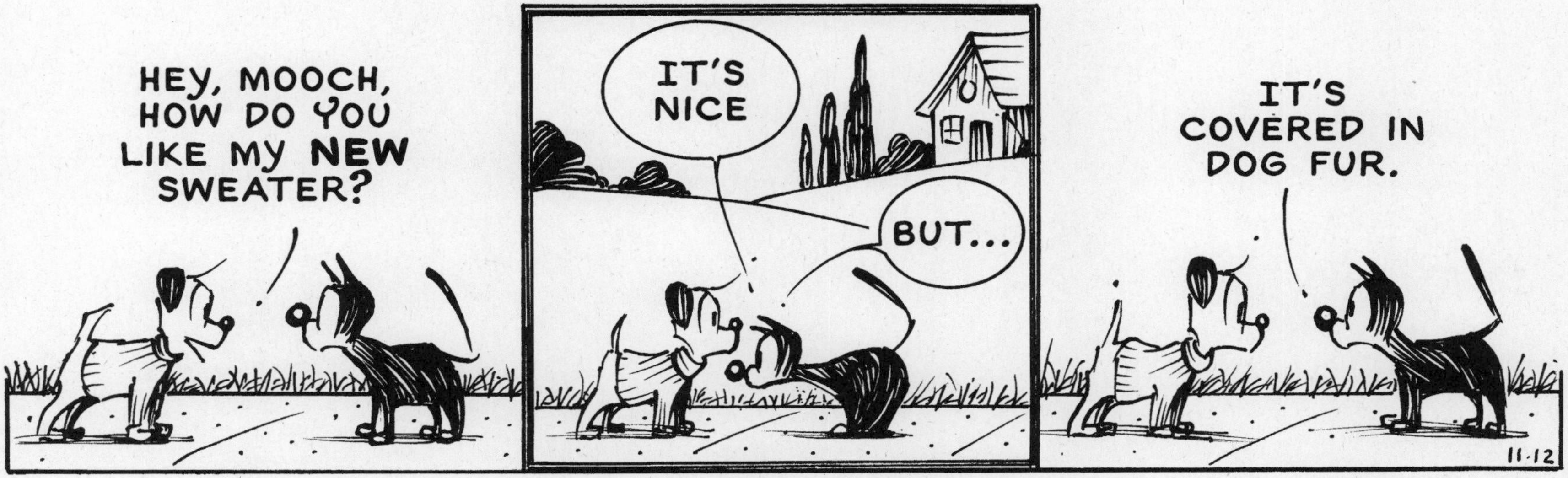
HEY, MOOCH, HOW DO YOU LIKE MY **NEW** SWEATER?
IT'S NICE
BUT...
IT'S COVERED IN DOG FUR.
11-12

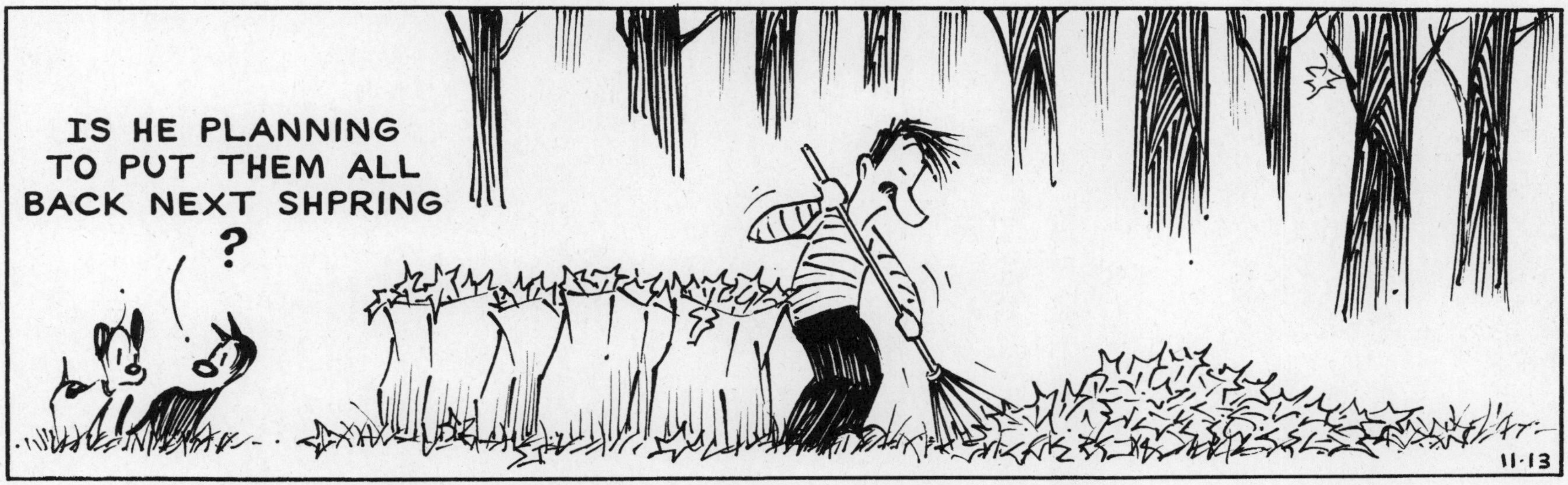
IS HE PLANNING TO PUT THEM ALL BACK NEXT SHPRING ?
11-13

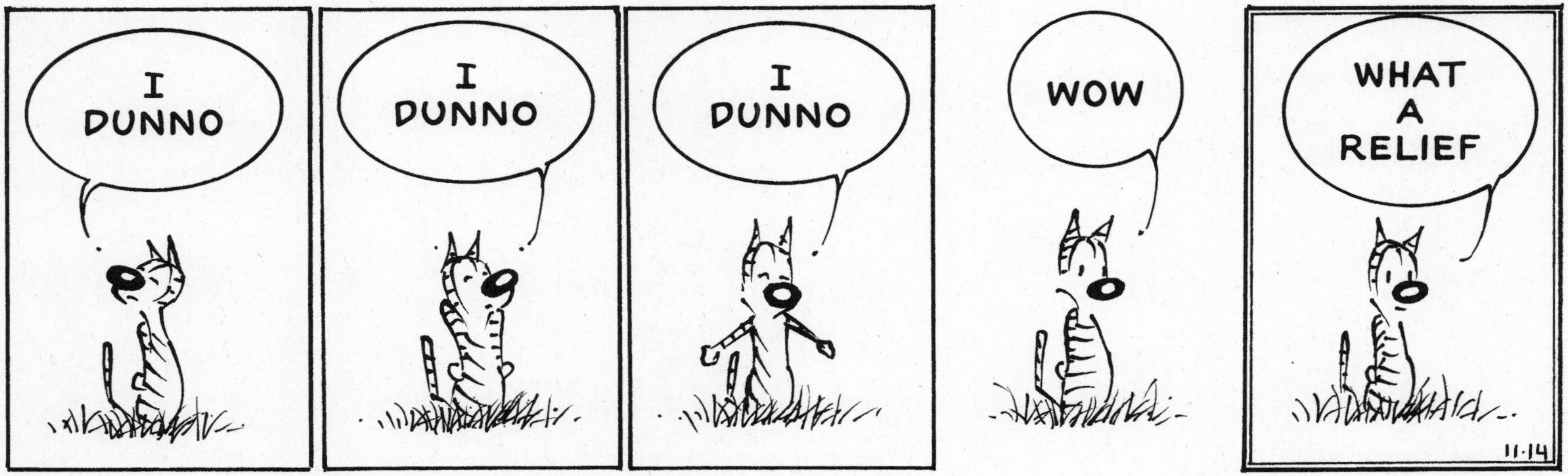
I DUNNO
I DUNNO
I DUNNO
WOW
WHAT A RELIEF
11·14

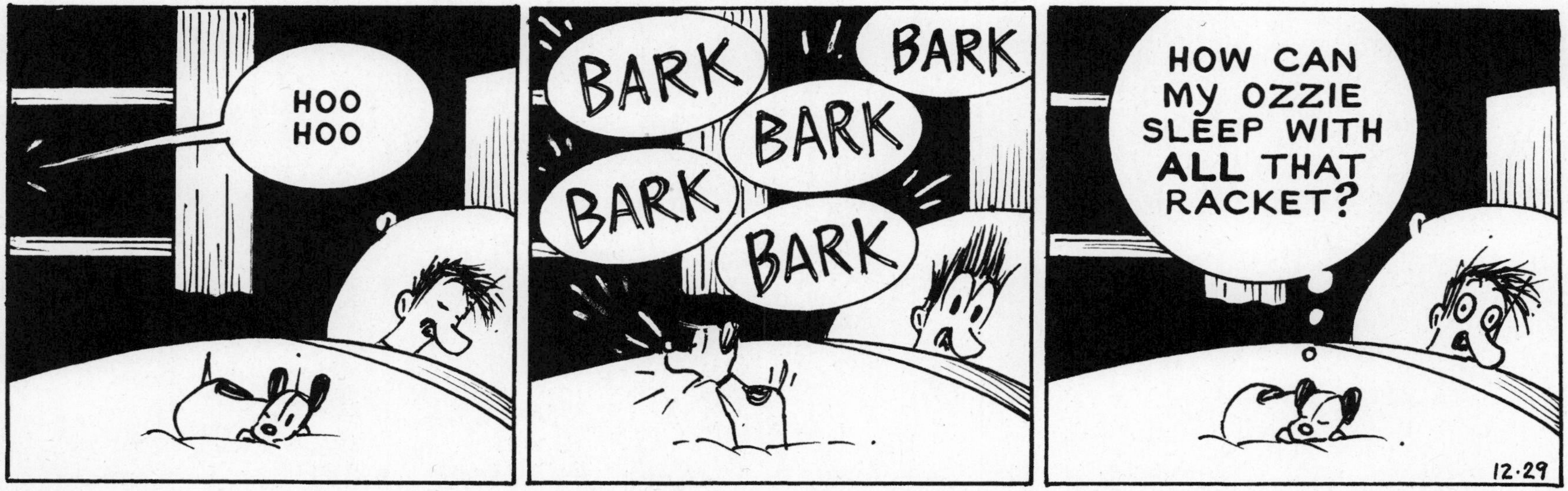
HOO HOO
BARK
BARK
BARK
BARK
BARK
HOW CAN MY OZZIE SLEEP WITH ALL THAT RACKET?
12·29

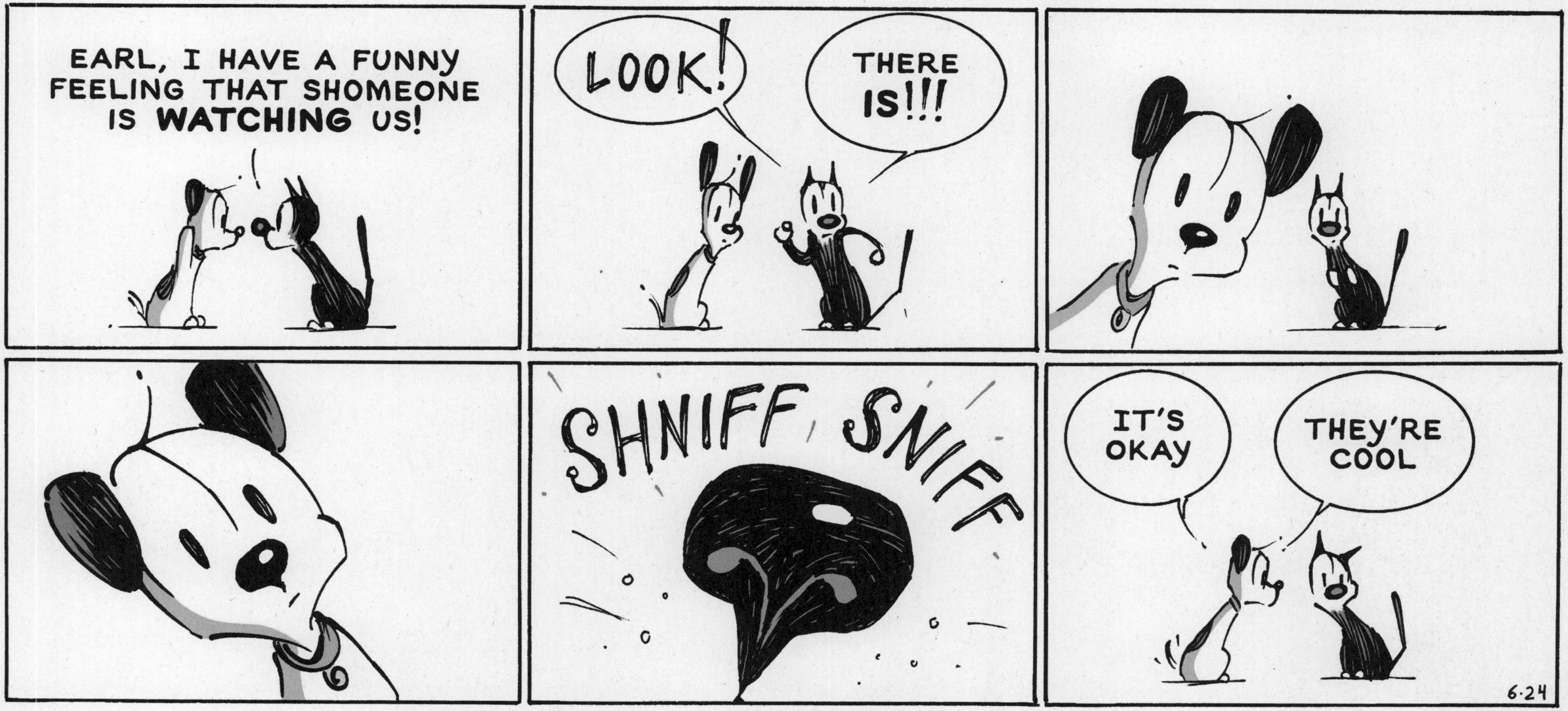
EARL, I HAVE A FUNNY FEELING THAT SHOMEONE IS WATCHING US!
LOOK!
THERE IS!!!
SHNIFF SNIFF
IT'S OKAY
THEY'RE COOL
6·24

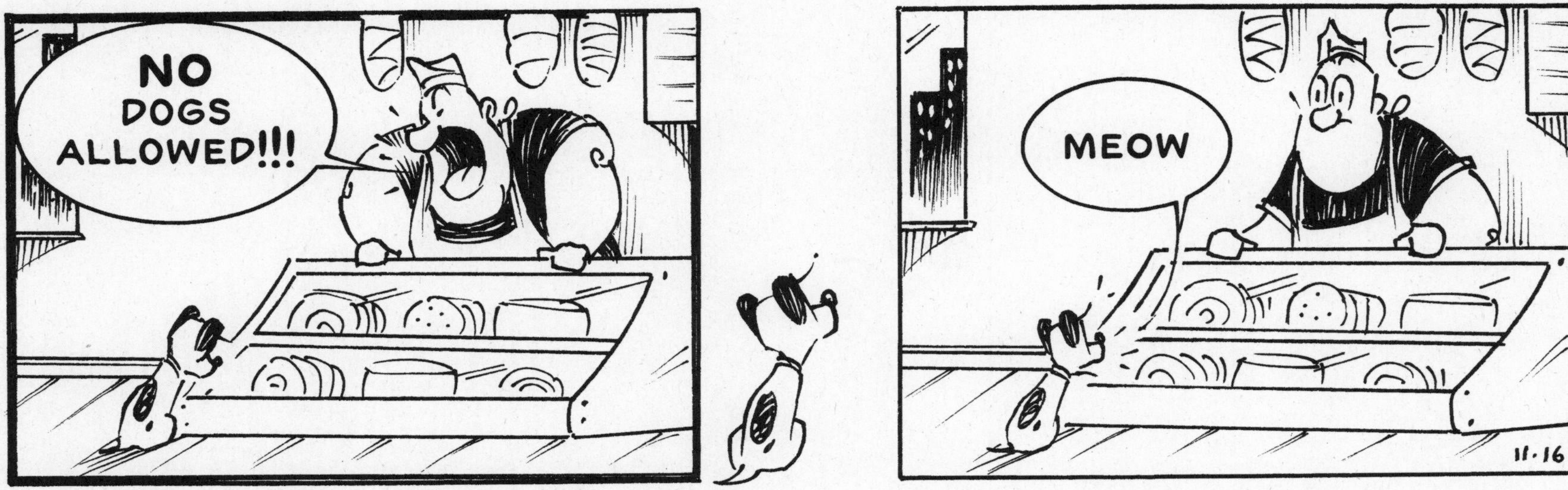
NO DOGS ALLOWED!!!
MEOW
11·16

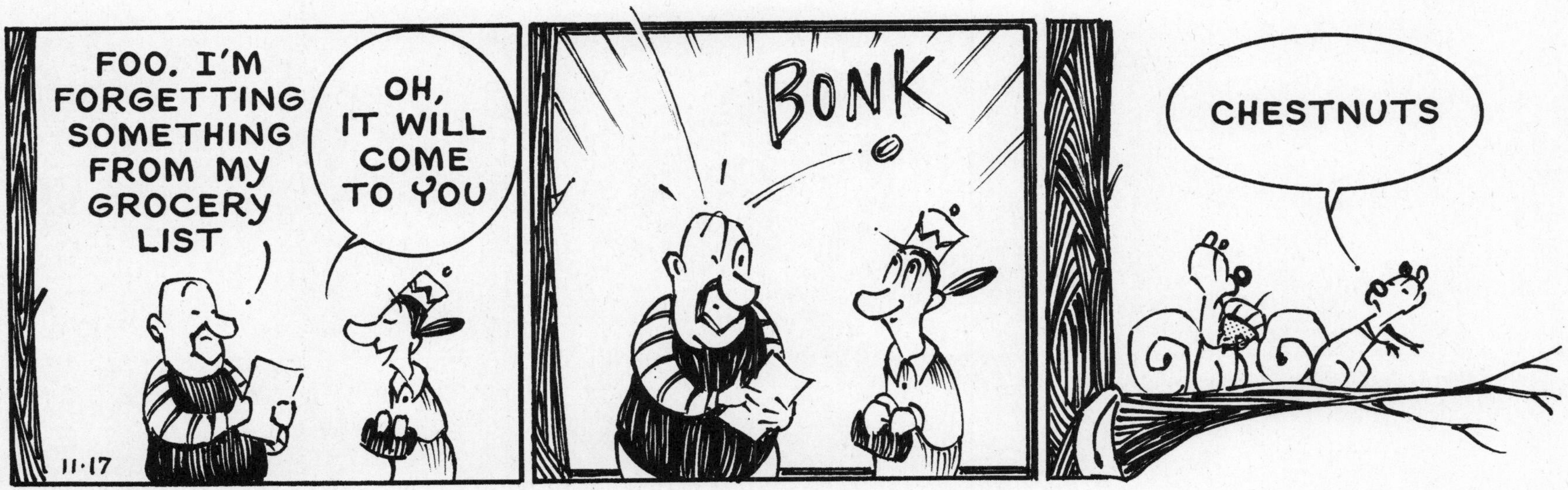
FOO. I'M FORGETTING SOMETHING FROM MY GROCERY LIST
OH, IT WILL COME TO YOU
11·17
BONK
CHESTNUTS

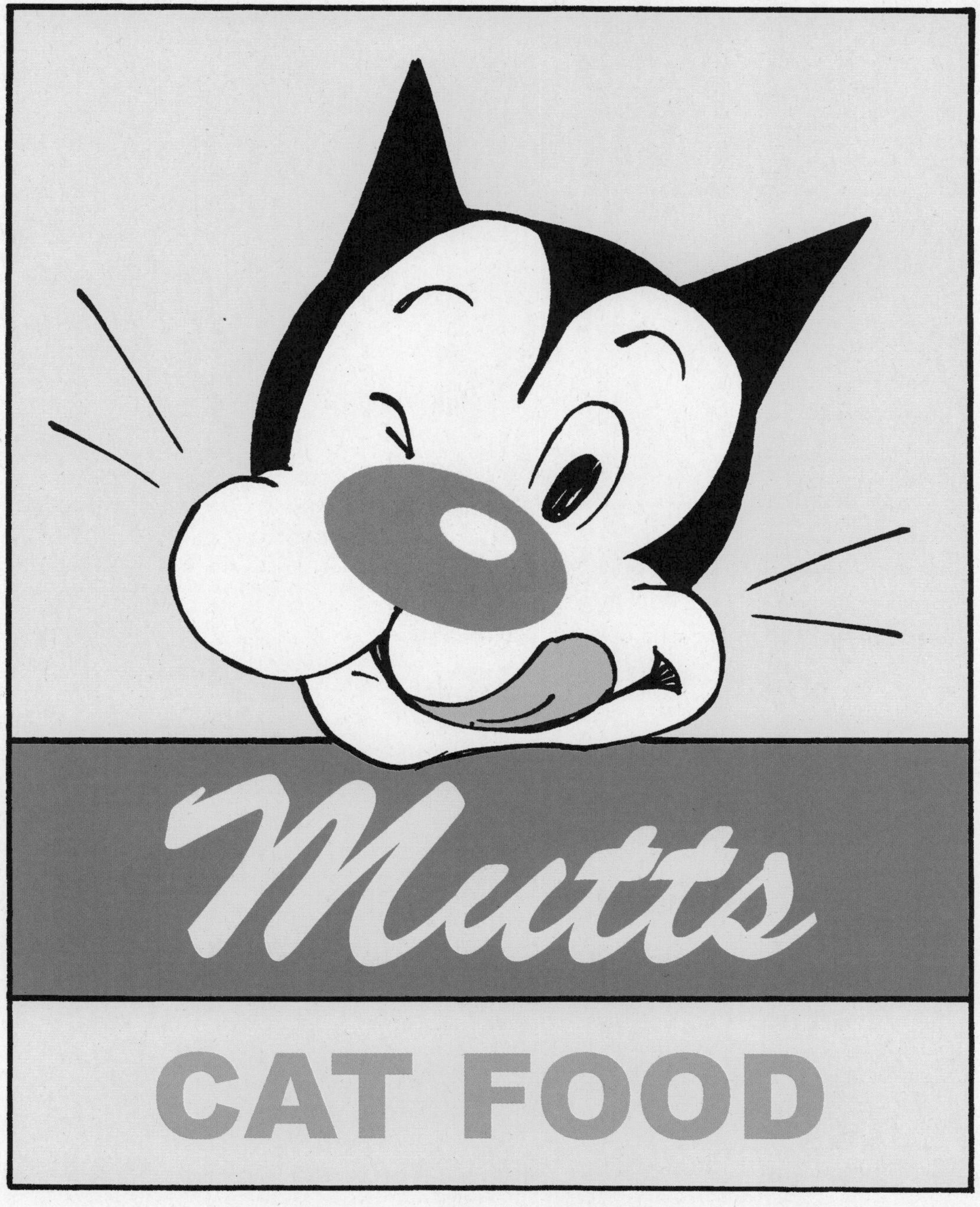
Mutts
CAT FOOD

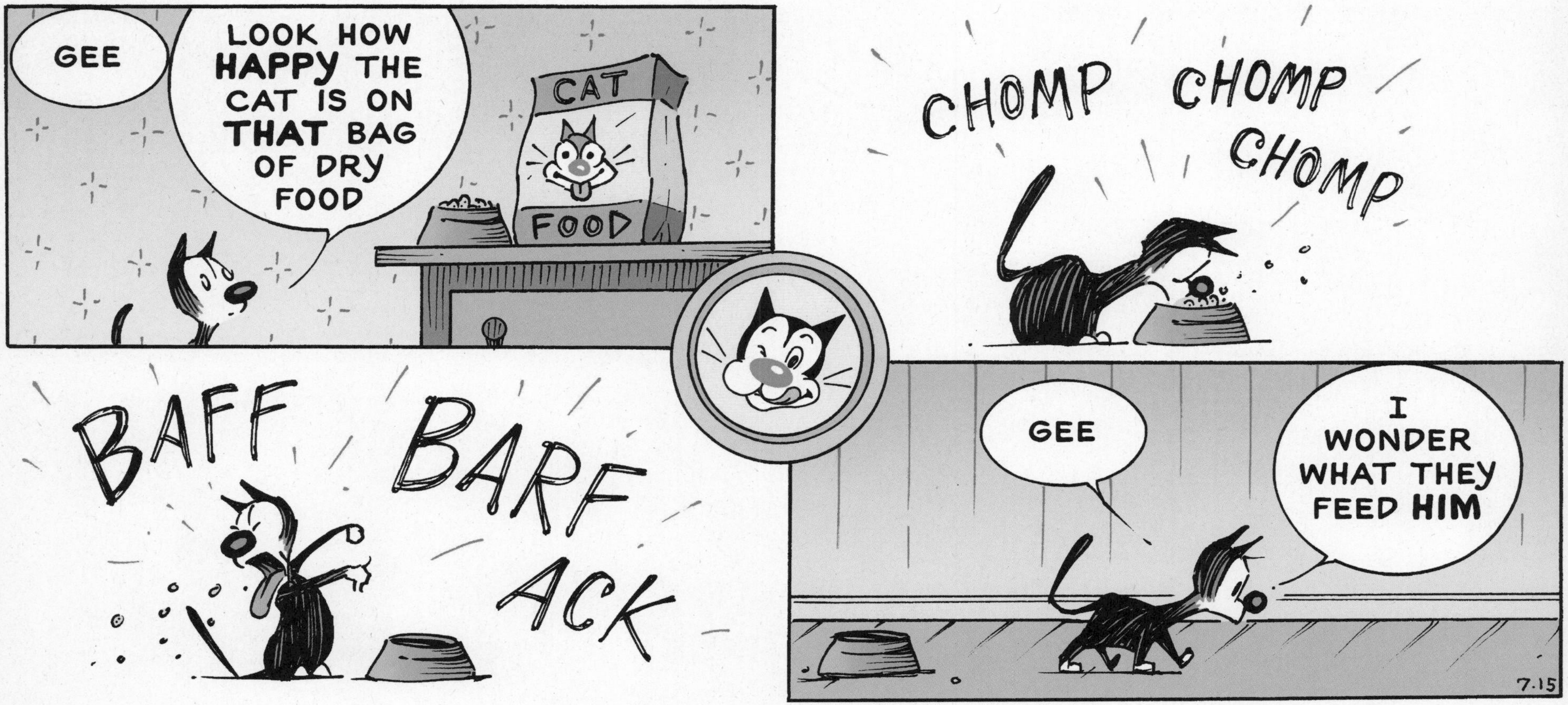
GEE
LOOK HOW HAPPY THE CAT IS ON THAT BAG OF DRY FOOD
CAT
FOOD
CHOMP CHOMP
CHOMP
BAFF
BARF
ACK
GEE
I WONDER WHAT THEY FEED HIM
7.15

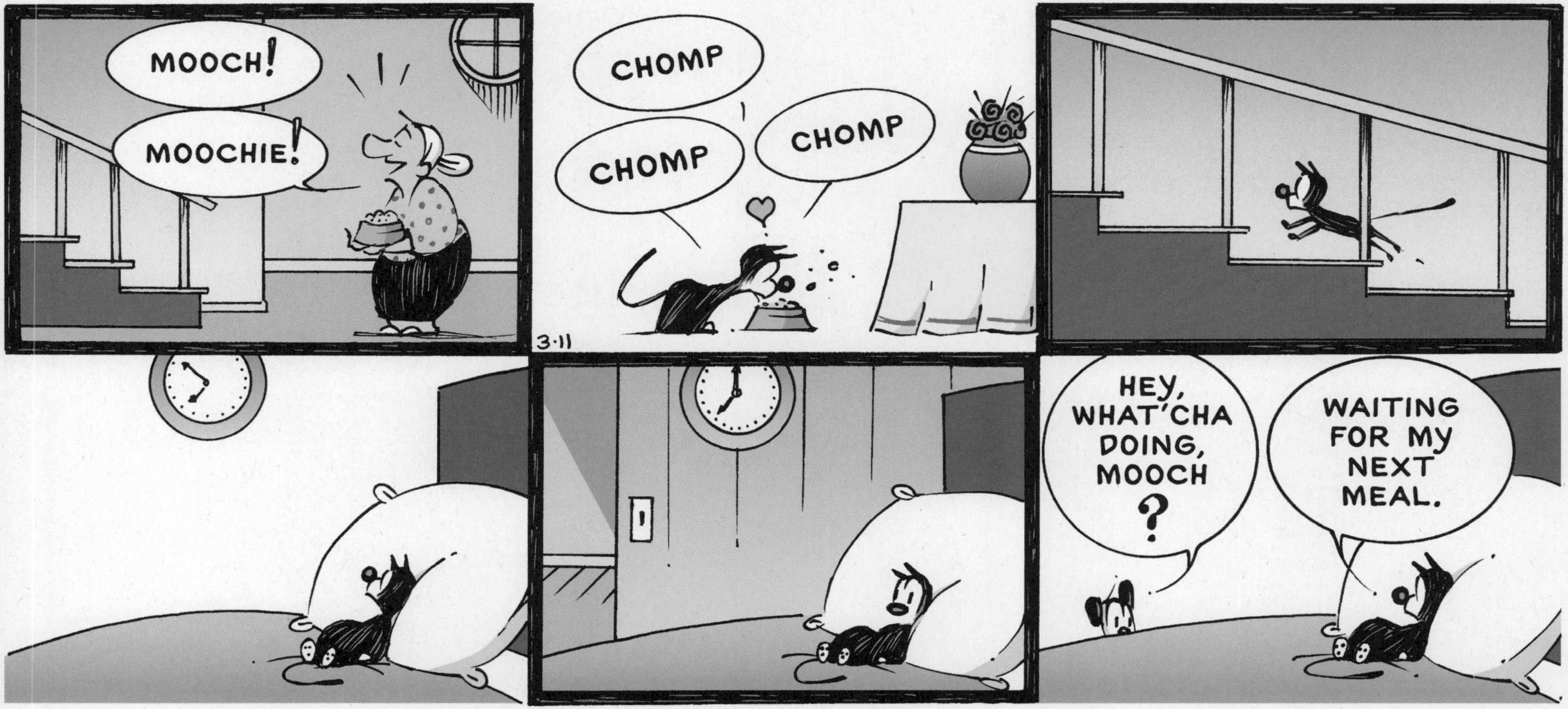
MOOCH!
MOOCHIE!
CHOMP
CHOMP
CHOMP
3·11
HEY, WHAT'CHA DOING, MOOCH ?
WAITING FOR MY NEXT MEAL.

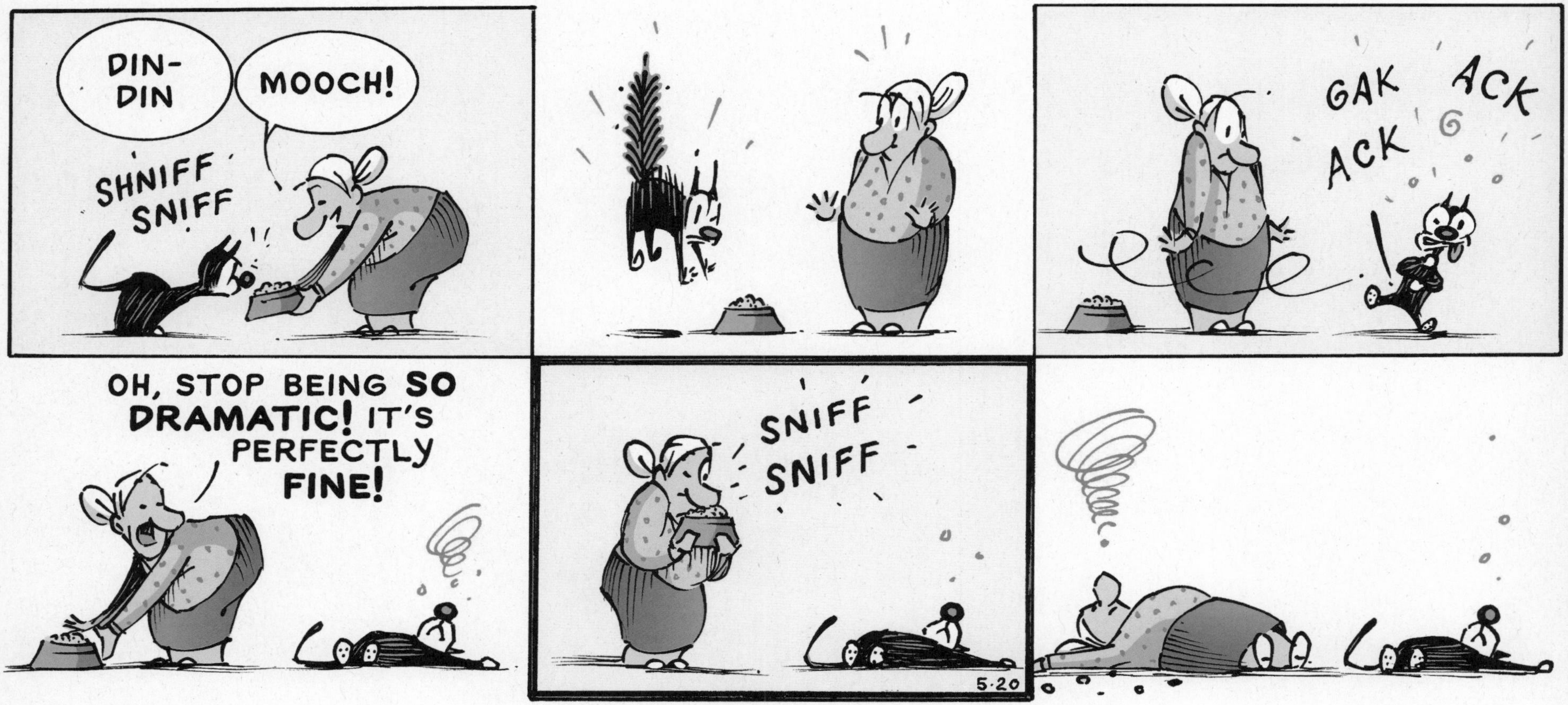
DIN-DIN
MOOCH!
SHNIFF SNIFF
GAK ACK
ACK
OH, STOP BEING SO DRAMATIC! IT'S PERFECTLY FINE!
SNIFF SNIFF
5·20

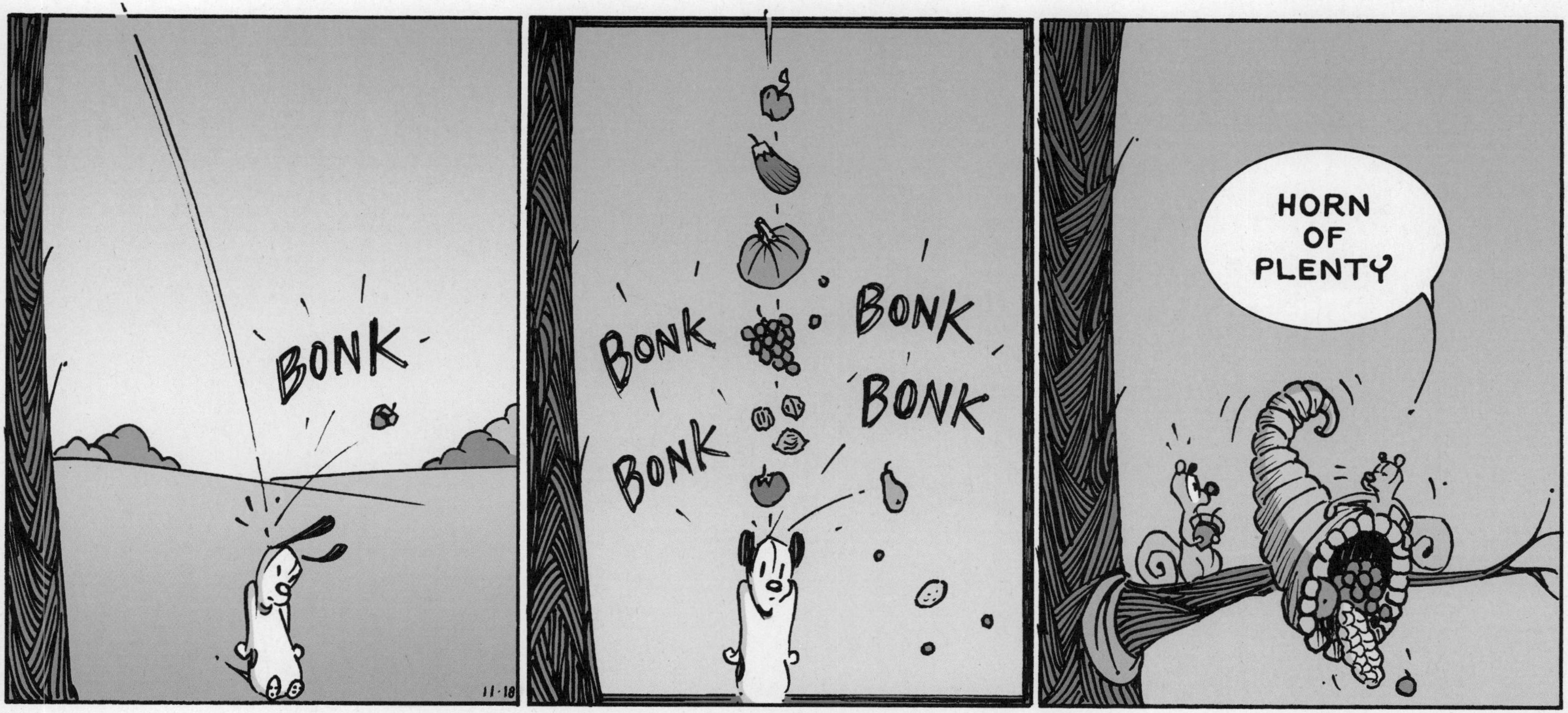
BONK
11-18
BONK
BONK
BONK
BONK
HORN OF PLENTY

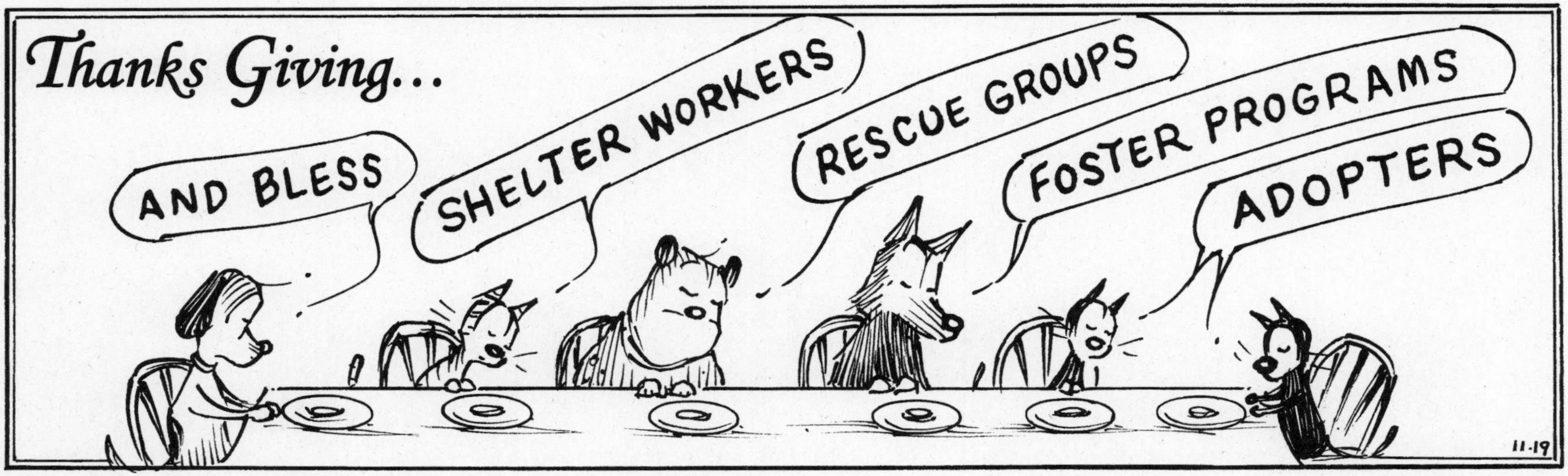
Thanks Giving...
AND BLESS
SHELTER WORKERS
RESCUE GROUPS
FOSTER PROGRAMS
ADOPTERS
11-19

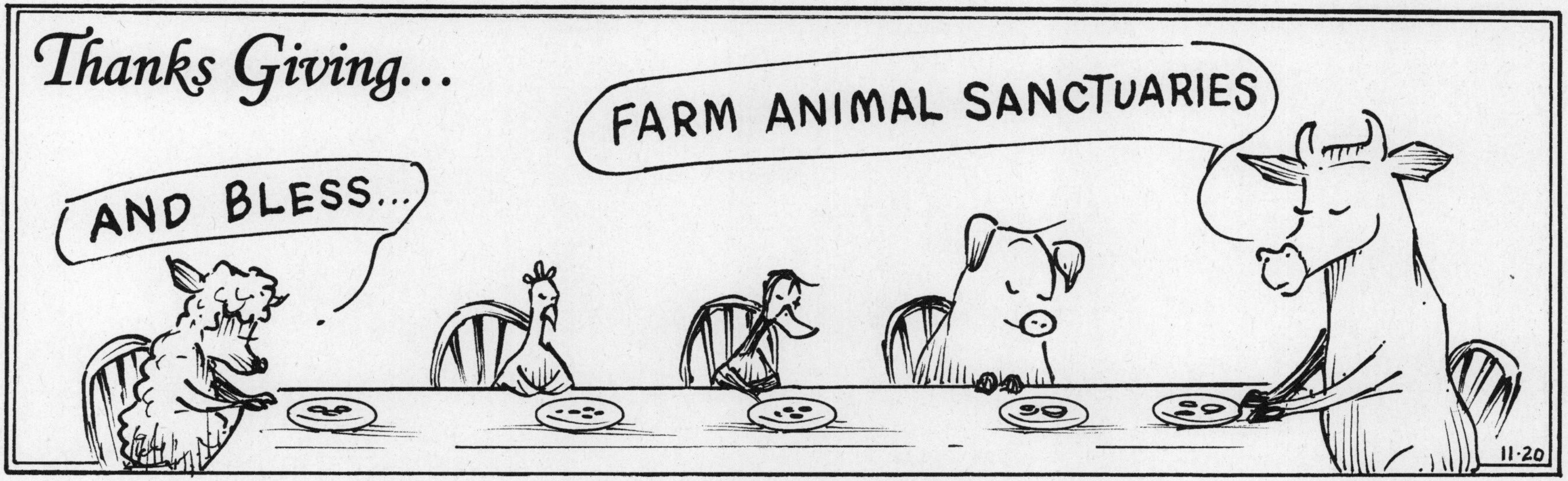

Thanks Giving...
AND BLESS...
FARM ANIMAL SANCTUARIES
11·20

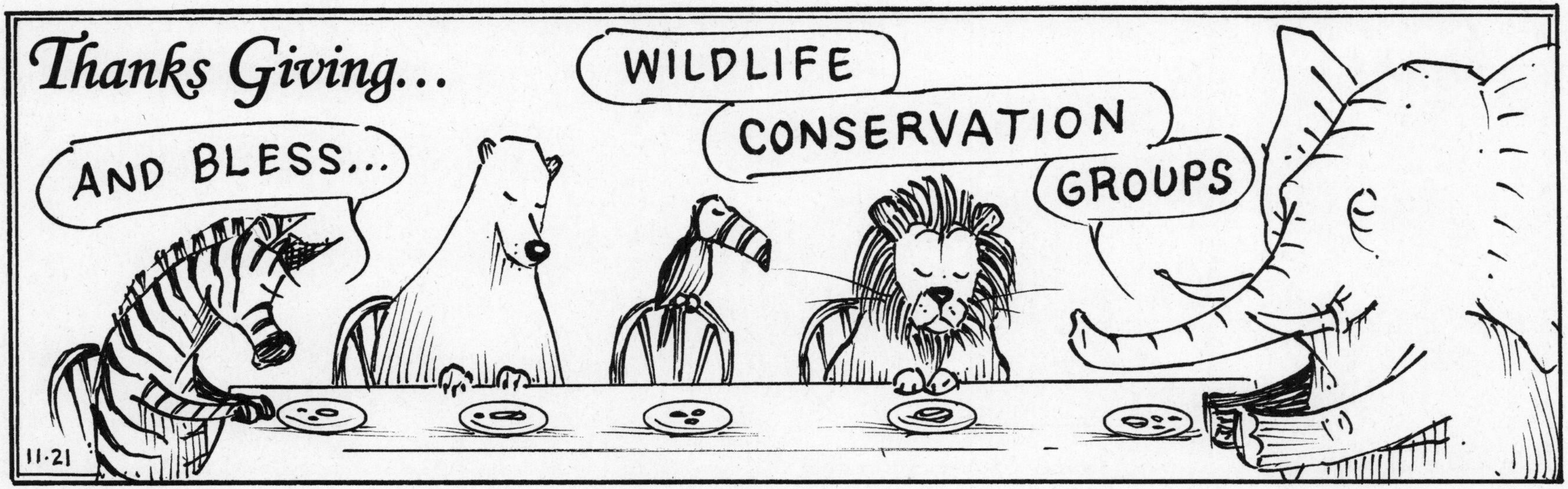
Thanks Giving...
AND BLESS...
WILDLIFE
CONSERVATION
GROUPS
11·21

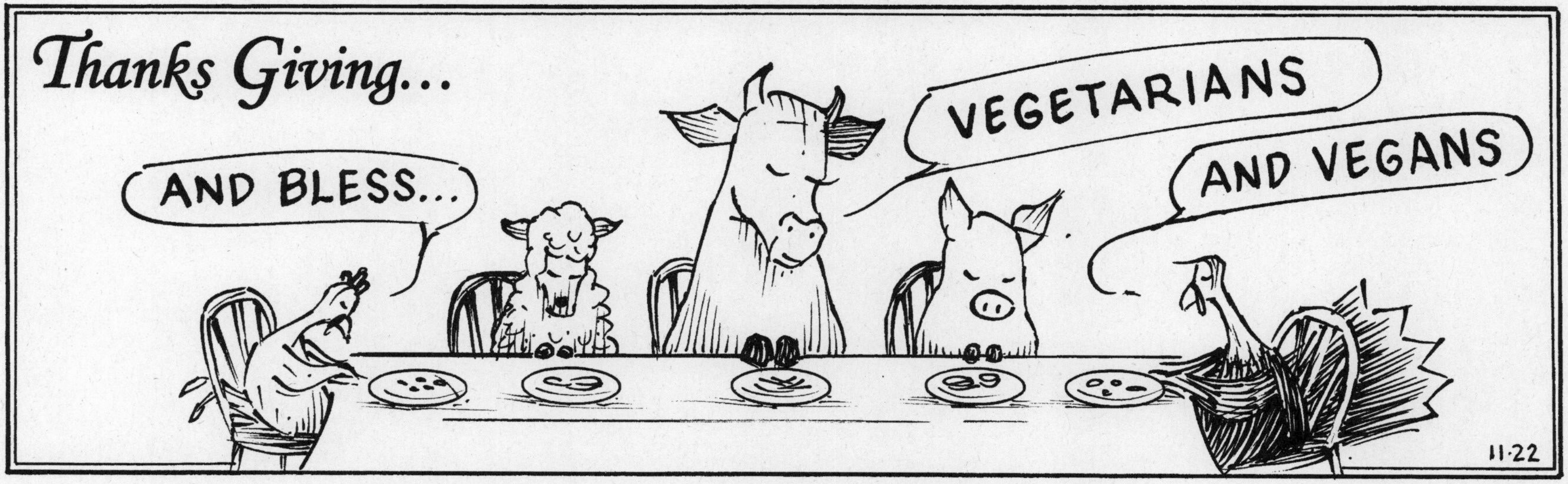
Thanks Giving...
AND BLESS...
VEGETARIANS
AND VEGANS
11·22

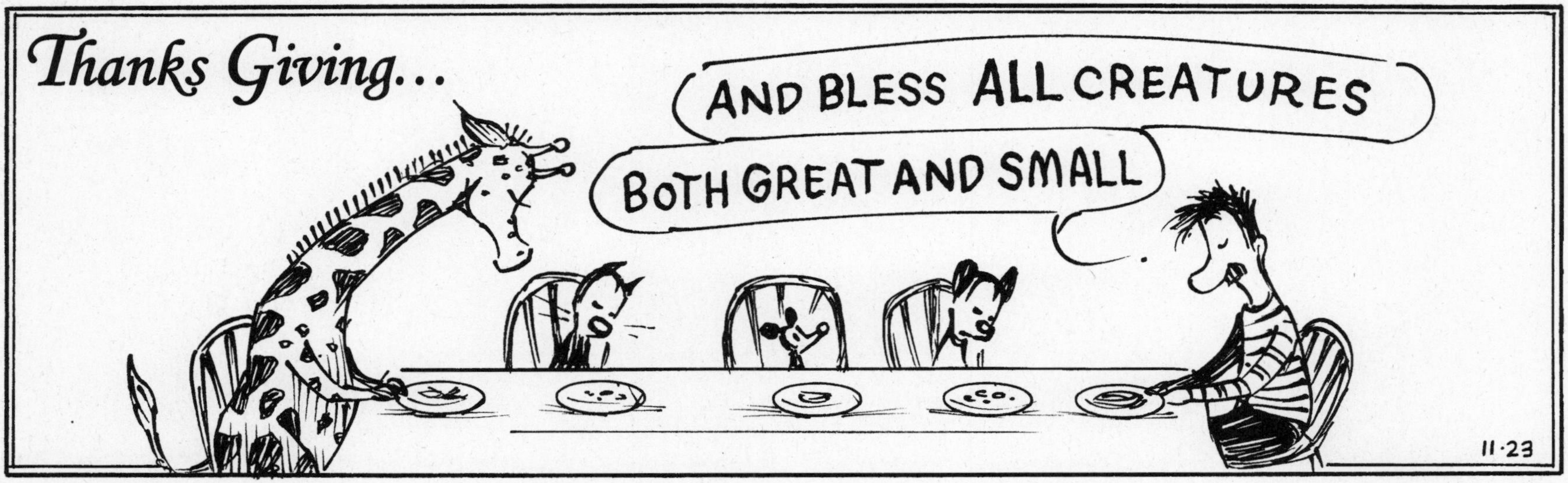
Thanks Giving...
AND BLESS ALL CREATURES
BOTH GREAT AND SMALL
11·23

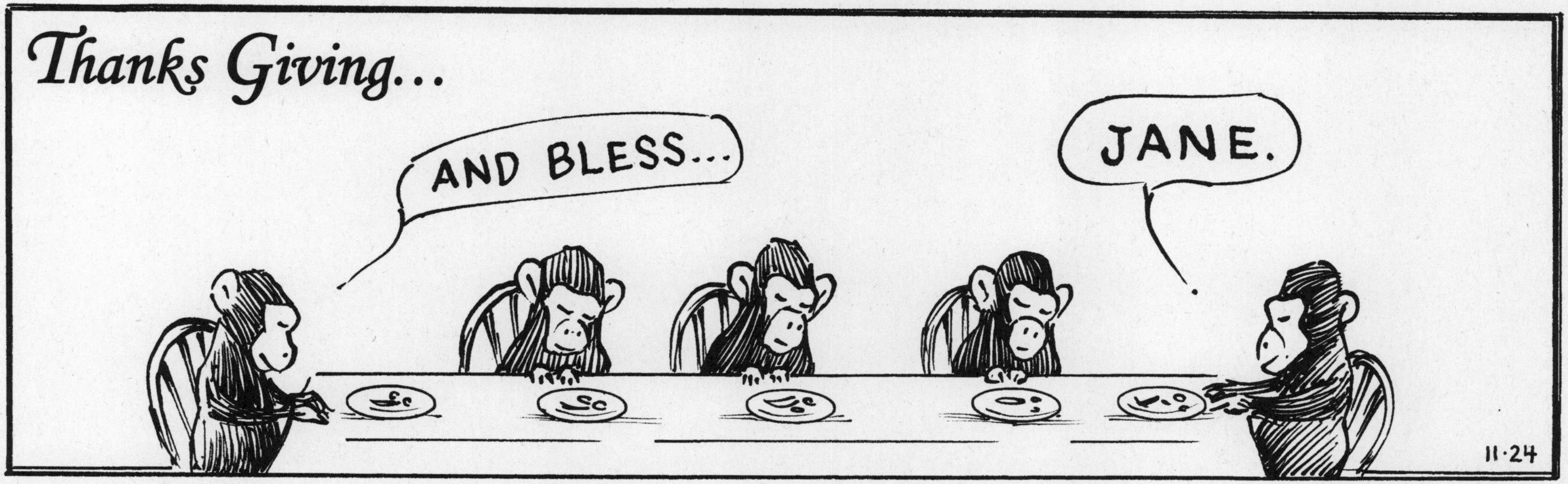
Thanks Giving...
AND BLESS...
JANE.
11·24

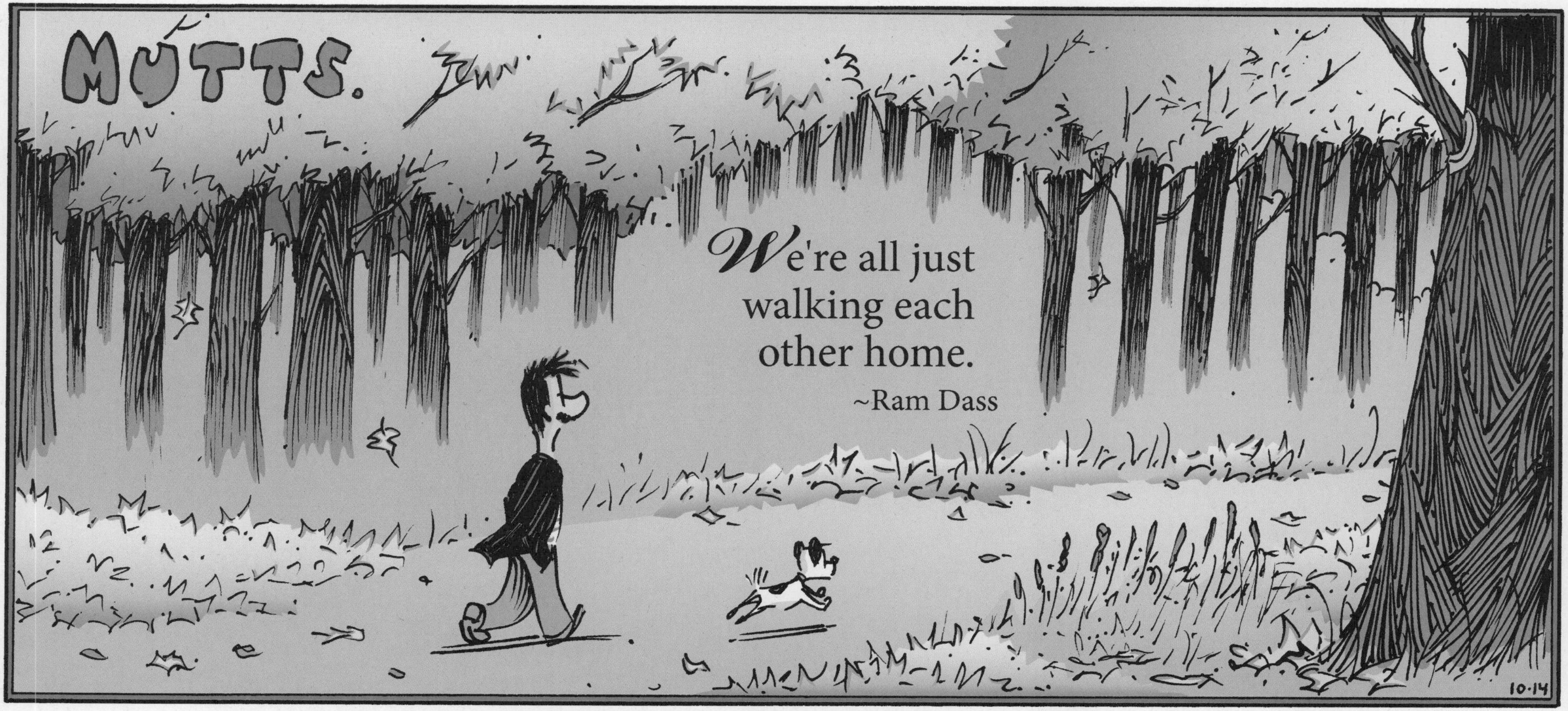
MUTTS.
We're all just walking each other home.
~Ram Dass
10·14

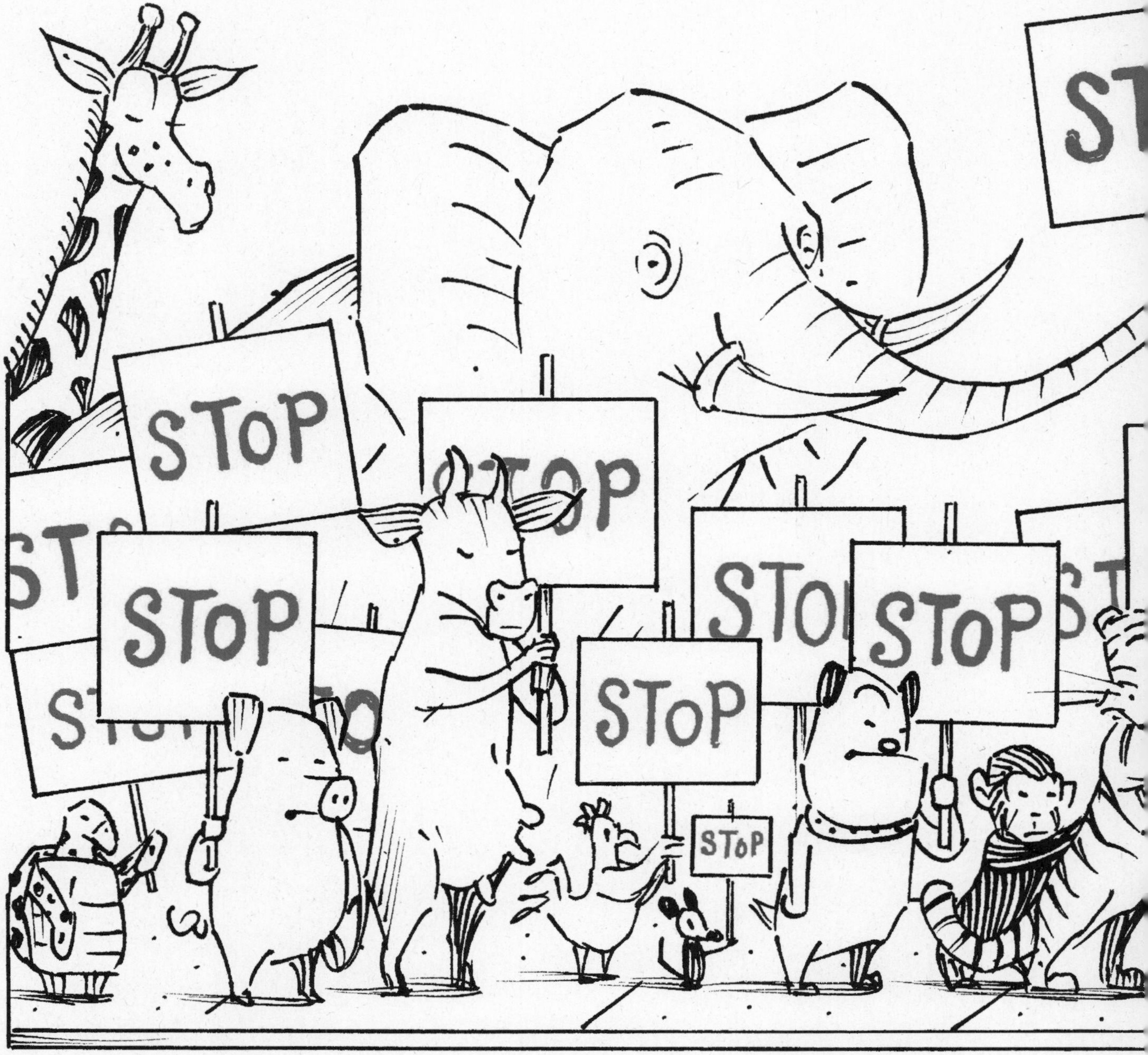
STOP
STOP
STOP
STOP
STOP
STOP

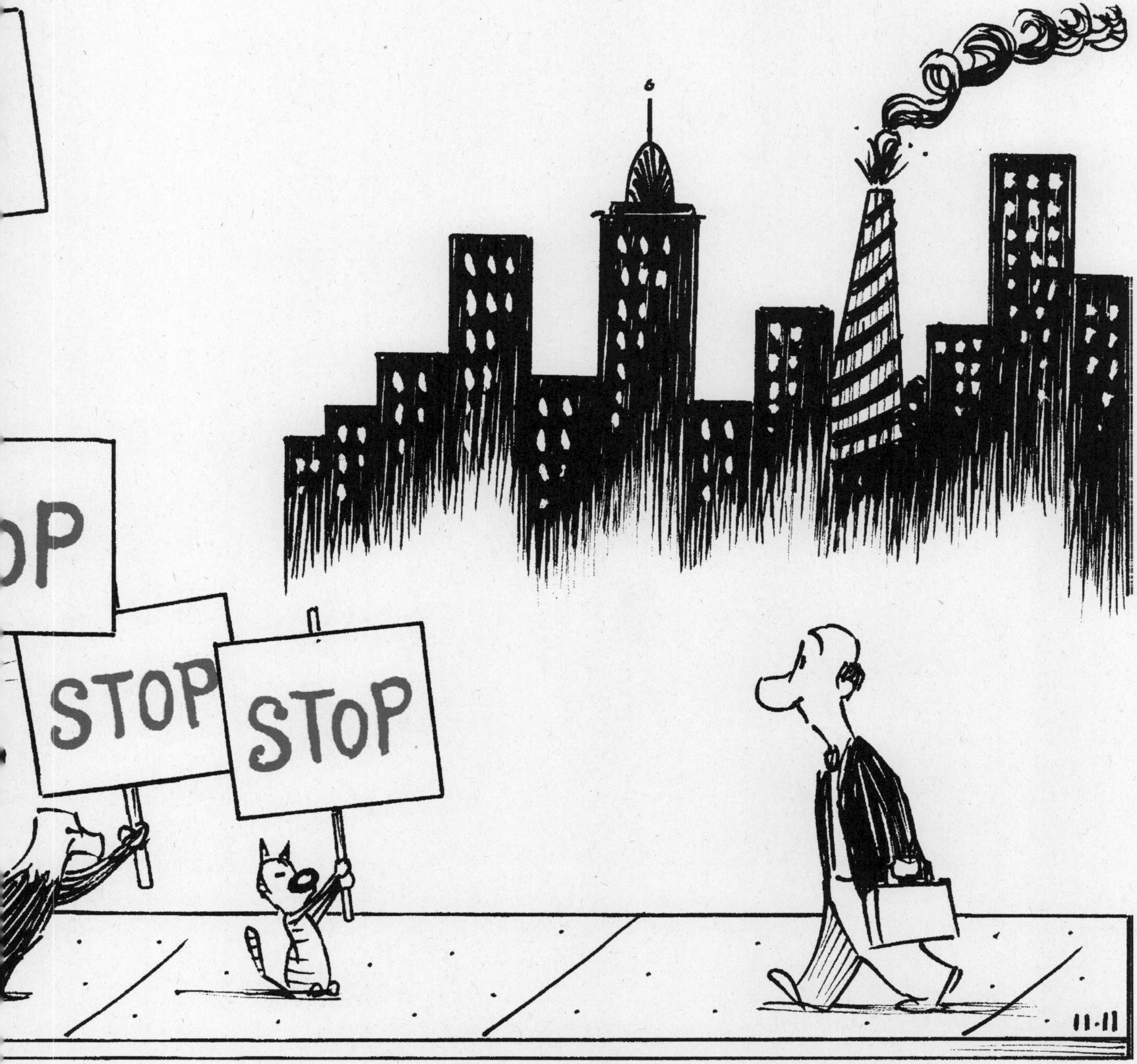
OP
STOP
STOP
6
11-11

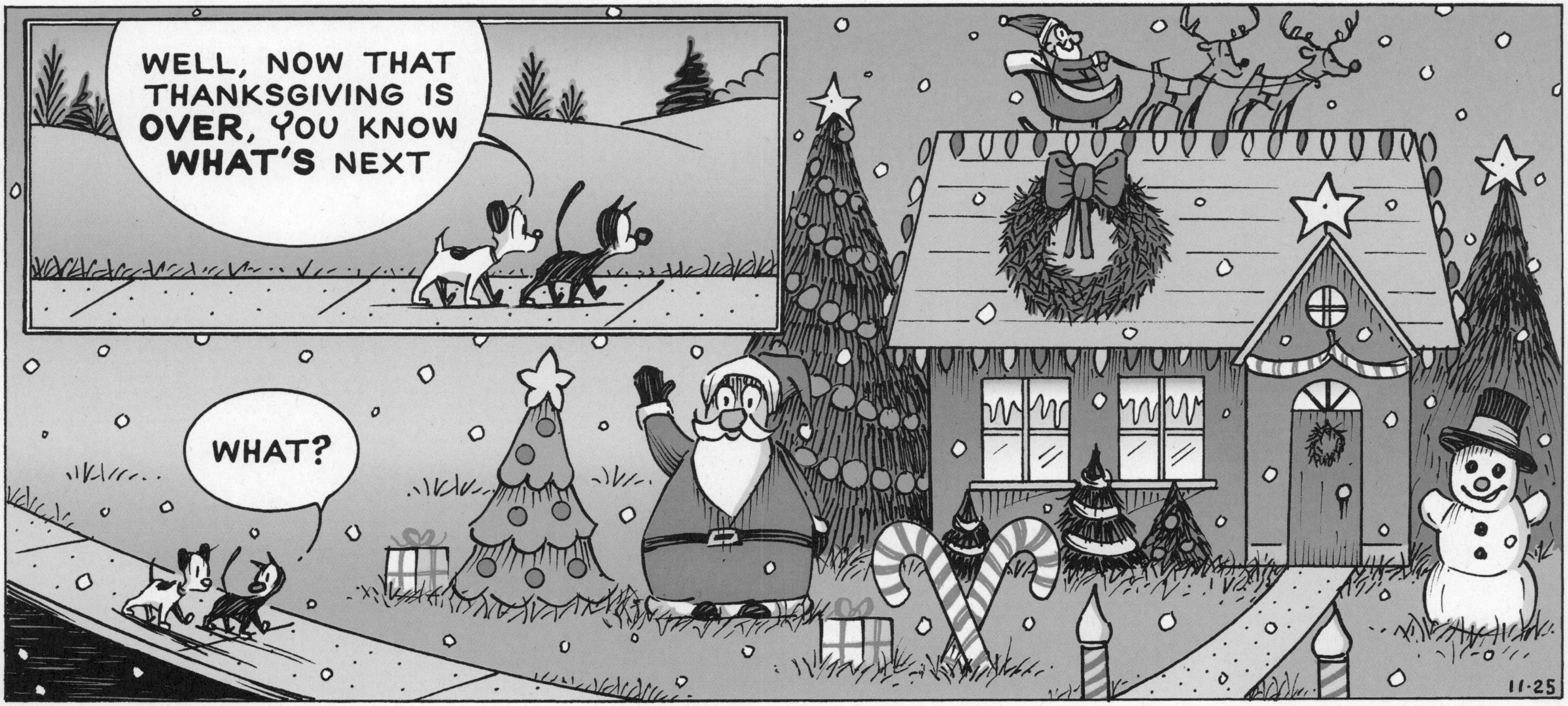
WELL, NOW THAT THANKSGIVING IS OVER, YOU KNOW WHAT'S NEXT
WHAT?
11·25

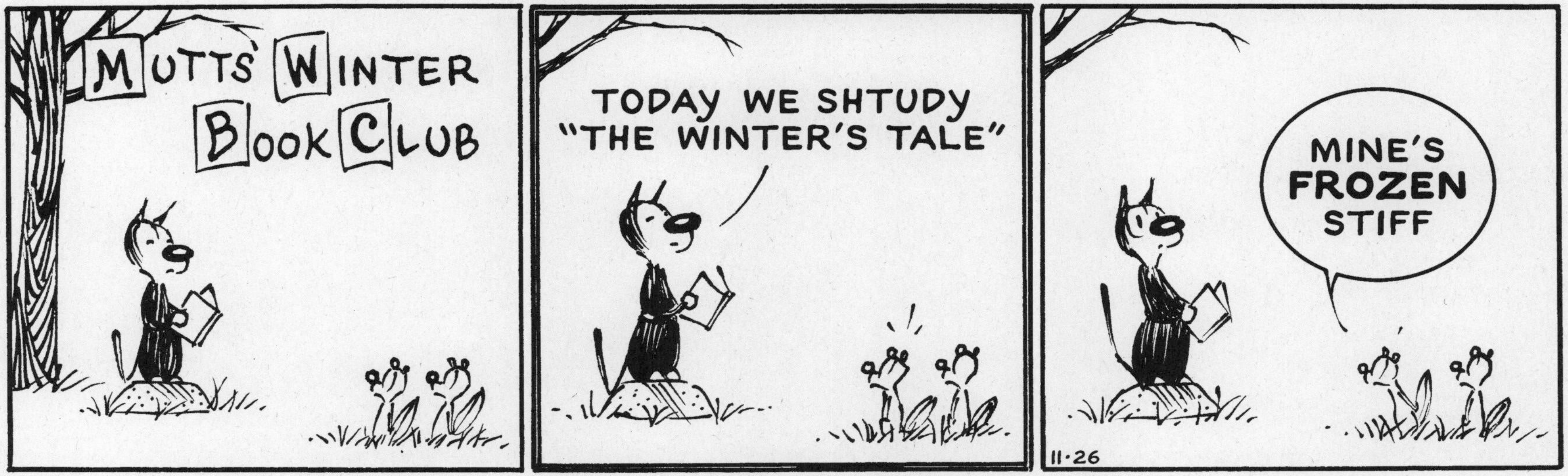
MUTTS WINTER BOOK CLUB
TODAY WE SHTUDY "THE WINTER'S TALE"
MINE'S **FROZEN** STIFF
11·26

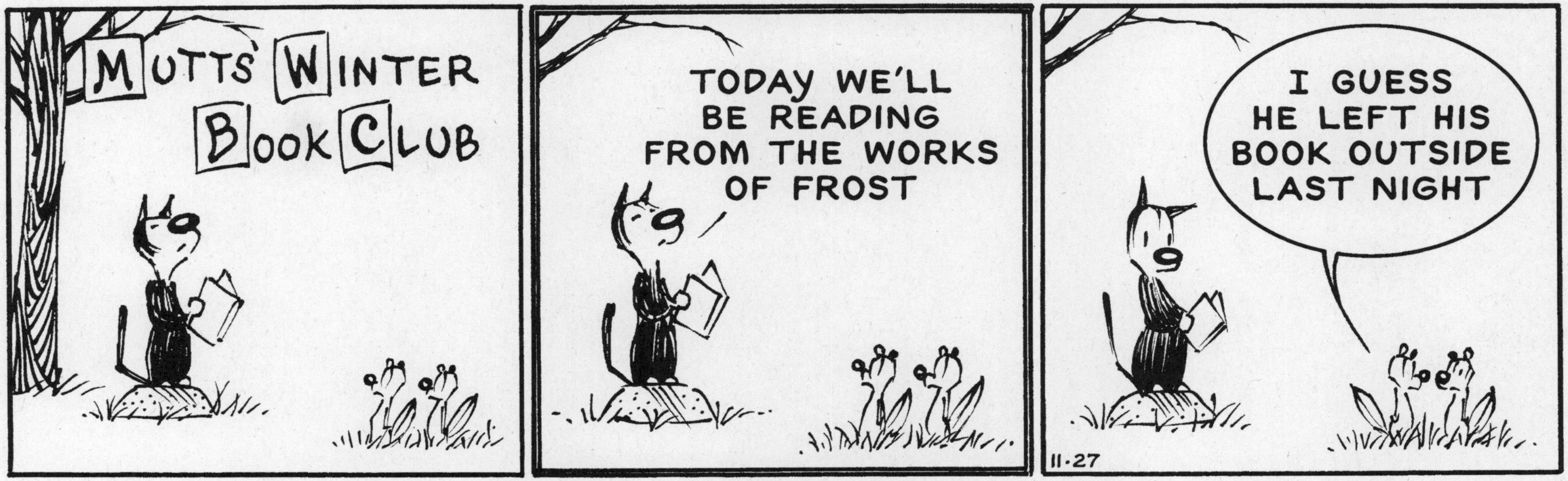
MUTTS WINTER BOOK CLUB
TODAY WE'LL BE READING FROM THE WORKS OF FROST
I GUESS HE LEFT HIS BOOK OUTSIDE LAST NIGHT
11·27

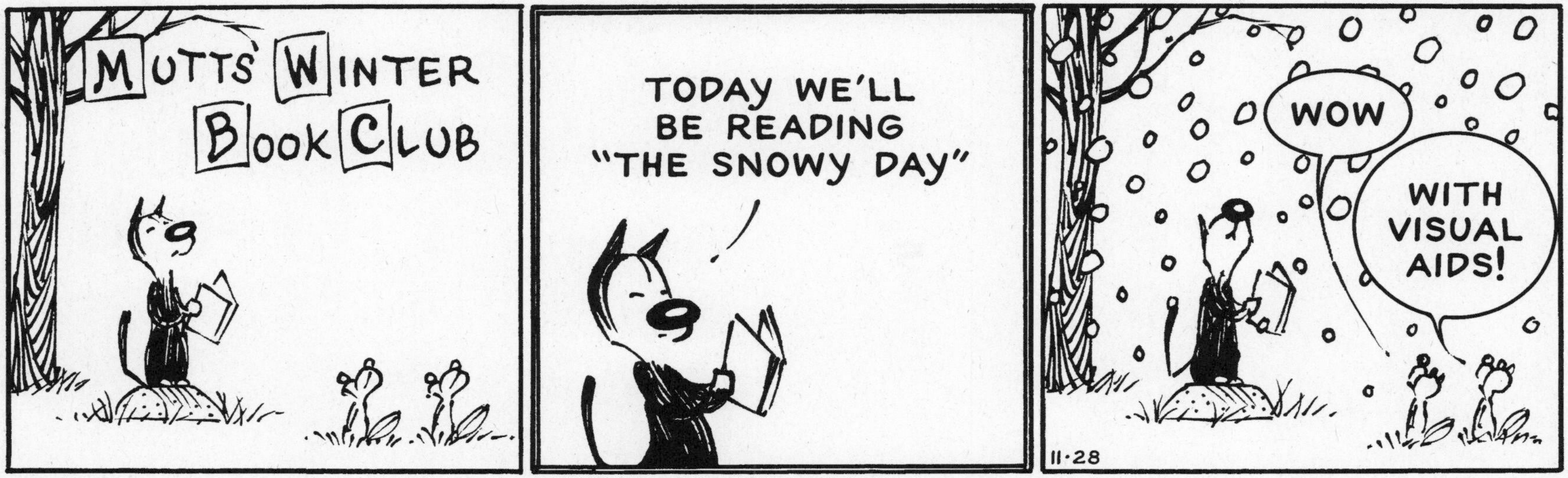
MUTTS WINTER BOOK CLUB
TODAY WE'LL BE READING "THE SNOWY DAY"
WOW
WITH VISUAL AIDS!
11·28

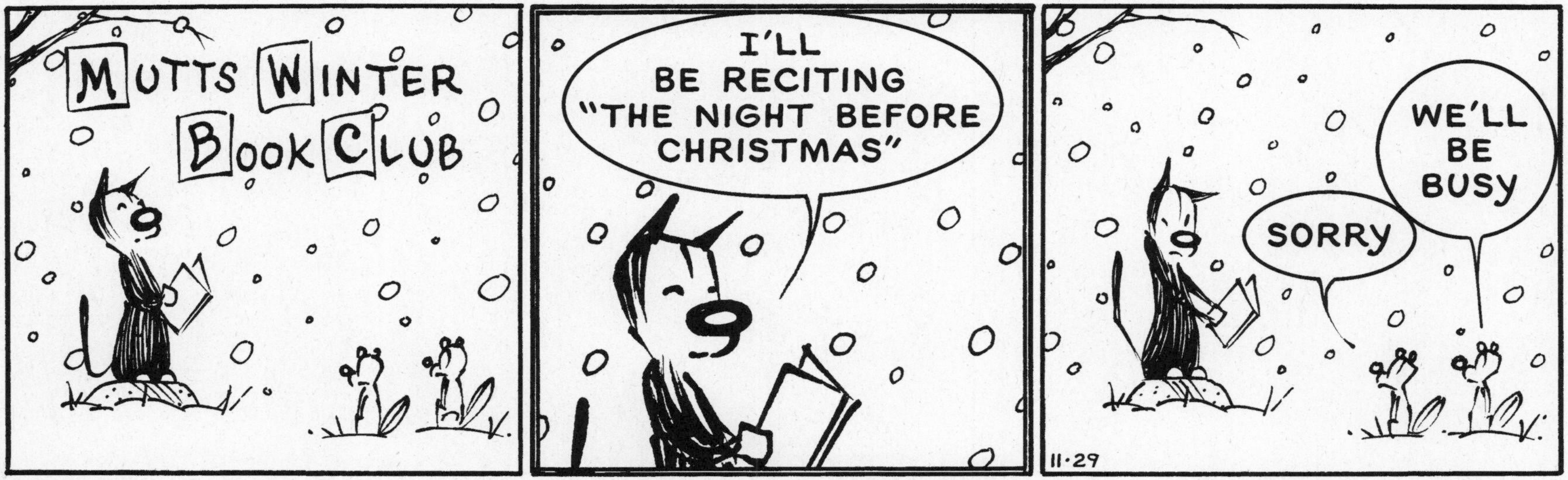
MUTTS WINTER BOOK CLUB
I'LL BE RECITING "THE NIGHT BEFORE CHRISTMAS"
SORRY
WE'LL BE BUSY
11·29

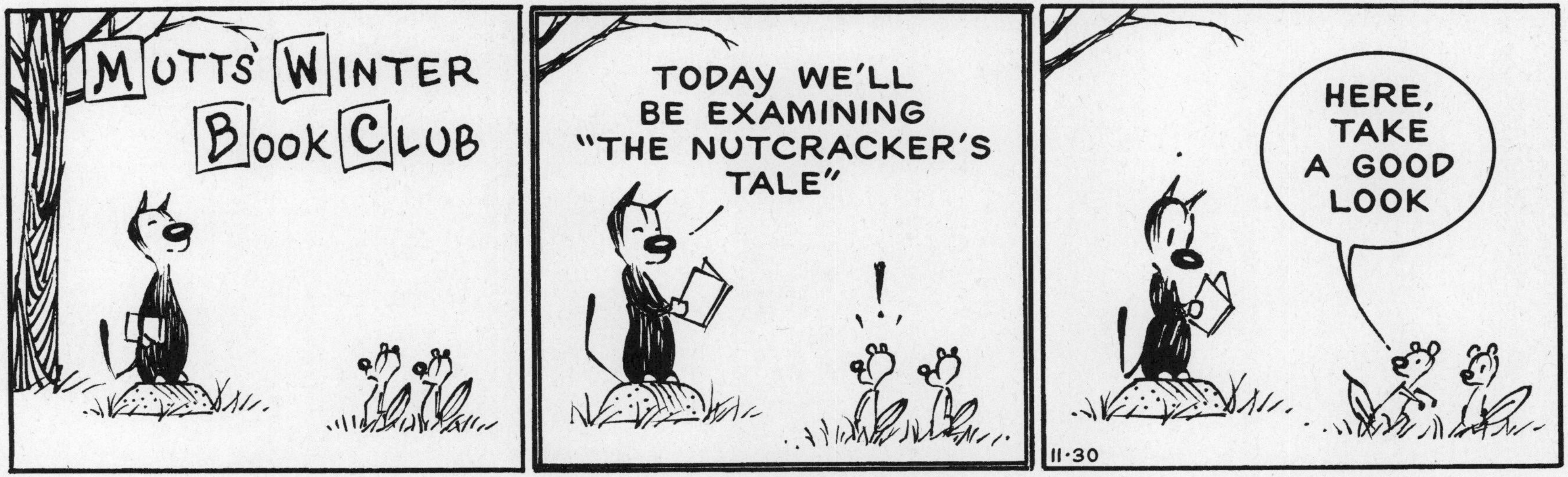
MUTTS WINTER BOOK CLUB
TODAY WE'LL BE EXAMINING "THE NUTCRACKER'S TALE"
!
HERE, TAKE A GOOD LOOK
11·30

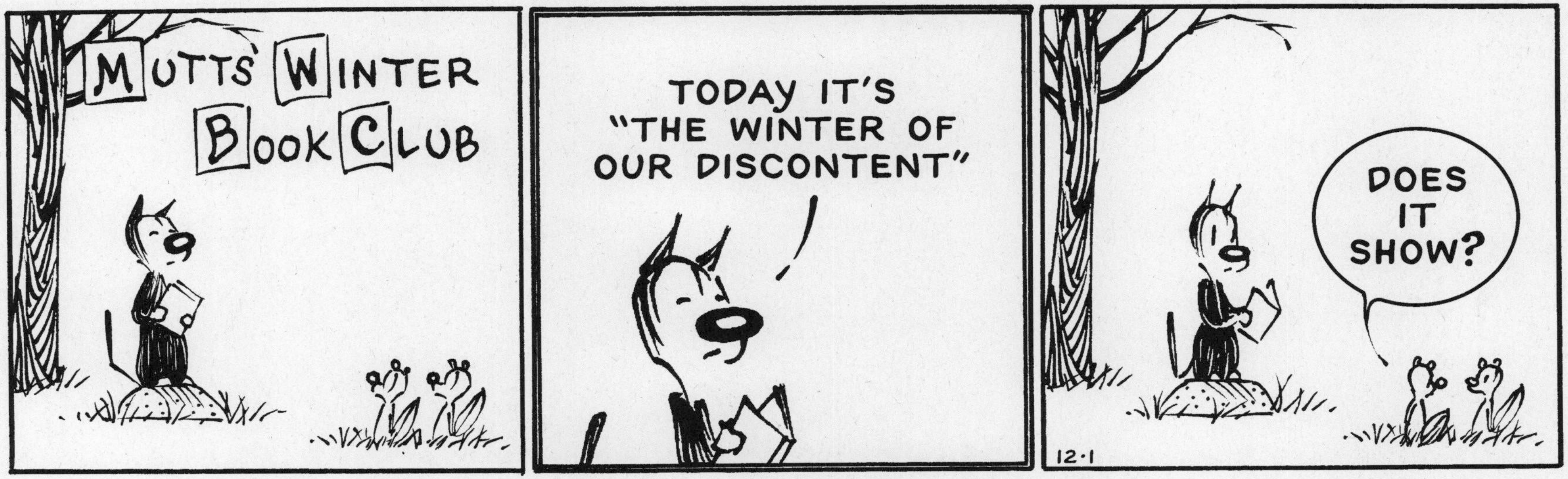
MUTTS WINTER BOOK CLUB
TODAY IT'S "THE WINTER OF OUR DISCONTENT"
DOES IT SHOW?
12·1

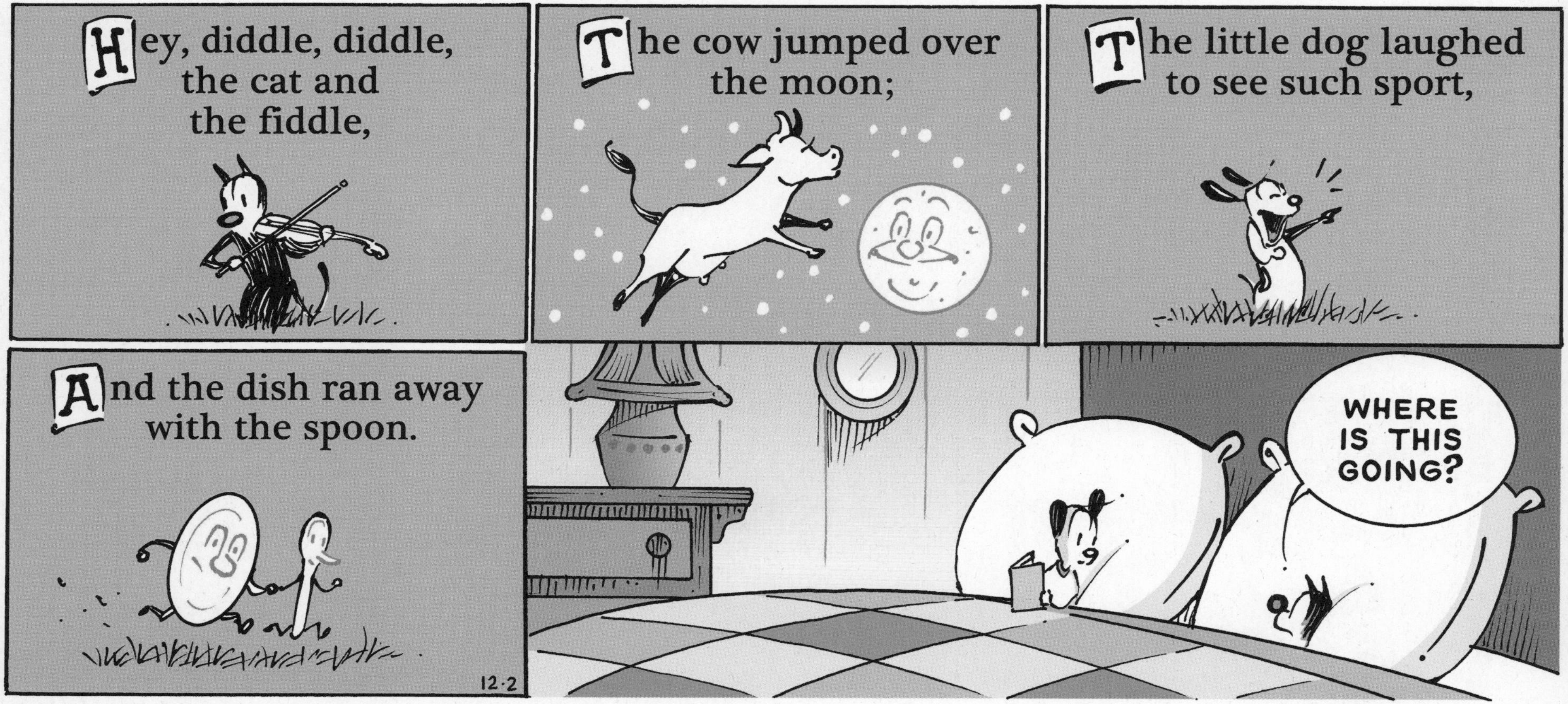
Hey, diddle, diddle, the cat and the fiddle,
The cow jumped over the moon;
The little dog laughed to see such sport,
And the dish ran away with the spoon.
12·2
WHERE IS THIS GOING?

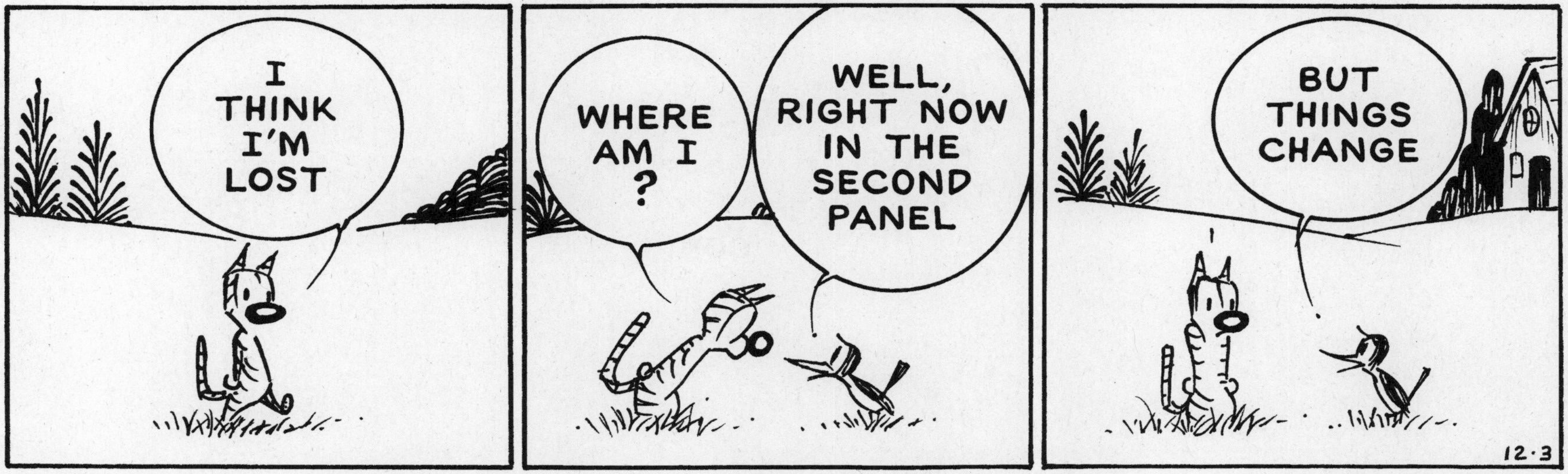
I THINK I'M LOST
WHERE AM I ?
WELL, RIGHT NOW IN THE SECOND PANEL
BUT THINGS CHANGE
12·3

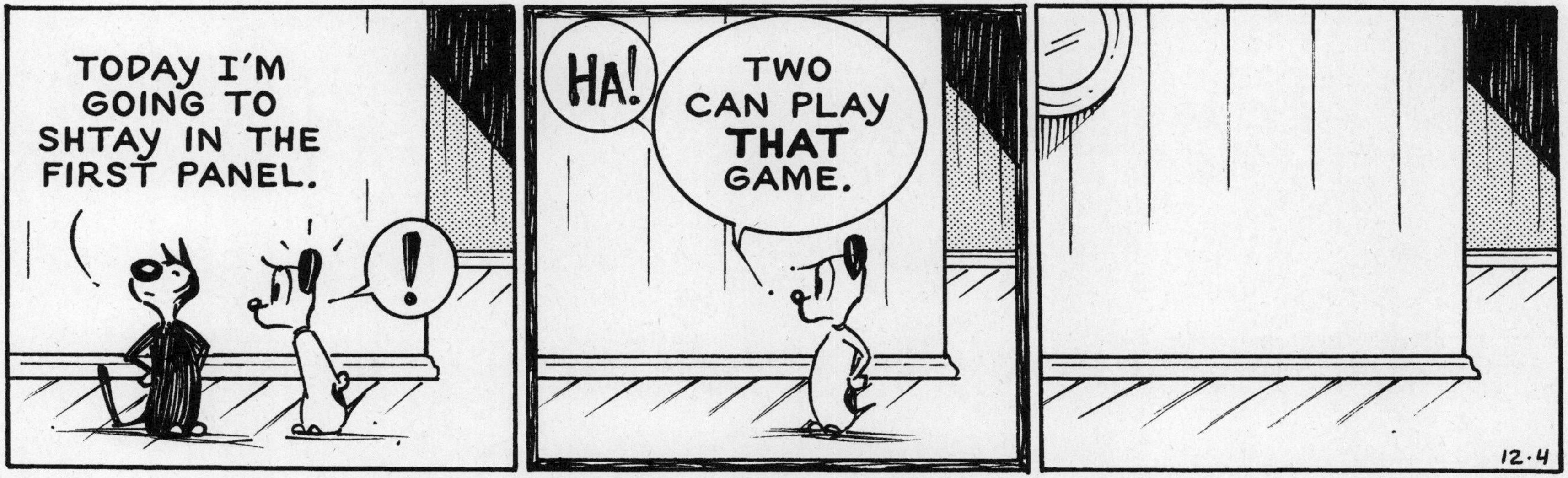
TODAY I'M GOING TO SHTAY IN THE FIRST PANEL.
!
HA!
TWO CAN PLAY **THAT** GAME.
12·4

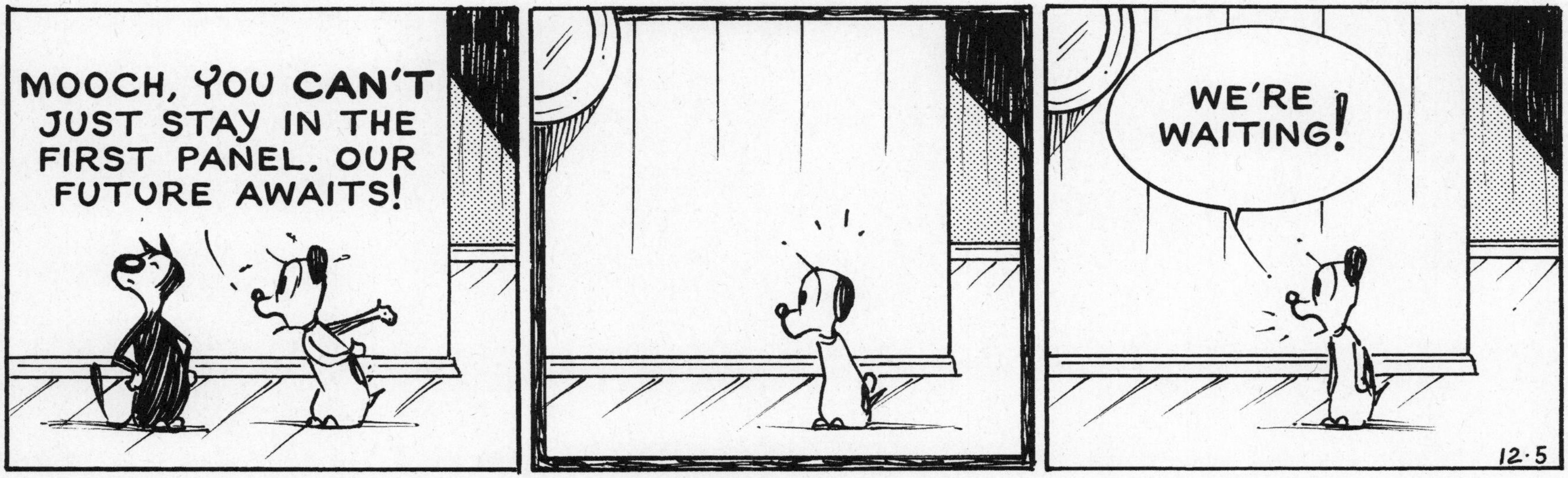
MOOCH, YOU CAN'T JUST STAY IN THE FIRST PANEL. OUR FUTURE AWAITS!
WE'RE WAITING!
12·5

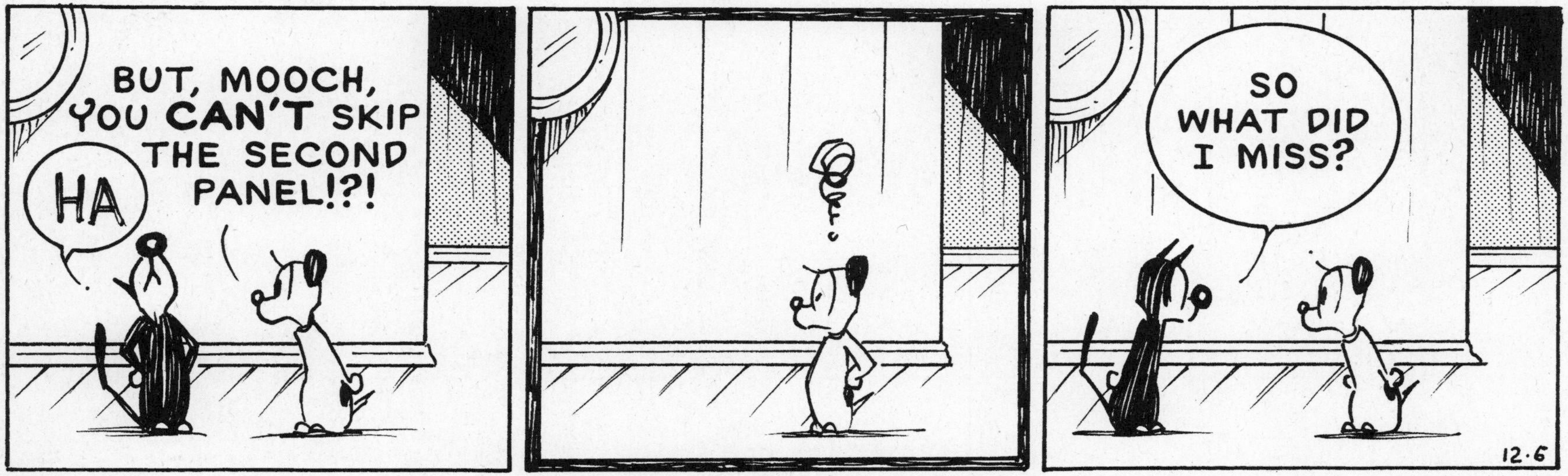
BUT, MOOCH, YOU CAN'T SKIP THE SECOND PANEL!?!
HA
SO WHAT DID I MISS?
12·6

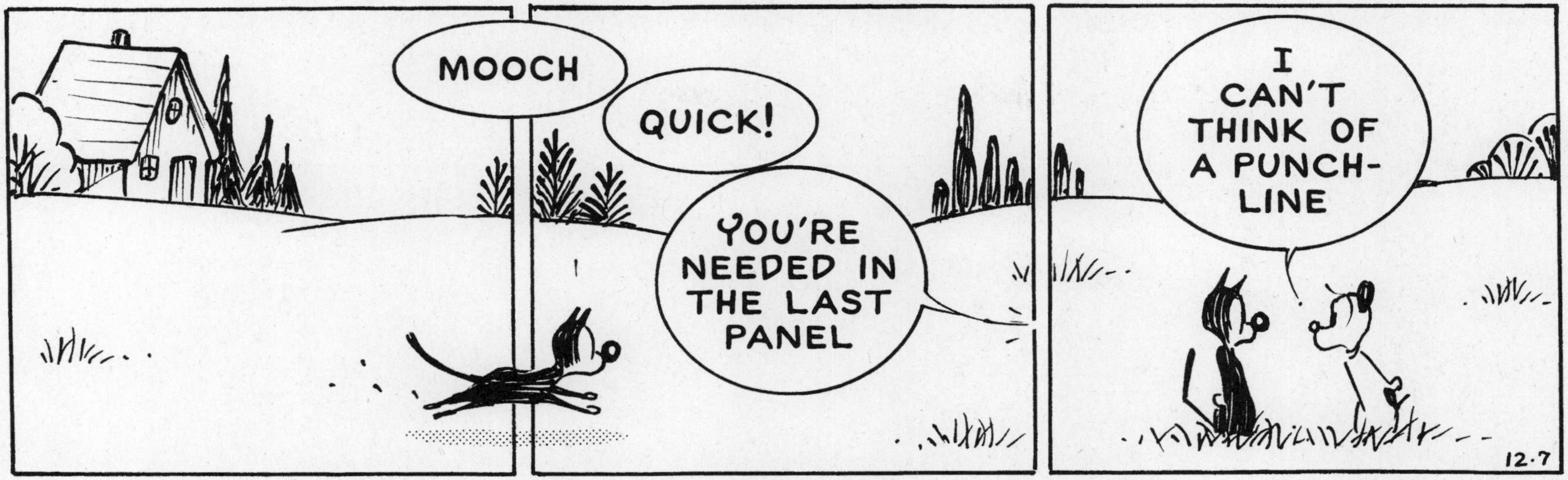
MOOCH
QUICK!
YOU'RE NEEDED IN THE LAST PANEL
I CAN'T THINK OF A PUNCH-LINE
12·7

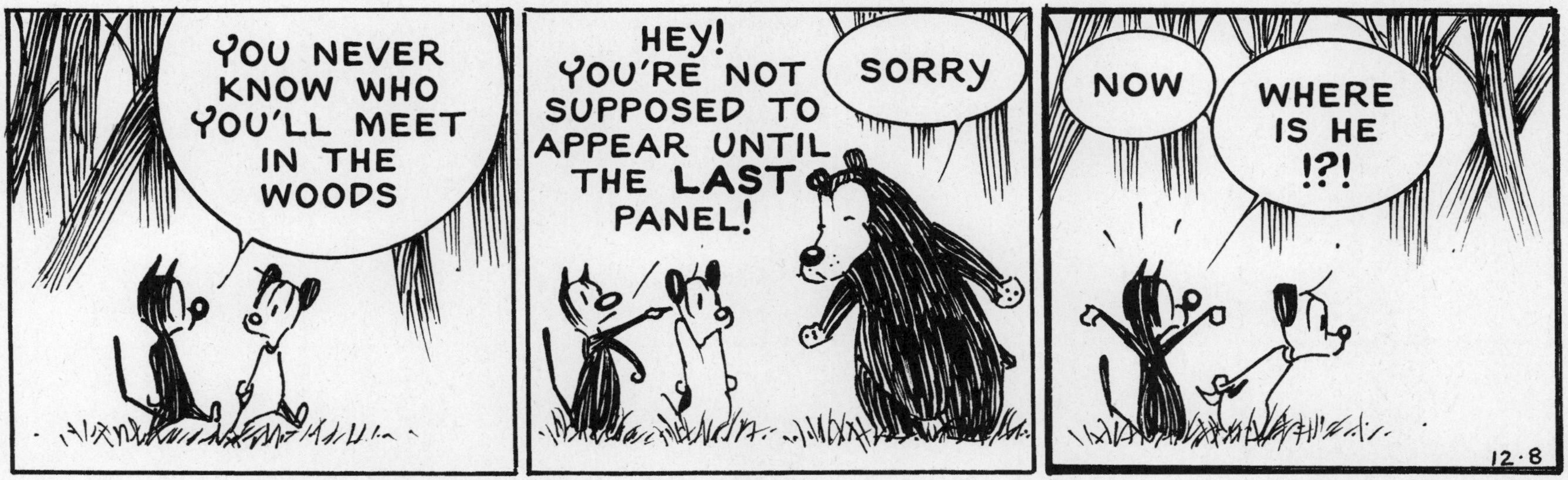
YOU NEVER KNOW WHO YOU'LL MEET IN THE WOODS
HEY! YOU'RE NOT SUPPOSED TO APPEAR UNTIL THE LAST PANEL!
SORRY
NOW
WHERE IS HE !?!
12·8

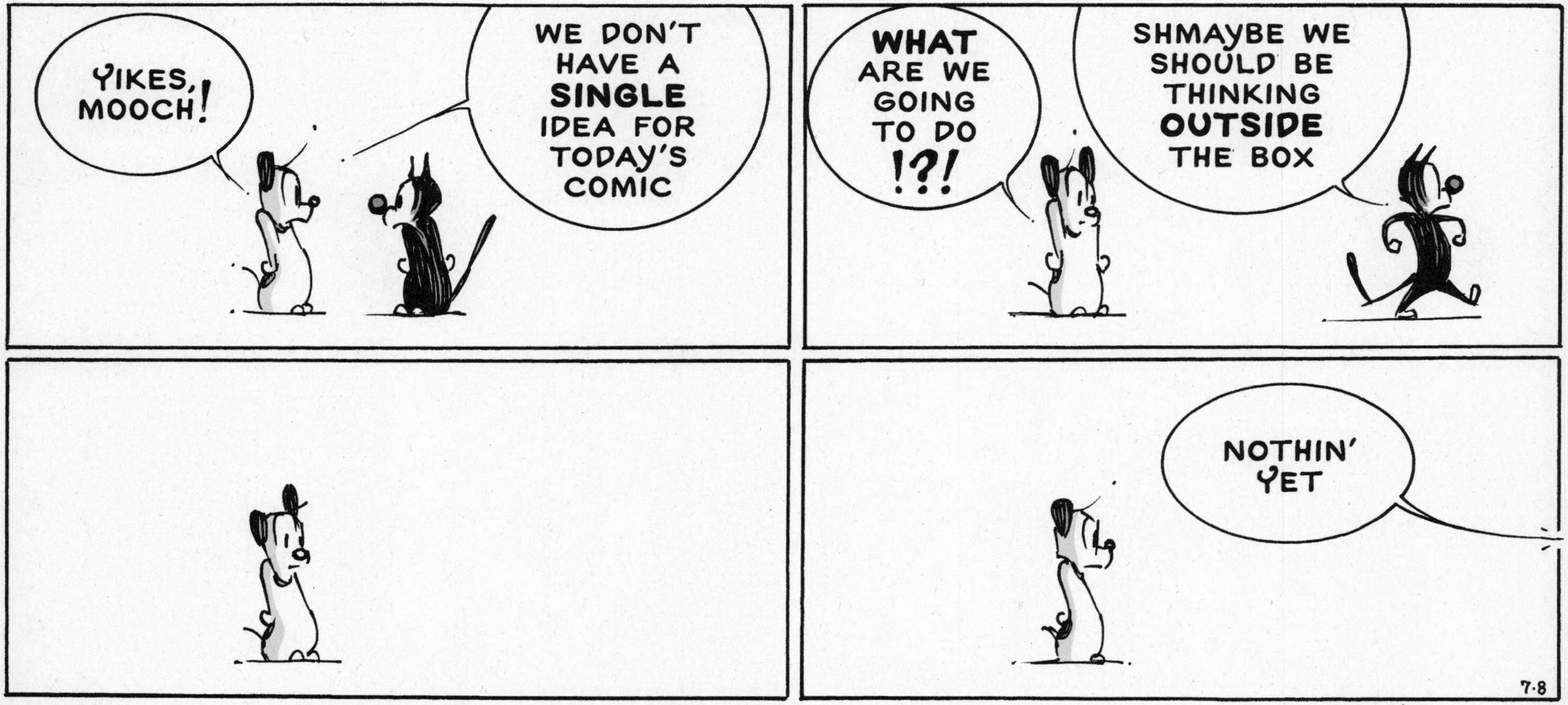
YIKES, MOOCH!
WE DON'T HAVE A SINGLE IDEA FOR TODAY'S COMIC
WHAT ARE WE GOING TO DO !?!
SHMAYBE WE SHOULD BE THINKING OUTSIDE THE BOX
NOTHIN' YET
7·8

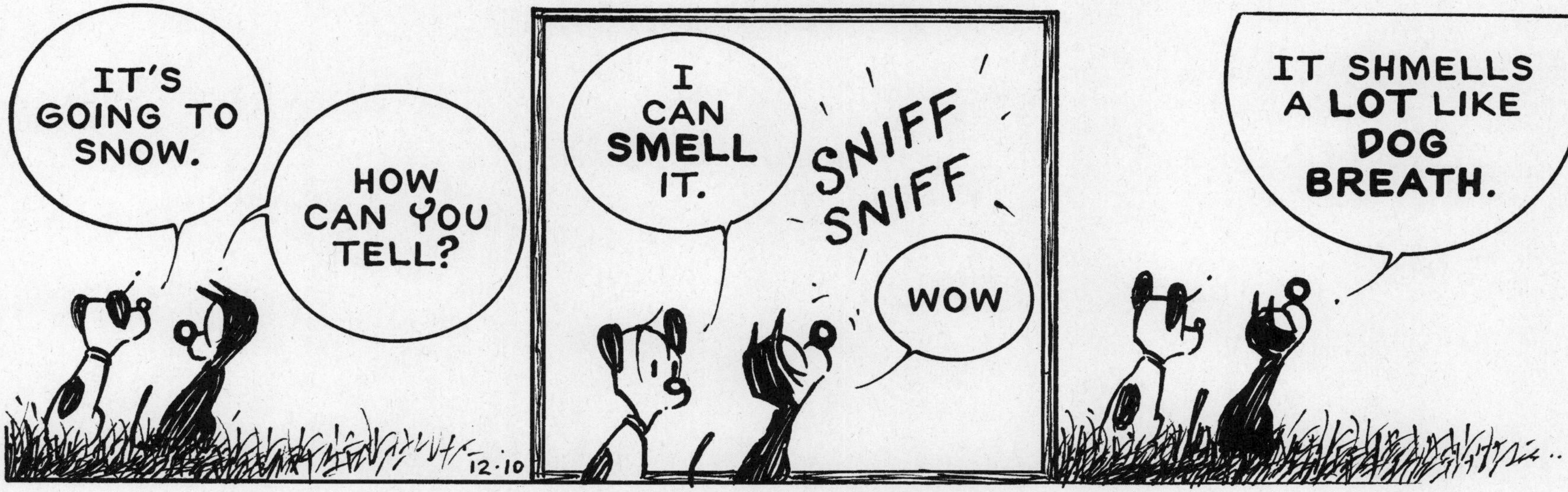
IT'S GOING TO SNOW.
HOW CAN YOU TELL?
12·10
I CAN SMELL IT.
SNIFF SNIFF
WOW
IT SHMELLS A LOT LIKE DOG BREATH.

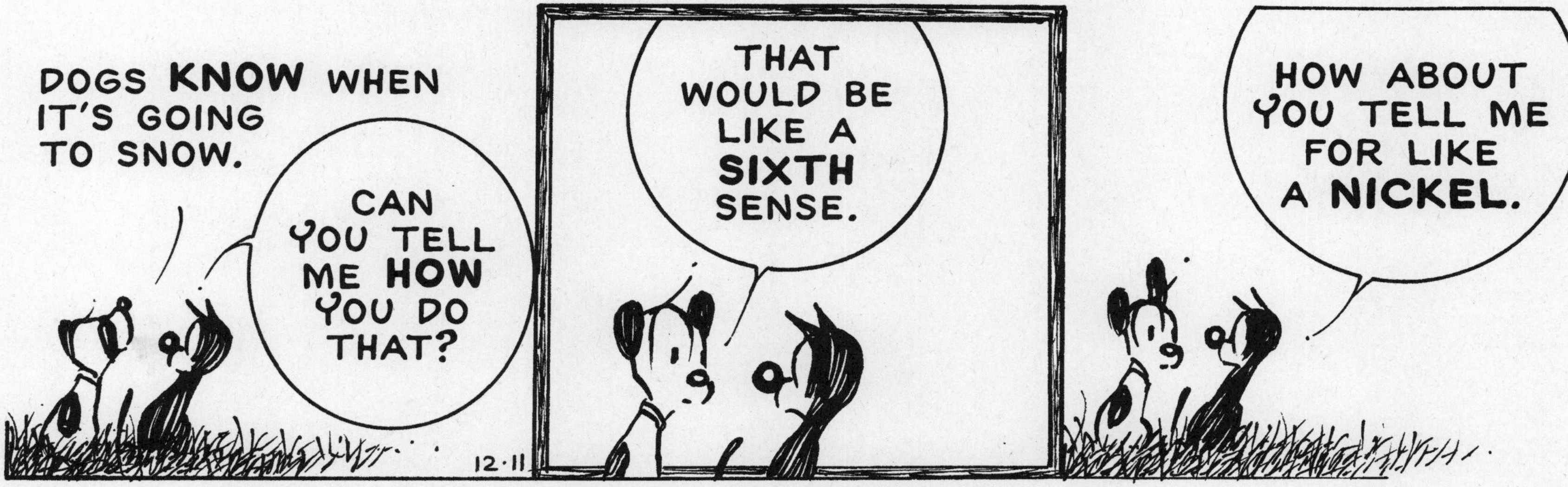
DOGS KNOW WHEN IT'S GOING TO SNOW.
CAN YOU TELL ME HOW YOU DO THAT?
12·11
THAT WOULD BE LIKE A SIXTH SENSE.
HOW ABOUT YOU TELL ME FOR LIKE A NICKEL.

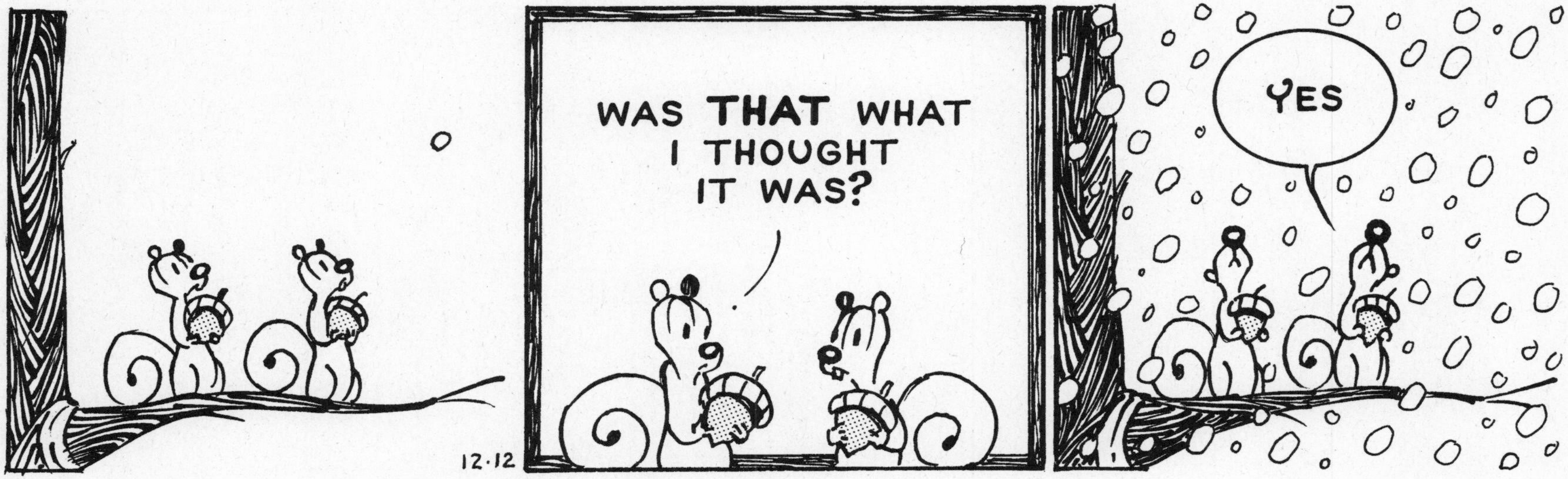
12·12
WAS THAT WHAT I THOUGHT IT WAS?
YES

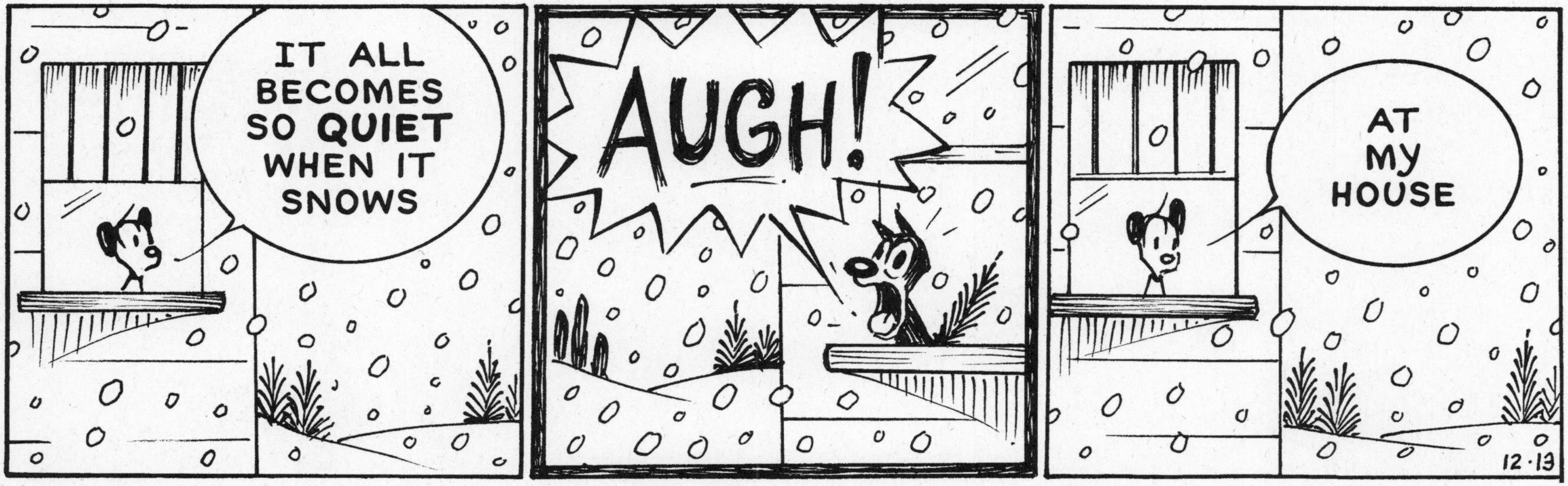
IT ALL BECOMES SO QUIET WHEN IT SNOWS
AUGH!
AT MY HOUSE
12·13

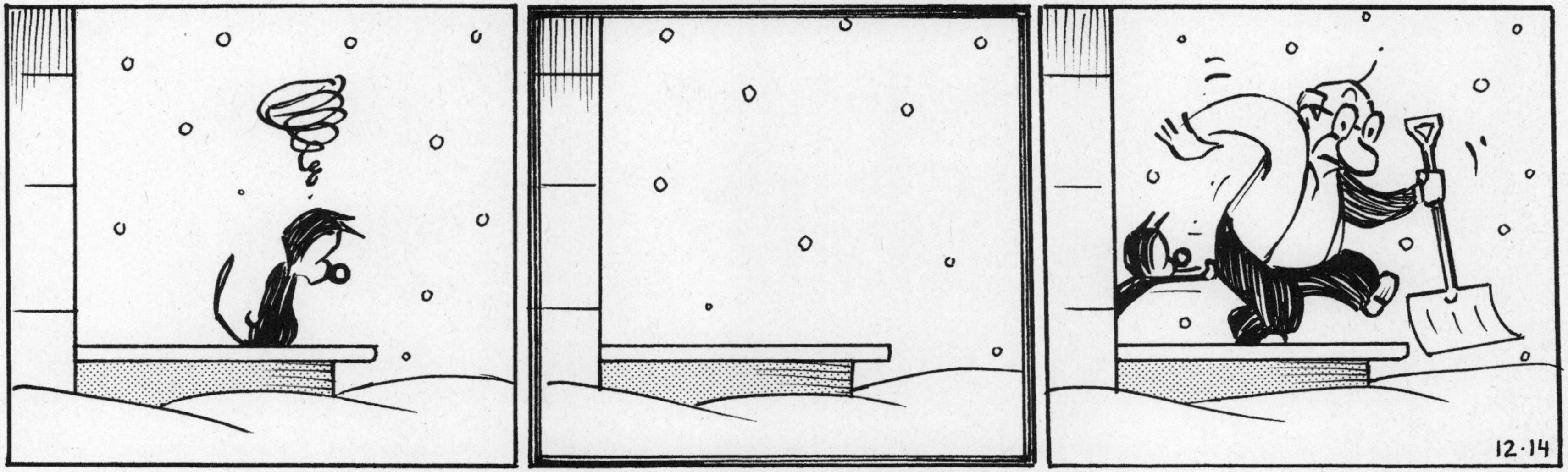
12·14

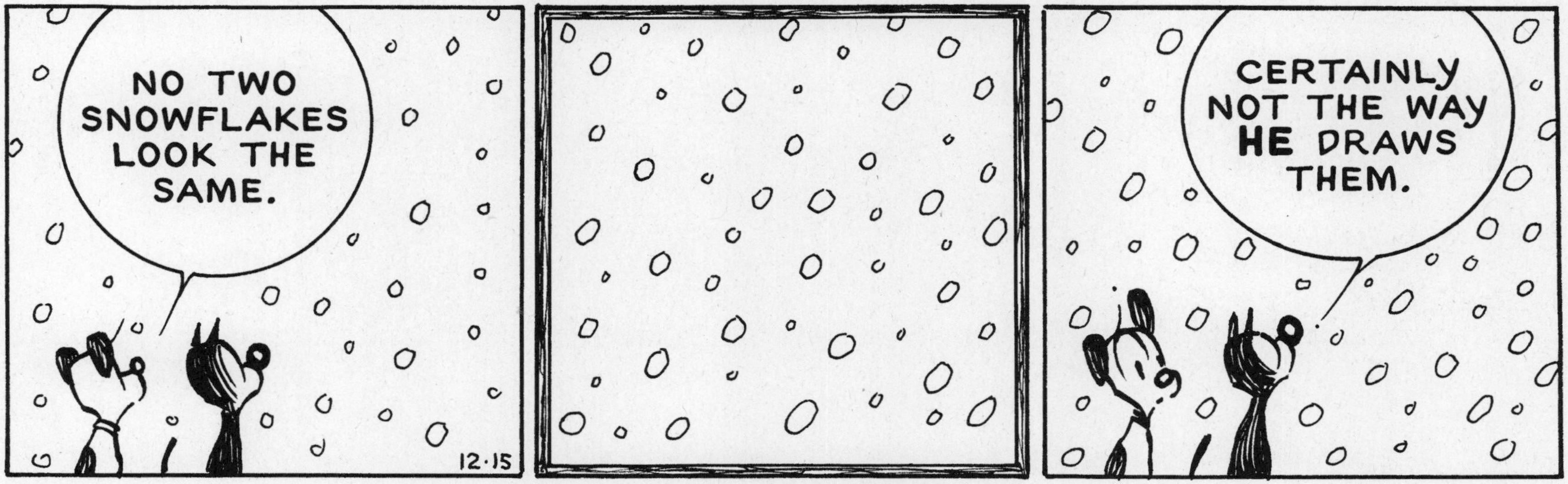
NO TWO SNOWFLAKES LOOK THE SAME.
12·15
CERTAINLY NOT THE WAY **HE** DRAWS THEM.

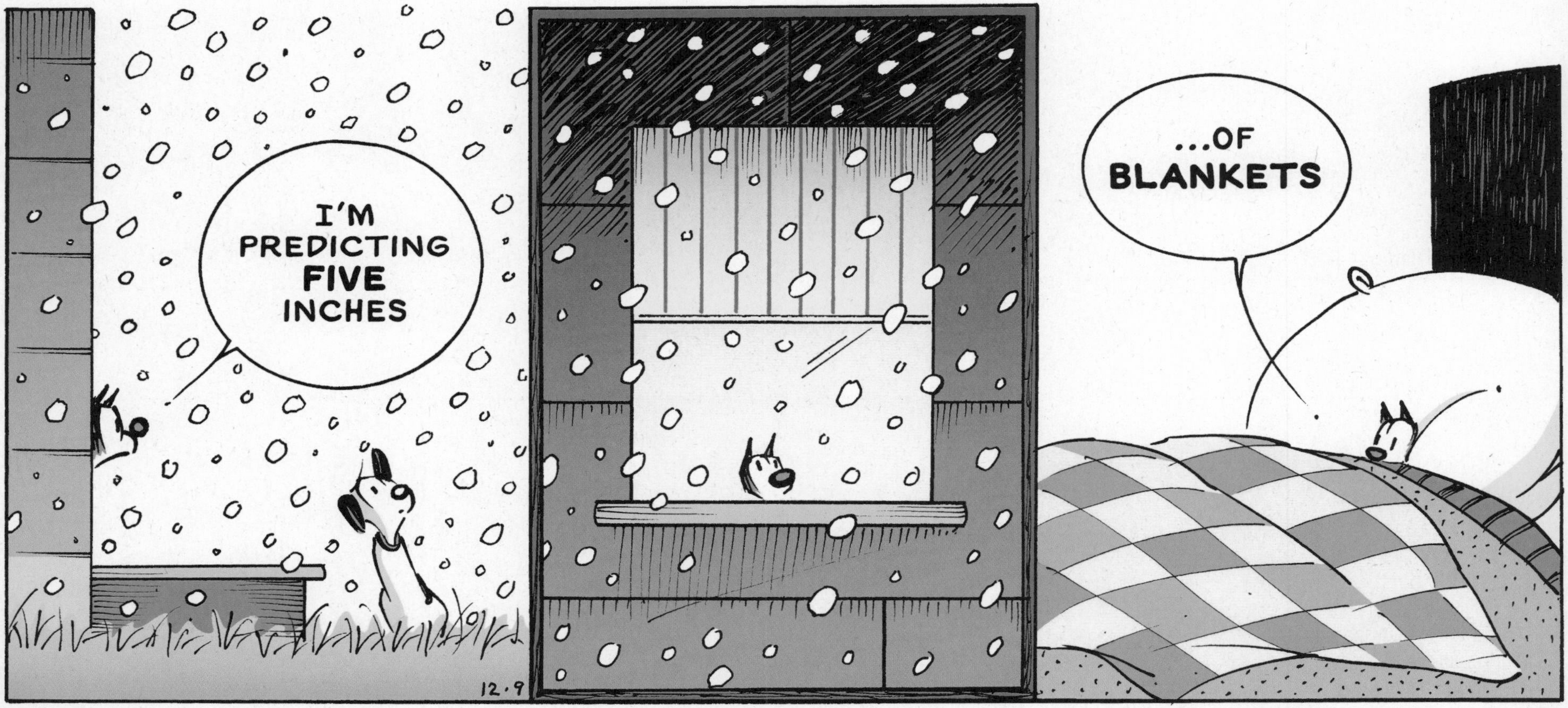
I'M PREDICTING FIVE INCHES
12·9
...OF BLANKETS

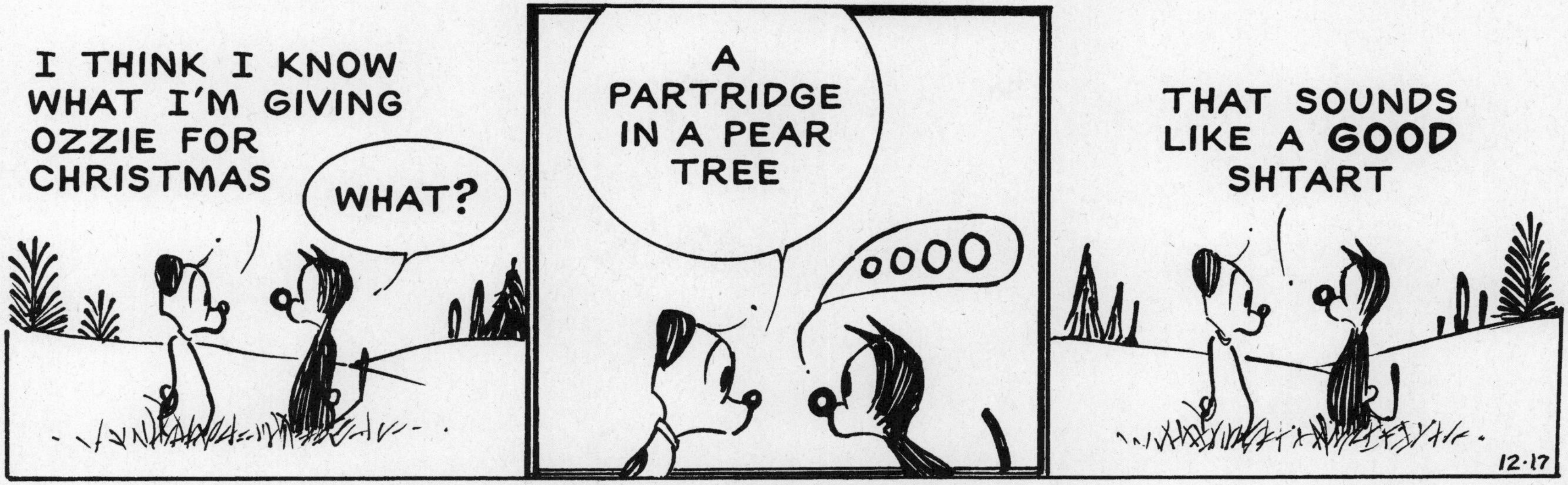
I THINK I KNOW WHAT I'M GIVING OZZIE FOR CHRISTMAS
WHAT?
A PARTRIDGE IN A PEAR TREE
oOOO
THAT SOUNDS LIKE A **GOOD** SHTART
12·17

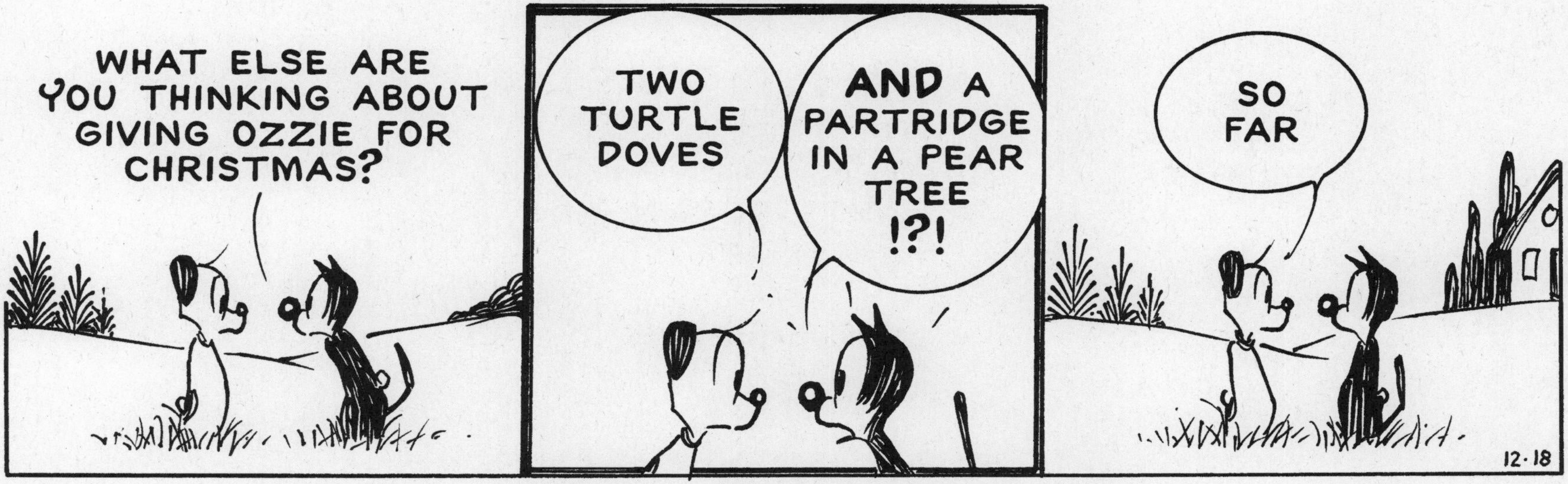
WHAT ELSE ARE YOU THINKING ABOUT GIVING OZZIE FOR CHRISTMAS?
TWO TURTLE DOVES
AND A PARTRIDGE IN A PEAR TREE !?!
SO FAR
12·18

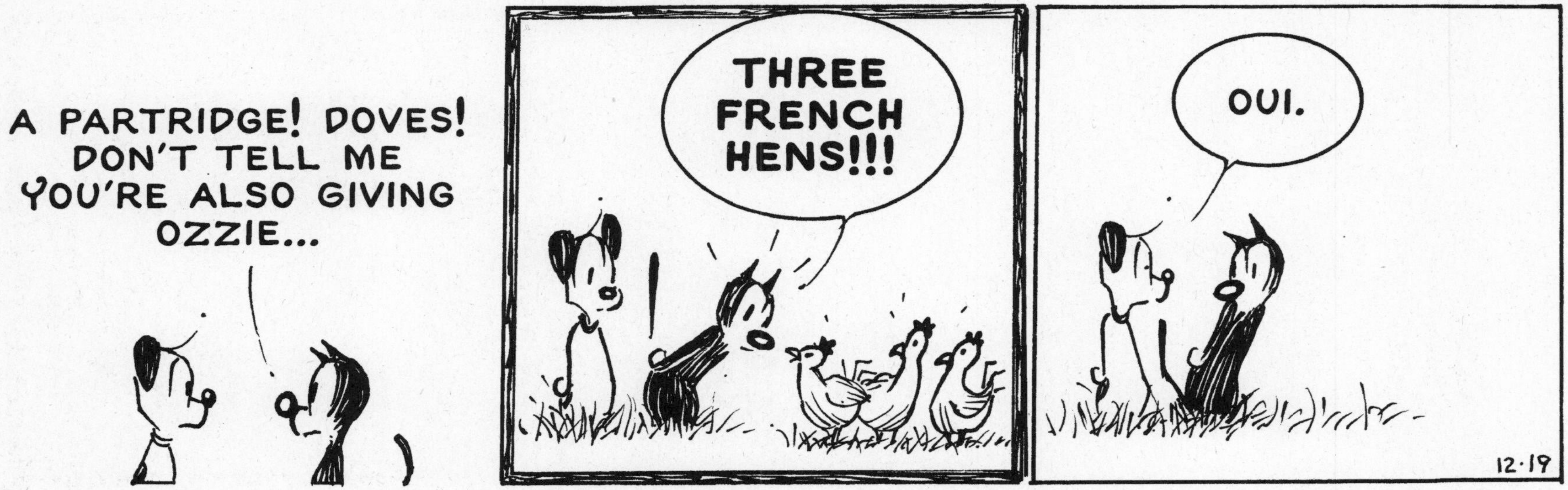
A PARTRIDGE! DOVES! DON'T TELL ME YOU'RE ALSO GIVING OZZIE...
THREE FRENCH HENS!!!
OUI.
12·19

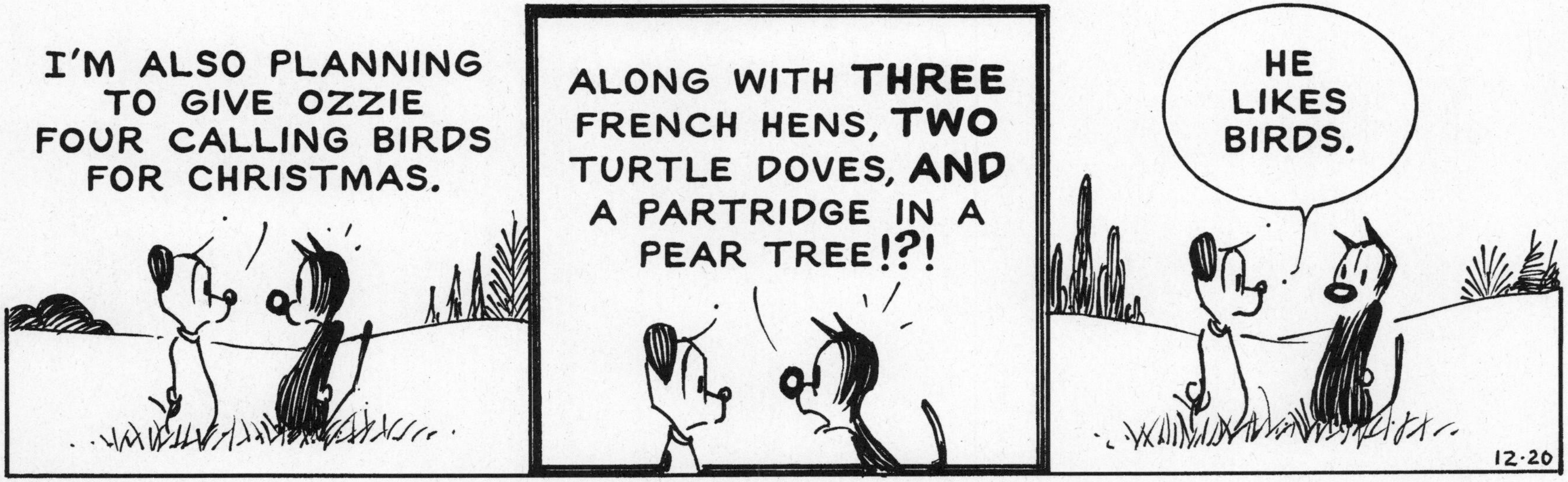
I'M ALSO PLANNING TO GIVE OZZIE FOUR CALLING BIRDS FOR CHRISTMAS.
ALONG WITH THREE FRENCH HENS, TWO TURTLE DOVES, AND A PARTRIDGE IN A PEAR TREE!?!
HE LIKES BIRDS.
12·20

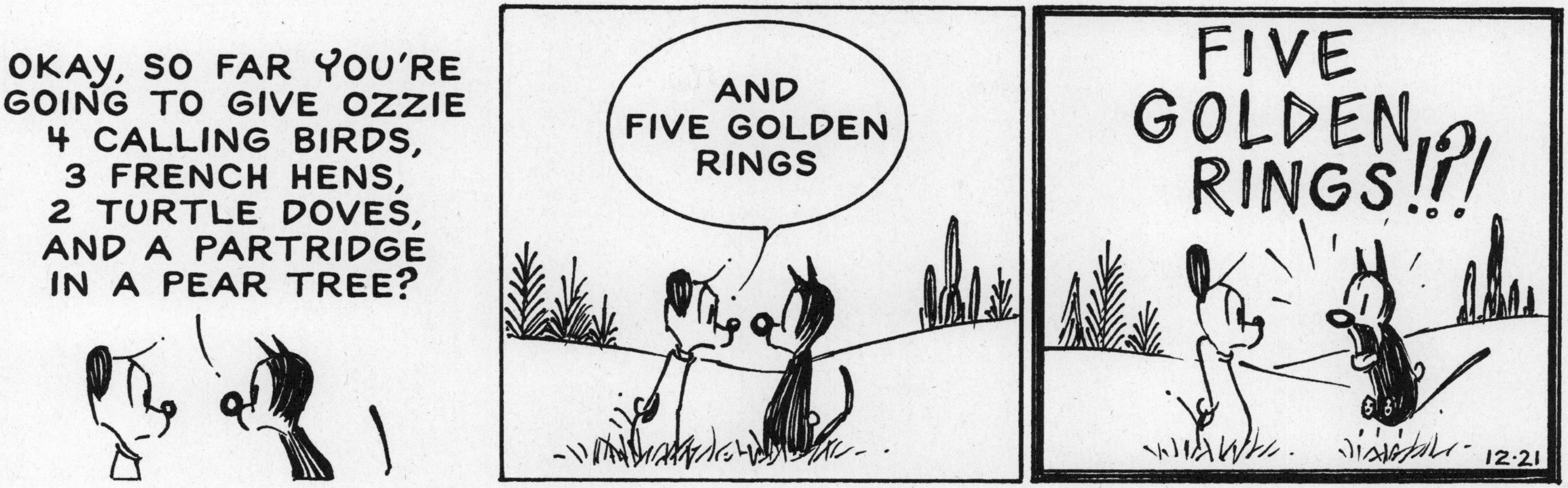
OKAY, SO FAR YOU'RE GOING TO GIVE OZZIE 4 CALLING BIRDS, 3 FRENCH HENS, 2 TURTLE DOVES, AND A PARTRIDGE IN A PEAR TREE?
AND FIVE GOLDEN RINGS
FIVE GOLDEN RINGS!?!
12·21

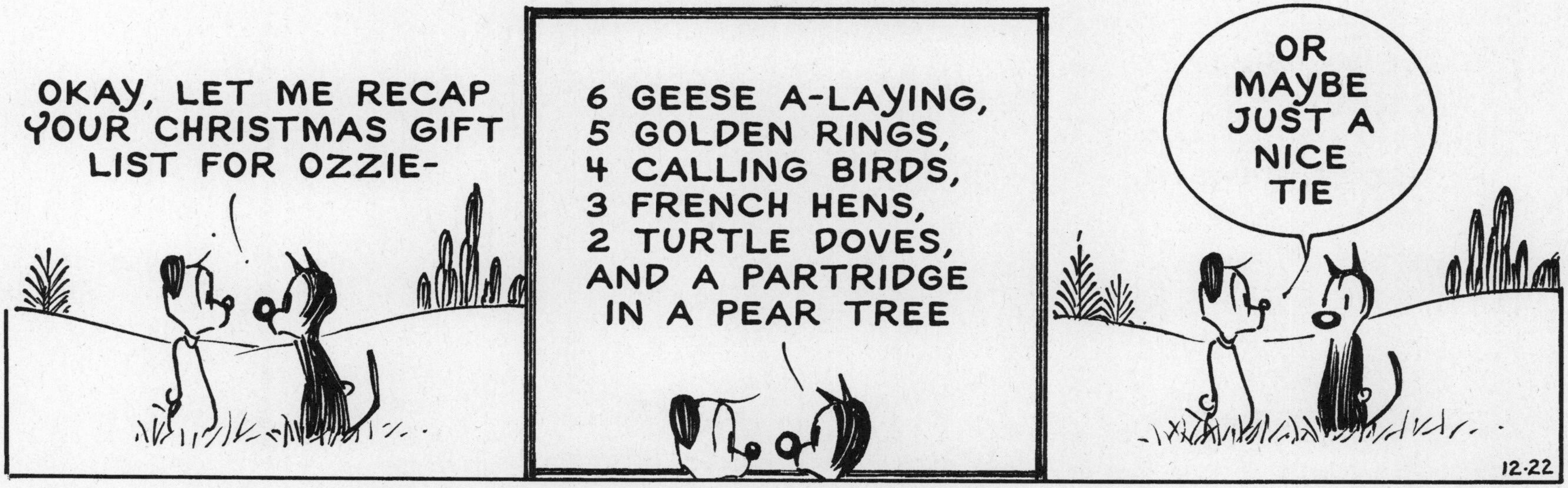
OKAY, LET ME RECAP YOUR CHRISTMAS GIFT LIST FOR OZZIE-
6 GEESE A-LAYING, 5 GOLDEN RINGS, 4 CALLING BIRDS, 3 FRENCH HENS, 2 TURTLE DOVES, AND A PARTRIDGE IN A PEAR TREE
OR MAYBE JUST A NICE TIE
12·22

MUTTS

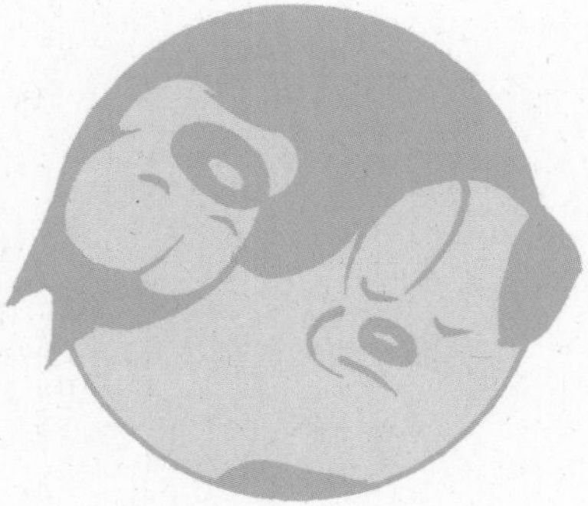

Patrick McDonnell

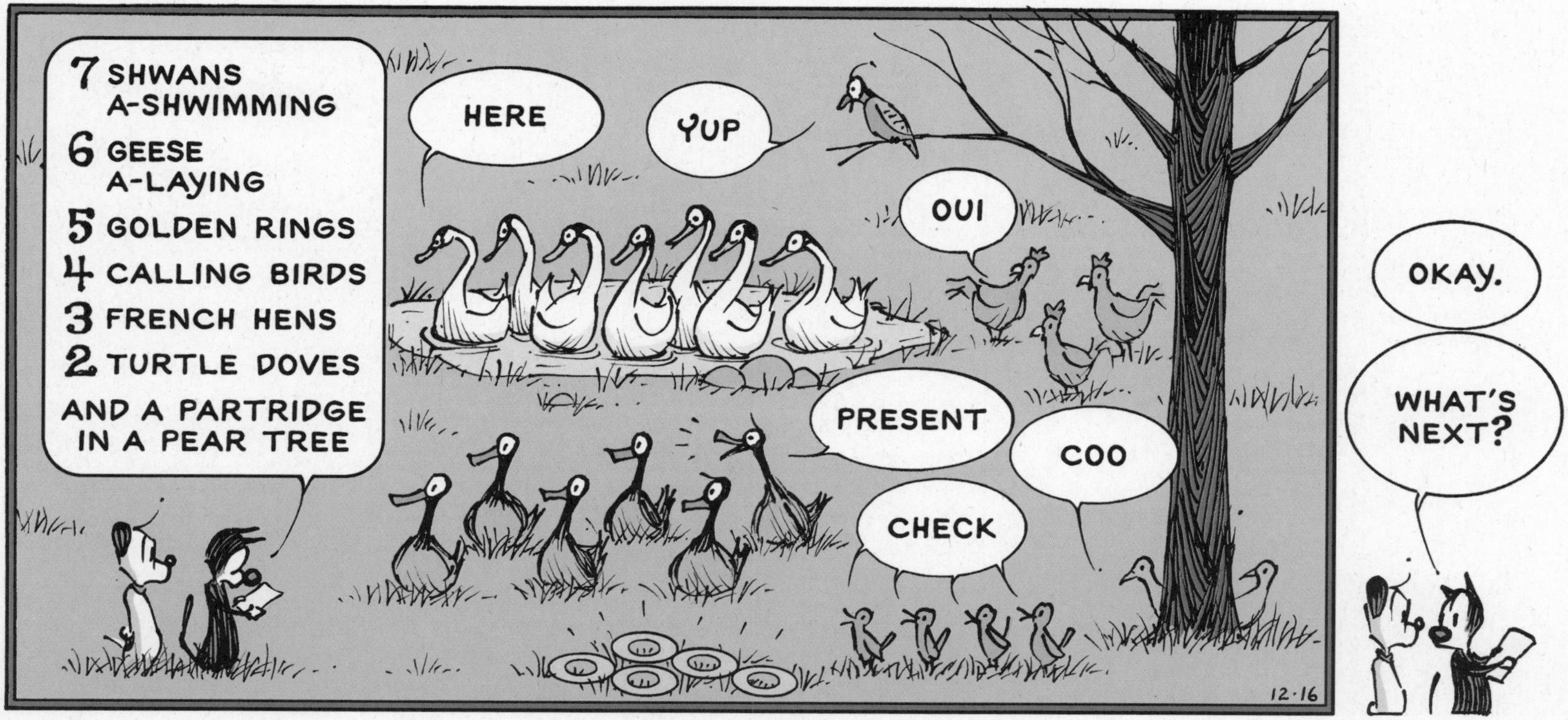
7 SHWANS A-SHWIMMING
6 GEESE A-LAYING
5 GOLDEN RINGS
4 CALLING BIRDS
3 FRENCH HENS
2 TURTLE DOVES
AND A PARTRIDGE IN A PEAR TREE
HERE
YUP
OUI
PRESENT
COO
CHECK
12·16
OKAY.
WHAT'S NEXT?

MUTTS

Patrick McDonnell

FATTY SNAX DELI
MEET
SANTA
HO
HO!
I LIKE THE NEW OWNER
HO
HO
12·23

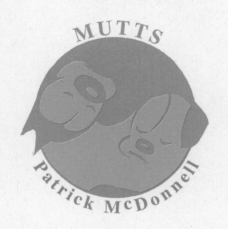

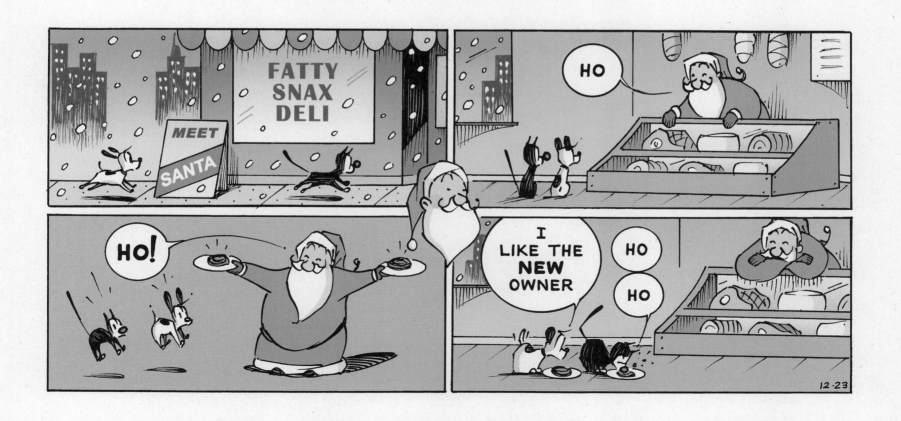

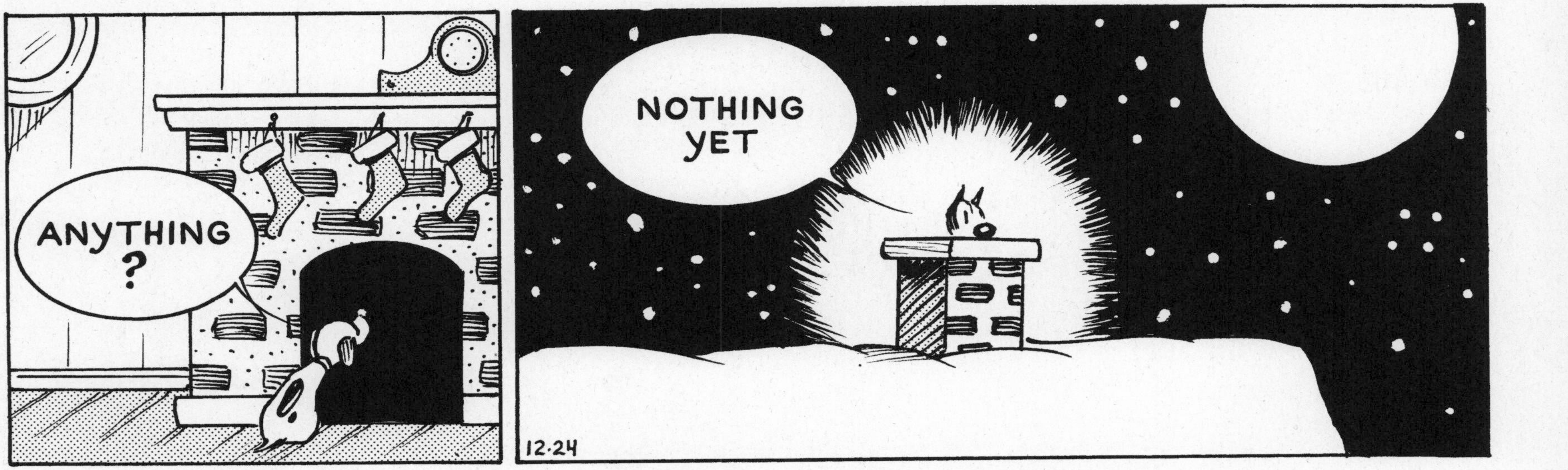
ANYTHING ?
NOTHING YET
12·24

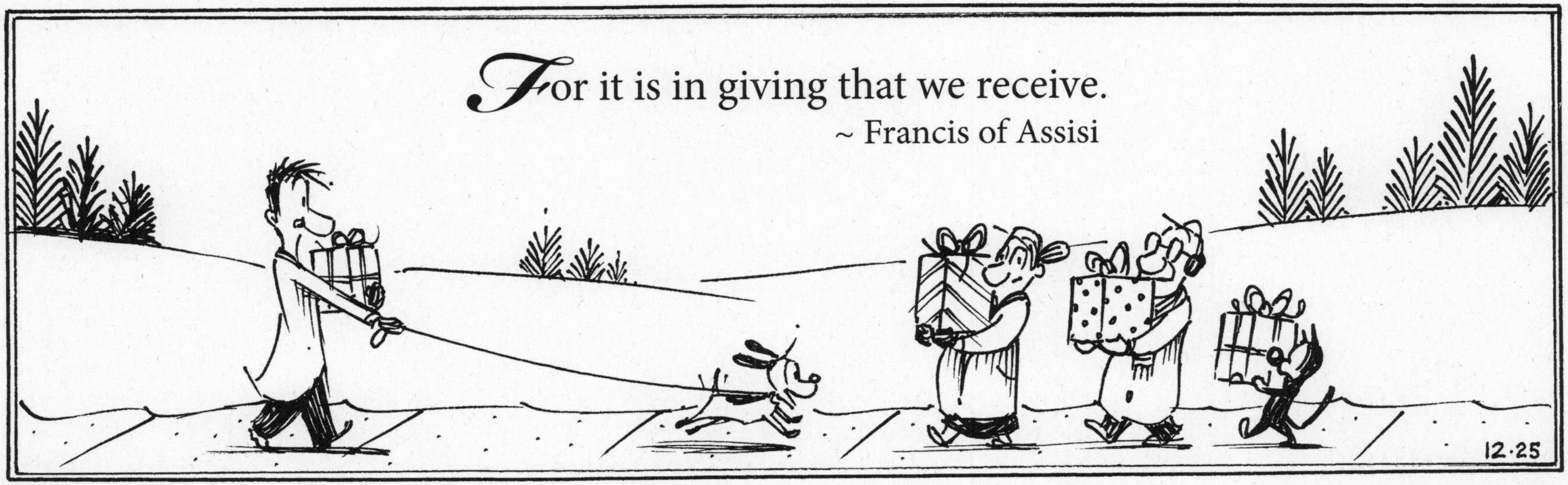
For it is in giving that we receive.
~ Francis of Assisi
12·25

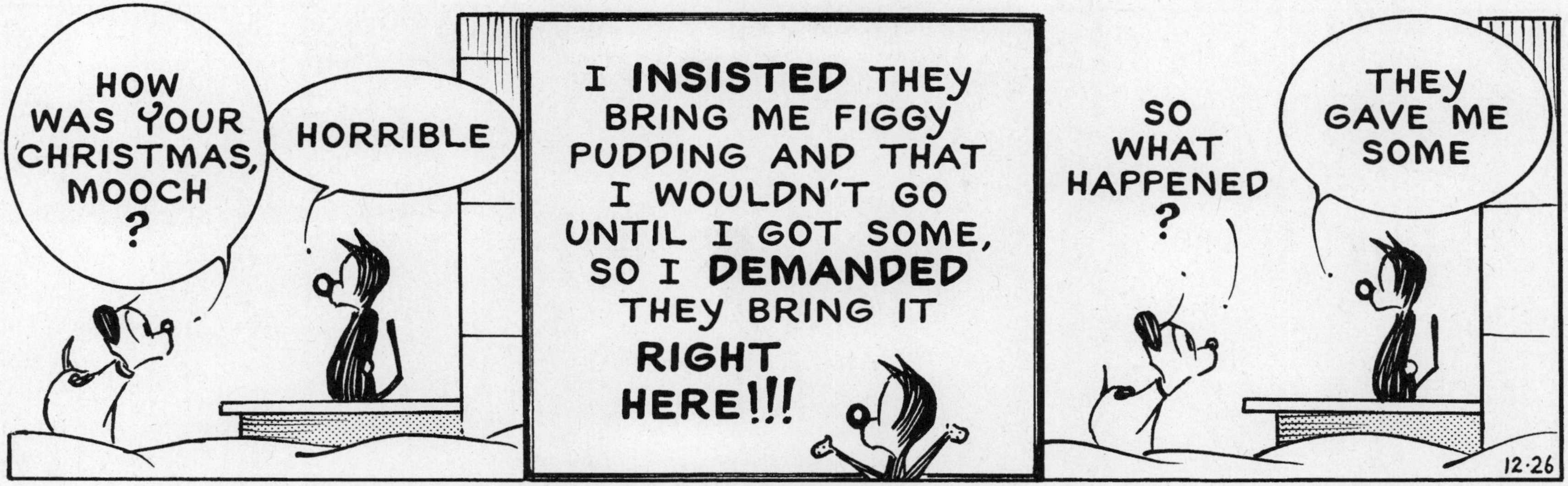
HOW WAS YOUR CHRISTMAS, MOOCH ?
HORRIBLE
I **INSISTED** THEY BRING ME FIGGY PUDDING AND THAT I WOULDN'T GO UNTIL I GOT SOME, SO I **DEMANDED** THEY BRING IT **RIGHT HERE!!!**
SO WHAT HAPPENED ?
THEY GAVE ME SOME
12·26

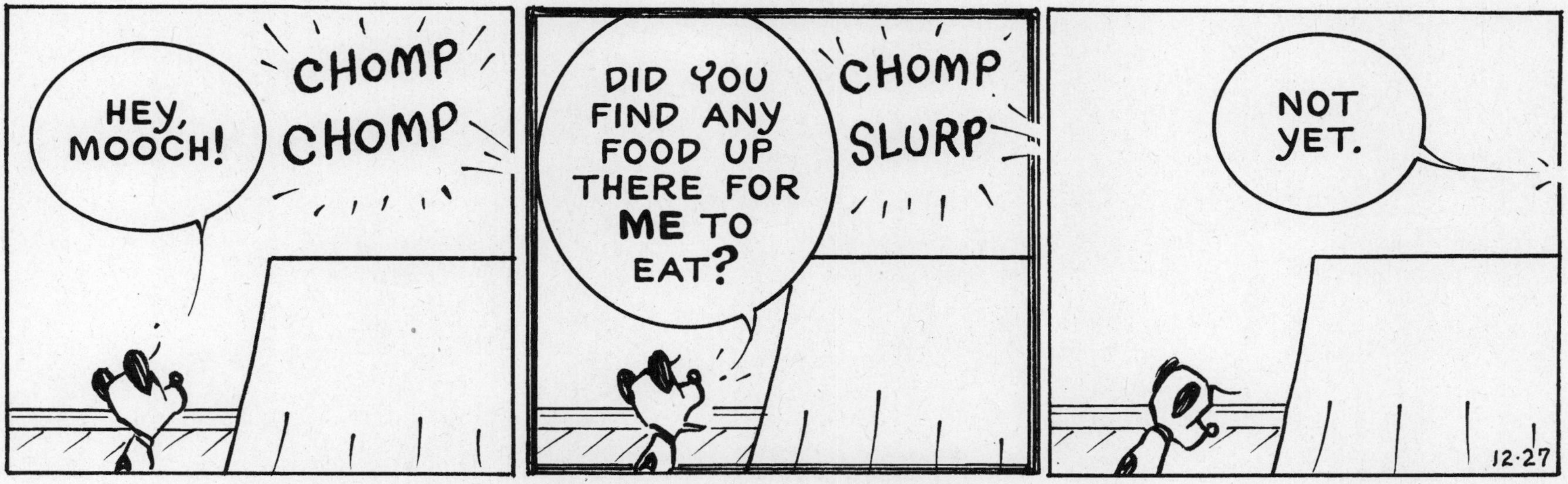
HEY, MOOCH!
CHOMP CHOMP
DID YOU FIND ANY FOOD UP THERE FOR **ME** TO EAT?
CHOMP SLURP
NOT YET.
12·27

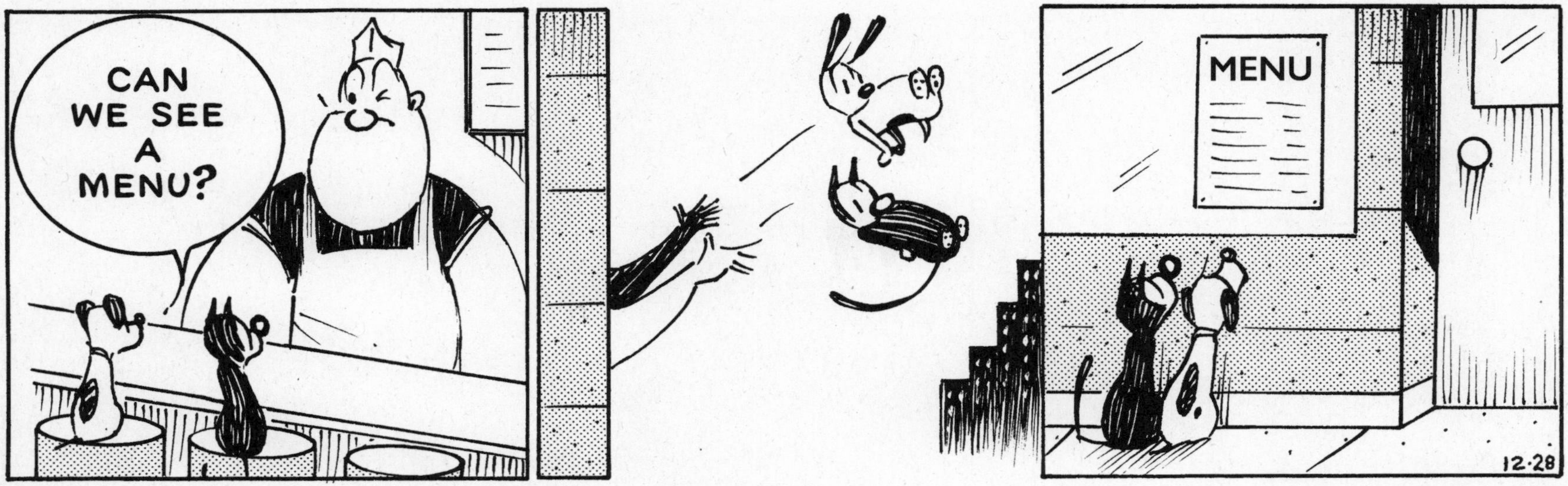
CAN WE SEE A MENU?
MENU
12-28

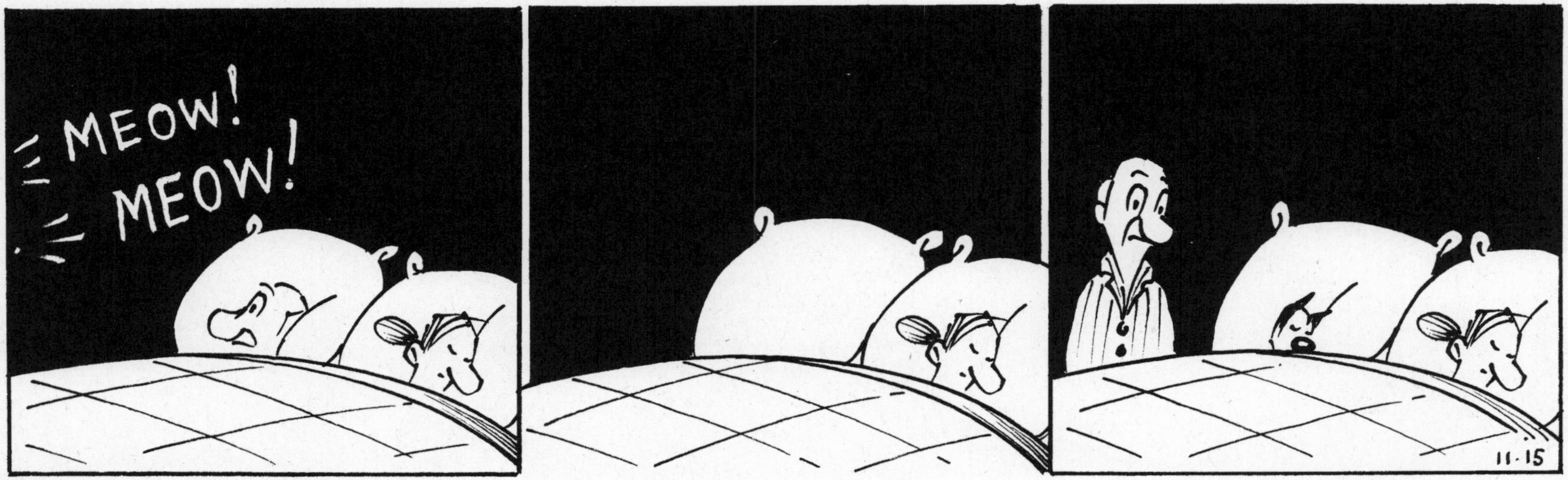
MEOW!
MEOW!
11-15

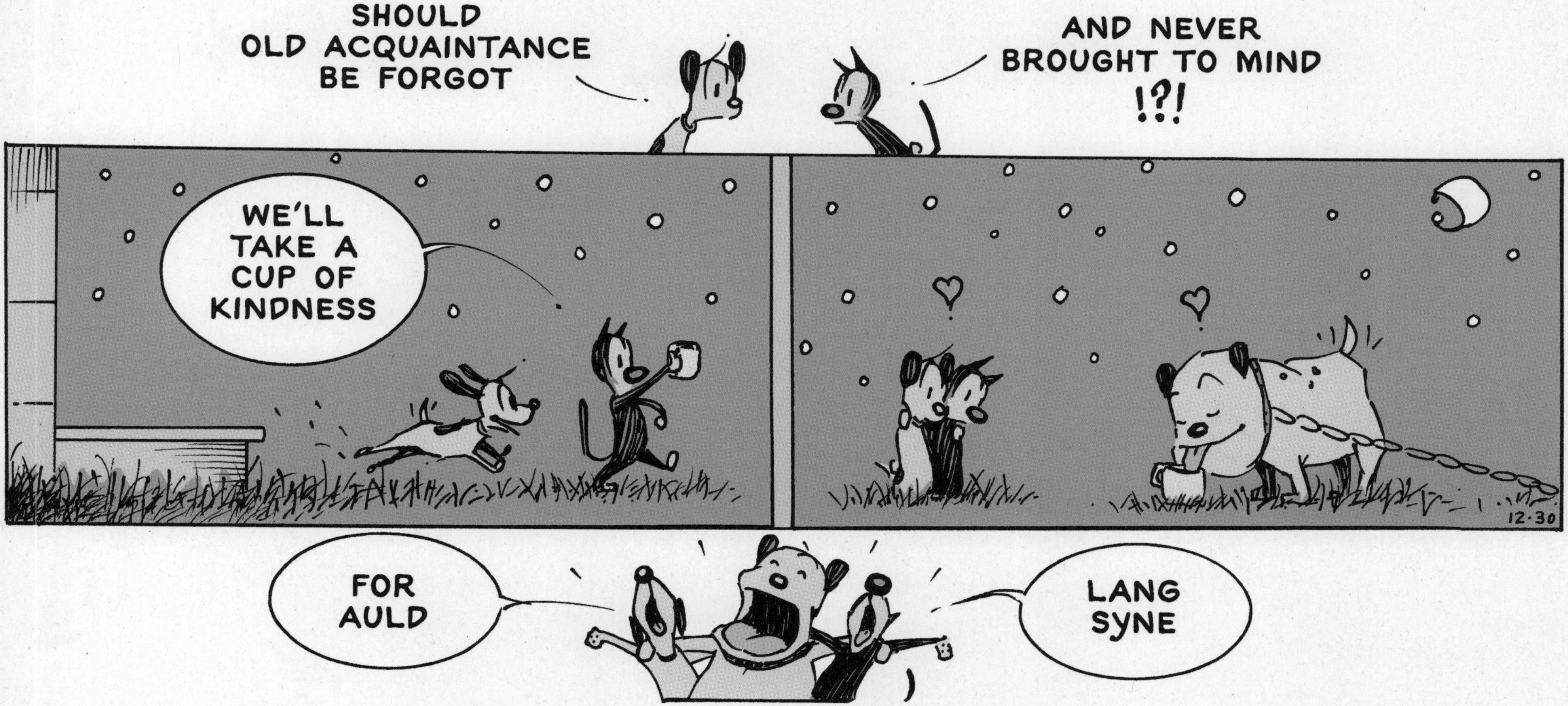
SHOULD OLD ACQUAINTANCE BE FORGOT
AND NEVER BROUGHT TO MIND !?!
WE'LL TAKE A CUP OF KINDNESS
12·30
FOR AULD
LANG SYNE

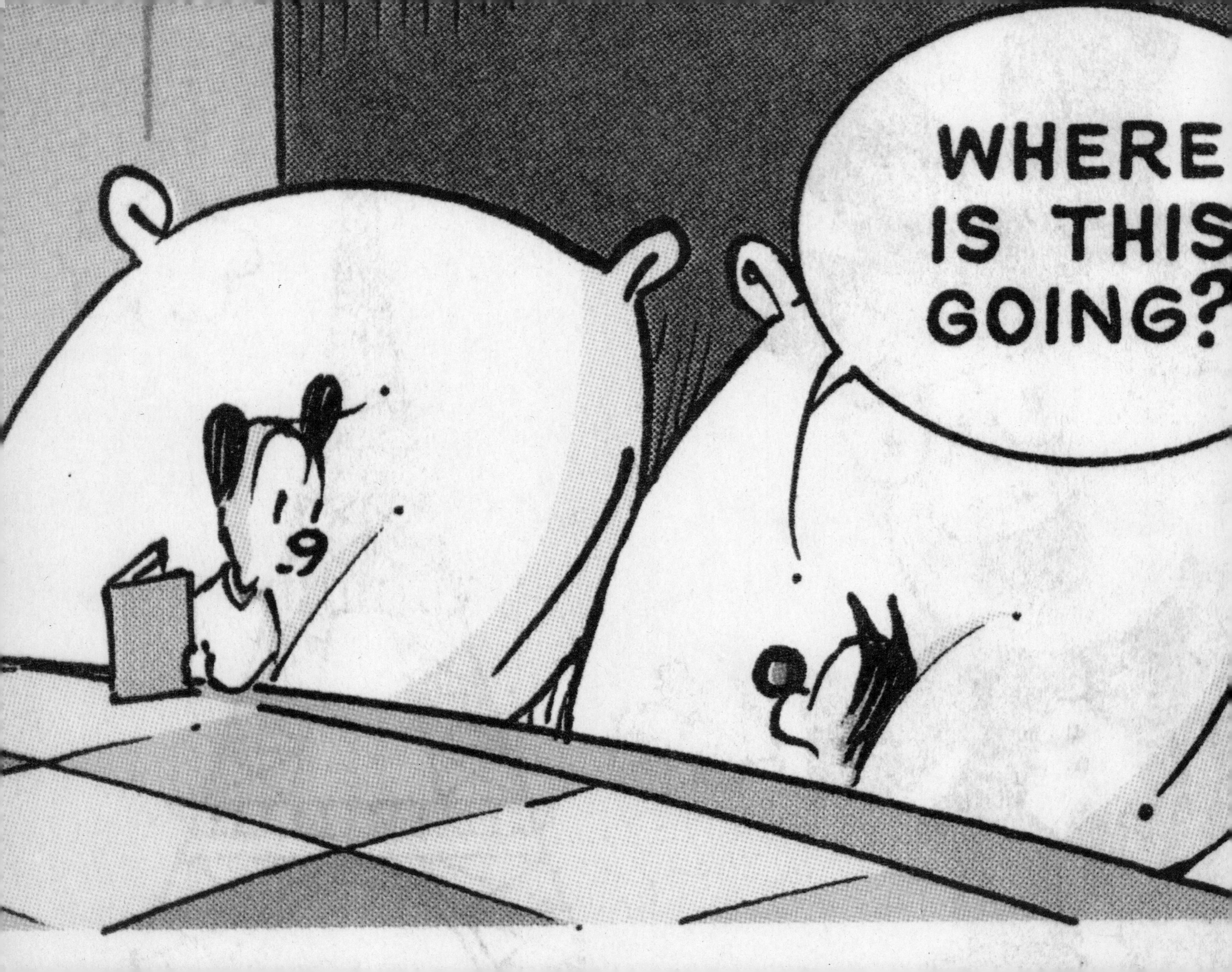
WHERE IS THIS GOING?